Human–Computer Interaction Series

Editors-in-Chief

Desney Tan
Microsoft Research, Redmond, WA, USA

Jean Vanderdonckt
Louvain School of Management, Université catholique de Louvain,
Louvain-La-Neuve, Belgium

The Human–Computer Interaction Series, launched in 2004, publishes books that advance the science and technology of developing systems which are effective and satisfying for people in a wide variety of contexts. Titles focus on theoretical perspectives (such as formal approaches drawn from a variety of behavioural sciences), practical approaches (such as techniques for effectively integrating user needs in system development), and social issues (such as the determinants of utility, usability and acceptability).

HCI is a multidisciplinary field and focuses on the human aspects in the development of computer technology. As technology becomes increasingly more pervasive the need to take a human-centred approach in the design and development of computer-based systems becomes ever more important.

Titles published within the Human–Computer Interaction Series are included in Thomson Reuters' Book Citation Index, The DBLP Computer Science Bibliography and The HCI Bibliography.

More information about this series at http://www.springer.com/series/6033

Wai Tat Fu · Herre van Oostendorp
Editors

Understanding and Improving Information Search

A Cognitive Approach

 Springer

Editors
Wai Tat Fu
Raytheon BBN Technologies
Cambridge, MA, USA

Herre van Oostendorp
Utrecht University
Utrecht, The Netherlands

ISSN 1571-5035   ISSN 2524-4477   (electronic)
Human–Computer Interaction Series
ISBN 978-3-030-38827-0   ISBN 978-3-030-38825-6   (eBook)
https://doi.org/10.1007/978-3-030-38825-6

This Springer imprint is published by the registered company Springer Nature Switzerland AG
The registered company address is: Gewerbestrasse 11, 6330 Cham, Switzerland

Contents

1 **Introduction** 1
   Wai Tat Fu and Herre van Oostendorp

Part I Foundation and Background

2 **Challenges for a Computational Cognitive Psychology
   for the New Digital Ecosystem** 13
   Peter Pirolli

3 **How Cognitive Computational Models Can Improve
   Information Search** 29
   Wai Tat Fu

4 **Cognitive Modeling of Age and Domain Knowledge Differences
   in Information Search** 47
   Saraschandra Karanam and Herre van Oostendorp

Part II Methods and Tools

5 **An Evolving Perspective to Capture Individual Differences
   Related to Fluid and Crystallized Abilities in Information
   Searching with a Search Engine** 71
   Mylène Sanchiz, Franck Amadieu, and Aline Chevalier

6 **Semantic Relevance Feedback on Queries and Search Results
   for Younger and Older Adults** 97
   Herre van Oostendorp and Saraschandra Karanam

7 **Designing Multistage Search Systems to Support the Information
   Seeking Process** 113
   Hugo C. Huurdeman and Jaap Kamps

8   Search Support Tools 139
     Kazutoshi Umemoto, Takehiro Yamamoto, and Katsumi Tanaka

**9   Eye-Tracking as a Method for Enhancing Research on
     Information Search** 161
     Jacek Gwizdka and Andrew Dillon

Part III   Areas of Applications

**10   Children's Acquisition of Text Search Strategies:
     The Role of Task Models and Relevance Processes** 185
     Jean-François Rouet, Julie Ayroles, Mônica Macedo-Rouet,
     and Anna Potocki

**11   Trainings and Tools to Foster Source Credibility Evaluation
     During Web Search** 213
     Yvonne Kammerer and Saskia Brand-Gruwel

**12   Computer-Supported Collaborative Information Search
     for Geopolitical Forecasting** 245
     Ion Juvina, Othalia Larue, Colin Widmer, Subhashini Ganapathy,
     Srikanth Nadella, Brandon Minnery, Lance Ramshaw,
     Emile Servan-Schreiber, Maurice Balick, and Ralph Weischedel

13   Conversational Interfaces for Information Search 267
     Q. Vera Liao, Werner Geyer, Michael Muller, and Yasaman Khazaen

Contributors

Franck Amadieu University of Toulouse, Toulouse, France

Julie Ayroles Centre National de la Recherche Scientifique (CNRS) and Université de Poitiers, Poitiers, France

Maurice Balick Hypermind, LLC, Paris, France

Saskia Brand-Gruwel Open University of the Netherlands, Heerlen, The Netherlands

Aline Chevalier University of Toulouse, Toulouse, France

Andrew Dillon Information eXperience Lab, School of Information, University of Texas at Austin, Austin, TX, USA

Wai Tat Fu Raytheon BBN Technologies, Cambridge, MA, USA

Subhashini Ganapathy Wright State University, Dayton, OH, USA

Werner Geyer IBM Research AI, Cambridge, MA, USA

Jacek Gwizdka Information eXperience Lab, School of Information, University of Texas at Austin, Austin, TX, USA

Hugo C. Huurdeman University of Amsterdam, Amsterdam, The Netherlands

Ion Juvina Wright State University, Dayton, OH, USA

Yvonne Kammerer Leibniz-Institut für Wissensmedien, Tübingen, Germany; Open University of the Netherlands, Heerlen, The Netherlands

Jaap Kamps University of Amsterdam, Amsterdam, The Netherlands

Saraschandra Karanam User Experience Group, The MathWorks, Bangalore, India

Yasaman Khazaen IBM Research AI, Cambridge, MA, USA

Othalia Larue Wright State University, Dayton, OH, USA

Q. Vera Liao IBM Research AI, Yorktwon Heights, New York, NY, USA

Mônica Macedo-Rouet University of Paris 8, Saint-Denis, France

Brandon Minnery Kairos Research, Dayton, OH, USA

Michael Muller IBM Research AI, Cambridge, MA, USA

Srikanth Nadella Kairos Research, Dayton, OH, USA

Peter Pirolli Florida Institute for Human and Machine Cognition, Pensacola, FL, USA

Anna Potocki Centre National de la Recherche Scientifique (CNRS) and Université de Poitiers, Poitiers, France

Lance Ramshaw Raytheon BBN Technologies, Cambridge, MA, USA

Jean-François Rouet Centre National de la Recherche Scientifique (CNRS) and Université de Poitiers, Poitiers, France

Mylène Sanchiz University of Toulouse, Toulouse, France

Emile Servan-Schreiber Hypermind, LLC, Paris, France; School of Collective Intelligence, Mohammed VI Polytechnic University, Ben Guerir, Morocco

Katsumi Tanaka Kyoto University, Kyoto, Japan

Kazutoshi Umemoto NICT/The University of Tokyo, Tokyo, Japan

Herre van Oostendorp Department of Information and Computing Sciences, Utrecht University, Utrecht, The Netherlands

Ralph Weischedel Information Sciences Institute, University of Southern California, Los Angeles, CA, USA

Colin Widmer Kairos Research, Dayton, OH, USA

Takehiro Yamamoto University of Hyogo, Kobe, Japan

Chapter 1
Introduction

Wai Tat Fu and Herre van Oostendorp

Abstract This book adopts a cognitive perspective to provide breadth and depth to state-of-the-art research related to understanding, analyzing, predicting, and improving one of the most prominent and important classes of behavior of modern humans: *information search*. This book is timely as the broader research area of cognitive computing and cognitive technology has recently attracted much attention, and there has been a surge in interest to develop systems that are more compatible with human cognitive abilities. The goal of this book is to introduce a coherent set of theories, methods, computational models, and empirical results that highlight how cognitively compatible systems can and should be developed to improve information search by humans. This edited book includes contributions from cognitive, social, information, and computer scientists around the globe, including researchers from Europe (France, Netherlands, Germany), the USA, and Asia (India, Japan), providing their unique but coherent perspectives to the set of core issues and questions most relevant to our current understanding of information search behavior. We expect this book will be of interest to information scientists, psychologists, and computer scientists.

1.1 The Goal of This Book

This book adopts a cognitive perspective to provide breadth and depth to state-of-the-art research related to understanding, analyzing, predicting, and improving one of the most prominent and important classes of behavior of modern humans-information search. This book is timely as the broader research area of cognitive computing and cognitive technology has recently attracted much attention, and there has been a surge in interest to develop systems that are more compatible with human

W. T. Fu (✉)
Raytheon BBN Technologies, Cambridge, MA, USA
e-mail: wai.fu@acm.org

H. van Oostendorp
Utrecht University, Utrecht, The Netherlands
e-mail: H.vanOostendorp@uu.nl

© Springer Nature Switzerland AG 2020
W. T. Fu and H. van Oostendorp (eds.), *Understanding and Improving Information Search*, Human–Computer Interaction Series,
https://doi.org/10.1007/978-3-030-38825-6_1

cognitive abilities. The goal of this book is to introduce a coherent set of theories, methods, computational models, and empirical results that highlight how cognitively compatible systems can and should be developed to improve information search by humans. This edited book includes contributions from cognitive, social, information, and computer scientists around the globe, including researchers from Europe (France, Netherlands, Germany), the USA, and Asia (India, Japan), providing their unique but coherent perspectives to the set of core issues and questions most relevant to our current understanding of information search behavior. We expect this book will be of interest to information scientists, psychologists, and computer scientists.

1.2 Applying a Cognitive Approach to Improve Information Search

There has been a recent rise of research and applications on various *cognitive technologies*, which we broadly refer to as machines that are capable of performing tasks that are traditionally done solely by humans (e.g., driving a car, engaging in a conversation, or finding relevant information from large databases). Naturally, cognitive technologies that aim to *replace* humans tend to leverage a range of existing techniques that are traditionally developed in the domain of artificial intelligence. For various reasons, building autonomous machines that completely replace humans are sometimes not possible or not desirable. As a result, there has been a recent surge of interest in developing machines that can work *along with* humans, in ways that allow humans to more effectively perform their tasks. To build machines that facilitate this kind of *human–machine collaboration*, one needs to have a good understanding of how humans process information, derive meanings from various symbolic structures (e.g., language, signs, or pictorial symbols), communicate with each other, make decisions, or make inferences. A better understanding of these cognitive functions not only allows machines to be built to help humans accomplish their tasks, but they can also be built to behave in ways that are more cognitively compatible with humans to enhance human cognitive functions (e.g., make better decisions or inferences).

The goal of this book is to focus on this cognitive approach in developing information search technologies. While there has been a long tradition of research from areas such as psychology, linguistics, and information sciences that focus on understanding of human cognitive functions in various situations, there has been relatively less research that provides a unified cognitive perspective on how to conduct research in ways that allow researchers to understand information search in meaningful contexts. Psychologists often focus on controlled experiments that lack realism. Information scientists often focus on generic processes of information flows that lack foundations from psychological theories. Computer scientists often focus on developing generic systems and interfaces for all users that lack sensitivity to unique challenges faced by different user populations. This book intends to integrate multiple perspectives from psychology, information science, and computer science to provide synergistic insights into the spectrum of topics that are relevant to developing more cognitively compatible systems for information search.

1.3 About This Book

This book has three main parts. In the *first* part, there are three chapters to provide a few foundational concepts, theories, and frameworks of this book. The main focus is on how the cognitive approach is distinct from traditional approaches in information sciences and information retrieval research in computer sciences. In fact, the cognitive approach combines these approaches in ways that allow it to provide unique perspectives that inform the development of applications to improve information search. Specifically, the first part of this book focuses on the computational cognitive modeling framework that integrates information retrieval metrics into cognitive simulations of user behavior in the broader information search process. This allows theoretical constructs in information sciences to be operationalized into computational terms to provide descriptive and prescriptive propositions to the broader set of activities related to information search behavior.

Having laid the foundational framework, in the *second* part, there are five chapters on the methods and tools that support the cognitive approach. The goal of this part is *not* to provide an exhaustive list. Rather, these chapters serve to provide examples demonstrating how empirical and computational methods and tools are used to investigate the cognitive aspects of information search. For instance, a chapter is devoted to describing how eye tracking can be a very informative technique to better understand an information searcher's interaction with a system. In addition, there are a few chapters that focus on interface features that support information search, particularly on ways that support the broader set of behavior that emerges from more complex search tasks. There is also a chapter on discussing how human cognitive abilities influence information search behavior and their implications on the development of useful tools that support users with varying cognitive abilities.

To highlight the practical aspect of the cognitive approach, in the *third and last* part, there are four chapters that demonstrate how the cognitive approach can inform the development of tools to improve information search and related activities. These four chapters not only demonstrate the utility of applying scientific understanding of information search to develop better tools and technologies, but also provide a snapshot of the emerging new application areas of information search. For example, educational interventions such as instructions or training often hinge on effective information search strategies to find relevant knowledge to solve problems. Better information search skills, however, have not yet been incorporated into mainstream educational curricula. This is partly due to the lack of principled understanding of how we should train people to perform better information search, especially for children and younger adults. Another timely issue is how to ensure that people can judge whether the information they consume is credible and not fabricated to influence people's beliefs, attitudes, or decisions. A better understanding of how users evaluate credibility will lead to better tools that help users make better credibility judgements. An important and challenging area is how people can harness the massive amount of available information to make better forecasts. Finally, an increasingly important trend is to leverage artificial intelligence tools, such as conversational agents, to facilitate the various steps in the broader information search process.

In the following parts, we will preview the contents of each part to give the reader a more detailed overview of this book.

1.3.1 Part I Foundation and Background

In Part I, we begin with the chapter by Peter Pirolli. Pirolli's chapter (Chapter 2) provides a general, yet succinct, overview of the history of computational cognitive models, and how they can (and should) be applied in the new digital ecosystem afforded by the emerging new information technologies that shape the everyday lives of most people. Pirolli coined the term human–information interaction (HII) as an emerging area of research that demands new perspectives on repurposing traditional psychological concepts and methodologies to understand the complex set of interlocking processes that allow people to find, collect, understand, and act on the diverse set of information from various dynamic sources. The key idea is that a comprehensive understanding of HII requires integration of psychological theories and concepts into computational predictive models to maintain both theoretical and computational integrity and efficiency (Gardner 1985). The chapter demonstrates the utility of computational cognitive models in predicting and explaining how people understand and develop effective knowledge representations of a topic (a process referred to as "sense-making"), judge the credibility of information and its sources, and make decisions based on these processes.

The second chapter by Wai Fu (Chapter 3) argues that information search is seldom an isolated activity. Rather, information search is often an essential element among a broader set of activities that allow a person to achieve his or her goal. For example, when one searches for a new computer laptop online, the search activity is likely initiated by the goal of purchasing a new laptop. The broader set of activities may include understanding what (new) functions or capabilities of laptop are important and relevant, how they impact the prices and thus may influence the decisions on focusing on laptops that have good trade-offs between prices and functions. Fu argues that, rather than an isolated episode of information search, these activities are better studied as a series of interdependent processes of search, learning, and decision making. Fu's chapter shows how cognitive modeling has the benefit of having a solid theoretical framework of information behavior based on research from psychology, cognitive sciences, and information sciences, and at the same time, it is capable of generating concrete computational simulations and predictions of behavior that emerge from a set of complex set of activities. In a nutshell, computational cognitive models have the distinctive advantage of providing precise computational predictions based on behavioral theories.

In the third chapter of Part I, Saraschandra Karanam and Herre van Oostendorp (Chapter 4) show how computational cognitive models can be used to explain and predict the influence of age-related cognitive abilities and domain knowledge on information search behavior. Specifically, they showed that their model, called CoLiDeS+, is capable of predicting the differences in information search and navigation behavior among people with different cognitive abilities and domain knowledge. The chapter not only demonstrates again the foundational concepts and background of computational cognitive models, but also demonstrates the utility of these models and the distinctive advantage of applying these models to provide theoretical and prescriptive propositions to improve information search.

1.3.2 Part II Methods and Tools

Information search is not only influenced by the quality of the search system, but is also influenced by the characteristics of the user. For instance, users' cognitive abilities, computer experiences, age (and many more) play a decisive role in information search behavior. Complex information search tasks often require the user to issue a number of search queries, demanding strategic reformulations of keywords after every query. Users can be supported by the search system during this phase of information search by getting feedback about what the next query should be. Also, one can imagine that when conducting a complex information search task, the support that a user needs from the search system in the beginning stages of search may be quite different from that in later stages. This part provides an overview of the development of different types of support for search. To evaluate the quality of a search system, it is common that the number and nature of queries, the time needed to solve the information problem, clicks on the search result pages (SERPs), etc. are measured, analyzed, and studied. A recent development is the use of eye tracking in order to measure where users look at and attend to, e.g., to which links on a Web page or results page they look at and for how long. An important advantage of the eye-tracking technique is that it can be done unobtrusively, that is, the search process is less likely influenced by the extra interactions imposed on the user by the system.

Part II begins with an introduction to the above issues. The part begins with the chapter by Mylène Sanchiz, Franck Amadieu and Aline Chevalier (Chapter 5), who address the role of cognitive abilities and search strategies of the user in information search. They describe important individual differences in search strategies and performance and focus on how fluid and crystallized abilities may influence the different stages of the search and how they can provide an account for users' difficulties in the search tasks. Fluid abilities refer to the abilities that support executive functioning and include cognitive flexibility like switching of attentional focus; while crystallized abilities refer to abilities that are acquired throughout life like prior knowledge, and vocabulary skills (Horn and Cattell 1967). Purpose of the chapter is to provide a theoretical and methodological foundation to better understand the role of these abilities. To this point, recent empirical studies are reviewed and analyzed in a new framework. It is demonstrated how fluid and crystallized abilities impact updating processes in working memory when searching for information.

Providing feedback on the adequacy and progress of the search and search queries can be helpful and support the direction in which the search progresses. Herre van Oostendorp and Saraschandra Karanam report in their chapter (Chapter 6) the empirical research in which the influence of providing feedback on the semantic relevance of queries and search results was examined with younger and older adults when they reformulated their search queries. In previous research, it is demonstrated that information scent (Pirolli and Card 1999), the semantic similarity between the search goal and link labels during Web search, can provide good explanations of Web navigation behavior. A similar approach is adopted in this chapter. Based on the computational modeling approach as put forward in the CoLiDeS+ model (see the chapter by Saraschandra Karanam and Herre van Oostendorp, Chapter 4), it is assumed that the information scent between a query and target information (i.e., page containing the requested information) can predict the query process if users receive at least sufficient information back from the search system. Providing feedback in this respect should be helpful to users, particularly to older users, because it is known that their executive functions including their cognitive flexibility, in general, called fluid abilities (Horn and Cattell 1967), decline with age (see specifically the chapter by Mylène Sanchiz et al., Chapter 5). More specifically, the idea examined in this chapter is that providing feedback on the semantic relevance of search queries and search results can increase the semantic relevance of future search queries as they are reformulated by the users.

Next, we discuss the idea that traditional search engines are not as well suited for more sustained and complex information search tasks. During complex information search tasks, various stages during the tasks may demand varying support needs from users (Savolainen 2018). Hugo Huurdeman and Jaap Kamps address this issue in their chapter (Chapter 7), which focuses on the question of how to design search interfaces with enhanced support for the macro-level process. They begin with a review of previous research, followed by a framework for supporting complex information search tasks, which explicitly connects the temporal development of solving complex tasks with different levels of support by search interface features. This is followed by a discussion of examples of concrete search systems that include elements of their framework in an exploratory search and sense-making context.

In the next chapter (Chapter 8), we present an overview of recent search systems including the support they offer. This is done by Kazutoshi Umemoto, Takehiro Yamamoto and Katsumi Tanaka. Their chapter provides in-depth reviews of search tools for supporting information search. With a brief introduction of cutting-edge search support tools, the authors describe the key ideas behind the tools and implications for design. They also discuss the limitations of conventional search interfaces to explore directions for future research on search support tools.

Finally, we pay attention to a relatively new technique to study information search, the eye-tracking method as studied by Jacek Gwizdka and Andrew Dillon (Chapter 9). Eyes play an essential role in information acquisition from the external world. The eye-mind link hypothesis states that human attention is where our eyes are focused (Just and Carpenter 1980). Even though covert attention phenomenon is known, it is also known that to acquire sufficient detail, for example, the meaning of text, humans need to fixate on an information object in their foveal (high-acuity) vision. Eye-mind link hypothesis together with the limited area of foveal vision and eye movement are the theoretical basis that makes eye tracking possible. In the simplest terms, eye tracking can be used to measure aspects of visual attention and task performance and it has been used to better understand a user's interaction with information. Examples are provided to demonstrate how eye-tracking data has been used to infer information relevance, user expertise, search task, reading style, and how it could be used in an adaptive information retrieval system.

1.3.3 Part III Areas of Applications

In this part, we focus on a number of different areas of applications. Searching texts both online and in print has become an essential skill for twenty-first-century students. Although most children can read fluently and comprehend short texts by the age of 10, research suggests that older students and even adults experience difficulties when searching for digital information inside digital texts, such as navigating and inspecting different Web sites in order to solve an information problem. It is important to know what difficulties young children have and how to teach the needed skills to these young users. A separate problem that has become more and more prominent is the problem of fake news or untruthful information accessed while solving information tasks. Unlike traditional news media, anyone can publish information on the Internet, often without any review or endorsement by professional gatekeepers. Thus, in order to avoid comprehending incomplete or inaccurate information, Web searchers need to critically evaluate the credibility of online information or its source. However, research has indicated that Internet users of all ages seldom engage in credibility evaluation spontaneously during Web search (Fogg 2003). Therefore, in recent years, various interventions have been developed and tested to foster individuals' credibility evaluation during Web search. Often information search is embedded in an integrated work environment for searching within and across documents supporting highlighting, annotating, and organizing information. In these complex information tasks, often called *information-intensive tasks*, users often make use of sense-making tools and sometimes this work is done collaboratively. A specific example is forecasting, that is, the process of generating judgments of probability for a wide variety of future (geopolitical) events. Recent progress in information search extends to applications that rely on conversational interactions, from speech-based devices to robots and virtual agents. Conversational interfaces are becoming widely accepted as utility tools, where a common function is to satisfy users' information needs. However, we are only starting to understand information-seeking behaviors and design opportunities when moving from conventional graphical user interfaces to conversational user interfaces.

The issues raised above introduce the chapters that will be discussed in Part III. More specifically, the four chapters in this part address the following topics. The chapter by Jean-Francois Rouet, Julie Ayoroles, Monica Macedo-Rouet and Anna Potocki (Chapter 10) synthesizes various theoretical models of the processes involved in information search, drawing from information science as well as cognitive psychology. They identify three key processes that may represent specific challenges for young students: constructing a task model, selectively scanning, and assessing the relevance of information. The evidence is reviewed regarding children's ability to search for information, and the importance of the task model is stressed on subsequent search processes (Vakkari 2003).

The next chapter (Chapter 11) by Yvonne Kammerer and Saskia Brand-Gruwel provides an overview of interventions in training credibility evaluation. Specifically, the chapter distinguishes between three different types of interventions or support tools. These are comprehensive long-term training programs that teach students the entire process of conducting Web search (of which credibility evaluation is only one aspect), short-term trainings that focus explicitly on aspects of credibility evaluation during Web search, and computer-based applications that provide prompts or cues that help evaluate the credibility of online information during Web search. The different types of approaches are compared and critically discussed in terms of both their effectiveness and limitations.

Information intensive tasks like (geopolitical) forecasting are discussed in the chapter by Ion Juvina, Othalia Larue et al. (Chapter 12). In this chapter, relevant literature is reviewed from the areas of decision making, psychology, and human–machine interaction, and the authors suggest how findings from these areas could contribute to improvements in forecasters' performance. Also, data and insights gained from the experience of the authors as competitors in a government-funded forecasting tournament are presented.

In the chapter on conversational interfaces (Chapter 13) by Vera Liao, Werner Geyer, Michael Muller, and Yasaman Khazaen, the authors start by reviewing recent work in the emerging area of conversational interfaces and layout their opportunities for supporting information search tasks. The authors then present insights from their experience deploying a chatbot supporting information search in a large enterprise. They demonstrate how a conversational interface impacts user search behavior and offers new opportunities for improving search experience, in particular for user modeling.

1.4 Summary

The three parts of this book aim to provide a solid foundation and reference for researchers and practitioners in areas related to information search. We expect that readers will find that the cognitive approach can provide unique advantages in providing a theoretical and descriptive framework for predicting how people behave in various information search task environments afforded by the emerging technological ecosystems. We also demonstrate how such framework can inform the design of better tools and technologies for people to leverage information search to improve performance in various tasks. The framework is timely as the broader research area of cognitive computing and cognitive technology has recently attracted much attention, as better computational models of human behavior are increasingly needed to complement traditional statistical approaches in machine learning to create systems that are more compatible with human social and cognitive abilities.

The chapters of this book are written for a wide and diverse audience who may or may not be experts in information search, but are interested in integrated approaches to information search. In particular, we hope that researchers and practitioners from computer science, information science, psychology, and human factors will find this book useful for their work, research, and teaching. Contributors of this book are from diverse disciplines and geographical locations, including cognitive, social, information, and computer scientists from Europe, the USA, and Asia.

References

Fogg BJ (2003) Prominence-interpretation theory: explaining how people assess credibility online. In Cockton G, Korhonen P (eds) Proceedings of CHI'03 extended abstracts on human factors in computing systems. ACM Press, New York, pp. 722–723

Gardner H (1985) The mind's new science. Basic Books, New York

Horn JL, Cattell BR (1967) Age differences in fluid and crystallized intelligence. Acta Physiol (Oxf) 26:107–129

Just MA, Carpenter PA (1980) A theory of reading: from eye fixations to comprehension. Psychol Rev 87(4):329–354

Pirolli P, Card S (1999) Information foraging. Psychol Rev 106(4):643–675

Savolainen R (2018) Information seeking processes of stage-based and cyclic approaches. J Assoc Inf Sci Technol 69(6):787–797

Vakkari P (2003) Task-based information searching. Ann Rev Inf Sci Technol 37(1):413–464

Part I
Foundation and Background

Chapter 2
Challenges for a Computational Cognitive Psychology for the New Digital Ecosystem

Peter Pirolli

Abstract Advances in computational cognitive psychology have played an important role in understanding and engineering human–information interaction systems. These computational models include several addressing the cognition involved in the human sensemaking process, user models that capture the knowledge that humans acquire from interaction, and how people judge the credibility of online Twitter users who influence decision-making. The models presented in this chapter build on earlier information foraging models in which it is important to model individual-level knowledge and experience because these clearly influence human–information interaction processes. This chapter concludes with a discussion of challenges to computational cognitive models as digital information interaction becomes increasingly pervasive and complex.

2.1 Introduction

Human–information interaction is concerned with how people interact with and process outwardly accessible information (Pirolli 2007a). It is an application field in which new systems can benefit from cognitive engineering models that synthesize results from sound cognitive science and provide predictions about technology and information designs. In turn, interactive digital systems serve as testbeds for integrated psychological theories that provide the foundation for cognitive engineering.

In this chapter, I provide a brief review of some of the advances that have been made in computational cognitive psychology that have been relevant to understanding and engineering human–information interaction systems. This chapter focuses on cognitive models of the human sensemaking process, user models that capture the knowledge that they acquire from interaction, and how people judge the credibility of online Twitter users who influence decision-making. These models address tasks

P. Pirolli (✉)
Florida Institute for Human and Machine Cognition, Pensacola, FL, USA
e-mail: ppirolli@ihmc.us

© Springer Nature Switzerland AG 2020
W. T. Fu and H. van Oostendorp (eds.), *Understanding and Improving Information Search*, Human–Computer Interaction Series,
https://doi.org/10.1007/978-3-030-38825-6_2

in which people have prolonged interactions with digital media and are shaped and influenced by their experiences.

Scientific understanding and prediction in the field of HII require integrative psychological theories. Theories need to provide predictions at multiple time-scales of phenomena and provide explanations in multiple ways (Orr et al. 2019). Theories also have to integrate across the typical subdivisions of psychological theory (Newell 1990). *Computational cognitive modeling* is an approach to understanding human psychology and behavior using concepts and tools from the computational sciences. Depending on the specific theoretical approach, the concepts may utilize computational algorithms, representations, processes, and mechanisms that may be specified as programs to capture the essence of human perception, attention, memory, thinking, actions, learning, and other functions. The predictions of computational cognitive models are often explored using computer simulations, although mathematical formulations are also often used. Modern cognitive psychology and cognitive science would not exist in its current form without computational cognitive models (Gardner 1985).

One of the significant subfields within the computational cognition approach is the development of theories of *cognitive architectures* (Kotseruba and Tsotsos 2018), which strive to unify results from disparate studies into a unified theory of how the structures and mechanisms of the mind work together to produce intelligent behavior in a wide diversity of environments. Recently, a standard model of cognition has emerged as a consensus among these cognitive architecture theories (Fig. 2.1). The early work of Card et al. (1983)—a seminal monograph in the field of human–computer interaction—had a significant impact on theories of cognitive architecture and the emergence of the *standard model of the mind*. Card et al. (1983) set out to propose what they called a *cognitive engineering model* called the Model Human Processor that was a synthesis of findings from a diverse set of cognitive psychology paradigms. Cognitive engineering models are aimed at supporting prediction about human factors in the applied contexts (Gray 2008). A designer with a cognitive engineering model in hand can explore and explain the quantitative and qualitative effects of

Fig. 2.1 Standard model of the mind (Laird et al. 2017)

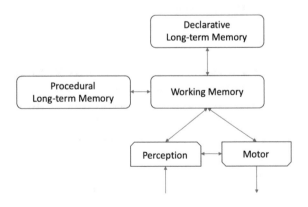

different design decisions before the heavy investment of resources for implementation and testing. This exploration of design space is more efficient because the choices among different design alternatives are better informed: Rather than operating solely by intuition, the designer is in a position to know which avenues are better to explore and which are better to ignore. Over the decades, there has been a continued symbiotic relationship among computational cognitive architectures and cognitive engineering models.

The standard model of the mind consists of independent modules that have distinct functions for perception, motor action, working memory, declarative long-term memory, and procedural long-term memory. Complex internal processing and external behavior arise from sequential *cognitive cycles*, each cycle performing a single deliberate act that might involve (for instance) initiating processing of a visual perception, initiating a retrieval of knowledge from long-term declarative memory, performing a step of abstract reasoning, or initiating a motion action. The memory components store, maintain, and retrieve content. Procedural memory stores pattern-driven knowledge about how to select and execute internal and external actions and generally provides the flow of control for the cognitive cycles. Working memory provides a temporary store of the outputs of perception and retrievals from declarative long-term memory. Long-term declarative memory stores knowledge, facts, and experiences. The standard model includes long-term learning mechanisms that incrementally adapt procedural and long-term declarative memories.

Cognitive architectures provide an integrated theory of human cognition and are consequently a good source of applied cognitive engineering theory for HII. Developing computational cognitive models forces deeper understanding and insights for HII because of the rigor required. The tools of computational simulation support the prediction of performance and failure modes without the need for uniformed experimentation (Gray et al. 1993). Often, they serve as a foundation for the development of new design principles, tools, and methods.

Table 2.1 presents a sample of HII engineering questions that have been addressed by cognitive models. In contrast to conceptual models, such as process diagrams

Table 2.1 Sample of questions that can be answered by cognitive engineering models (expanded from Pirolli [1999, 2007a])

Questions answered by cognitive models	
• What is the time it would take to perform elementary tasks, like inserting, deleting, or moving text? • How long will it take to learn the skills required for basic text editing? • Will knowledge of other applications, such as a spreadsheet, transfer to the text editor? • Will a user be able to figure out how to perform tasks (e.g., by exploration of the interface) without explicit instruction?	• What arrangement of information on a display yields more effective visual search? • How difficult will it be for a user to find information on a World Wide Web site? • What will this person learn from this Web session? • Will this person be biased in their information search? • Will this person judge this Twitter user to be a credible source?

prevalent in the field of information retrieval (e.g., Chapter 3, Hearst 2009), cognitive models provide quantitative predictions. Earlier versions of this summary have appeared in handbook chapters (Pirolli 1999, 2007a), and a comparison among them illustrates the continuing progress of the cognitive modeling and engineering approach. Only the first question about elementary HCI operations could be answered by the modeling approaches in Card, Moran, and Newell (Card et al. 1983). The last three questions have been addressed by models published since Pirolli (2007a) and are the focus of the research reviewed in this chapter. Recent research extending cognitive models to online social behavior (Orr et al. 2019) and mobile health systems for personalized behavior change (Pirolli et al. 2018) suggest these models will continue to address an ever-broadening array of engineering issues.

2.2 Sensemaking

Although many information seeking tasks are short and transactional in nature, there is a pervasive category of tasks that involve *sensemaking* (Klein et al. 2006a, b; Pirolli and Russell 2011; Russell et al. 1993). Sensemaking is the term that has emerged for human behavior surrounding the collecting and organizing information for deeper understanding. It involves finding information and learning from it, solving ill-structured problems, acquiring situation awareness, and participating in social exchanges of knowledge. Sensemaking is also a conceptual framework for the process of forming and working with meaningful representations in order to facilitate insight and subsequent intelligent action (Klein et al. 2006a, b; Pirolli and Card 2005).

As summarized in Pirolli and Russell (2011), there are actually several variants of conceptual frameworks for sensemaking. The macro-cognitive model of sensemaking (Klein et al. 2006a, b) also called the data/frame theory proposes that *situation awareness* can be considered a state-of-knowledge about the world, involving a form of mental model representation. It assumes that meaningful representations called *frames* define what counts as *data* and how those data are structured for mental processing. Frames can be expressed in a variety of forms including stories, maps, organizational diagrams, or scripts. Whereas frames define and shape data, data can mandate changes to frames. In this framework, sensemaking can involve the elaboration of a frame (e.g., filling in details), questioning a frame (e.g., due to the detection of anomalies), or reframing (e.g., rejecting a frame and replacing it with another). The data/frame theory proposes backward-looking processes are involved in forming mental models that explain past events and forward-looking mental simulations that predict how future events will unfold (see Fig. 2.2).

A similar conceptual model of Pirolli and Card (2005) derives from the study of intelligence analysts. The overall process is organized into two major loops of activities: (1) a *foraging loop* that involves processes aimed at seeking and filtering information, as well as reading and extracting information into a mental model organizing framework (Pirolli and Card 1999), and (2) a *sensemaking loop* (Russell et al. 1993) that involves iterative development of representational schemas that best fit the evidence and provide a basis for understanding the data.

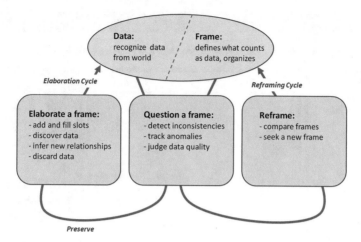

Fig. 2.2 Data/frame model (*Source* Image reproduced from Klein et al. [2006b])

2.2.1 Cognitive Model of Geospatial Sensemaking and Cognitive Biases

Lebiere et al. (2013) present a computational cognitive model of people performing a sensemaking in an experiment with a geospatial intelligence information system. The interface was map-based, and provided different layers that superimposed visual information on the map to communicate various kinds of intelligence that had been obtained (Fig. 2.3). The superimposed data layers included HUMINT (human intelligence), IMINT (image intelligence), MOVINT (movement intelligence), SIGINT (signal intelligence), and SOCINT (socio-cultural intelligence). The information foraging subtasks involved clicking through the various layers to obtain information. The users' goal was to use this information to update hypotheses about what various simulated insurgent groups were about to do next. These tasks involve an iterative process of requesting new intelligence (evidence) from available sources and using that evidence to update hypotheses about potential adversaries.

The experiment used the COIN AHA tasks, developed as part of the IARPA ICArUS program. In the COIN AHA tasks, simulated enemy groups attack at sites on roads in an area of interest. Users are assigned the problem of inferring probabilistic hypotheses about the perpetrators of the attacks. The AHA tasks included some that focused on a kind of statistical learning based on patterns of attacks by insurgent groups located on a map-like layout, and another subset of tasks that required reasoning with a set of rules (Bayesian update rules) concerning the relation of observed evidence to inferences about the likelihood of attack by different insurgent groups. Across the tasks, users had to infer which groups were responsible for attacks, allocate troops for protection, infer geographical distribution of the insurgent groups, and predict the probability of an imminent attack by each known group.

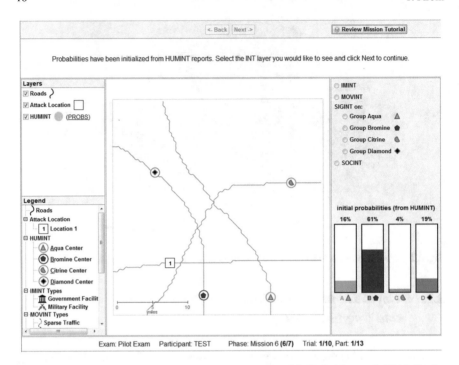

Fig. 2.3 Sample screen from a geospatial intelligence task modeled in Lebiere et al. (2013). Participants must make sense of information in the map and estimate the likelihood that a given "event" (denoted by the "1") was produced by one of four possible insurgent groups (groups aqua, bromine, citrine, or diamond). Different layers can be selected to reveal different features (layers HUMINT, MOVINT, SOCINT, and IMINT). As they process the information revealed in the different layers, participants must update their probability estimates about the group that instigated the given event using the bars in the lower right

A total of $N = 45$ people participated in an experiment using the AHA tasks. Lebiere et al. (2013) developed simulation models in ACT-R (Anderson 2007) of the information-foraging and hypothesis-updating processes involved in this sensemaking experiment. The ACT-R simulation environment is a computational architecture that supports the development of specific models. ACT-R is composed of *modules*, processing different kinds of content, which are coordinated through a centralized *production module*. Each module theoretically corresponds to a brain region. Each module is assumed to access and deposit information into *buffers* associated with the module, and the central *production module* can only respond to the contents of the buffers.

The development of the geospatial sensemaking model involved first performing an analysis and decomposition of the overarching task into *unit tasks* (Card et al. 1983). Unit tasks reflect a rational analysis of the task structure to a temporal granularity at which cognitive mechanisms can be specified to achieve those tasks. The bulk of the simulated sensemaking behavior in ACT-R was produced using a general-purpose mechanism, whereby situation-action-outcome-utility experiences are stored and retrieved as memory chunks in ACT-R declarative memory. These memory-based experiences are used to drive sensemaking behavior using a variation of *instance-based learning theory (IBLT)* (Gonzalez et al. 2003). IBLT is particularly pertinent to modeling naturalistic decision-making in complex dynamic situations. Not only did the sensemaking model provide good fits to the human performance, it accounted for data regarding the levels of cognitive biases (Nickerson 1998; Tversky and Kahneman 1974), exhibited by participants for confirmation bias, anchoring, representativeness, and probability matching. Thus, a cognitive architecture and IBLT provided a unified account of performances and biases in a complex sensemaking task. A related IBLT model is discussed below that address data about human credibility judgment.

2.3 Topic Learning and Knowledge-Tracing in Sensemaking Tasks

One common subclass of sensemaking tasks involves acquiring knowledge of some new (to the user) technical or scientific domain in order to answer questions and/or make decisions. For instance, following a medical diagnosis, most people attempt to make sense of available information in order to make medical decisions. Professional jobs frequently require that people stay up-to-date on emerging technical areas related to their work. Exploratory search technologies (Marchionini 2006; White et al. 2006) aim to provide users with means that go beyond query-based search engines, to provide users with improved ways of understanding the topical and navigational landscape of available content, and to provide improved ways of making sense of that content to achieve users' goals.

To study such topic learning with novel exploratory browsers, we developed an experimental paradigm called the *topic learning paradigm*. This paradigm is illustrated in Fig. 2.4. Participants are asked to perform as sensemaking task that involves foraging for information and making sense of it in order to answer questions, and develop a short summary that addresses certain questions. The users' conceptual model of the domain is probed and tracked over the course of the task. In earlier work, we used methods as simple as asking people to draw trees of the concepts and subconcepts in the corpus of interest (Pirolli et al. 1996) or asking them to generate precise queries (Kammerer et al. 2009). Figure 2.3 captures a variant of this paradigm used in Pirolli and Kairam (2013) in their model of sensemaking using a tagging and notebook system called Spartag.us (Nelson et al. 2009). The experiment asked users to learn about the then-new domain of Web-based mashup technology, with users tested for the knowledge of the domain before and after their sensemaking tasks. Detailed traces of each user's interactions with Spartag.us were used to diagnose user knowledge states as they interacted with the system and to make predictions about their performance on the post-experimental knowledge tests.

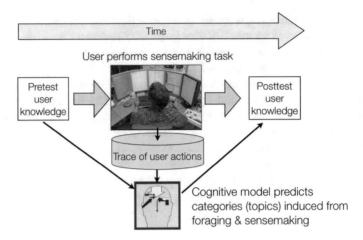

Fig. 2.4 Topic learning paradigm for studying sensemaking

A *knowledge-tracing* model (Pirolli and Kairam 2013) was developed as a user model. This knowledge-tracing model is induced from the documents tagged by an expert in a social tagging system. Tags identified with "expertise" in a domain can be used to identify a corpus of domain documents. That corpus can be fed to an automated process that distills a topic model representation (Griffiths et al. 2007) characteristic of the domain. As a user navigates and reads online material, inferences can be made about the degree to which topics in the target domain have been learned. This approach could also be used to perform new kinds of student modeling for educational purposes (Brusilovsky et al. 2016).

The Pirolli and Kairam (2013) knowledge-tracing model was developed in three stages. First, a topic model was developed to represent user knowledge states. This stage involved the use of latent Dirichlet allocation (LDA; Blei et al. 2003) to induce the latent topics inherent in the subject domain. Knowledge of the domain can be represented as the possession of different degrees of latent ability (or "strength-of-knowledge" of a topic, see Fig. 2.5) with respect to each of these underlying latent topics. Second, a measurement framework (using a Rasch model; Rasch 1960) was developed to assess users' knowledge profiles across those latent topics. Users' responses to questions and their Web browsing traces can be used to measure knowledge of the latent topics. Third, the modeling and measurement predictions were tested against the observed pre- and post-test questions about the target domain from a topic learning study (Nelson et al. 2009). In the Nelson et al. (2009) study, the sensemaking task involved learning about the then-novel domain of Web 2.0 mashups, and example pre- and post-test items were questions such as "Intel is strongly involved in building a Web mashup maker" or "Web mashup software is typically written in XML." The predictions concerned the individual learning gains made by each user as they engaged in the sensemaking task, using recorded traces of their behavior collected with Spartag.us. Gain scores for each

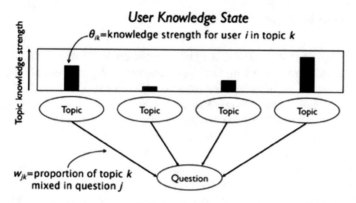

Fig. 2.5 Knowledge-tracing user model (Pirolli and Kairam 2013) is a profile of strength-of-knowledge weights (indicated by bar heights). A user's knowledge profile is modified by the mix of topics that they read while sensemaking. The likelihood that a user will be able to answer a given question is predicted by the user's knowledge profile over the topic mix embedded in the question

individual were calculated as *gain* = (*posttest score* – *pretest score*)/(*max score* – *pretest score*). These learning gains predicted by the knowledge-tracing model, and the observed gains, are reproduced in Fig. 2.6.

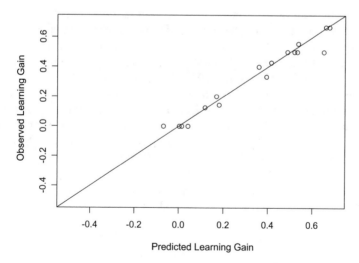

Fig. 2.6 Observed learning gains against learning gains predicted by a knowledge-tracing model (Pirolli and Kairam 2013)

2.4 Credibility

Cognitive models (Pirolli 2007a, b, c) of information foraging explain and predict human browsing and search with Web-based content. A major aspect of such models concerns how cues are perceived and used to judge information scent. These models assess how complex cues are processed to make judgments about relevance, and how those judgments affect decisions about actions to take to get to the most useful information (i.e., how to optimize information foraging).

Beyond the use of information scent to guide information navigation, an additional concern is how people assess cues about online information sources (e.g., the Web; Twitter; Facebook) to judge their credibility, and how those credibility judgments bias decision-making. In making decisions about what products to buy, which destinations to visit on vacation, or who to vote for in an election, people frequently take in information from online sources that vary in their credibility (Birnbaum 1979; Hovland et al. 1953). Early models developed to address credibility judgments about Web sites generally fell into two categories. One category involved stage models that focus on the iterative process of credibility evaluation, i.e., how the assessment takes place when users open a page, read the contents, and are further involved with the site (Diana et al. 2016). The other main category follows a bottom-up approach attempting to empirically establish what elements on a Web page impact users' credibility judgment.

Inspired by both of these approaches, Liao et al. (2012) developed a detailed ACT-R cognitive model covering both the iterative processes of stage models and the impact on credibility judgment of specific-user interface cues in different task and content contexts. The model addressed data from an earlier study of the Twitter microblogging service (Canini et al. 2011). In that study, participants were presented with a page generated to represent individual Twitter users. Each of these generated pages included a user name and icon, a set of social status statistics (number of following, followers, and tweets), 40 tweets by the user, and a word cloud summarizing the Twitter user's generated content. Among other things, each participant was asked to rate presented Twitter users' credibility in making judgments in the specific domain of car purchases. The Canini et al. (2011) study manipulated the content domain in which credibility judgments were made, as well as cues about the presented Twitter user's social status, and the type of visualization used by the participants.

The ACT-R model of credibility judgment relies primarily on the instance-based learning theory mechanisms discussed above. The ACT-R credibility model is set up with declarative memory content that is intended to represent word semantics and topics that model the knowledge and experience of an average user. This declarative memory content includes word chunks, topic chunks, and credibility chunks, and optionally, contextual cue chunks capturing the perceived social status of encountered Twitter users based on their follower/followee statistics (Canini et al. 2011). These chunks are created by processing a corpus of tweets collected from 1,800 Twitter accounts randomly chosen from different WeFollow directories.[1] From these data, word chunks were created to represent the 3,000 highest frequency words in the corpus. Latent Dirichlet allocation (LDA) topic modeling (Blei et al. 2003) was used to induce topic chunks. The ACT-R model for Twitter page credibility judgment uses two buffers in addition to the basic ACT-R buffers: a word buffer and a credibility cue buffer. The content of the word buffer reflects the text that the model attends to and holds in a short-term memory. The credibility cue buffer contains cues identified by the model which may potentially have an impact on credibility judgments. This model performs a three stage process: (1) perception and attention to the words in tweets, (2) the identification of information cues that impact credibility judgment that uses the spreading activation mechanism of ACT-R, (3) use of the information cues to make a credibility judgment using the declarative memory blending mechanism in ACT-R (Gonzalez et al. 2003).

This ACT-R credibility model was matched to data from participants who rated a Twitter author's credibility for giving recommendation on topics such as car prices. Figure 2.7 shows the participant results and model results for credibility ratings about ten users chosen from the WeFollow directories of cars. The fit between human and model results for credibility judgments about car prices is $R^2 = 0.56$.

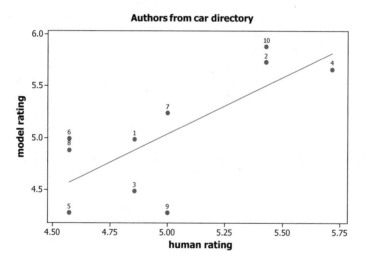

Fig. 2.7 Predicted credibility ratings against human ratings for ten users from WeFollow (Liao et al. 2012) (Numbers above the data points index specific users)

---

[1] https://twitter.com/wefollow?lang=en.

2.5 Conclusion

This chapter illustrates a continued expansion of the domain of cognitive engineering models (Table 2.1). More specifically, the models presented here build on earlier information foraging models in which it became important to model individual-level knowledge and experience because it clearly influences human–information interaction processes. There are numerous challenges to the continued development of rigorous cognitive engineering models. These challenges arise from the reality that in the time since the origins of research on the psychology of human–computer interaction (Card et al. 1983), information systems have advanced at an extraordinary rate. Cognitive models have been useful in the design of novel information foraging techniques (Olston and Chi 2003; Suh et al. 2002) and techniques addressing bias and credibility in sensemaking (Vydiswaran et al. 2012a, b) and knowledge gains from sensemaking (Brusilovsky et al. 2016).

One challenge is that people are now engaged in *prolonged modes of interaction with pervasive digital infrastructure*. Since the days of the 1980s desktop, our interaction with information systems has evolved to become pervasive throughout our daily lives and it involves richer and more prolonged modes of interaction. How people make sense of the online world and are influenced by their experiences drives much of the current engineering of the online universe. The models presented here are an attempt to capture just a fraction of these prolonged engagements.

Another challenge is the need for expansion of computational cognitive theory. Human psychology and behavior in this new digital ecology of everyday life require the expansion of existing computational theories of cognition. Existing theory needs to be expanded to embrace the richness of psychological phenomena at multiple time-scales (Orr et al. 2019) and the importance of modeling the unique individual knowledge and experience that accumulates with near-continuous online interactions.

A further challenge is the need for new methods. Because information systems have become so pervasive in everyday life, a significant challenge for experimental behavioral science is the ability to generalize from results obtained in the laboratory to be able to say something scientific and relevant about the meaningful activities people perform in their daily lives (Baumeister et al. 2007). Pervasive digital infrastructure provides new challenges—as well as new opportunities—for experimental methods to study such behavior. One area in which new rigorous methods are being explored is digital health platforms (Pirolli et al. 2018). For instance, the sequential multiple assignment randomized trial method (SMART; Collins et al. 2007) is suited for understanding sequentially delivered interventions–for instance, a sequence of tests that compare treatment versus control conditions. Micro-randomized trials (Klasnja et al. 2015) combine aspects of within-participant and between-participant experimental designs in ways that greatly increase statistical power. Each of these methods extends traditional experimental designs and statistical techniques in ways that are more congruent with how digital platforms actually operate and collect rich data. In commercial systems, it is commonplace to engineer systems having user models that track individuals over the long term, that utilize data from all levels of time-scales, and that are refined through continuous experimental testing. Continued evolutions of science-based cognitive models will likely need to meet these challenges using similar, although more scientifically justified techniques.

References

Anderson JR (2007) How can the human mind occur in the physical universe? Oxford University Press, Oxford, UK

Baumeister RF, Vohs KD, Funder DC (2007) Psychology as the science of self-reports and finger movements: whatever happened to actual behavior? Perspect Psychol Sci 2(4):396–403. https://doi.org/10.1111/j.1745-6916.2007.00051.x

Birnbaum MH (1979) Source credibility in social judgment: bias, expertise, and the judge's point of view. J Pers Soc Psychol 37(1):48–74

Blei DM, Ng AY, Jordan MI (2003) Latent Dirichlet allocation. J Mach Learn Res 3:993–1022

Brusilovsky P, Somyurek S, Guerra J, Hosseini R, Zadorozhny V, Durlach PJ (2016) Open social student modeling for personalized learning. IEEE Trans Emerg Top Comput 4:450–461. https://doi.org/10.1109/TETC.2015.2501243

Canini K, Suh B, Pirolli P (2011) Finding credible information sources in social networks based on content and social structure. Paper presented at the IEEE international conference on social computing, SocialCom 2011, Boston, MA

Card SK, Moran TP, Newell A (1983) The psychology of human-computer interaction. Lawrence Erlbaum Associates, Hillsdale, NJ

Collins LM, Murphy SA, Strecher V (2007) The multiphase optimization strategy (MOST) and the sequential multiple assignment randomized trial (SMART): new methods for more potent eHealth interventions. Am J Prev Med 32(5 Suppl):S112–118. https://doi.org/10.1016/j.amepre.2007.01.022

Diana F, Bahry S, Masrom M, Masrek MN (2016) Website credibility and user engagement: a theoretical integration. Paper presented at the 2016 4th international conference on user science and engineering (i-USEr), 23–25 August 2016

Gardner H (1985) The mind's new science. Basic Books, New York

Gonzalez C, Lerch JF, Lebiere C (2003) Instance-based learning in dynamic decision making. Cogn Sci 27:591–635

Gray WD (2008) Cognitive modeling for cognitive engineering. In: Sun R (ed) The Cambridge handbook of computational psychology. Cambridge University Press, Cambridge, pp 565–588

Gray WD, John BE, Atwood ME (1993) Project Ernestine: A validation of GOMS for prediction and explanation of real-world task performance. Hum-Comput Interact 8:237–309

Griffiths TL, Steyvers M, Tenenbaum JB (2007) Topics in semantic representation. Psychol Rev 114(2):211–244

Hearst MA (2009) Search user interfaces. Cambridge University Press, New York

Hovland CI, Janis IL, Kelley HH (1953) Communication and persuasion. Yale University Press, New Haven, CT

Kammerer Y, Nairn R, Pirolli P, Chi EH (2009) Signpost from the masses: learning effects in an exploratory social tag search browser. Paper presented at the proceedings of the 27th international conference on human factors in computing systems, Boston, MA, USA

Klasnja P, Hekler EB, Shiffman S, Boruvka A, Almirall D, Tewari A, Murphy SA (2015) Micro-randomized trials: an experimental design for developing just-in-time adaptive interventions. Health Psychol: Official J Div Health Psychol, Am Psychol Assoc 34:1220–1228. https://doi.org/10.1037/hea0000305

Klein G, Moon B, Hoffman RR (2006a) Making sense of sensemaking 1: alternative perspectives. IEEE Intell Syst 21(4):70–73

Klein G, Moon B, Hoffman RR (2006b) Making sense of sensemaking 2: a macrocognitive model. IEEE Intell Syst 21(5):88–92

Kotseruba I, Tsotsos JK (2018) 40 years of cognitive architectures: core cognitive abilities and practical applications. Artif Intell Rev. https://doi.org/10.1007/s10462-018-9646-y

Laird JE, Lebiere C, Rosenbloom PS (2017) A standard model of the mind: toward a common computational framework across artificial intelligence, cognitive science, neuroscience, and robotics. AI Mag 38:13–16. https://doi.org/10.1609/aimag.v38i4.2744

Lebiere C, Pirolli P, Thomson R, Paik J, Rutledge-Taylor M, Staszewski J, Anderson JR (2013) A functional model of sensemaking in a neurocognitive architecture. Comput Intell Neurosci 2013:921695. https://doi.org/10.1155/2013/921695

Liao QV, Pirolli P, Fu W (2012) An ACT-R model of credibility judgment of micro-blogging Web pages. Proceedings of the international conference on cognitive modeling (ICCM 2012). Universitätsverlag der TU Berlin, Berlin, pp 103–108

Marchionini G (2006) Exploratory search: from finding to understanding. Commun ACM 49(4):41–46. http://doi.acm.org/10.1145/1121949.1121979

Nelson L, Held C, Pirolli P, Hong L, Schiano D, Chi EH (2009) With a little help from my friends: examining the impact of social annotations in sensemaking tasks. Paper presented at the proceedings of the 27th international conference on human factors in computing systems, Boston, MA, USA

Newell A (1990) Unified theories of cognition. Harvard University Press, Cambridge, MA

Nickerson RS (1998) Confirmation bias: a ubiquitous phenomenon in many guises. Rev Gen Psychol 2(2):175–220. https://doi.org/10.1037/1089-2680.2.2.175

Olston C, Chi EH (2003) ScentTrails: integrating browsing and searching on the Web. ACM Trans Comput-Hum Interact 10(3):177–197

Orr MG, Lebiere C, Stocco A, Pirolli P, Pires B, Kennedy WG (2019) Multi-scale resolution of neural, cognitive and social systems. Comput Math Organ Theor 25(1):4–23. https://doi.org/10.1007/s10588-018-09291-0

Pirolli P (1999) Cognitive engineering models and cognitive architectures in human-computer interaction. In: Durso FT, Nickerson RS, Schvaneveldt RW, Dumais ST, Lindsay DS, Chi MTH (eds) Handbook of applied cognition. Wiley, West Sussex, England, pp 441–477

Pirolli P (2007a) Cognitive models of human-information interaction. In: Durso FT (ed) Handbook of applied cognition, 2nd edn. Wiley, West Sussex, England, pp 443–470

Pirolli P (2007b) Information foraging theory: adaptive interaction with information. Oxford University Press, Oxford; New York

Pirolli P (2007c) Information foraging: a theory of adaptive interaction with information. Oxford University Press, New York

Pirolli P, Card SK (1999) Information foraging. Psychol Rev 106:643–675

Pirolli P, Card SK (2005) The sensemaking process and leverage points for analyst technology. Paper presented at the 2005 international conference on intelligence analysis, McLean, VA

Pirolli P, Kairam S (2013) A knowledge-tracing model of learning from a social tagging system. User Model User-Adap Inter 1–30. https://doi.org/10.1007/s11257-012-9132-1

Pirolli P, Russell DM (2011) Introduction to this special issue on sensemaking. Hum-Comput Inter 26:1–8

Pirolli P, Schank P, Hearst M, Diehl C (1996) Scatter/Gather browsing communicates the topic structure of a very large text collection. Proceedings of the conference on human factors in computing systems, CHI '96. ACM Press, Vancouver, BC, pp 213–220

Pirolli P, Youngblood GM, Du H, Konrad A, Nelson L, Springer A (2018) Scaffolding the mastery of healthy behaviors with fittle + systems: evidence-based interventions and theory. Hum–Comput Interact, 1–34. https://doi.org/10.1080/07370024.2018.1512414

Rasch G (1960) Probabilistic models for some intelligence and attainment tests. Danish Institute for Educational Research, Copenhagen

Russell DM, Stefik MJ, Pirolli P, Card SK (1993) The cost structure of sensemaking. Paper presented at the INTERCHI '93 conference on human factors in computing systems, Amsterdam

Suh B, Woodruff A, Rosenholtz R, Glass A (2002) Popout prism: adding perceptual principles to overview + detail document interfaces. CHI 2002, ACM Conf Hum Fact Comput Syst, CHI Lett 4(1):251–258

Tversky A, Kahneman D (1974) Judgment under uncertainty: heuristics and biases. Science 185:1124–1131

Vydiswaran V, Zhai C, Roth D, Pirolli P (2012) Unibiased learning of controversial topics. In Proceedings of the annual meeting of the American Society for Information Science and Technology (ASIST), ASIST, Baltimore, MD.

Vydiswaran VGV, Zhai C, Roth D, Pirolli P (2012) BiasTrust: teaching biased users about controversial topics. In CIKM 2012. ACM, Maui, Hawaii

White RW, Kules B, Drucker SM, schraefel mc (2006) Supporting exploratory search: introduction. Commun ACM 49(4):36–39. http://doi.acm.org/10.1145/1121949.1121978

Chapter 3
How Cognitive Computational Models Can Improve Information Search

Wai Tat Fu

Abstract This chapter discusses why and how a computational cognitive model that captures the broader set of processes of information search is important and useful. The first reason why this can be useful is when information search is only one component of a broader task. A better understanding of the broader process of information search can lead to better metrics of relevance that are specific to the broader task in which the user is engaged. The second reason is that it helps to develop better personalized tools that are more compatible with the individual users as they search information for different purposes. Two examples of such computational cognitive models are presented. The first model, SNIF-ACT, demonstrates the value of adopting a theory-based mechanism, called the Bayesian satisficing mechanism (BSM), that selects information search strategies based on ongoing assessment of the information scent cues encountered by a user as he or she navigates across Web pages. The second model, ESL, tracks both learning of knowledge structures and search behavior in a social tagging system over a period of eight weeks as they continuously search for Web documents. These computational cognitive models generate explicit predictions on what users will do when they interact with different information retrieval systems for different tasks in different contexts. Computational cognitive models therefore complement existing computational techniques that aim to improve information or document retrieval. At the same time, they allow researchers to develop and test unified theories of information search by integrating the vast literature on information search behavior in different contexts.

3.1 Introduction

Information search has become one of the most common human activities in modern societies. Typically, information search is initiated when a person needs information to accomplish a task, such as solving a problem, making a decision, or learning a new

W. T. Fu (✉)
Raytheon BBN Technologies, Cambridge, MA, USA
e-mail: wai.fu@acm.org

© Springer Nature Switzerland AG 2020
W. T. Fu and H. van Oostendorp (eds.), *Understanding and Improving Information Search*, Human–Computer Interaction Series,
https://doi.org/10.1007/978-3-030-38825-6_3

topic. There has been a long history of research that aims to improve information search, and they can be generally put into two major categories. One line of research aims to improve an information retrieval system by optimizing metrics that characterize the relevance of retrieved documents (e.g., Web pages) to the query terms entered by a user. This line of research often relies on computational techniques that improve the indexing and ranking of documents based on relevance metrics such as semantic relatedness (e.g., Manning and Schütze 1999). Another line of research aims to investigate the broader process of information search that users engage in (e.g., Kuhlthau 1991, 2004). This line of research often combines both quantitative and qualitative analysis of user behavior, such as how they represent and express their information goals, how they evaluate relevance of information, or how they decide to select different information sources to accomplish their goals. User behavior is often expressed as descriptive models that characterize the general stages or phases of the broader information search process. These models are useful for guiding design of information search interfaces or systems and inform features that can support user search behavior.

Although these two lines of research have demonstrated their importance in providing useful guidelines for improving information search, there have been relatively few attempts to integrate the approaches. For example, while new computational techniques have led to more powerful and efficient online search engines, it is not clear how these computational techniques can improve the broader information search process in different contexts and how they can be personalized for individual users. Similarly, while descriptive models of information search are useful for understanding the nuances of user search behavior in different contexts, the qualitative nature of these models make it difficult to directly inform better computational techniques for information retrieval systems. To better integrate these approaches, one may need a unifying computational framework that is compatible with common metrics used in optimization of information retrieval systems, and at the same time, capable of computationally characterizing the broader information search process. The goal of this chapter is to introduce such framework—a computational cognitive modeling framework that integrates information retrieval metrics into cognitive simulations of user behavior in the broader information search process.

Developing a computational model that captures the broader process of information search is important for at least two reasons. First, understanding how information can inform and help people to perform their tasks will likely lead to better metrics of relevance that are specific to the tasks. For example, when deciding to purchase a consumer product, say a laptop computer, users may not know what attributes are important. One way that they can learn more about how to choose is to browse attributes of multiple laptop computers online, read reviews about these computers, and understand the importance of, for example, screen sizes, displays, weights, memory sizes, and how they may impact the prices of the computers. They can use the information to learn how to evaluate attributes that are more personally important to them. This initial phase of exploration not only helps users identify important attributes, but also helps them formulate their subsequent searches (e.g., they may look for and compare only laptops weighing less than 6 lb) and evaluate available options (knowing that they tend to be in a certain price range). In contrast to item-specific search (e.g., looking for the address of a restaurant), in such exploratory search situations, search engines may benefit from the use of diversity measures in the metric of relevance such that search results can be more useful. For example, without knowing what attributes are important to users, search engines may sample laptop computers that vary in multiple dimensions (instead of picking the most popular one) to help users to identify attributes that are important to them.

The second reason to develop computational models of the broader process of information search is to develop better personalized tools that are more compatible with the individual users as they search information for different purposes. As the example above shows, when users are learning a new topic by information search, tools that help them incrementally build up their knowledge as they encounter new information will likely lead to more effective learning environments. For example, tools that allow people to establish semantic relations among concepts, causal relations among events, or different perspectives that people have on social issues may help people develop a better higher-level understanding of information.

Traditionally, computational cognitive models are predictive models or computer programs that simulate mental operations and human behavior in different contexts (e.g., ACT-R, SOAR, etc.). These simulations can be useful for understanding, evaluating, and improving information search by, for example, highlighting how information search behavior dynamically adapts to environmental structures (e.g., search results returned from a query). In this chapter, I will describe two examples of how computational cognitive models can improve information search. In the first example, I will discuss a model called SNIF-ACT (Fu and Pirolli 2007), which predicts how the history of information cues encountered by a user will impact the strategies of information search. In the second example, I will discuss a model called exploratory search and learning (ESL) that aims to predict search and learning behavior when the user is engaged in online learning (Fu and Dong 2012). In the initial phases of online learning, the goal of information search is ambiguous and ill-defined. Through iterative cycles of searching and learning, the goal becomes incrementally more focused and well-defined. A more well-defined information search goal in turn leads to more focused information search behavior. The ESL model is useful for understanding how one can build better tools to improve information search that is more explorative in nature, in which the user learns new information to better articulate their information search goals over time. The main goal of this chapter is to show how computational cognitive models can generate simulations of user behavior of the broader information search process in different contexts, and how these simulations can be useful for design of intelligent interfaces that improve information search.

3.2 The SNIF-ACT Model

SNIF-ACT, which stands for Scent-based Navigation and Information Foraging in the ACT (adaptive control of thought) architecture, provides an account of how people use information scent cues, such as the text associated with Web links, to make Web navigation decisions such as evaluating which link to go next or when to give up on a particular path of information search. SNIF-ACT is shaped by rational analyses of the Web developed by combining the Bayesian satisficing model (BSM; Fu and Gray 2006) with the information foraging theory (Pirolli and Card 1999), and is implemented in a modified version of the ACT-R cognitive architecture (Anderson et al. 2004). While it is beyond the scope of the chapter to review these theories and cognitive architecture, it is useful to point out that the model calculates relevance of information scent cues (e.g., link text) to information goal (e.g., query terms) by the semantic similarities between the cues and the goal. The calculation of semantic similarities is similar to many existing computational methods in text analysis (see e.g., Chapter 3, Karanam and van Oostendorp, this volume; Karanam et al. 2016; Landauer et al. 2007; Manning and Schütze 1999), which statistically estimates how likely two words have similar meanings based on analysis of large text corpuses.

SNIF-ACT is a computational cognitive model that predicts information search strategies of human users by simulating the mental or physical steps that allow the users to follow information scent cues to accomplish their information goals. For example, when a user enters query terms into a search engine, s/he will evaluate the search results, click on a Web link, evaluate the page, then decide to click on another link on the page, go back to the previous page, or go back to the search engine and enter different query terms to search. SNIF-ACT assumes a set of elementary mental or physical (which can be perceptual, cognitive, or motor) steps such as evaluate-link, click-link, go-back, etc. Each step is expressed as a *production*, a term that refers to such a mental or physical step in the ACT-R architecture. A production is essentially an *if-then* rule. The *if* part of the production specifies the conditions under which the production can potentially match the current conditions (e.g., the goal = enter search terms, memory contents = search terms retrieved from memory, physical states of the environment = search box is shown on a Web page). The then part of the production specifies what actions will be taken (e.g., click on a link). When the *if* part of a production matches the current conditions, it will be put in a conflict set. On each model cycle, productions in the conflict set will be evaluated based on the values of the *utilities*. Calculations of these utilities will be discussed below.

In SNIF-ACT, the utilities are calculated as a function of the information scent values of cues that the model encounters. As a result, the model is able to dynamically change its behavior based on different information scent cues that it encounters as it navigates across dynamic Web pages. To illustrate this point, a simple example is presented in Fig. 3.1, in which it shows the utilities of three productions: Click-Link, Attend-to-Link, Backup-a-page change over model cycles, and how the changes influence the probabilities that each production will be selected and executed. In this example, the information scent values of the link are decreasing as the model goes down the page (e.g., in a typical search results page). As the evaluation of individual links progresses, the experience of decreasing value of information scent leads to an increase in the probability that the model will stop evaluating and select the link with a higher information scent value that it encountered before (based on the Bayesian satisficing mechanism, Fu and Gray 2006).

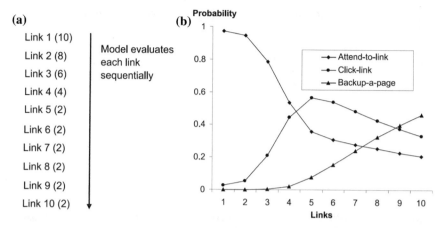

Fig. 3.1 SNIF-ACT 2.0 dynamically adjusts the utilities and probability values of productions as it evaluates each link sequentially on an example Web page (adapted from Fu and Pirolli 2007)

3.2.1 Validation of the Model

To illustrate how the model is useful for predicting user behavior, we validated the model using data from tasks performed on help.yahoo.com (the help system section of Yahoo!). 30 Participants using the Yahoo sites were tested with a set of eight tasks, for a total of eight tasks (See Fu and Pirolli 2007 for details). For each task, the user was given an information goal in the form of a question. Users were explicitly asked not to use the search feature of the site, given our interests in how people navigated using Web links. Whenever the user wanted to abandon a task, or if they felt they had achieved the goal, the user clicked on a button signifying the end of the task. All pages they accessed and the keystrokes they entered (if any) were recorded.

Figure 3.2 shows the scatter plots of the number of times the links on all Web pages were selected by the model and participants. If the model's predictions were perfect, all points should lie on the straight line that passes through the origin with a slope of 1. The results show that, in general, the model did a good job describing the data, ($R^2 = 0.91$). These results show that, in general, links frequently chosen by participants were also chosen frequently by the model. This is important because this demonstrates the ability of SNIF-ACT 2.0 to identify the links most likely chosen by the participants across a wide range of tasks.

To highlight the predictive power of the BSM in SNIF-ACT 2.0, we compared the simulation results to those produced by a Position model. The Position model predicts only the ranks of links on a given Web page based on the position of links and did not depend on its information scent value. We see that for the Position model, we obtained $R^2 = 0.45$, which had worse fit than SNIF-ACT 2.0. Figure 3.2 shows that the Position model was worse at identifying many of the "attractor" pages (i.e., pages selected by many users through multiple links), as shown by the data points lying on or close to the x-axis. On the other hand, the Position model frequently chose links

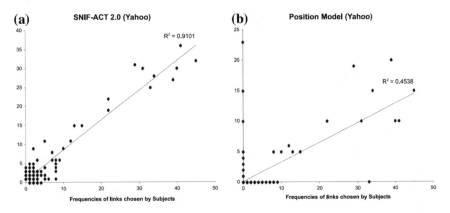

Fig. 3.2 Results of SNIF-ACT 2.0 and the Position model in predicting information search behavior. *Y*-axis is frequencies of links chosen by the SNIF-ACT model

that were not chosen by the participants, as shown by the data points lying on the *y*-axis. The results were consistent with the assumption of the SNIF-ACT 2.0 model: Participants tended to "satisfice" on "reasonably good" links presented earlier on the Web page rather than exhaustively finding the best links on the whole Web page. This highlights the importance of including dynamic mechanisms that take ongoing assessments of link context into account when describing detailed user interactions with the Web page.

3.2.2 Summary

The SNIF-ACT model integrates a computational metric of relevance called information scent into a cognitive model that simulates the elementary mental operations in the broader information search process. The model was capable of predicting that link selection is influenced by the history of links encountered by a user. Specifically, a Bayesian satisficing process that dynamically adjusts the values of information scent is used to decide when a link will be selected and when to go back to the previous page. This dynamic process allows the model to simulate the broader information search process in real Web pages, and was shown to match well to how different users look for information across a wide range of information search tasks. In particular, compared to models that do not adapt to histories of link evaluation during the search process, SNIF-ACT was more accurate in predicting "attractor" pages that were chosen frequently by users.

SNIF-ACT demonstrates how computational simulations of the broader search process can be useful for improving information search. For example, one may want to evaluate different metrics of relevance in search engines. In addition to performance in document retrievals (e.g., using precision and recall measures), one can use SNIF-ACT to understand how different search engines may impact the broader information search process. It is possible that, for example, search engines that promote diversity of search results could be more useful for certain tasks and users (e.g., when exploring for options) and not others (e.g., when search for information related to a specific event or topic). A computational cognitive model can be very useful for improving information search by simulating how users evaluate search results and how they make subsequent navigation decisions. In the next section, I will demonstrate how computational cognitive models can also simulate mental processes that influence subsequent search behavior, such as those that are involved in concept learning.

3.3 The Explorative Search and Learning (ESL) Model

A common and important goal of information search is online learning. In such situation, a user starts with a general, often ambiguous and poorly defined, information goal, and slowly learns more information that allows the goal to become more specific over time (e.g., knowing more specifically what information to search for), which in turn influences evaluation and selection of information (Marchionini 2006). This kind of information search has become more common, especially with the rise of the *participatory Web*. The possibilities for using participatory Web technologies for learning are endless. One form of learning that has attracted much attention is when multiple users engage in knowledge exploration in a social tagging system—a platform that allows multiple users to annotate information for others to use. In a social tagging system, when users assign tags (a small number of keywords) to Web pages, the choice of tags is not only influenced by the information contents of the Web page, but also how other users have tagged the same or similar Web pages (Cattuto et al. 2007; Golder and Huberman 2006; Fu et al. 2010b). For example, when a person is browsing for Web pages related to the topic of "anti-aging," he or she may initially believe that pages related to skin care will be relevant to the topic. However, when the person sees that a Web page on genetic engineering has been assigned the tag "anti-aging," he or she may start to realize that the concepts of genetic engineering and anti-aging are related to each other. Similarly, as the person sees other tags that co-occur with the tag "anti-aging" (or tags that are assigned to the same or similar documents), he or she may learn that these tags (or concepts behind these tags) are also associated with the concept of anti-aging. In other words, as a person explores for information related to a topic, the person will learn the context (i.e., related topics) associated with the topic based on the tag-document and tag-tag structures contributed by other users of the system.

Learning through online search involves finding and evaluating relevant documents related to the topic, comprehending and extracting information from the documents, and integrating extracted information with existing knowledge. Social tagging systems can therefore potentially facilitate learning as users perform knowledge exploration through the guidance of social tags in the system. They also serve as a good testbed for online learning, as social tags created by multiple users can provide important insights into how users index new information, and how these indices change as they learn more about a topic.

As people search through a social tagging system, new knowledge is learned. This process of knowledge growth can be traced to the Piaget's (1975) developmental model of equilibration of cognitive structures in children, and it has also been adopted by other prominent theories of knowledge representation and acquisition. According to Piaget, there are at least two processes through which new experiences interact with existing schemas. When new experiences are modified to fit existing schemas, the process is defined as *assimilation*. In this case, existing schemas influence how we *interpret* new information extracted from documents. In contrast, *accommodation* is an adaptation process of knowledge acquisition that changes the schemas in order to fit the new experience, or the person creates an entirely new schema in order to accommodate new data that does not fit any of their existing schemas. Through the process of knowledge assimilation and accommodation, people can adapt to new experiences that they obtain from their interactions with others, such as when they discuss, share, or exchange information.

The explorative search and learning (ESL) model is a computational cognitive model that simulates how knowledge structures are changed with new information that is acquired through the assimilation and accommodation processes described above (details of these computational mechanisms can be found in Fu et al. 2009, 2010a; Fu and Dong 2010). In general, the ESL model assumes that internal knowledge representations will influence how users interpret information in different Web pages, the tags created by others, as well as the tags they assign to Web pages that they bookmark. This assumption is consistent with a number of previous research that shows that domain expertise can significantly influence document selection and Web navigation (Cole et al. 2011; Juvina and van Oostendorp 2008; Karanam et al. 2017). To a certain extent, these internal representations are shared among others through the external representations (tags) of the information content of the Web pages. While users may contribute tags to different Web pages, they may also need to interpret tags created by others as they navigate in the system.

In previous research, we have shown that the interpretation process will influence users' own internal knowledge representations through a *semantic imitation* process (Fu et al. 2010b). The major characteristics of this semantic imitation process are that:

1. both internal and external representations may influence the search and interpretation of the Web document, and
2. the understanding and interpretation of Web documents may influence both the internal (concepts) and external representations (tagged contents) of knowledge.

Fu et al. (2010b) showed that semantic imitation may be one of the spontaneous processes in social information systems that contribute to emergent behavioral patterns and structures in the systems (Fu et al. 2009; Golder and Huberman 2006).

To formalize the analysis, the ESL model is developed to simulate how users search and learn through interactions with a social tagging system. Figure 3.3 shows

Fig. 3.3 General structure of the explorative search and learning (ESL) model

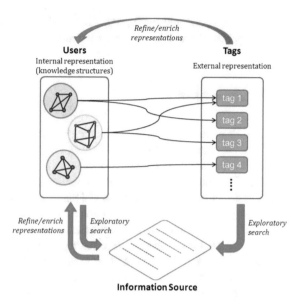

the structure of the model. The model assumes that a user can perform *exploratory search* by using social tags in the system as navigational cues to help them to explore for relevant information sources. Interpreting the tagged information contents allows the user to learn more relevant topics and how these topics are indexed (tagged) by other users, thus allowing the user to refine and enrich their internal knowledge representations of the topics. The user can also create tags based on his or her interpretation of the information contents, enriching the external folksonomies in the system. The model assumes that people will naturally categorize Web documents and their associated context (such as tags created by other users, related documents, or related links presented on a social information system) as they interact and comprehend the contents and the tags of the documents. Tags assigned to documents become features that allow users to predict the unobserved contents of the documents, thus allowing users to more correctly evaluate the relevance of the information.

3.4 Validating the ESL Model—An Empirical Study

An empirical study was conducted to validate the model, in which a set of exploratory learning tasks was given to participants. In all tasks, participants were given a rough description of the topic and gradually acquired knowledge about the topic through an iterative search-and-learn knowledge exploration cycle. Following the tradition of representative design (Brunswik 1955; Hammond 1996; Fu 2008), we chose to follow a small number of subjects over a period of eight weeks to closely keep track of their interactions with the system. This choice greatly increased the complexity of the experiment and constraints to the model.

3.4.1 Procedure

Participants were told to imagine that they wanted to understand the given topic and to write a paper and give a talk on the given topic to a diverse audience. Two general topics were chosen: (1) "Find out relevant facts about the independence of Kosovo" and (2) "Find out relevant facts about anti-aging." These two tasks were chosen after a series of pilot studies that showed that they were representative of the general exploratory search tasks. In addition, the two tasks were chosen to represent the two very different distributions of the information ecology. Specifically, because the first task (independence of Kosovo) referred to a specific event, information related to it tended to be more specific, and there were more Web sites containing multiple pieces of well-organized information relevant to the topic. For example, on pages that contain information about Kosovo, they all have information related to the city, such as its history, the population, and the geographic locations. Because these pieces of information have a higher tendency to co-occur, the overlap of concepts related to the independence of Kosovo event tends to be higher. The second task (anti-aging), on the other hand, was more ambiguous and was related to many disjoint areas such as cosmetics, nutrition, or genetic engineering. Because Web sites relevant to the first task have more overlapping concepts than those relevant to the second task, they will be called high-overlap and low-overlap tasks, respectively. The other characteristic is that because the low-overlap task was more general, the tags tended to be more generic (such as "beauty" and "health"); in contrast, for the high-overlap task, tags tended to be more "semantically narrow" (such as "Kosovo"), and thus had higher cue validity than generic tags.

Each student performed the task for eight 30-min sessions over a period of eight weeks, with each session approximately one week apart. Students were told to think aloud during the task in each session. All verbal protocols and screen interactions were captured using the screen recording software *Camtasia*. All tags created were recorded manually from their del.icio.us accounts after each session. Students were instructed to provide a verbal summary of every Web page they read before they create any tags for the page. They could bookmark the Web page and create tags for the page. After they finished reading a document, they could either search for new documents by initiating a new query or selecting an existing tag to browse documents tagged by others. This exploratory search-and-tag cycle continues until a session ended. All tags used and created during each session were extracted to keep track of changes in the shared external representations, and all verbal description on the Web pages were also extracted to keep track of changes in the internal representations during the exploratory search process.

After the last session, participants were asked to perform a sorting task. Participants were given printouts of all Web pages that they read and bookmarked during the task, and were given the tags associated with the pages (either by themselves or other members in del.icio.us). They were then asked to "put together the Web pages that go together on the basis of their information content into as many different groups as you would like." The schemas (categories of Web pages) formed by the participants were then matched to those predicted by the assimilation and accommodation processes in the ESL model.

3.5 Results

Given that the impact of the interfaces on knowledge acquisition will likely depend much on each subject's idiosyncratic learning patterns and background knowledge, we analyzed the results for each individual subject separately and compared them to the model rather than matching model results to group averages. Separate model simulations were performed for each participant based on the documents and tags that they interacted with. Figure 3.4 shows the proportion of new tags assigned by each participant and the corresponding model simulations. Interestingly, even though

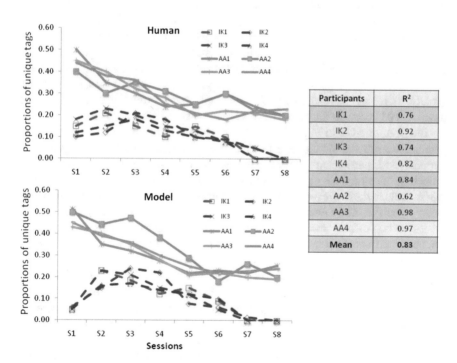

Fig. 3.4 Mean proportions of unique tag assignment for the high-overlap (IK) and low-overlap (AA) tasks by participants (top) and the model (bottom) across the eight sessions. IK1 represents participant 1 in the IK task, AA1 represents participant 1 in the AA task, etc. The table (right) shows the match between the model and the each of the participants

participants assigned fewer tags in the low-overlap task, the *proportions* of new tag assignment over total number of tag assignment were higher in the low-overlap task than in the high-overlap task. This was consistent with the lower rate of return of relevant information (the rate of return can be measured by the proportion of relevant information contained on a page returned from a search engine) in the lower-overlap task, and this lower rate could be caused by fact that the existing tags on del.icio.us were less informative for the lower-overlap task. Indeed, concepts extracted from the documents by the participants in the lower-overlap task were more often different from the existing tags than in the high-overlap task, suggesting that the existing tags did not serve as good cues to information contained in the documents. The general trends and differences between the two tasks were closely matched by the model (average $R^2 = 0.83$, min $= 0.62$, max $= 0.98$). Nevertheless, the current results demonstrated the good match of the model in keeping track of the tag assignments for *each* participant based on their histories of processing of Web pages across a period of eight weeks.

One core assumption of the ESL model was that the assignment of tags and the selection of links were dynamically related to the set of mental concepts (i.e., clusters of terms that are perceived to belong to the same category of information) formed during the knowledge exploration cycles. It is therefore critical to verify that the set of mental concepts formed by the model matched those formed by the participants. To do this, correlations between the mental concepts formed by the model and the participants were calculated by constructing "match" tables for each participant and model. Items that are in the same mental concepts will be given a value 1, otherwise a 0. For example, two possible partitions (categorization) for the set (a, b, c, d, e) are (ab), (c, d), (e) and (a, b, c), (d, e). In this example, their correlation can be calculated as $r = 0.102$ based on the match table as shown at the top in Fig. 3.5.

The bottom table in Fig. 3.5 shows the number of mental concepts formed by each participant and the model, as well as the correlations between their partitions. As predicted, participants formed more mental concepts in the low-overlap task, reflecting the structures of the information sources. However, as discussed earlier, participants in the low-overlap task also had lower rate of return in their information search, and thus had fewer tags (but more unique tags, see Fig. 3.4). Some of the most common mental concepts by the low-overlap group were "nutrition," "cosmetics," and "skin-care," while those by the high-overlap group were "Kosovo War," "Serbian–Albanian," and "history." Apparently, mental concepts in the low-overlap group tended to be more general than those in the high-overlap group, presumably because documents saved by participants in the low-overlap group had less overlap in the contents and were therefore grouped under more general mental concepts. In contrast, documents in the high-overlap group tended to be more specifically related to the independence of Kosovo, and thus the mental concepts were more specific. The correlations between the participants and the models were high in both tasks, suggesting that the model not only created similar number of mental concepts as participants, but the partitions of the mental concepts were also similar as participants, even though the inherent information structures were different between the two tasks.

Fig. 3.5 (a) An example of the match table that calculates that correlation between two partitions of objects. (b) Number of categories formed by each participant and model, and the correlations of the partitions of the categories of the models and the students calculated using the match tables. Hi = High-overlap task, Lo = Low-overlap task, S1 = participant 1, S2 = participant 2, and so on

(a)

	{a,b},{c,d},{e}				{a,b,c},{d,e}			
	a	b	c	d	a	b	c	d
b	1				1			
c	0	0			1	1		
d	0	0	1		0	0	0	
e	0	0	0	0	0	0	0	1

(b)

	#categories (human)	#categories (model)	Correlations of partitions
Hi-S1	6	6	0.71
Hi-S2	5	6	0.68
Hi-S3	7	7	0.81
Hi-S4	5	6	0.86
Lo-S5	12	13	0.59
Lo-S6	10	11	0.67
Lo-S7	11	12	0.79
Lo-S8	10	10	0.87

3.5.1   Summary

The ESL model demonstrates how a computational cognitive model can predict changes in internal knowledge structures (mental concepts or categories) as people engage in iterative search-and-learn cycles over a period of eight weeks. Predicting these changes are important because internal knowledge structures of the users directly influence search behavior, which in turns leads to learning of new knowledge. The interdependent processes of searching and learning demand an approach that can keep track of the dynamic cognitive computations involved as users interact with an information-rich environment.

The ESL model highlights the value of a computational cognitive model in improving information search in the context of online learning. The computational model can simulate changes in internal knowledge structures as new information is assimilated and accommodated into existing knowledge structures, which are processes that directly reflect learning. It also highlights the fact that the perceived relevance of information is a dynamic function of the existing knowledge structures of the individual users. In the context of online learning, users initially have relatively shallow knowledge structures of a topic. Consequently, they will likely have inaccurate judgment of relevance of information. This is consistent with the large body of literature on the importance of domain expertise on information search (Cole et al. 2011; Duggan and Payne 2008; Juvina and van Oostendorp 2008; Karanam et al. 2017). A search engine that derives relevance metrics by applying statistical language modeling techniques on large text corpora may therefore provide information to users that are perceived to be irrelevant, when the users do not yet have the background knowledge to correctly interpret the search results. The use of computational cognitive models can provide more accurate predictions on how users may be more effectively search and learn using an information retrieval system.

3.6   Conclusion and General Discussion

This chapter presented two examples of how computational cognitive models can improve information search. The first model, SNIF-ACT, demonstrates the value of adopting a theory-based mechanism, called the Bayesian satisficing mechanism (BSM), that selects information search strategies based on ongoing assessment of the information scent cues encountered by a user as he or she navigates across Web pages. The model shows a better fit to how humans selected Web links, decided to go back to previous pages or leave a Web site than a Position model that relied only on positions of links on a Web page. Results provide not only validation to the use of BSM as a computational model of link evaluation and selection, but also a theory of how the history of the perceived relevance (measure by information scent value) of information cues influences navigational choices in a general information search process: such as when navigating through pull-down menus to find the right commands (Brumby and Howes 2008), or when programmers debug their codes (Lawrance et al. 2013).

The second model, ESL, aims to track both learning of knowledge structures and search behavior in a social tagging system. The model shows a good fit to how humans develop more refined knowledge structures of a topic over a period of eight weeks as they continuously search for Web documents. These structures allow them to better judge the relevance of documents, which increases their efficiency in learning more about the topic. Results not only provide support to the assumed processes of assimilation and association in knowledge growth during information search, but they provide a mechanistic account of why domain expertise helps information search (White et al. 2009; Karanam et al. 2017). The model provides a foundation for a theoretical framework for developing and evaluating metrics of relevance to account for different levels of domain expertise, which are useful for developing search tools that can be personalized for individuals with different background knowledge. Results also have important implication on design of information systems that support online learning, especially how they can be designed such that learning can be coupled to search behavior in the system.

Traditionally, computational cognitive models are developed to understand and predict cognitive behavior. The computational nature of these models requires the researcher to be precise and explicit about behavioral predictions (e.g., what actions will a person select in a given situation) that verbal or descriptive models do not. When computational cognitive models are developed to simulate information search behavior, explicit predictions allow these models to predict what users will do when they interact with different information retrieval systems for different tasks. Computational cognitive models therefore complement existing computational techniques that aim to improve information or document retrieval. At the same time, they allow researchers to develop and test unified theories of information search by integrating the vast literature on information search behavior in different contexts, including those by Sanchiz et al., Karanam and Oostendorp, Rouet et al., Brand-Gruwel and Kammerer, Juvina et al., and Liao et al. in this book.

There are many opportunities to apply computational cognitive models to improve information search. For example, models such as SNIF-ACT allow realistic simulations to be created to predict how likely users will be able to navigate a Web site and find information they need for different information tasks. These simulations can also provide suggestions on changes on link structures, textual information cues, and presentation of search results from search engines. For example, the simulations may identify pages that users had trouble reaching through links from other pages given their information search goals, as well as pages that may encourage inefficiency in browsing behavior, such as those general information Web page that tends to "attract" users to visit but may distract users from finding more specific information. Lastly, these computational models can be repurposed to act as intelligent agents to provide real-time support as people are searching for information. For example, it may provide guidance on navigation paths (e.g., by visualizing upcoming Web pages that contain relevant search terms) or semantically related search terms that can be found in linked Web pages.

The ESL model shows that by simulating the learning process of users, it is capable of adapting to individual users who are acquiring semantic knowledge as they search over an extended period of time. This kind of longer-term exploratory search is not supported by traditional search engines, which are originally designed for one-time item-specific retrieval. The ESL model demonstrates how exploratory search engines can be developed by incorporating a learning model that keeps track of individual users' knowledge structures, in ways that allow search results to change to provide better cognitive compatibility with users' internal knowledge structures. This kind of exploratory search engines will benefit knowledge workers who need to conduct extensive search tasks over a longer period of time, such as intelligent analysts who need to learn and keep track of changes in certain communities, patent and trademark officers who need to find related inventions to decide whether to approve or disapprove a new invention application, or students who need to learn a new subject or topic through online resources. These types of domain-specific search engines have already been developed and used by knowledge specialists for different industrial or academic purposes, and research on adaptive and personalizable search technologies will likely benefit from the success of computation cognitive models in tracking internal cognitive structures and processes of users.

References

Anderson JR, Bothell D, Byrne M, Douglass D, Lebiere C, Qin Y (2004) An integrated theory of mind. Psychol Rev 111:1036–1060

Brumby DP, Howes A (2008) Strategies for guiding interactive search: an empirical investigation into the consequences of label relevance for assessment and selection. Hum-Comput Interact 23(1):1–46

Brunswik E (1955) Representative design and probabilistic theory in a functional psychology. Psychol Rev 62:193–217

Cattuto C, Loreto V, Pietronero L (2007) Semiotic dynamics and collaborative tagging. Proc Natl Acad Sci 104(5):1461–1464

Cole MJ, Zhang X, Liu C, Belkin NJ, Gwizdka J (2011) Knowledge effects on document selection in search results pages. In: Proceedings of the 34th international ACM SIGIR conference on research and development in information retrieval, ACM, New York, pp 1219–1220

Duggan GB, Payne SJ (2008) Knowledge in the head and on the web: using topic expertise to aid search. In: Proceedings of the SIGCHI conference on human factors in computing systems, ACM, New York, pp 39–48

Fu W-T (2008) The microstructures of social tagging: a rational model. In: Proceedings of the 2008 ACM conference in computer supported cooperative work (CSCW 2008), ACM, pp 229–238

Fu W-T, Dong W (2010) Facilitating knowledge exploration in folksonomies: expertise ranking by link and semantic structures. In: Proceedings of the 2010 international conference on computational science and engineering, Minneapolis, MN

Fu W-T, Dong W (2012) From collaborative indexing to knowledge exploration: a social learning model. IEEE Intell Syst 27(1):39–46

Fu W-T, Gray WD (2006) Suboptimal tradeoffs in information-seeking. Cogn Psychol 52:195–242

Fu W-T, Kannampallil T, Kang R (2009) A semantic imitation model of social tag choices. In: Proceedings of the 2009 IEEE international conference on social computing, IEEE CS, pp 66–72

Fu W-T, Kannampallil T, Kang R (2010a) Facilitating exploratory search by model-based navigational cues. In: Proceedings of the international conference on intelligent user interfaces, Hong Kong, China, pp 199–208

Fu W-T, Kannampallil TG, Kang R, He J (2010b) Semantic imitation in social tagging. ACM Trans Comput-Hum Interact 17(3), article 12

Fu W-T, Pirolli P (2007) SNIF-ACT: a cognitive model of user navigation on the world wide web. Hum-Comput Interact 22(4):355–412

Golder SA, Huberman BA (2006) Usage patterns of collaborative tagging systems. J Inf Sci 32(2):198–208

Hammond KR (1996) Human judgment and social policy: irreducible uncertainty, inevitable error, unavoidable injustice. Oxford University Press, New York

Juvina I, van Oostendorp H (2008) Modeling semantic and structural knowledge in web navigation. Discourse Processes 45(4–5):346–364

Karanam S, van Oostendorp H, Fu WT (2016) Performance of computational cognitive models of web-navigation on real websites. J Inf Sci 42(1):94–113

Karanam S, Jorge-Botana G, Olmos R, van Oostendorp H (2017) The role of domain knowledge in cognitive modeling of information search. Inf Retr J 20(5):456–479

Kuhlthau CC (1991) Inside the search process: information seeking from the user's perspective. J Am Soc Inf Sci 42(5):361–371

Kuhlthau CC (2004) Seeking meaning: a process approach to library and information services. Libraries Unlimited, London

Landauer TK, McNamara DS, Dennis S, Kintsch W (2007) Handbook of latent semantic analysis. Erlbaum, Mahwah, NJ

Lawrance J, Bogart C, Burnett M, Bellamy R, Rector K, Fleming SD (2013) How programmers debug, revisited: an information foraging theory perspective. IEEE Trans Software Eng 39(2):197–215

Manning CD, Schütze H (1999) Foundations of statistical natural language processing. MIT Press, Cambridge, MA, USA

Marchionini G (2006) Exploratory search: from finding to understanding. Commun ACM 49(4):41–46

Piaget J (1975) The equilibration of cognitive structures. University of Chicago Press, Chicago

Pirolli P, Card SK (1999) Information foraging. Psychol Rev 106:643–675

White RW, Dumais ST, Teevan J (2009) Characterizing the influence of domain expertise on web search behavior. In: Proceedings of the second ACM international conference on web search and data mining, ACM, New York, pp 132–141

Chapter 4
Cognitive Modeling of Age and Domain Knowledge Differences in Information Search

Saraschandra Karanam and Herre van Oostendorp

Abstract Several cognitive processes are involved in the process of information search on the Internet: memory, attention, comprehension, problem solving, executive control and decision making. Several cognitive factors such as aging-related cognitive abilities and domain knowledge in turn influence either positively or negatively these cognitive processes. Traditional click models from information retrieval community that predict user clicks do not fully consider the effect of the above cognitive factors. We demonstrate how the capabilities of computational cognitive models to simulate the effects of various cognitive factors can be used to improve our understanding of information search behavior. In this direction, we present some outcomes of modeling and predicting individual differences in information search due to age and domain knowledge using a computational cognitive model called CoLiDeS+. We also present some thoughts on how to model the influence of cognitive factors such as spatial ability and need for cognition in CoLiDeS+.

Keywords Information search · Aging · Domain knowledge · Individual differences · Cognitive modeling

4.1 Introduction

Searching for information on the Internet is usually carried out either by formulating queries relevant to one's goal (search by query) or by navigating websites (search by navigation) or a combination of both (Olston and Chi 2003). Many times, important

Saraschandra Karanam: User Experience Group, The MathWorks—This work was carried out by the author when he was working as a postdoctoral researcher at Utrecht University.

S. Karanam
User Experience Group, The MathWorks, Bangalore, India
e-mail: skaranam@mathworks.com

H. van Oostendorp (✉)
Utrecht University, Princetonplein 5, 3584CC Utrecht, The Netherlands
e-mail: H.vanOostendorp@uu.nl

© Springer Nature Switzerland AG 2020
W. T. Fu and H. van Oostendorp (eds.), *Understanding and Improving Information Search*, Human–Computer Interaction Series,
https://doi.org/10.1007/978-3-030-38825-6_4

information that is needed to solve the main search problem is present in the intermediate pages leading to the target page, and issuing a query is simply not sufficient. In such cases, when one has to navigate through the intermediate pages, it is important to evaluate the information on each page and take a decision on which hyperlink to click next, based on the information that is already processed. Users acquire new knowledge not only at the end of an information search process after reaching the target page, but also during the intermediate pages through which they reach the target page.

Learning from contextual information as users navigate on the Internet through hyperlinks involves complex cognitive processes that dynamically influence the evaluation of link texts and Web contents (Fu 2012; Fu and Dong 2012; see also Fu, Chapter 3, this volume). These include cognitive processes such as memory (by keeping track of previously viewed information), attention (understanding the visual layout of the websites and search engine result pages, and directing the perceptual–cognitive system to some location on a page and not to others), problem solving (information can be found in multiple locations and there could be multiple paths leading to them, and solving the problem which path to follow), comprehension (evaluating the relevance of search results, understanding the content of websites), decision making (choosing a relevant search result) and executive control (reformulating an unfruitful search query, backtracking to earlier webpages, comparing new information to what was found earlier). These processes are particularly relevant when the user is engaged in a less well-defined search goal, in which the user is not certain about what it is that they will find, and they must incrementally update their knowledge to evaluate the relevance of information as they encounter it. These cognitive processes, in turn, are known to be affected by one or more cognitive factors such as age (Sanchiz et al. 2017a, b; Chevalier et al. 2015) and domain knowledge (Sanchiz et al. 2019; Wildemuth et al. 2018; Monchaux et al. 2015; see also Chapter 5 of Sanchiz et al., this volume).

Technologies that enable us to find information on the Internet, such as search engines, however, assume a homogeneous class of users and follow a one-size-fits-all model. Furthermore, they are largely focused on the end-result—retrieving the webpage containing the information that the user is searching for—while ignoring the intermediate steps that, as we argued above, are important when the search description and query is not clear from the beginning. Many experiments examining the relationships between the cognitive factors that influence the cognitive processes underlying information search and the performance of users have been conducted by researchers from the domain of cognitive psychology and the broader area of human–computer interaction. However, using laboratory studies to understand these relationships requires participation from real users, who are not always available. Also, as the number of factors in the experiment increases, the complexity of the experiment and the number of experiments required to investigate all possible relationships also increase. This is not only expensive but also time-consuming and difficult to scale up. Computational models, on the other hand, allow us to simulate user behavior without performing the experiment(s) itself. Modeling and simulation of user behavior during information search has therefore been an active area of research in the information retrieval community. Many click models to simulate and predict user behavior during information search have been proposed (Chucklin et al. 2015). Except for a few models like (Ruotsalo et al. 2018; Xing et al. 2013; Shen et al. 2012), most of them do not consider variations caused by cognitive factors. Moreover, they provide only limited process description.

4.2   Computational Cognitive Modeling Approach

Our focus in this chapter would be on computational cognitive models. Based on theories of cognitive psychology and cognitive science, the main goal of these computational cognitive models is to use well-tested cognitive mechanisms to characterize more complex information search behavior (Pirolli and Card 1999; see also Pirolli, Chapter 2, this volume).

In addition to a strong theoretical basis, another important advantage of using computational cognitive models to analyze and predict Web behavior is that the models can be used to capture effects of individual differences in cognitive abilities, domain-specific knowledge and Internet experience on information search behavior and outcomes. By doing so, these computational cognitive models can provide much-needed insights into how each of the above cognitive factors influences information search behavior and performance, thereby enhancing our understanding of information search behavior in general. Given that computational cognitive models are often implemented as computer programs to simulate behavior, they can be used to conduct automatic assessment of websites and simulations of Web behavior in different Web designs by individual users with varying cognitive abilities and background knowledge (Blackmon et al. 2007; Chi et al. 2003). By comparing the simulated behavior of different computational cognitive models, one can gain much insight into how variations in cognitive abilities and knowledge will impact their information search performance.

One can also provide model-generated support by highlighting the hyperlinks/search results predicted by the model. Results, from earlier studies we did, showed that information-seeking performance in terms of the probability of finding what you are looking for and how efficiently you find it is enhanced considerably when support based on cognitive models of Web navigation is provided (Van Oostendorp and Juvina 2007; Juvina and Van Oostendorp 2008; Karanam et al. 2011; Aggarwal et al. 2014; Van Oostendorp and Karanam 2016). We discuss in detail how computational cognitive models can be used to generate automatic support in the chapter (Van Oostendorp and Karanam 2020) and also in Juvina and Van Oostendorp (2008). The focus of computational cognitive models is on the process that leads to the target information relevant to the search problem and is therefore more capable of providing opportunities to incorporate behavioral differences due to variations in cognitive factors.

In this chapter, we propose some preliminary ideas that can be incorporated into computational cognitive models to simulate the behavioral differences in information search performance due to the variations in cognitive factors such as age and domain knowledge. Several computational cognitive models (Kitajima et al. 2000; Fu and Pirolli 2007; Juvina and Van Oostendorp 2008; Van Oostendorp et al. 2012; Karanam et al. 2012) exist in literature that tries to characterize information search and navigation behavior. In the next section, we describe in detail two computational cognitive models of Web navigation called CoLiDeS and CoLiDeS+. In Sect. 4.4, we discuss the influence of two cognitive factors—age and domain knowledge on information search performance. We also present preliminary analysis of our ideas on simulating and predicting individual difference in information search performance due to age and domain knowledge using the computational cognitive model CoLiDeS+. We discuss some thoughts on how to model the influence of other cognitive factors such as spatial ability and need for cognition on information search performance using CoLiDeS+. We conclude the chapter with a summary of our findings and ideas for further research directions in Sect. 4.5.

4.3   Computational Cognitive Models

4.3.1   CoLiDeS

CoLiDeS, or Comprehension-based Linked Model of Deliberate Search, developed by Kitajima et al. (2000) explains user navigation behavior on websites. It divides user navigation behavior into four stages of cognitive processing: *parsing* the webpage into high-level schematic regions, *focusing* on one of those schematic regions, elaboration or *comprehension* of the screen objects (e.g., hyperlink text) within that region, and evaluating and *selecting* the most appropriate screen object (e.g., hyperlink text) in that region. CoLiDeS is based on information foraging theory (Pirolli and Card 1999) and connects to the construction–integration theory of text comprehension (Kintsch 1998). The notion of *information scent*, defined as the estimate of the value or cost of information sources represented by proximal cues (such as hyperlinks), is central to CoLiDeS. Information scent was found to be one of the driving factors steering navigation. The higher the information scent of a cue (or hyperlink) is, the higher the probability of a user clicking on it is. It is operationalized as the semantic similarity between the user goal and each of the hyperlinks. The model predicts that the user is most likely to click on that hyperlink which has the highest semantic similarity value with the user goal, i.e., the highest information scent. This process is repeated for every new page until the user reaches the target page.

CoLiDeS uses latent semantic analysis (LSA, henceforth) introduced by Landauer et al. (1998) to compute the semantic similarities. LSA is an unsupervised machine learning technique that employs singular value decomposition to build a high-dimensional semantic space using a large corpus of documents that is representative of the knowledge of the target user group. The semantic space contains a representation of terms from the corpus along a low number of dimensions, typically between 250 and 350, and is orthogonal, abstract and latent (Landauer et al. 1998). CoLiDeS has been successful in simulating and predicting user link selections, though the websites and webpages used were very restricted (Blackmon et al. 2007). The model has also been successfully applied in finding usability problems, by predicting links that would be unclear to users (Blackmon et al. 2007).

4.3.2 CoLiDeS+

CoLiDeS+ (Juvina and Van Oostendorp 2008) shares the main theoretical foundations: Construction–integration theory of text comprehension (Kintsch 1998) and information foraging theory (Pirolli and Card 1999) on which it is based with its predecessor CoLiDeS (Kitajima et al. 2000). CoLiDeS+ further augments CoLiDeS and makes it more consistent with its theoretical assumptions by drawing inspiration from work on text comprehension that lays emphasis on the role of context. For example, when reading a text, it has been shown that contextual information helps users in comprehending new incoming sentences better, especially those with potentially multiple interpretations (Budiu and Anderson 2004). Analogously, when interacting with a search engine or navigating on a website, users often encounter information that is varying in its degree of ambiguity and context can help to select the appropriate link.

CoLiDeS+ takes a task description as input and assumes it to be a representation of the user goal. It parses a webpage into several regions and a particular region is focused on (e.g., a set of hyperlinks). These set of hyperlinks are comprehended (based on how semantically similar to the user's goal they are) and one hyperlink (the one that is most similar to the user's goal) is selected. This opens a new webpage and if it is not (yet) the page with the target information, the cycle is repeated. Until this step, CoLiDeS+ runs exactly in the same fashion as CoLiDeS. However, CoLiDeS+ retains in memory the selected links which are used, starting from the second cycle, to compute *navigation path* and *path adequacy* (PA) in addition to information scent. The navigation path is defined as the sequence of hyperlinks clicked by a user at any given moment. CoLiDeS+ computes the path adequacy as the semantic similarity between the user goal and the navigation path. Only if the information from an incoming hyperlink increases in information scent (i.e., the semantic similarity with the user goal), it is considered for selection. If it does not increase in information scent, path adequacy is checked. If path adequacy increases, then the incoming hyperlink is selected even when it does not increase in information scent. In other words, first semantic similarity is locally evaluated based on information scent, and only when it is not satisfying, a more effortful evaluation of the context is performed by checking the path adequacy. If path adequacy does not increase, a latent impasse is said to have occurred and CoLiDeS+ invokes backtracking strategy, i.e., backtracking to other regions within the same page and eventually to the previously visited pages. CoLiDeS+ stops when the user declares the current page is the page with the target information.

Figure 4.1 shows a schematic diagram of the steps involved in CoLiDeS+. The most important steps are, first, check whether the current webpage contains the target page including the searched information. Second, if the target page does not contain the searched information, focus on the area with the link(s). Third, comprehend and select the link with the highest semantic similarity to the goal. Fourth, determine if the semantic similarity is increasing. If so, go to the next page. If not, calculate path adequacy based on current path in working memory. Next step, if there is an increase, the incoming link with the highest path adequacy is selected. If not, go back, refocus or select the next-best link, etc.

When both CoLiDeS and CoLiDeS+ were tested on real websites, CoLiDeS+ was found to not only locate the target page more often than CoLiDeS but also reach closer to the target page than CoLiDeS, whenever the target page was not located (Karanam et al. 2016). Also, by comparing selections made by users with the selections that CoLiDeS+ would have made for a set of tasks on a mockup website, Juvina and Van Oostendorp (2008) found that CoLiDeS+ was able to predict 54.9% of actual user clicks, slightly better than CoLiDeS, which could predict 46.9% of actual user clicks, lending evidence to the assumptions of CoLiDeS+.

Both CoLiDeS and CoLiDeS+ models are developed to describe the navigation path within websites but it has been shown that they can also be applied to the interaction with search engines (Karanam et al. 2015, 2017a). In brief, each search

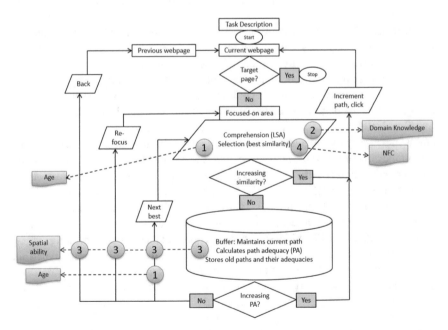

Fig. 4.1 Schematic diagram of CoLiDeS+. Shaded circles indicate the locations where individual differences are involved (1: Age, 2: Domain Knowledge, 3: Spatial Ability and 4: Need for cognition). See also later in text references to these locations

engine result page (SERP, henceforth) is considered as a page of a website. And, each of the search engine results is considered as a hyperlink within a page of a website. The problem of predicting which search engine result to click is now equivalent to the problem of predicting which hyperlink to click within a page of a website. Semantic similarity is computed between the query and the title and the snippet combinations of the search results on a SERP using LSA. The search result with the highest LSA value is selected. Note that the CoLiDeS model can predict only one search result per query using this methodology, whereas users, in reality, click on more than one search result per query. CoLiDeS+, on the other hand, can select more than one search result if it increases path adequacy. If none of the search results increases path adequacy or if all the search results are exhausted, the model decides to reformulate the query (Karanam et al. 2017a). Please note that the CoLiDeS/CoLiDeS+ modeling so far does not incorporate any effect of individual differences and that is what we will focus on in the remainder of this chapter. Due to its additional features like backtracking strategies and incorporation of contextual information into modeling, CoLiDeS+ is better equipped to model individual differences than CoLiDeS (Karanam et al. 2017a), and therefore, we will use CoLiDeS+ to describe how to model individual differences.

4.4   Individual Differences

In this section, we will describe the influence of the following two cognitive factors: age and domain knowledge on the cognitive processes underlying information search. Next to the description of the influence of each cognitive factor, we present some preliminary thoughts on how the variations in information search behavior caused by the differences in cognitive factors can be incorporated into the computational cognitive model CoLiDeS+. We will also present some outcomes based on CoLiDeS+ simulations. We will end the section with some ideas on how the influence of two other cognitive factors—spatial ability and need for cognition—can be incorporated into CoLiDeS+. Table 4.1 summarizes the four cognitive factors, their influence on information search behavior and the corresponding feature of CoLiDeS+ that we think could be used to model their influence on information search behavior. Figure 4.1 also marks the exact location in the CoLiDeS+ model where the manipulation occurs.

4.4.1   Age

Aging leads to a natural decline in motor skills and fluid intelligence involving processing speed, cognitive flexibility or ability to switch processing strategies, attentional control and visuospatial span (Horn and Cattell 1967; Horn 1982; Wang and

Table 4.1 Relation between cognitive factors discussed, their influence on search behavior and the CoLiDeS+ model

Cognitive Factor	Influence on information search behavior	Feature of CoLiDeS+
Age	Younger adults—explore more and exploit less Older adults—exploit more and explore less	Number of times next-best strategy is applied; LSA threshold value
Domain knowledge	Higher the domain knowledge is, higher the estimation of semantic relevance is	Semantic space in LSA
Spatial ability	Users with high spatial ability make higher number of revisits to already visited pages and use back button more often than users with low spatial ability	Depth of backtracking Number of hyperlinks on navigation path when computing path adequacy
Need for cognition	Users with high NFC would evaluate information more thoroughly and take more informed decisions on clicking than users with low NFC	Threshold value for elaboration process in LSA

Kaufman 1993). However, crystallized knowledge (vocabulary skills and knowledge in a specialized domain such as health) seems stable or even increases with age.

Some of these cognitive abilities directly influence the cognitive processes underlying information search resulting in lower efficiency of older adults on information search tasks. For example, lower processing speed could lead to longer time in evaluating search results or hyperlinks on a website, difficulty in switching strategies could lead to difficulty in reformulating unsuccessful queries or difficulty in getting out of an unsuccessful path, lack of attentional control could lead to inefficient handling of relevant and irrelevant search results or hyperlinks and finally lower visuospatial span could mean less efficient exploration of the search result page or a website. Many studies have shown that older adults generate less queries, use less keywords per query, reformulate less, spend longer time evaluating the search results, spend more time evaluating the content of websites opened from SERPs, switch less often between SERPs and websites and find it difficult to reformulate unsuccessful queries (Queen et al. 2012; Pak and Price 2008; Dommes et al. 2011). Older adults were found to allocate less resources to exploration (fewer keywords, fewer clicks on search results, etc.) and more resources to exploitation (longer time on a search result page, deeper navigation into websites opened from the search results) compared to younger adults (Chin et al. 2015; Sanchiz et al. 2019). In one of our own studies (Karanam and van Oostendorp 2016), we examined the effect of age and task difficulty on search performance in terms of task completion time and task accuracy. For simple tasks, participants in most cases could find the answer easily either in the snippets of the search engine results or in one of the websites referred

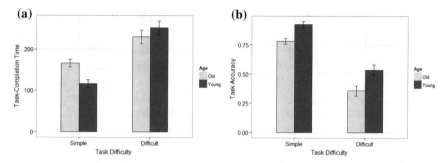

Fig. 4.2 Analysis of search performance (means and standard errors) in terms of **a** task completion time, **b** accuracy in relation to age and task difficulty

to by the search engine results. For difficult tasks, users had to frame queries using their knowledge and understanding of the task, the answer was not easily found in the snippets of search engine results and often they had to evaluate information from multiple websites. Results were found to be in line with prior outcomes from aging-related literature. As shown in Fig. 4.2, older adults were found to take significantly more time than younger adults when performing simple tasks. Also, when the time spent on SERPs and the time spent on websites are analyzed separately, older adults were found to spend significantly more time than younger adults on SERPs (for both simple and difficult tasks) and significantly less time than younger adults on websites when performing difficult tasks. Accuracy of difficult tasks was significantly lower than that of simple tasks and the accuracy of older adults was significantly lower than that of younger adults. These findings provide more evidence to the fact that older adults are less efficient than younger adults.

Behavioral outcomes from this study were used to compute mean semantic relevance of search queries (SRQ, henceforth) with target information sought, for each reformulation cycle, as a function of age and task difficulty. SRQ gives us an estimate of how close in semantic similarity the queries generated by the participants are to the target information. So, in general, the higher the SRQ value is, the more relevant the query is. Results indicated that for both simple and difficult tasks, as older adults reformulated, they produced search queries that were further away from the target information, whereas, for younger adults, it remained constant.

In a follow-up study (Karanam and van Oostendorp 2017), we manipulated task difficulty using a different metric called *task preciseness*. Task preciseness measures the degree to which the task description overlaps in meaning with the content of the target page(s) containing the answer to the task (using LSA). Tasks with a high LSA value of task preciseness provide better, more precise contextual information pointing to the target information. Tasks with a low LSA value of task preciseness would, on the other hand, require the user to engage in higher-level cognitive activities such as using his/her own knowledge to understand the task, generating relevant queries, examining search results and determining their usefulness. Results were largely in line with our earlier study (Karanam and van Oostendorp 2016). Low precise tasks demanded significantly more time and were significantly less accurate than high precise tasks. Younger adults were significantly faster in completing tasks compared to older adults. The accuracy of older adults was significantly lower than that of younger adults, especially for low precise tasks. We used behavioral data from this study to examine the semantic relevance of search queries across reformulations, that is, the relevance per cycle of queries submitted by an individual. Younger adults were found to reformulate much longer, i.e., more cycles, than older adults. Furthermore, as older adults reformulated, they produced search queries that were further away from the target information, whereas, for younger adults, the mean SRQ remained constant for high precise tasks and even increased for low precise tasks. These findings are also in line with our earlier study (Karanam and van Oostendorp 2016).

4.4.2 Cognitive Modeling of Age-Related Differences in Information Search

We first evaluated the ability of CoLiDeS and CoLiDeS+ in modeling age-related differences in information search behavior. The search queries from the study Karanam and van Oostendorp (2016) were used to run simulations of CoLiDeS and CoLiDeS+. We evaluated the performance of the models by computing the number of matches between the model predictions and the actual user clicks for each query and its corresponding SERP (Karanam et al. 2017a) outcomes of which are shown in Fig. 4.3. If a search result clicked by user is also a search result predicted by the model, then we consider that the model prediction matches with the actual user behavior. The number of matches for this scenario is 1. However, if a search result clicked by user is not a search result predicted by the model, then we consider that the model prediction does not match with the actual user behavior. The number of matches for this

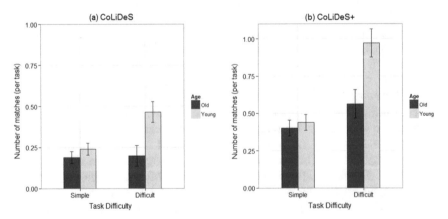

Fig. 4.3 Mean number of matches (and standard errors) per task with **a** CoLiDeS and **b** CoLiDeS+ in relation to age and task difficulty

scenario is 0. This process is repeated for all the queries of a particular task. Every time, there is a match between the model prediction and the actual user behavior, the number of matches is incremented by 1 for that task. At the end of this step, we would have available with us the total number of matches between the user clicks and the model-predicted clicks for one task. This process is then repeated for all the tasks of a participant and finally for all the participants. Using this data, the mean number of matches per task between the user clicks and the model-predicted clicks was computed in relation to age and task difficulty for both CoLiDeS and CoLiDeS+. The higher the number of matches is, the better the match between the model and the actual user behavior is. Firstly, results indicate that CoLiDeS+ matched actual user behavior significantly better than CoLiDeS, especially for difficult tasks.

Please note that the CoLiDeS model can predict only one search result per query using this methodology because CoLiDeS does not possess a backtracking mechanism, whereas users, in reality, click on more than one search result per query. The main reason why CoLiDeS+ seems to perform much better than CoLiDeS is because CoLiDeS+ gives importance not only to the local cue, that is, the incoming new search results, but also to the global context, that is, the query and the search results already clicked in the preceding session. Also, CoLiDeS+ can go back, if necessary, to already visited pages, change route and explore a new path to find the target page. CoLiDeS, on the other hand, always focuses on current information and does not utilize any historical information. It is only capable of linear forward search. Secondly, we also found that CoLiDeS+ matched actual user behavior significantly better than CoLiDeS, especially on difficult tasks, and thirdly, the model predictions matched significantly better with the actual behavior of younger adults compared to older adults, especially for difficult tasks. These interaction effects occur because difficult tasks by nature require integration of information from multiple sources, which in turn requires more queries, more clicks on the SERPs generated by the queries, more switches between SERPs and websites and overall more detours. Younger adults, owing to their higher fluid capabilities and lower switching costs, are more capable of performing all the above activities better than older adults. This is coherent with the discussion in the chapter by Sanchiz et al. (Chapter 5 of this book) that fluid intelligence correlates positively with exploration strategies. Therefore, we think that CoLiDeS+ is better equipped in terms of backtracking and next-best strategies to model individual differences in search performance due to variations in age.

We present here some preliminary ideas to simulate the differences in the number of search results clicked by younger and older adults on a SERP. We vary the number of times the next-best strategy is applied (ranging from 0 to 9) by CoL-iDeS+. This measure indicates how often a participant, after clicking on a search result and exploring the content of the corresponding website, comes back to the search result page to select one or more of the other search results. If the number of times the next-best strategy is applied is high, the model would come back and select the next-best search result more often than when the number of times the next-best strategy is applied is low. We also vary the minimum LSA value of a search result (computed in relation to the query, ranging from 0 to 0.9) which is an estimate of its relevancy. If the minimum LSA value of a search result is set high, the number of search results selected by the model would be low. Similarly, if the minimum LSA value of a search result is set low, the number of search results selected by the model would be high. Therefore, we expect that the information search behavior of older adults can be modeled with a low value for number of times the next-best strategy is applied and a high value for the minimum LSA value of a search result. This is in line with "explore less and exploit more" strategy of older adults (Chin et al. 2015). Similarly, we expect that the information search behavior of younger adults can be modeled with a high value for number of times next-best strategy is applied and a low value for the minimum LSA value of a search result. This is in line with "exploit less and explore more" strategy of younger adults (Chin et al. 2015).

The steps involved in CoLiDeS+ that get affected by these variations have been marked with 1 in Fig. 4.1. To demonstrate these variations, we ran simulations using CoLiDeS+ under all possible combinations of the two parameters (number of next-best strategy applied and LSA threshold) on twelve information search tasks and matched the model predictions with actual user clicks from the study in Karanam and van Oostendorp (2016). We used only difficult tasks for this analysis as the age-related differences are more prominent for difficult tasks as opposed to simple tasks.

Therefore, we expect the difference in the mean number of matches between younger and older adults to increase as the number of times the next-best strategy is applied is increased and the minimum LSA value of a search result is decreased.

Results showed that there is no significant difference in the mean number of matches between younger and older adults when the number of times the next-best strategy is applied is 0 (Fig. 4.4a) or when the minimum LSA value is very high: 0.7–0.9 (Fig. 4.4b). However, opposed to this, the match with younger adults increases much more than the match with older adults as the number of times the next-best strategy is applied is increased, or as the minimum LSA value is decreased (0.6–0). These outcomes are in line with our expectations. They imply that the optimal model simulations for older and younger adults should be based on different parameter values for the number of times the next-best strategy is applied for each search query and the LSA value of search results. Overall, our outcomes suggest that by varying the number of times the next-best strategy is applied and adjusting the critical LSA value into computational cognitive models, it is possible to simulate differences in the selection of search results due to differences in age.

4.4.3   Prior Domain Knowledge (PDK)

Users with high domain knowledge have more appropriate mental representations characterized by more relevant concepts, higher activation values and stronger connections between different concepts in the conceptual space compared to users with low domain knowledge (Kintsch 1998). Users with high domain knowledge, therefore, can comprehend the search results and the content of the websites better and

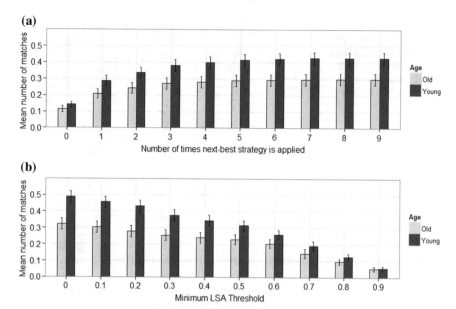

Fig. 4.4 Mean number of matches (and standard errors) in relation to variations in **a** number of times next-best strategy is applied and **b** minimum LSA value of a search result

evaluate the relevancy more thoroughly and easily than users with low domain knowledge (Kintsch 1998).

Variations in search behavior due to the differences in domain knowledge of users have been well researched and documented in the cognitive psychology community (Monchaux et al. 2015; Cole et al. 2011). In the study by Monchaux et al. (2015), domain experts were found to find more correct answers in shorter time and via a path closer to the optimum path than non-experts. This difference was stronger as the difficulty of the task increased. Higher domain knowledge enables a user to formulate more appropriate queries and comprehend the search results and the content in the websites better, which in turn, enables them to take informed decisions regarding which hyperlink or a search result to click next. Domain experts are also known to evaluate search results more thoroughly and click more often on relevant search results compared to non-experts. This is because their higher domain knowledge enables them to differentiate between a relevant and a non-relevant search result better (Cole et al. 2011).

We used the data from the study of Karanam and van Oostendorp (2016) to compute mean semantic relevance between search queries and the target information sought. We divided the participants into two groups of high (25 participants) and low (23 participants) prior domain knowledge (PDK) by taking the median score on the prior domain knowledge test. Results (in Fig. 4.5) showed that participants with high

Fig. 4.5 Mean semantic relevance of queries (with standard errors) with target information in relation to prior domain knowledge (PDK) and task difficulty

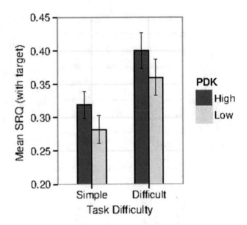

prior domain knowledge generated queries with significantly higher semantic relevance to target information compared to participants with low prior domain knowledge. These findings are consistent with the discussion in the chapter by Sanchiz et al. (Chapter 5 of this book) that crystallized intelligence correlates positively with exploitation strategies.

Therefore, we think that the step involving comprehension and selection of a hyperlink or a search result in CoLiDeS+ can get affected by variations in prior domain knowledge of users (marked with 2 in Fig. 4.1).

4.4.4 Cognitive Modeling of Domain Knowledge Differences in Information Search

To simulate the differences in evaluation of relevancy of search results due to the differences in the domain knowledge of users in CoLiDeS+, we use the semantic space in LSA. A semantic space in LSA is an approximate representation of a given user population's knowledge. It is possible to create two semantic spaces that reflect two different user population's knowledge levels. Based on this idea, we collated two different corpora (a non-expert corpus and an expert corpus, each consisting of 70,000 articles in Dutch) varying in the amount of medical- and health-related information. The *non-expert corpus*, representing the knowledge of low domain knowledge users, contained 90% news articles and 10% medical- and health-related articles, whereas the *expert corpus*, representing the knowledge of high domain knowledge users, contained 60% news articles and 40% medical- and health-related articles. The expert corpus was used to create the expert semantic space and the non-expert corpus was used to create the non-expert semantic space using the software package Gallito (Jorge-Botana et al. 2013). More details on construction and evaluation of these semantic spaces can be found in Karanam et al. (2017b). We expect that the expert semantic space would give higher semantic relevance values for a medical concept compared to the non-expert semantic space. Therefore, expert semantic space would model information search behavior (number of clicks on search results) of high domain knowledge users better than low domain knowledge users and vice versa.

Participants from Karanam and van Oostendorp (2016) were divided into low and high domain knowledge groups based on a domain knowledge test. Actual search queries were used to run simulations on six difficult information search tasks. Subsequent matching with actual behavioral data showed that the efficacy of the modeling of user interaction in terms of the number of matches (Fig. 4.6). With efficacy, we mean here that for each participant and for each task of the participant, we analyzed how many actual selections of search results were successfully predicted by the model. We found that the efficacy is significantly higher with the expert semantic space compared to the non-expert semantic space for *high* domain knowledge participants while for *low* domain knowledge participants, it is the other way around (so a significant interaction effect). Low prior domain knowledge participants seem to be confronted with more distracting information underlying the search results because it is too detailed for them.

It is important to note that this interaction effect is lost when semantic space is not used as a factor in the analysis of variance. That is, if we would not have used semantic space as a factor, we would have concluded that there is no difference in model performance between the participants with high and low domain knowledge levels. This would have been a (too) hasty conclusion because we saw that when we included semantic space as a factor in the analysis, there was an effect of PDK, but it was dependent on the type of semantic space.

Fig. 4.6 Mean number (and standard errors) of matches (per task) in relation to semantic space and prior domain knowledge (PDK)

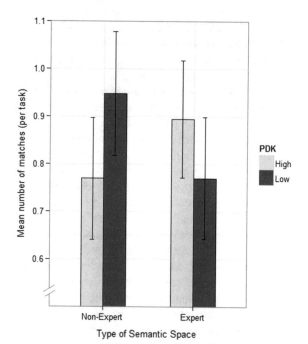

Overall, our outcomes suggest that using appropriate semantic spaces—a semantic space with high domain knowledge represented for high domain knowledge users and a semantic space with low domain knowledge represented for low domain knowledge users—gives better prediction outcomes. These outcomes imply that by incorporating differentiated domain knowledge levels into computational cognitive models, it is possible to simulate differences in the evaluation of relevancy of search results due to differences in domain knowledge.

4.4.5   *Spatial Ability*

Spatial ability is the ability to form visual or mental representations, process spatial information and remember the spatial relationships among different objects. Visuospatial skills are of great importance for success in solving many tasks in everyday life: for instance, using a map to navigate through an unfamiliar city, understanding the layout of a new building, merging into high-speed traffic, etc. (Diehl et al. 1995; Pak et al. 2006; Van Oostendorp and Karanam 2013). Since the structure or architecture of the information space of the Internet can be represented spatially as a graph, it is plausible that the (spatial) ability of a user to mentally form an equivalent representation of the information space has an influence on search performance. Users with high spatial ability would form a more accurate mental representation of the hyperspace that they are navigating through, compared to users with low spatial ability. They would be more aware of their current location in the hyperspace and therefore would be able to navigate themselves forward and backward with little effort. Whereas, users with low spatial ability usually do not understand their current location in the hyperspace and most often get lost. Research showed that spatial ability correlates with the number of revisits made by users to already visited pages, number of times the back button is used, etc. (Tamborello and Byrne 2005). Many studies have repeatedly shown that spatial ability correlates highly with information search and navigation performance (e.g., Juvina and Van Oostendorp 2008).

To simulate differences in number of times users revisit already visited pages or the number of times they use the back button, due to differences in their spatial ability, we can vary the frequency and the depth of backtracking behavior in CoLiDeS+ (marked with 3 in Fig. 4.1). Depth of backtracking measures the number of levels (of hyperlinks) a user would backtrack. If the depth of backtracking is set high, the model would visit higher number of already visited pages, and if the depth of backtracking is set low, the model would visit lower number of already visited pages. We assume that setting a high value for both frequency and depth of backtracking would model the information search behavior of users with high spatial ability and setting a low value would model the information search behavior of users with low spatial ability. We can also vary the amount of context that is taken into consideration when computing path adequacy in CoLiDeS+. If we assume that users with high spatial ability can utilize more contextual information than users with low spatial ability, we can vary the number of hyperlinks from the preceding session that are used to compute path adequacy (that is, the length of path adequacy). If length of path adequacy is set high, the model would use higher number of already visited hyperlinks to compute path adequacy, whereas, if the length of path adequacy is set low, the model would use lower number of already visited hyperlinks to compute path adequacy. Therefore, we propose that we should use a higher number of links (greater amount of context) for users with high spatial ability and a smaller number of links (smaller amount of context) for users with low spatial ability. Again, we can model variations in these parameters and examine the fit to behavioral search results of users differing in spatial ability.

4.4.6 Need for Cognition

Cohen et al. (1955) describe need for cognition (NFC, henceforth) as *"a need to structure relevant situations in meaningful, integrated ways."* If this need is not satisfied, it can result in feelings of tension and deprivation that can lead to *"active efforts to structure the situation and increase understanding"* (p. 291). It is an indication of the urge to make sense of the world. Users with high NFC are more likely to put efforts to clear all ambiguities and uncertainty in the presented information compared to users with low NFC. Therefore, we expect that NFC will have influence on the cognitive processes of comprehension, decision making and executive control during information search. Users with high NFC would evaluate information more thoroughly and take more informed decisions on clicking, reformulating and backtracking than users with low NFC.

Indeed, users with high NFC were found to spend more time on accessing relevant information, prefer formal sources for reliable information to informal ones, select up-to-date resources, value high-quality information, use advanced search options for formulating queries, prefer to select information sources with complex and multi-dimensional contents rather than simple ones (Mokhtari et al. 2013). In other studies, users with high NFC were found to explore more information from multiple sources (Ho 2005) and evaluate available information more thoroughly than users with low NFC (Liu and Zhang 2008). Therefore, we think that the most important step in CoLiDeS+ that can be affected by variations in NFC is the step involving comprehension of a hyperlink or a search result (marked with 4 in Fig. 4.1). The process of elaboration simulates the cognitive processes of activation of semantically related terms to a piece of text that is present in our working memory through a spreading activation mechanism. These elaborations are known to assist in better comprehension of what is being read (Kintsch 1998). Using LSA, the model can extract words that are close in semantic similarity to the target text. By varying the threshold value of the LSA semantic similarity, the number of words extracted and their degree of semantic similarity to the target text can be varied. If the threshold is set high, the model would take a fewer number of words that are very close in semantic similarity to the target text for elaboration, whereas, if the threshold is set low, the model would take greater number of words—also words that are not so close in semantic similarity to the target text for elaboration. We conjecture that this threshold value should be high for users with high NFC and low for users with low NFC. A higher threshold value ensures less ambiguity, whereas a lower threshold value leads to greater ambiguity. Similar to the modeling of spatial ability, we can again model variations in these parameters and examine the fit to behavioral search results of users differing in need for cognition.

4.5 Conclusions and Discussion

In this chapter, using a computational cognitive model called CoLiDeS+, we presented ideas to simulate variations in information search behavior due to the variations in cognitive factors such as age and domain knowledge. Preliminary analysis of our ideas on predicting individual differences due to age and domain knowledge effects showed promising outcomes.

By varying the number of times the next-best strategy is applied by CoLiDeS+ and the minimum LSA value of a search result, we were able to simulate the variations in the number of search results clicked by younger and older adults on SERPs. It appeared that the difference in mean number of matches between the model-predicted clicks and the actual user clicks between younger and older adults increased as the number of times the next-best strategy is *in*creased (Fig. 4.4a), and as the minimum LSA value of a search result *de*creased (Fig. 4.4b). These findings add empirical evidence to the discussion in the chapter by Sanchiz et al. (Chapter 5 of this book), regarding variations in exploration and exploitation strategies during information search behavior.

To simulate differences in evaluating the relevancy of search results due to the differences in prior domain knowledge, we used two different semantic spaces that varied in the amount of medical- and health-related information (the non-expert semantic space had lower medical- and health-related knowledge than the expert semantic space) to compute LSA values corresponding to information scent and path adequacy. The efficacy of the modeling in terms of the number of matches between the model-predicted clicks (Fig. 4.6) was found to be higher with the expert semantic space compared to the non-expert semantic space for high domain knowledge participants while for low domain knowledge participants, it was the other way around. Consequently, it appeared important to adapt the semantic space to the prior domain knowledge of the participants.

Overall, our outcomes suggest that using appropriate semantic spaces—a semantic space with high domain knowledge represented for high domain knowledge users and a semantic space with low domain knowledge represented for low domain knowledge users—gives better prediction outcomes—as we expect it to be. Similarly, variations wherein the number of times the next-best strategy is applied or variations in critical LSA threshold can be used to model individual differences in search performance due to age. These outcomes demonstrate that the efficacy of cognitive models can be enhanced by incorporating variations in information search performance due to variations in cognitive factors. This is an important finding with practical implications because improved predictive capacity of these models can lead to more accurate model-generated support for search and navigation which, in turn, leads to enhanced information-seeking performance as some studies have already shown (Karanam et al. 2011; Van Oostendorp and Juvina 2007). For each task, navigation support was generated by recording the step-by-step decisions made by the cognitive model which in turn are based on the semantic relatedness of hyperlinks to the user goal (given by a task description). The model predictions were presented to the user in the form of visually highlighted hyperlinks. In both studies, the navigation performance of participants who received such support was found to be more structured and less disoriented compared to participants who did not receive such support. This was found to be true, especially for participants with a particular cognitive deficit, such as low spatial ability. Model-generated support for information search contributes to the knowledge acquisition process of users as it helps them in efficiently filtering unnecessary information. It gives them more time to process and evaluate relevant information during the intermediate stages of clicking on search results and webpages within websites before reaching the target page. This helps in reducing user's effort in turn lessening cognitive load. This can lead to better comprehension and retention of relevant material because contextual information relevant to the user's goal is emphasized by model-generated support. In the chapter (Van Oostendorp and Karanam 2020), we present details of studies in which the influence of presenting the estimates of semantic relevance of search results as computed by the computational cognitive model CoLiDeS are examined.

More experiments are required to empirically verify all the ideas presented in this chapter corresponding to age, domain knowledge, spatial ability and need for cognition. We do not claim that the ideas presented in this chapter fully explain the variations in information search behavior due to the variations in cognitive factors, but we hope that they could be starting points for further research. We demonstrated modeling of individual differences in one particular aspect of the overall information search and navigation process; for example, for age, we also demonstrated modeling differences in selection of search results, and apart from that, for domain knowledge, we demonstrated differences in evaluation of relevancy of search results. It has to be seen what results are when more than one factor is varied at the same time. In general, the findings reported in this chapter support the framework put forward by Sanchiz et al., Chapter 5 of this book. Prior knowledge as part of crystallized abilities influences information processing (see their Fig. 5.1) and updating information in working memory plays a role in applying strategies such as the next-best strategy as part of fluid abilities,

Furthermore, modeling individual differences in cognitive factors in every stage of the information search and navigation process is a promising direction for future research. The influence of each of the cognitive factors discussed in this chapter on the psychological processes during information search can be simulated in more than one location, that is, as part of different subprocesses in the model (Fig. 4.1). It is not clear, at this moment, if the influence on one location in the model is more significant than the other. Also, there exist other cognitive factors but not discussed in this chapter such as Internet experience, gender, complexity of a task and interface characteristics which can have an influence on information search behavior.

Acknowledgements Much of the work reported here was supported by the Netherlands Organization for Scientific Research (NWO) Open Research Area Plus project MISSION (464-13-043).

References

Aggarwal S, van Oostendorp H, Indurkhya B (2014) Automating web-navigation support using a cognitive model. In: Akerkar R, Bassiliades N, Davies J, Ermolayev V (eds) Proceedings of the 4th international conference on web intelligence, mining and semantics (WIMS'14). ACM, New York, pp 1–6

Blackmon MH, Mandalia DR, Polson PG, Kitajima M (2007) Automating usability evaluation: cognitive walkthrough for the web puts LSA to work on real-world HCI design problems. In: Landauer TK, McNamara DS, Dennis S, Kintsch W (eds) Handbook of latent semantic analysis. Lawrence Erlbaum Associates, Mahwah, NJ, pp 345–375

Budiu R, Anderson JR (2004) Integration of background knowledge in language processing: a unified theory of sentence comprehension. Cogn Sci 28(1):1–44

Chevalier A, Dommes A, Marquié JC (2015) Strategy and accuracy during information search on the web: effects of age and complexity of the search questions. Comput Hum Behav 53:305–315

Chi EH, Rosien A, Supattanasiri G et al (2003) The bloodhound project: automating discovery of web usability issues using the InfoScent simulator. In: CHI letters, 5: proceedings of CHI 2003, pp 505–512

Chin J, Anderson E, Chin CL, Fu WT (2015) Age differences in information search: an exploration-exploitation tradeoff model. In: Proceedings of the human factors and ergonomics society annual meeting, vol 59(1). Sage CA: Los Angeles, CA: SAGE Publications, pp 85–89

Chucklin A, Markov I, de Rijke M (2015) Click models for web search. Synth Lect Inf Concepts, Retrieval Serv 7(3):1–115

Cohen AR, Stotland E, Wolfe DM (1955) An experimental investigation of need for cognition. J Abnorm Soc Psychol 51(2):291–294

Cole MJ, Zhang X, Liu C, Belkin JN, Gwizdka J (2011) Knowledge effects on document selection in search results pages. In Proceedings of the 34th international ACM SIGIR conference on research and development in information retrieval. ACM, pp 1219–1220

Diehl M, Willis SL, Schaie KL (1995) Everyday problem solving in older adults: observational assessment and cognitive correlates. Psychol Aging 10(3):478–491

Dommes A, Chevalier A, Lia S (2011) The role of cognitive flexibility and vocabulary abilities of younger and older users in searching for information on the web. Appl Cogn Psychol 25(5):717–726

Fu WT (2012) From Plato to the WWW: exploratory information foraging. In: Todd PM, Robbins T (eds) Cognitive search. MIT Press

Fu WT, Dong W (2012) Collaborative indexing and knowledge exploration: a social learning model. IEEE Intell Syst 27(1):39–46

Fu WT, Pirolli P (2007) SNIF-ACT: a cognitive model of user navigation on the World Wide Web. Hum Comput Interact 22(4):355–412

Ho SY (2005) An exploratory study of using a user remote tracker to examine web users' personality traits. In Proceedings of the 7th international conference on electronic commerce. ACM, pp 659–665

Horn JL (1982) The theory of fluid and crystallized intelligence in relation to concepts of cognitive psychology and aging. In: Craik FJM, Trehub SE (eds) Aging and cognitive processes. Plenum Press, New York, pp 847–870

Horn JL, Cattell BR (1967) Age differences in fluid and crystallized intelligence. Acta Physiol 26:107–129

Jorge-Botana G, Olmos R, Barroso A (2013) Gallito 2.0: a natural language processing tool to support research on discourse. In Proceedings of the 13th annual meeting of the society for text and discourse. University of Valencia, Spain

Juvina I, van Oostendorp H (2008) Modeling semantic and structural knowledge in web navigation. Discourse Process 45(4–5):346–364

Karanam S, van Oostendorp H, Indurkhya B (2011) Towards a fully computational model of web-navigation. In: International conference on industrial, engineering and other applications of applied intelligent systems. Springer, Berlin, Heidelberg, pp 327–337

Karanam S, van Oostendorp H, Indurkhya B (2012) Evaluating CoLiDeS+ Pic: the role of relevance of pictures in user navigation behaviour. Behav Inf Technol 31(1):31–40

Karanam S, van Oostendorp H, Sanchiz M, Chevalier A, Chin J, Fu WT (2015) Modeling and predicting information search behavior. In Proceedings of the 5th international conference on web intelligence, mining and semantics, Article Number 7, ACM

Karanam A, van Oostendorp H, Fu WT (2016) Performance of computational cognitive models of web-navigation on real websites. J Inf Sci 42(1):94–113

Karanam S, van Oostendorp H (2016) Age-related differences in the content of search queries when reformulating. In Proceedings of the 2016 CHI conference on human factors in computing systems. ACM, pp 5720–5730

Karanam S, van Oostendorp H, Sanchiz M, Chevalier A, Fu WT (2017a) Cognitive modeling of age-related differences in information search behavior. J Assoc Inf Sci Technol 68(10):2328–2337

Karanam S, Jorge-Botana G, Olmos R, van Oostendorp H (2017b) The role of domain knowledge in cognitive modeling of information search. Inf Retrieval J 20(5):456–479

Karanam S, van Oostendorp H (2017) Age-related effects of task difficulty on the semantic relevance of query reformulations. In Proceedings of the IFIP conference on human-computer interaction, interact 2017. Springer, pp 77–96

Kintsch W (1998) Comprehension: a paradigm for cognition. Cambridge University Press, Cambridge

Kitajima M, Blackmon MH, Polson PG (2000) A comprehension-based model of web navigation and its application to web usability analysis. In: Mc Donald S, Waern S, Cockton G (eds) People and computers XIV—usability or else!. Springer, London, pp 357–373

Landauer TK, Foltz PW, Laham D (1998) An introduction to latent semantic analysis. Discourse Process 25(2–3):259–284

Liu J, Zhang X (2008) The effect of need for cognition on search performance. Proc Am Soc Inf Sci Technol 45(1):1–12

Mokhtari H, Davarpanah M-R, Dayyani M-H, Ahanchian M-R (2013) Students' need for cognition affects their information seeking behavior. New Libr World 114(11/12):542–549

Monchaux S, Amadieu F, Chevalier A, Marine C (2015) Query strategies during information searching: effects of prior domain knowledge and complexity of the information problems to be solved. Inf Process Manage 51(5):557–569

Olston C, Chi EH (2003) ScentTrails: integrating browsing and searching on the web. ACM Trans Comput Hum Interact (TOCHI) 10(3):177–197

Pak R, Roger WA, Fisk AD (2006) Spatial ability sub-factors and their influence on a computer-based information search task. Hum Factors 48(1):154–165

Pak R, Price MM (2008) Designing an information search interface for younger and older adults. Hum Factors: J Hum Factors Ergon Soc 50(4):614–628

Pirolli P, Card S (1999) Information foraging. Psychol Rev 106(4):643–675

Queen TL, Hess TM, Ennis GE, Dowd K, Grühn D (2012) Information search and decision making: effects of age and complexity on strategy use. Psychol Aging 27(4):817–824

Ruotsalo T, Peltonen J, Eugster MJ, Głowacka D, Floréen P, Myllymäki P, Jacucci G, Kaski S (2018) Interactive intent modeling for exploratory search. ACM Trans Inf Syst (TOIS) 36(4):44

Sanchiz M, Amadieu F, Chevalier A (2019) Does pre-activating domain knowledge foster elaborated online information search strategies? comparisons between young and old web user adults. Appl Ergon 75:201–213

Sanchiz M, Chevalier A, Amadieu F (2017a) How do older and young adults start searching for information? impact of age, domain knowledge and problem complexity on the different steps of information searching. Comput Hum Behav 72:67–78

Sanchiz M, Chin J, Chevalier A, Fu WT, Amadieu F, He J (2017b) Searching for information on the web: impact of cognitive aging, prior domain knowledge and complexity of the search problems. Inf Process Manage 53(1):281–294

Shen S, Hu B, Chen W, Yang Q (2012) Personalized click model through collaborative filtering. In Proceedings of the fifth ACM international conference on web search and data mining. ACM, pp 323–332

Tamborello II FP, Byrne MD (2005) Information search: the intersection of visual and semantic space. In CHI'05 extended abstracts on human factors in computing systems. ACM, pp 1821–1824

Van Oostendorp H, Juvina I (2007) Using a cognitive model to generate web navigation support. Int J Hum Comput Stud 65(10):887–897

Van Oostendorp H, Karanam S, Indurkhya B (2012) CoLiDeS+ Pic: a cognitive model of web-navigation based on semantic information from pictures. Behav Inf Technol 31(1):17–30

Van Oostendorp H, Karanam S (2013) Navigating in a virtual environment with model-generated support. In Proceedings of the European conference on cognitive ergonomics. ACM, New York

Van Oostendorp H, Karanam S (2016) Supporting information search by older adults. In: Proceedings of the European conference on cognitive ergonomics. ACM, New York, p 12

Van Oostendorp H, Karanam S (2020) Semantic relevance feedback on queries and search results for younger and older adults. In: Fu W-T, van Oostendorp H (Eds) Understanding and improving information search: a cognitive approach. Springer, Cham, Switzerland, pp 97–111

Wang JJ, Kaufman AS (1993) Changes in fluid and crystallized intelligence across the 20-to 90-year age range on the K-BIT. J Psychoeducational Assess 11(1):29–37

Wildemuth BM, Kelly D, Boettcher E, Moore E, Dimitrova G (2018) Examining the impact of domain and cognitive complexity on query formulation and reformulation. Inf Process Manage 54(3):433–450

Xing Q, Liu Y, Nie J-Y, Zhang M, Ma S, Zhang K (2013) Incorporating user preferences into click models. In: Proceedings of 22nd ACM international conference on information & knowledge management (CIKM), pp 1301–1310

Part II
Methods and Tools

Chapter 5
An Evolving Perspective to Capture Individual Differences Related to Fluid and Crystallized Abilities in Information Searching with a Search Engine

Mylène Sanchiz, Franck Amadieu, and Aline Chevalier

Abstract Interacting with a search engine to search for information is an essential component in our information society. Yet, information search can be a complex task as users can face challenges when processing a staggering amount of information. Research in cognitive psychology and ergonomics has shown important individual differences in search strategies and performance. In this chapter, we describe how fluid and crystallized abilities may influence search behavior all along the task and how they can account for users' difficulties. Our purpose is to provide a theoretical and methodological foundation to better understand the role of these abilities. To this point, we first review recent insights on the behavioral data collected in studies. Next, we present a new framework to analyze such data and discuss how fluid and crystallized abilities can impact information processing when searching for information. Illustrations of how this work can contribute to the development of useful information search support tools are discussed.

5.1 Introduction

In our information and communication society, we process information every day to make informed decisions, to acquire new knowledge, to complete a specific goal, to get up-to-date news or for leisure. The development of the web and information technologies has granted individuals a somewhat easy access to a huge mass of information. Search engines are burgeoning on the web, and despite how intuitive they may look at first, interacting with them to search for information can be complex for some users. The literature on cognitive psychology and ergonomics has documented how children (Bilal and Kirby 2002), disabled adults (Giraud et al. 2018) and older adults (Dommes et al. 2011; Wagner et al. 2010; Sanchiz et al. 2017a, b, 2019a) can face challenges when using a search engine to search for information. Users' difficulties can come from a wide variety of cognitive, social or emotional factors

M. Sanchiz (✉) · F. Amadieu · A. Chevalier
University of Toulouse, 5 Allée Antonio Machado, Toulouse Cedex 9, 31058 Toulouse, France
e-mail: Mylene.Sanchiz@gmail.com

© Springer Nature Switzerland AG 2020

W. T. Fu and H. van Oostendorp (eds.), *Understanding and Improving Information Search*, Human–Computer Interaction Series,
https://doi.org/10.1007/978-3-030-38825-6_5

71

(such as low prior topic knowledge, lack of familiarity with the device, low self-perceived efficiency on the web, anxiety toward new technologies) (Hölscher and Strube 2000; Sharit et al. 2008).

The current chapter addresses two particular types of cognitive factors that have received an increased interest over the last few years: fluid and crystallized abilities (Crabb and Hanson 2014; Dommes et al. 2011; Eppinger et al. 2007; Sanchiz et al. 2019a; Sharit et al. 2015). These abilities allow individuals to reason and interact with their environment. Fluid abilities correspond to the ability to think, reason and solve problems independently of learning, experience and education, whereas crystallized abilities refer to the skills and knowledge individuals acquire throughout their life (such as prior knowledge or vocabulary skills) (Cattell 1971; Horn and Cattell 1967). These abilities can impact people's behavior and performance (Park et al. 1996; Park 2000), and they are particularly crucial for problem-solving tasks involving working memory (such as information search). However, their role on information search (IS) with a search engine is still to be better documented, particularly for growing populations of users on the web such as older adults. Better capturing individual differences related to such abilities are crucial in order to: (i) predict adequately the behavior and search performance of users with particular needs and (ii) develop adapted IS support tools. Adopting a cognitive approach to study IS strategies could complement approaches in information science to understand the decisions taken by users with particular needs. For instance, combining cognitive and computing approaches could help future research integrate the impact of users' navigational and processing decisions all along the search task in order to better predict users' difficulties and performance. In addition, such knew knowledge would also provide more validation for the inferences and conclusions drawn from empirical data in the future works.

With this in mind, we will first begin the chapter with a brief overview of the theoretical frameworks of IS that are compatible with the inclusion of fluid and crystallized abilities. Next, a synthesis of the empirical findings related to the influence of these abilities on IS will be provided. Then, we will present an original methodological framework to study the impact of fluid and crystallized abilities on IS performance (i.e., efficiency) and behavior (i.e., searching strategies). The chapter will conclude with the introduction of a new theoretical perspective to guide future research works and better account for the role of fluid and crystallized abilities.

5.2   Current State of the Art on the Role of Fluid and Crystallized Abilities in Information Search Behavior and Performance

5.2.1   Review of the Theoretical Construct of IS

Research in cognitive psychology and ergonomics has defined IS as a complex problem-solving activity that involves several high-level processes such as comprehension, reasoning and decision-making. IS starts with the elaboration of a mental representation of a search need (i.e., user's search goal) and is followed by several cycles in which the user has to evaluate information relevance, select pieces of information that are related to the search goal and possibly navigate between several content webpages (Fu and Pirolli 2007; Sharit et al. 2008, 2015; van Oostendorp et al. 2012). Searching for information with a search engine usually involves three steps: planning, evaluating information and navigating (Sharit et al. 2008, 2015). First, search engines require users to formulate an initial query that represents their search goal and enter it in the search engine box. To formulate their query, users can rely on information provided in the search context (such as the keywords contained in their information need or in the search problem statements) and their prior topic knowledge (Monchaux et al. 2015; Sanchiz et al. 2019a). The production of the initial query corresponds to the planning stage of the activity (Sharit et al. 2008). This initial query will allow the search engine to retrieve a set of links that users can process to access websites. Then, in a second stage, users have to evaluate the relevance of the search results (i.e., analyze the search engine result page—SERP) and select website(s) to open up. In optimal situations, users should process the links provided on the SERP to locate the best way(s) to find their target information (i.e., select the most useful website(s)). Finally, in a third stage, Sharit and his collaborators (2008, 2015) showed that users can process in deeper detail the websites they opened up (i.e., spend time reading information provided on the website or go deeper to it by navigating into several webpages). IS is a cycling activity: Users can move forward or backward through this step as long as their search need is not fulfilled. Users can, for instance, reformulate their query, update their mental model thanks to new pieces of information, evaluate again the SERP to select a new website, consult more SERPs and so on. The cycling aspect of IS represents the critical part of this activity as it may require users to engage in complex and uncertain decision-making. How users strategically decide to process and update information and navigate between pages to solve their search need is often the key to success or failure.

Models of information search describe the mechanisms that underlie the evaluation and the selection of links (SNIF-ACT models by Fu and Pirolli 2007 or CoLiDeS + Pic by van Oostendorp et al. 2012 for instance). Individuals rely on the information link(s) that concentrate(s) the highest information scent (i.e., highest perceived utility with regard to the search goal). Then, through an activation spreading mechanism, pieces of information semantically related to the search goal are activated in memory and help users decide which link to open up. However, using these computing approaches to predict users' search behavior and performance can be difficult because of the cycling and strategic features of IS. While users move forward through their search, they will allocate their attention to a different information. Consequently, the information scent of one particular piece of information will vary all along the task. In other words, some information that was first highly useful and relevant to the search goal might still be relevant but no longer useful for users. In addition, these computing models often fall short of taking into account users' search strategies and inner resources. Yet, they can have a major impact on users' difficulties and search performance. Research in cognitive psychology showed that IS strategies during the different steps of the search can be supported (or impaired) by several cognitive factors related to crystallized or fluid abilities (Dommes et al. 2011; Sharit et al. 2008).

5.2.2 Review of the Theoretical Construct of Fluid and Crystallized Abilities

Fluid abilities involve processing speed, update in working memory, inhibition, attentional focus or cognitive flexibility (Cattell 1971; Chevalier and Chevalier 2009; Horn and Cattell 1967; Eppinger et al. 2007; Slegers et al. 2012). These abilities help individuals plan, coordinate and regulate the cognitive operations required to perform a task. In other words, fluid abilities support adaptive decision-making and allow individuals to switch between different processing strategies in order to adapt to environment changes and constraints (Lindow and Betsch 2019). Fluid abilities support executive functioning (Salthouse et al. 2003) and are particularly critical in IS:

1. *Cognitive flexibility*: ability to switch attentional focus to different stimuli and manipulate at the same time several mental models (Verhaeghen and Cerella 2002). Lower level of cognitive flexibility can increase individuals' sensitivity to interfering or unpredictable input stimuli. This is particularly critical for IS as this activity heavily relies on alternating between the different mental models elaborated (i.e., representation of users' search goal, of the different search results, websites processed, etc.).

2. *Inhibition*: ability to access, suppress and restrict access to information in working memory (Hasher and Zacks 1988). Inhibitory mechanisms help individuals allocate attentional resources to more goal-relevant items and filter useless information (for instance in reading comprehension). Inhibition can thus be a key to support the exclusion of seductive, salient or irrelevant pieces of information in an environment in which a huge mass of information is easily accessible. Interestingly, goal-directed inhibitory mechanisms are particularly crucial during the

initial stage of IS to avoid the allocation of resources to irrelevant items. Additionally, empirical studies also demonstrated that inhibitory mechanisms could work as a "search and destroy" process (Kawashima and Matsumoto 2018; Moher et al. 2014): While proceeding through a task, the irrelevant items to be ignored are first selected and then inhibited in favor of more relevant items.

3. *Update in working memory*: ability to maintain in working memory an active and up-to-date mental representation. This mechanism helps, for instance, individuals replace pieces of information that are no longer accurate or needed by more relevant ones (Morris and Jones 1990). Three components are at stake in updating mechanism: retrieval, transformation and substitution of information (Ecker et al. 2010). As such, this process allows users to maintain the mental representation of their search need active in working memory and transform it in order to adapt to situational changes (such as the discovery of new information that invalidates previously read ones).

Crystallized abilities correspond to skills and knowledge that an individual acquires throughout life (Cattell 1971; Sharit et al. 2008). They include prior knowledge, knowledge schemata or vocabulary skills. Crystallized abilities are particularly useful to perform actions in an optimal way (i.e., without engaging too much cognitive resources). For instance, when navigating in an environment (as in an unknown train station for instance), individuals may engage automatic processes if they do possess relevant schemata (e.g., find the main hall and train departure/arrival information to know where to go next). Such schemata, acquired through experience, eventually support the planning and executions of actions without much effort.

5.2.3 Overview of the Relation Between Fluid and Crystallized Abilities and IS Behavior and Performance

A large body of research has shown how fluid and crystallized abilities can impact strategies in visual search tasks. For instance, when individuals are asked to locate a target item (e.g., a word and a figure), inhibition mechanisms support the filtering of irrelevant distractors and the localization of relevant items (Kawashima and Matsumoto 2018). However, fewer researches have documented the impact of fluid abilities on information search with search engines or websites. Prior findings have reported that fluid abilities affect search performance and the elaboration of appropriate search strategies (Chin et al. 2009; Pak and Price 2008; Sharit et al. 2008, 2015). For instance, when users have to search for information in a complex fact-finding search task, low cognitive flexibility can alter the number of query reformulations and the number of new keywords produced by participants (Dommes et al. 2011; Crabb and Hanson 2014). Cognitive flexibility is also reported to support the processing of websites' structures and the decision to explore a larger part of the problem space of the search (Brand-Gruwel et al. 2009; Chin et al. 2015).

Crystallized abilities, such as prior topic knowledge or vocabulary, can support users' search performance (Downing et al. 2005; Hölscher and Strube 2000; Monchaux et al. 2015; Sanchiz et al. 2017a; Tabatabai and Shore 2005) and the production of more relevant keywords (Vakkari et al. 2003; Wildemuth 2004). Prior knowledge and IS skills are among the most common dimensions of crystallized abilities used in empirical studies (Downing et al. 2005; Duggan and Payne 2008; Hembrooke et al. 2005; Hölscher and Strube 2000; Monchaux et al. 2015; Sharit et al. 2008, 2015; Tabatabai and Shore 2005; Wildemuth 2004). Prior topic knowledge corresponds to declarative (i.e., semantic content), procedural (knowledge about specific strategies on how to process concepts for instance) and/or metacognitive knowledge (knowledge about how to self-evaluate and regulate the strategies engaged for instance) that are related to a particular knowledge domain (i.e., topic). IS skills correspond to more domain-independent expertise in IS itself (such as the development of relevant schemata to apply or search strategies) (Smith 2015). Prior knowledge, IS skills and more largely crystallized abilities influence how users allocate their resources when processing information (Hölscher and Strube 2000; Monchaux et al. 2015). Prior empirical works have indeed demonstrated that prior topic knowledge supports the formulation of semantically more appropriate keywords (Vakkari et al. 2003; Wildemuth 2004), of more relevant reformulation strategies (such as using more unique queries or making more important transformations when reformulating queries: Hembrooke et al. 2005; Zhang et al. 2005) and search performance (Downing et al. 2005). Prior knowledge can also help users select more relevant websites (Hölscher and Strube 2000) and evaluate information more rapidly (i.e., greater number of webpages visited in a smaller amount of time (Sihvonen and Vakkari 2004; Wildemuth 2004).

Overall, these findings show that prior knowledge and more largely crystallized abilities foster the elaboration of a more coherent mental model of the search need, the articulation of more accurate queries and more efficient processing of information. Hence, low topic knowledgeable users face a double challenge. First, they tend to start searching for information with a less coherent mental model and a less accurate query (which will degrade the quality and relevance of the results retrieved by the search engine). Secondly, less knowledgeable users have fewer resources to evaluate information relevance and to integrate information while they proceed through the search. In sum, crystallized abilities, such as prior knowledge use, can help users process information more efficiently, at lower cognitive costs. They can also improve the relevance and accuracy of the search strategies elaborated.

As illustrated in the above section, a large number of empirical works have documented the impact of crystallized abilities on IS performance and behavior. However, fewer studies examined how fluid abilities can influence users' behavior. In addition, the majority of these empirical studies focused either on large scope indicators of search behavior (such as the time spent searching for information: Sharit et al. 2008, 2015, or the number of queries produced: Dommes et al. 2011) or on very precise indicators but they failed to relate them to the cognitive processes they reflect (such as the number of new keywords produced in query or the query length, e.g., Hembrooke et al. 2005). To fully understand how fluid and crystallized abilities can impact search behavior, research needs to provide a more global framework to analyze these data. Such ambition is quite a challenge as many indicators can be confusingly used as a proxy of several cognitive or metacognitive processes. For instance, the number of queries produced by users can reflect deeper processing (i.e., cognitive processes, such as comprehension or inference-making) or regulation strategies (i.e., metacognitive processes). In the present chapter, we argue that one way to override this challenge would be to identify high-level common features between online indicators (i.e., *do they reflect an attempt to access new information? to keep digging for particular pieces of information?*) and/or contextualize their analyses with regard to the different steps of the activity.

5.3 The Value of Studying Behavioral Data: A Review of Methodological Perspectives to Better Understand the Role of Fluid and Crystallized Abilities

A burgeoning amount of empirical studies use online data to investigate users' search performance and strategies. For instance, indicators of efficiency include the time spent to perform the task (Chin and Fu 2010; Kammerer and Gerjets 2014; Karanam and van Oostendorp 2016; Lazonder et al. 2000; Sharit et al. 2015; Thatcher 2006; Vanderschantz and Hinze 2017) or the task completion speed (i.e., time taken to complete the search task in relation to the success or failure, Aula and Nordhausen 2006; Sanchiz et al. 2017a, b). A staggering amount of indicators of online search strategies can be found in the literature:

- Querying: number of queries formulated, number of new keywords, semantic depth of queries, types of query reformulations, etc (Bilal and Gwizdka 2018; Dommes et al. 2011; Hembrooke et al. 2005; Hölscher and Strube 2000; Monchaux et al. 2015; Phan et al. 2007; Sanchiz et al. 2017a, b, 2019a; Thatcher 2006; Vakkari 2001; Vanderschantz and Hinze 2017; van Deursen and van Dijk 2009).
- Navigational behavior: number of websites visited, number of content webpages opened up, time spent processing websites, etc (Barsky and Bar-Ilan 2012; Downing et al. 2005; Duggan and Payne 2008; Hölscher and Strube 2000; Sanchiz et al. 2017a, b; Scholer et al. 2013).

As a reminder, one of the main challenges in accurately using online data to understand users' search strategies is that most empirical findings analyze behavior to get a better understanding of what users *do* and *why*. However, most of these studies fall short of relating such data to the processes they may reflect. Among the many examples we could cite, Bilal and Kirby (2002) showed in a study that children were less capable than adults to effectively recover from breakdowns or impasses by adapting their search strategies (such as using new keywords in their queries). Such findings could reflect the impact of lower fluid abilities (which are not fully developed at this age), but it was not empirically investigated in the study. In addition, online behavioral indicators can sometimes be difficult to analyze as they may ambiguously represent several cognitive or metacognitive processes from one study to another. For instance, in the literature, the time spent processing the search results on a search engine result page is allotted to either deeper processing (i.e., a cognitive process), planning or evaluating (i.e., metacognitive processes) (Chin and Fu 2010; Dommes et al. 2011; Hahnel et al. 2018; Sharit et al. 2008). Hence, better relating online indicators to the actual processes they underlie and improving the methodological and theoretical frameworks used to analyze them would most likely help future research: (i) use online data with more precision and (ii) make more reliable conclusions about users' search strategies.

In the following section, we will discuss a new theoretical and methodological framework for the analysis of online behavioral data that accounts for the role of fluid and crystallized individual differences. First, we will present how using online indicators to distinguish between exploration and exploitation processes can better illustrate the role of fluid and crystallized abilities in IS. Secondly, we will highlight how contextualizing the analysis of online data to the search context and the different stages of IS can provide crucial insights on users' behavior, performance and cognitive processes.

5.3.1   *Distinguishing Exploration Vs. Exploitation*

Current empirical research provides interesting insights on users' search behavior and performance. For instance, we are better aware of the search strategies that can account for children's lower search performance (Bilal and Kirby 2002). Research has documented how users process information on websites (i.e., the time they spent reading content on websites for instance), how they explore the problem space (by consulting a new website for instance, Sharit et al. 2008, 2015) and how they can overcome impasses (by reformulating for instance, Bilal and Kirby 2002; Dommes et al. 2011). With regard to the theoretical models of IS (Brand-Gruwel et al. 2009; Fu and Pirolli 2007; Sharit et al. 2008, 2015; van Oostendorp et al. 2012), what readers are asked to do when searching for information (no matter if it is an explicit fact-finding task or a more complex sense-making search task, Bell and Ruthven 2004) is to *process information* and *explore their environment. Processing information* in IS implies assessing information relevance, selecting relevant information, comprehending semantic content, elaborating a coherent mental representation of the information retrieved (Hahnel et al. 2018; Sharit et al. 2008, 2015). *Exploring the environment* in IS implies selecting sources of information, navigating between different content webpages or websites, understanding how online documents are structured, how we can interact with them, etc (Sharit et al. 2008, 2015). In other words, indicators reflecting strategies to extensively navigate in different sources of information and initiate new branches/navigational paths in order to process an additional part of the problem space tend to reflect exploratory behavior.

Exploration processes are well documented in the literature. However, studies do not always refer to indicators of exploration as such. Instead, studies mostly refer to navigation or browsing behavior. Chin and her collaborators (2015) detailed the distinction between exploration and exploitation search strategies in IS. In line with information foraging theories (Pirolli and Card 1999), to search for information, individuals can either spend resources to forage for information among a particular source (or group of sources) of information or switch to a new one if the initial source(s) selected turned out to be useless/ not relevant. Due to the limited capacity of their working memory, individuals do not possess extensive resources to search for information. Hence, information searchers need to set a trade-off in order to decide whether or not to engage additional resources. Information foraging theories suggest that the likelihood for users to leave their current sources of information to consult a new one will increase if the expected additional value of visiting a new website exceeds the costs it will demand (Chin et al. 2015; Pirolli and Card 1999; Fu and Pirolli 2007). Indeed, deciding to leave a source of information and switch to a new one can be demanding as it requires users to engage resources to evaluate new information, select a new website, understand how this new website is structured, etc. Switching to a new source of information (i.e., exploring a broader part of the problem space of the search) requires high fluid abilities such as cognitive flexibility. In other words, exploration behavior corresponds to the initiation of new branches (as reflected by opening up a new website, for instance, or reformulating a new query) (Chin et al. 2015; Sanchiz et al. 2019b).

In contrast, exploitation behavior corresponds to perseveration behaviors (i.e., extended processing of similar pieces of information) such as visiting a high number of webpages from the same website (e.g., number of webpages revisited, Duggan and Payne 2008). Indicators reflecting deeper processing of the navigational branches elaborated tend to reflect exploitation strategies (Chin et al. 2015; Sanchiz et al. 2019b). For instance, to reformulate their queries, users can decide to change the entire content of their query, change some of the keywords (e.g., add/retrieve some keywords and change keywords by synonyms) or transform the organization of the query content (e.g., reverse keyword order). In empirical studies, some querying indicators correspond to narrow changes such as step-by-step reformulation strategies or reformulations that heavily rely on the content of the former query produced (i.e., number of times a keyword is reused and broadness of change in query reformulation; see Table 5.1 for example). Such indicators tend to reflect exploitation strategies: Users remain on similar or semantically extremely close information patches to search for information. In contrast, reformulation strategies that reflect broader changes (such as complete query transformation or production of new keywords) show exploration strategies (i.e., the new query formulated will most likely lead to a new and semantically more distant information patch). Table 5.1 provides a synthesis of indicators currently used in empirical works that tend to reflect exploitation strategies. To sum up, exploitation strategies mainly refer to: (i) the time spent processing the search paths initiated and/or (ii) the depth of the processing of the search paths initiated (i.e., the number of websites opened up per query, the number of SERPs consulted per query, etc.).

Table 5.1 Examples of online indicators reflecting exploitation strategies used in current research

Dimension	Indicators	Authors	Type of exploitation behavior
Website selection	Number of websites opened from SERPs per query	Duggan and Payne (2008), Guan (2014), Huang and Efthimiadis (2009)	Exploitation of a search path initiated by formulating a query
	Time taken on SERPs to select a link to visit	Chin and Fu (2010), Kelly et al. (2015)	
	Number of repeated links selected from SERP visits before adjusting queries (i.e., reformulating)	Vanderschantz and Hinze (2017)	
Webpages processing	Number of switches between content pages once on a website	Barsky and Bar-Ilan (2012), Lei et al. (2013), Wildemuth et al. (2018), Dommes et al. (2011)	Exploitation of a search path initiated through the visit to a website
	Number of content pages opened up per website visited	Chin et al. (2015) and Sanchiz et al. (2019b)	
	Number of content webpages visited multiple times	Barsky and Bar-Ilan (2012), Lei et al. (2013), Wildemuth et al. (2018)	
Query formulation	Number of times keywords/terms are used in queries	Hembrooke et al. (2005)	Exploitation of a search path initiated through a query formulation
	Number of keywords extracted from instructions/search problem statements	Dommes et al. (2011) and Sanchiz et al. (2017a, 2019a)	
	Broadness of changes in query reformulation	Hembrooke et al. (2005), Hölscher and Strube (2000), Vakkari (2001)	

It is to be noted that exploration and exploitation strategies cannot be generally associated with either good or bad search strategies per se (and thus cause good or bad performance). To determine whether exploring or exploiting information turns out to be the relevant thing to do, one must consider the search context (i.e., search goal and current stage of the activity) and the relevance of the information being processed. The following part of this section will discuss how research can connect online data with either exploration or exploitation strategies for navigation and querying. Figure 5.1 presents a schematic overview of the theoretical and methodological framework presented in this chapter.

Fig. 5.1 Overview of the role of fluid and crystallized abilities in exploration and exploitation search strategies

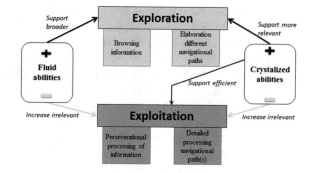

5.3.2   Presentation of the Construct of Exploration and Exploitation Behavior

As discussed in the above section, current research is burgeoning with online indicators showing how users navigate the web to search for information. Indicators of website selection, content webpage visits and time allotted to processing SERPs on webpages are among the most commonly used ones (Aula and Nordhausen 2006; Barsky and Bar-Ilan 2012; Dommes et al. 2011; Gerjets et al. 2011; Hölscher and Strube 2000). These indicators are particularly useful to understand to what extent users are engaged in an exhaustive or a superficial way in the task. However, it may be tricky to fully understand users' behavior without confronting these variables one with another (and thus get a clearer global representation of users' navigational behavior) and with the cognitive processes they reflect. As illustrated in Fig. 5.1, from a methodological point of view, the exploration–exploitation discrepancy can help research categorize raw data into two types of navigational behavior: (i) strategies to browse and process a broad part of the problem space and (ii) strategies to maximize the hoped utility of the sources of information accessed by digging deeper into them.

Discriminating different patches of information (i.e., the different sub-parts of the problem space) can be difficult (Chin et al. 2015). Indeed, users may go for another source of information, such as a new website, but they may keep looking for the same pieces of information. For instance, when searching for the name of *Luke Skywalker's ship* in the *Star Wars movies*, users may start by opening the first result provided on the SERP list and then go back to the SERP to open up a new one and look for further information. Consistently with prior works (Chin et al. 2015; Sanchiz et al. 2019b), we argue that initiating a new search path corresponds to exploration. New search paths can be elaborated through the evaluation of SERPs and the selection of new websites not previously seen or through a new query reformulation. Of course, exploratory behavior can be more or less extensive. Users may switch between two patches of information (i.e., parts of the problem space) that are semantically very similar. In contrast, users may also perform wider jumps between information patches. For instance, opening up a *Wikipedia* page tackling the different *ships* in *Star Wars* and jumping to a new website detailing the differences between the *Jedi* and the *Empire spaceships* correspond to a close jump (i.e., these two websites will most likely share a lot of common information). In contrast, returning to the SERP to open up a website describing the scenario of *Star Wars IV: A New Hope* corresponds to a wider jump as it focuses on more different pieces of information. Similar remarks can be made for querying strategies. Initiating a new search path is done by reformulating. To reformulate a query, either users can change parts of their previous query (i.e., transform, add or erase some keywords) or they may transform it completely (and use new keywords) (Bilal and Gwizdka 2018; Dommes et al. 2011; Duggan and Payne 2008; Kroustallaki et al. 2015; Lei et al. 2013; Sanchiz et al. 2017a, b, 2019a; Wildemuth et al. 2018). Complete reformulations, new keywords, unique queries are querying indicators reflecting a wide jump to a new information patch, whereas changing query length, suppressing keywords, keeping keywords used in the previous query correspond to a narrow jump.

5.3.3   Impact of Fluid Abilities on Exploration and Exploitation Behavior

Theoretically, fluid abilities mainly influence how individuals perform a task (i.e., the strategies engage to solve a problem for instance). In IS, fluid abilities support changes of search strategies in order to adapt to the constraints of the environment (Sharit et al. 2008, 2015). As discussed previously, exploratory behavior corresponds to more flexible search strategies in which users turn to different sources of information or different search patches to solve their search need (Sanchiz et al. 2019b). For instance, prior works have shown that fluid abilities such as cognitive flexibility can predict the number of reformulations and visits to new websites (Dommes et al. 2011; Sharit et al. 2008). Allocating extra resources to opening up a new website or reformulating queries requires users to: develop a new mental representation of the additional search path initiated, keep it active in working memory, update the overall global mental model of their search and inhibit some information already activated to put them on a second plan. All these processes particularly rely on users' fluid abilities. Indeed, current research has shown that users with lower fluid abilities (such as older adults) tend to visit fewer websites, reformulate less and initiate a smaller number of different navigational paths (Dommes et al. 2011; Sanchiz et al. 2019a, b). As another example, one could also cite how children with low fluid abilities tend to have difficulties to overcome impasses and reformulate less often (Bilal and Kirby 2002).

In a nutshell, fluid abilities, by supporting adaptation to environment changes and processing strategy switch (Eppinger et al. 2007; Sharit et al. 2008), tend to play a major role in broad exploration strategies and the development of adapted decisions when facing a breakdown. Indicators reflecting the will to find new information (i.e., exploratory behavior) can thus help research better grasp the actual role of fluid abilities in IS behavior. Operationally, when searching for information, users are more likely switching between exploration and exploitation strategies (i.e., users tend to initiate new branches/search paths and then process them in greater detail). Hence, high or low levels of fluid abilities will influence the trade-off between exploration and exploitation behaviors (Chin et al. 2015; Sanchiz et al. 2019b). Individuals with higher levels of fluid abilities should develop a larger proportion of exploration strategies. In contrast, for users with lower fluid abilities, the trade-off between exploration and exploitation strategies should be in favor of exploitation behavior (i.e., indicators of deeper processing of websites, multiple subsequent uses of similar keywords, etc.).

5.3.4   Impact of Crystallized Abilities on Exploration and Exploitation Behavior

Crystallized abilities, such as prior knowledge use or vocabulary skills, contribute to information processing efficiency (i.e., accurate evaluation of information relevance, efficient selection and integration of information, etc.) (Hölscher and Strube 2000; Monchaux et al. 2015; Sharit et al. 2008, 2015). In line with prior empirical studies reported in this chapter, we argue that crystallized abilities foster exploration strategies that are more relevant (e.g., selection of websites relevant with regard to users' search goal, production of accurate queries, etc.). For instance, high knowledgeable users should have enough cognitive resources available to browse a greater amount of information and elaborate a greater number of different navigational paths. Studies investigating the impact of IS skills showed that highly skilled searchers tend to conduct more parallel searches (such as processing several websites in multiple tabs) (Thatcher 2006). In contrast, less knowledgeable users tend to exhaust their cognitive resources in sense-making and coherence maintaining while processing information, which does not allow them to explore efficiently a broader part of the search problem space. In addition, crystallized abilities should support the efficient exploitation of the information patches consulted by users (see Fig. 5.1 for an overview). For instance, prior knowledge, vocabulary skills and IS skills can reduce the time spent processing information. They can also support the selection of coherent webpages once on a website through a more accurate evaluation of the website menus (Dommes et al. 2011; Hölscher and Strube 2000; Pak and Price 2008; Sanchiz et al. 2017a). In contrast, lower levels of crystallized abilities should reduce exploration strategies and increase the exploitation of irrelevant search patches. For instance, users with lower levels of prior topic knowledge or IS skills tend to narrow down their search activity and focus on a small amount of websites (link-dependent search strategies, Thatcher 2006) or visit a greater number of webpages once on a website (Sanchiz et al. 2017a).

Analyzing the impact of crystallized abilities on exploitation strategies represents a great challenge. Indeed, several empirical findings have clearly demonstrated to what extent these abilities can support more efficient and accurate exploration (or decrease exploration for users with lower crystallized abilities). However, very few studies have investigated how low levels of crystallized abilities can cause more unadapted exploitation of information patches (i.e., cause users to persevere on processing irrelevant sources of information). Indeed, to do so, research should first determine what is an irrelevant search path (an irrelevant website or query for instance). In IS, relevance is determined with regard to the features of the user's search goal (or the environments' constraints) (Balatsoukas and Ruthven 2012). When investigating navigation behavior, relevant sources of information thus correspond to sources that contain the target information or to webpages/websites that users have to go through in order to solve the search problem (either because these pages contain useful information to develop a more coherent mental representation of the search need or because the organization of the documents itself does not allow to jump over these pages). For some tasks, as in explicit fact-finding ones (Bell and Ruthven 2004), evaluating which sources of information are relevant can be easy. For instance, the level of topicality (i.e., semantic proximity between the website's contents and the search goal) and the quality of the source of information (i.e., credibility, authoritativeness of the author, etc.) are somewhat easy parameters to take into account in order to determine information source relevance. However, for more open-ended, sense-making and imprecise search tasks, such criterion might be more difficult to use. Indeed, when searching for information with a vague and unclear representation of the search need, users may deliberately want to access easy-to-understand documents that may not be the most relevant ones but that contain intuitive and familiar pieces of information that could contribute to get a clearer idea of what needs to be done to locate the target information. In other words, opening up a website that provides a general broad overview of a topic and browsing more or less randomly several webpages on this website could be considered as irrelevant exploitation behavior; yet, when considering the search context and the stage of the activity (i.e., early beginning of the search) such behavior may not necessarily be irrelevant.

Indeed, exploitation strategies mainly correspond to the over-processing of the search paths initiated through query formulation or website selection (Chin et al. 2015; Sanchiz et al. 2019b). However, to draw coherent conclusion on users' search behavior, researchers need to discriminate between coherent and necessary exploitation of information (i.e., such as deeper processing of useful webpages) and abusive/perseverating processing of information (such as going in circles and revisiting multiple times the same webpages). Ideally, to do so, researchers should distinguish between relevant/useful content and irrelevant ones. Some computerized tools may provide support to evaluate the semantic relevance of the links consulted for instance (see latent semantic analysis—LSA—as used in the CoLiDeS + Pic model by van Oostendorp et al. 2012). However, using LSA requires first to construct a database of documents in order to compute the degree of relevance of each link visited by users. Another less costly way to determine useful exploitation strategies *vs* irrelevant perseverating/exploitation strategies would be to distinguish between initial in-depth processing and subsequent ones. For instance, as stated earlier, the number of webpages consulted per website or per query is a commonly used indicator that reflects exploitation strategies (Barsky and Bar-Ilan 2012; Duggan and Payne 2008; Guan 2014; Huang and Efthimiadis 2009; Lei et al. 2013; Wildemuth et al. 2018). In line with Duggan and Payne's work (2008), research could take into account the number of different pages visited per query (or unique pages opened up per query) and the number of multiple visits to previously consulted webpages per query. Such indicator does not provide any information on the actual relevance or usefulness of the webpages consulted. However, it does distinguish between exploitation behavior that can reflect strategies to extensively comprehend the topic or process a search path and exploitation behavior that reflect more disorientation, unadapted decision-making or browsing difficulties. In addition, refining indicators of exploitation in such way could also improve the predictive power of search behavior on performance as exploitation behavior related to browsing difficulties (i.e., difficulties to select a useful webpage to visit) or disorientation is often associated with lower search performance (Wagner et al. 2010).

5.4 Contextualizing

5.4.1 Contextualizing Online Behavioral Data in Relation to the Evolution of the Search Behavior

As outlined in the previous section, indicators of exploration and exploitation strategies may provide more accurate insights on users' search behavior. However, to predict search performance (and thus relate exploration and exploitation strategies to IS outcome), one most likely needs to take into account the context of the search. One intuitive finding to understand how crucial it is to take into account the search context is the analysis of chronometry. Several prior works investigated, for example, the time spent processing the SERPs before selecting a link/website to open up (Chin and Fu 2010; Dommes et al. 2011; Kammerer and Gerjets 2014; Sanchiz et al. 2017a, 2019a). These studies showed, for instance, that users facing difficulties to select a relevant source of information can spend longer dwell times evaluating the search engine results. However, the value of the time spent processing the SERPs can be tremendously different from one task to another. For instance, in a simple fact-finding search task, such as *"when was Star Wars IV released in theaters?"*, no particular search strategies are required (provided that the user does formulate a relevant query that includes all important keywords). To find the target information, users need to read the top of the SERP in order to find the answer or to visit one website provided at the top of the result list to find it. In such cases, extensive dwell time spent on the SERP may reflect difficulties. However, in a more complex open-ended task, such as *"Which French political TV show, presented by two famous journalists has received political celebrities such as Georges Marchais and Francois Mitterrand in the seventies?"*, users most likely need to allocate more effort to the processing of the SERP in order to select one (or several) website(s) to find the target answer. In such contexts, dwell time on SERPs may not necessarily reflect difficulties but rather engagement in the task or careful processing. As illustrated in this example, the context of the search is determined by several factors such as the source of the information need (intern or extern) and the type of search task to perform (i.e., the complexity of the task and the constraints it puts on users). Taking into account the context of the search is particularly crucial to understand users' behavior and predict/explain search performance. Indeed, tasks of varying complexity do not require the same processes or the same amount of cognitive resources and they do not all share the same constraints for users. Bell and Ruthven (2004) presented a typology of search tasks in which the level of certainty/clarity of the information to be found and the way to access it represent major criteria of complexity. For instance, when the information to be found and the way to access it are clearly defined (the instructions provide relevant clues such as useful keywords: Dommes et al. 2011; Sanchiz et al. 2017a, b, 2019a) users are not particularly required to extensively process websites. In such context, deeper processing, such as a great number of different websites or multiple query reformulations, most likely reflects exploitation behavior. In contrast, when the search process is highly imprecise and uncertain, users are expected to process a greater amount of information and navigate in many websites to gather pieces of information (Chin and Fu 2010; Sanchiz et al. 2017a, b). In more complex search contexts, the above-mentioned indicators most likely reflect exploration strategies, at least at the early stages of the search.

Hence, one key to better analyze users' exploration and exploitation strategies and thus understand the respective role of fluid and crystallized abilities is to extract what users have to do to solve the search task (i.e., extract through a cognitive analysis the processes that users need to engage in order to be successful). No matter the level of complexity, or the amount of resources that users have (thanks to his/her own prior knowledge or thanks to a support tool), search tasks of similar nature (i.e., fact-finding ones, open-ended ones, sense-making ones, etc.) share some common general features that can help researchers make sense of the behavioral data they collect. As presented in Bell and Ruthven (2004) classification of task complexity, the more complex the task is, the more it requires exploration and exploitation strategies. However, as discussed above, understanding the task demands may sometimes not be enough to discriminate between exploration and exploitation strategies. In such cases, contextualizing the data collected (i.e., analyzing the data with regard to the ongoing step of the search) may bring more relevant insights.

5.4.2 Contextualizing Online Behavioral Data in Relation to the Search Task

Current indicators used in the literature provide a good overview of the strategies used during the entire search activity. These indicators tackle a wide spectrum of processes related to the exploration and exploitation of information in IS with a search engine. However, as outlined earlier in this chapter, research most often falls short of analyzing how users' search strategies evolve while proceeding through the task. Theoretical models of IS have explained how the different stages of the activity can rely on different processes. For instance, Sharit and collaborators (2008, 2015) showed that stage one particularly requires planning and the elaboration of a coherent mental representation of the search need/initial query. The second stage of the activity relies on evaluation processes (i.e., to assess information relevance and select websites). In contrast, the last stage of the activity requires navigation, sense-making processes to integrate information. This stage also requires users to maintain relevant information active in working memory and update them throughout the task. Finally, due to the cycling nature of IS, users may switch between these different stages, which particularly requires flexibility, evaluation and regulation processes. Hence, to draw stronger conclusions on users' search behavior and better predict search performance, analyzing online data with regard to the different stages of the activity represents a promising perspective.

Considering the different stages of IS is a burgeoning trend in the literature. For instance, prior works have developed operational indicators to understand how users start searching for information (such as the quality of the initial query produced and the time taken on the first SERP to access a website) (Downing et al. 2005; Kammerer and Gerjets 2014; Lei et al. 2013). Other studies developed indicators to investigate how users switch between browsing the web to process information and rereading the search problem instructions (to reactivate information in working memory for instance, Vakkari et al. 2003). In addition, studies focusing on information evaluation in Google-like environments (such as the SERP list) also created specific indicators based on eye-tracking measures to analyze how users initially process a search engine result before selecting a website (for instance: duration of the first-path fixation on a link or the duration of the first saccade, Oulasvirta et al. 2005: for a review, see Alemdag and Cagiltay 2018).

Analyzing the initial stage of the search is especially interesting because it can reflect how users engage in the task based on their own abilities and the information provided in the context without being influenced by how they processed information during the search (Sanchiz et al. 2017b). Hence, as illustrated in Table 5.2, retrieving precise indicators during the planning stage can help researchers identify whether users develop more exploratory strategies or exploitation strategies in relation to their fluid and crystallized abilities. For instance, Chin and Fu (2010) and Sanchiz and her collaborators (2017b, 2019b) showed that young adults (around 20 years old) used more bottom-up strategies when selecting the first website to open up (i.e., extremely short time spent on SERP before opening up a website and selection influenced by link position on the SERP list). In contrast, older adults (aged 60 years old and more) with lower fluid abilities used more top-down strategies and took more time to evaluate the SERP (i.e., they spent longer time on the initial SERP retrieved before deciding to opening up a website and mostly relied on their topic knowledge rather than link position).

In addition, computing indicators reflecting planning, evaluation, navigation and regulation stages of the activity can provide further insights to understand users'

Table 5.2 Examples of indicators investigated during the initial stage of the search in the literature (i.e., planning, Sharit et al. 2008, 2015)

Process targeted	Indicator	Author	Dimension of IS
Querying	Semantic specificity of initial query produced	Lei et al. (2013)	Level of relevance of the early mental representation elaborated (as measured by the semantic relevance of the query)
	Number of keywords extracted from the search problem statements in the first query	Sanchiz et al. (2017b)	Level of relevance of the early mental representation elaborated + inhibition of instruction-based keywords
	Number of new keywords (inferred by users based on their own prior knowledge) in the first query	Sanchiz et al. (2017b)	Level of relevance of the early mental representation elaborated + cognitive flexibility (adding new keywords)
	Analysis of the keywords contained in the initial query and query length	Jansen et al. (2007), Guan (2014), Vakkari (2001)	Level of relevance of the early mental representation elaborated + inhibition and cognitive flexibility
Navigation/website selection	Time taken to access the first relevant article	Downing et al. (2005), Kammerer and Gerjets (2014)	Evaluation of information relevance and sources
	Time spent evaluating the initial SERP	Sanchiz et al. (2017b, 2019b)	Evaluation of information
	Impact of the first query produced (number of websites accessed from initial SERP)	Guan (2014)	Level of exploitation of initial query
	Level of relevance of the initial document selected	Scholer et al. (2013)	Quality of evaluation processes

exploration and exploitation behavior. First, during the initial stage of the search, users try to reinforce the coherence of their mental representation of the search need (i.e., by extracting new information from the initial SERP or website and by determining whether the initial query produced is really relevant or not). At this stage, good information searchers should thus activate relevant prior knowledge and show flexible strategies in case they started the search with an irrelevant query or opened up an irrelevant website. In more complex open-ended tasks (Bell and Ruthven 2004), when the search need is imprecise, good searchers should more heavily rely on exploration strategies in order to browse a greater amount of information and find relevant pieces of information to improve their mental representation of the search need (and reformulate a better query). In contrast, exploitation of the initial search path elaborated (through the first query and/or the first website opened) might reflect a less adapted strategy. Stages 2 (evaluation) and 3 (deep processing) may however include a larger proportion of exploitation strategies as these two stages require users to process the relevance of the search path they elaborated (and thus determine whether it is a good way to find the target information or if they should switch back to earlier stages and regulate their behavior). Hence, exploitation of the search paths elaborated may, at first, not show particular difficulties. However, as users proceed through the search (for instance, after several phases of regulation such as multiple query reformulations), accumulation of exploitation strategies (such as extensive processing of a website through a larger number of content webpages accessed) most likely reflects that users face difficulties or are disoriented.

Finally, the number of SERPs—website switches and the number of query reformulations during the transitions between stages—could reflect adapted regulation strategies supported by the efficient use of fluid abilities (and thus reflect higher level of exploration).

5.5   Discussion

5.5.1   Theoretical Perspectives to Include Fluid and Crystallized Abilities to Theoretical Models

Overall, the current chapter discussed how aggregating online indicators as exploration or exploitation search strategies can help future research better understand the effects of interindividual differences related to fluid and crystallized abilities on IS behavior and performance. On a theoretical plan, the framework presented pointed out that IS requires two types of processes: (i) keeping active and refreshing information in working memory and (ii) processing information. Figure 5.2 provides a synthetic overview of the theoretical framework of IS that we introduce in order to better analyze how crystallized and fluid abilities impact IS performance and behavior.

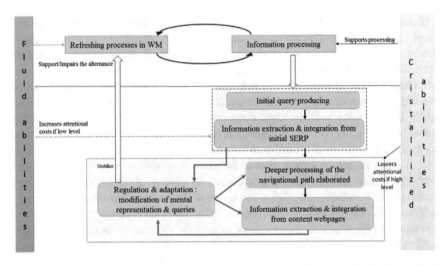

Fig. 5.2 Overview of the new theoretical framework to account for the role of fluid and crystallized abilities on IS

In line with several cognitive models of IS (Sharit et al. 2008, 2015), the information processing component of IS involves a wide set of processes such as elaborating mental models, evaluating information relevance and sources, etc. As illustrated in Fig. 5.2, information processing is argued to happen while users have to allocate resources to maintain information active and up to date in their working memory. For instance, users allocate their resources to elaborate a coherent mental representation of their search need and of each new source of information processed (and update their mental representation) in parallel to engaging in processing information (such as validating information, comprehension processes, sense-making). To perform these two types of processes in parallel all along the activity can particularly pose high demands on cognitive resources. Users' fluid and crystallized abilities are thus crucial as they can determine (i) the amount of resources available to perform the task and (ii) the amount of resources required by each operation. In other words, to search for information with a search engine, users need to alternatively allocate their attentional resources to updating processes in working memory and information processes. As discussed earlier, current empirical works have provided strong argument on the impact of fluid and crystallized abilities on each of these two components. As a reminder, updating information in working memory heavily relies on fluid abilities and is less demanding if users possess relevant prior topic knowledge or vocabulary skills (Eppinger et al. 2007; Sanchiz et al. 2019b; Sharit et al. 2008, 2015). Processing information (e.g., querying, SERP evaluation, navigation, comprehension processes) is also supported by high level of crystallized abilities such as IS skills or prior knowledge (Hölscher and Strube 2000; Monchaux et al. 2015). In addition, all along the evolution of the activity, processing information in an adapted way can be improved by high level of fluid abilities (Dommes et al. 2011; Sharit et al. 2008, 2015).

In this chapter, we discussed how lower levels of fluid abilities can also alter information processing by increasing exploitation and reducing exploration strategies (Chin et al. 2015; Sanchiz et al. 2019b). Overall, low fluid abilities tend to increase the cost in cognitive resources of information processes as early as the initial stage of the activity (Sanchiz et al. 2017b). They also cause difficulties for the stages that particularly require refreshing in both memory processes and information processes (such as the evaluation stage or regulation processes Sharit et al. 2008, 2015). For instance, a larger proportion of exploitation strategies on SERP evaluation and query reformulation could appear for users with lower fluid abilities. Regarding crystallized abilities, research has shown that the more users possess prior knowledge, vocabulary skills or IS skills, the lesser costly in cognitive resources information processes are. For instance, high knowledgeable users need fewer resources to produce a relevant initial query, to select relevant websites or reformulate (Hölscher and Strube 2000; Sanchiz et al. 2017a, b; Vakkari et al. 2003). Consequently, by lowering the cognitive costs of information processes, crystallized abilities can contribute to increase the amount of resources available for the task. In this way, they may facilitate the allocation of resources to refreshing in working memory processes and processing alternatively.

In general, our framework also includes the distinction between exploration and exploitation strategies in the information processing component of IS. As represented in the lower frame of Fig. 5.2, deeper processing and information integration (i.e., right branch of the frame) correspond to exploitation behavior. In these stages, users engage in comprehension processes to extract relevant information and integrate them into their mental model. The left branch (regulation and adaptation strategies) along with the gray arrows corresponds to exploration strategies (i.e., elaboration of new search paths through reformulation or selection of new website) and regulation stages.

5.5.2 Challenges and Perspectives for Future Works

Future works should deeper investigate how both components of IS are impacted by fluid and crystallized abilities when the search task actually serves a specific goal (such as writing an essay in an educational setting). In such contexts, users' attentional resources are particularly solicited by refreshing in working memory processes. Indeed, on a theoretical plan, the framework introduced may also explain why users with lower fluid and crystallized abilities can particularly have difficulties when the search task is conducted in parallel with another task. Conversely, such context may affect the amount of resources available for information processing and the trade-off between exploration and exploitation strategies (i.e., causing, for instance, too much irrelevant exploitation or shallow exploitation of the sources of information accessed).

Another challenge to be investigated for future works is the investigation of the final stage of the activity. Indeed, predicting when and why users stop searching for information (particularly in cases when they do not solve their search need) is a key leverage to understand their difficulties and develop useful IS support tools. To do so, we argue that pursuing the analyses of the different stages of the activity could help research better monitor users' difficulties.

Implications of this new framework provide insights on how to design useful support tools for users with particular needs. Indeed, our framework argues that IS support tools should not just attempt to cope with the decrease of attentional resources caused by lower fluid abilities (such as decreasing the amount of information on the screen or providing query suggestions) but should:

- Reduce all along the activity the amount of parallel processing (i.e., refreshing in working memory and information processing) to help users refresh information and elaborate adapted exploration and exploitation strategies.
- Support the alternative allocation of attentional resources between refreshing and information processing components. For instance, such tools could consist in metacognitive crutches that would help users keep active their search goal in working memory.

As an illustration, a study by Sanchiz and her collaborator (2019b) showed that a search interface designed to support the alternative allocation of resources to update in working memory and information processing could help older adults display more flexible search strategies. Displaying users' query at all time during the search (i.e., allowing users to have a glance at their current sub-goal at all time and at low cognitive costs) can help older adults evaluate information on content pages and reformulate new queries at lower cognitive costs. Such example shows how the framework introduced in this chapter can help the design of better system or search interface. Additionally, training users to strategically allocate resources to the two components of IS (i.e., update in working memory and information processing) could improve the search strategies and performance of users with lower fluid and crystallized abilities. Such training could also cope with the constraints of complex IS contexts.

References

Alemdag E, Cagiltay K (2018) A systematic review of eye tracking research on multimedia learning. Comput Educ 125:413–428. https://doi.org/10.1016/j.compedu.2018.06.023

Aula A, Nordhausen K (2006) Modeling successful performance in web searching. J Am Soc Inf Sci Technol 57(12):1678–1693. https://doi.org/10.1002/asi.20340

Balatsoukas P, Ruthven I (2012) An eye-tracking approach to the analysis of relevance judgments on the web: the case of Google search engine. J Am Soc Inf Sci Technol 63(9):1728–1746. https://doi.org/10.1002/asi.22707

Barsky E, Bar-Ilan J (2012) The impact of task phrasing on the choice of search keywords and on the search process and success. J Am Soc Inf Sci Technol 63(10):1987–2005. https://doi.org/10.1002/asi.22654

Bell DJ, Ruthven I (2004) Searcher's assessments of task complexity for web searching. In: European Conference on Information Retrieval. Springer, Berlin, Heidelberg, April, pp 57–71. https://doi.org/10.1007/978-3-540-24752-4_5

Bilal D, Gwizdka J (2018) Children's query types and reformulations in Google search. Inf Process Manag 54(6):1022–1041. https://doi.org/10.1016/j.ipm.2018.06.008

Bilal D, Kirby J (2002) Differences and similarities in information seeking: children and adults as web users. Inf Process Manag 38(5):649–670

Brand-Gruwel S, Wopereis I, Walraven A (2009) A descriptive model of information problem solving while using internet. Comput Educ 53(4):1207–1217. https://doi.org/10.1016/j.compedu.2009.06.004

Cattell RB (1971) Abilities: their structure, growth, and action. Houghton Mifflin, Boston

Chevalier A, Chevalier N (2009) Influence of proficiency level and constraints on viewpoint switching: a study in web design. Appl Cogn Psychol 23(1):126–137. https://doi.org/0.1002/acp.1448

Chin J, Anderson E, Chin C-L, Fu W-T (2015) Age differences in information search: an exploration-exploitation tradeoff model. In: Proceedings of the 59th annual meeting of the human factors and ergonomics society 2015. Human Factors and Ergonomics Society, Los Angeles, CA

Chin J, Fu W-T (2010) Interactive effects of age and interface differences on search strategies and performance. In: Proceedings of the 28th ACM conference on human factors in computing systems CHI'10. ACM Press, Atlanta, GA, pp 403–412. https://doi.org/10.1145/1753326.17

Chin J, Fu W-T, Kannampallil T (2009) Adaptive information search: age-dependent interactions between cognitive profiles and strategies. In: Proceedings of the 27th ACM conference on human factors in computing systems CHI'09. ACM Press, Boston, MA, pp 1683–1692. https://doi.org/10.1145/1518701.1518961

Crabb M, Hanson VL (2014) Age, technology usage, and cognitive characteristics in relation to perceived disorientation and reported website ease of use. In: Proceedings of the 16th international ACM SIGACCESS conference on computers & accessibility. ACM, October, pp 193–200. https://doi.org/10.1145/2661334.2661356

Dommes A, Chevalier A, Lia S (2011) The role of cognitive flexibility and vocabulary abilities of younger and older users in searching for information on the web. Appl Cogn Psychol 25(5):717–726

Downing RE, Moore JL, Brown SW (2005) The effects and interaction of spatial visualization and domain expertise on information seeking. Comput Hum Behav 21(2):195–209. https://doi.org/10.1016/j.chb.2004.03.040

Duggan GB, Payne SJ (2008) Knowledge in the head and on the web: using topic expertise to aid search. In: Proceedings of the SIGCHI conference on Human factors in computing systems. ACM, April, pp 39–48. https://doi.org/10.1145/1357054.1357062

Ecker UK, Lewandowsky S, Oberauer K, Chee AE (2010) The components of working memory updating: an experimental decomposition and individual differences. J Exp Psychol Learn Mem Cogn 36(1):170. https://doi.org/10.1037/a0017891

Eppinger B, Kray J, Mecklinger A, John O (2007) Age differences in task switching and response monitoring: evidence from ERPs. Biol Psychol 75(1):52–67. https://doi.org/10.1016/j.biopsycho.2006.12.001

Fu WT, Pirolli P (2007) SNIF-ACT: a cognitive model of user navigation on the World Wide Web. Hum Comput Interact 22(4):355–412. https://doi.org/10.1080/07370020701638806

Gerjets P, Kammerer Y, Werner B (2011) Measuring spontaneous and instructed evaluation processes during Web search: Integrating concurrent thinking-aloud protocols and eye-tracking data. Learn Instr 21(2):220–231. https://doi.org/10.1016/j.learninstruc.2010.02.005

Giraud S, Thérouanne P, Steiner DD (2018) Web accessibility: Filtering redundant and irrelevant information improves website usability for blind users. Int J Hum Comput Stud 111:23–35. https://doi.org/10.1016/j.ijhcs.2017.10.011

Guan DH (2014) Is the first query the most important: an evaluation of query aggregation schemes in session search. In: Proceedings of information retrieval technology 10th Asia information

retrieval societies conference, AIRS 2014, Kuching, Malaysia, 3–5 December 2014. https://doi.
org/10.1007/978-3-319-12844-3_8

Hahnel C, Goldhammer F, Kröhne U, Naumann J (2018) The role of reading skills in the evaluation of
online information gathered from search engine environments. Comput Hum Behav 78:223–234.
https://doi.org/10.1016/j.chb.2017.10.004

Hasher L, Zacks RT (1988) Working memory, comprehension, and aging: a review and a new view.
Psychol Learn Motiv 22:193–225

Hembrooke HA, Granka LA, Gay GK, Liddy ED (2005) The effects of expertise and feedback on
search term selection and subsequent learning. J Am Soc Inf Sci Technol 56(8):861–871. https://
doi.org/10.1002/asi.20180

Hölscher C, Strube G (2000) Web search behavior of Internet experts and newbies. Comput Netw
33(1–6):337–346. https://doi.org/10.1016/S1389-1286(00)00031-1

Horn JL, Cattell RB (1967) Age differences in fluid and crystallized intelligence. Acta Physiol
(Oxf) 26:107–129

Huang J, Efthimiadis EN (2009) Analyzing and evaluating query reformulation strategies in
web search logs. In: Proceedings of the 18th ACM conference on Information and knowledge
management. ACM, November, pp 77–86. https://doi.org/10.1145/1645953.1645966

Jansen BJ, Booth DL, Spink A (2007) Determining the user intent of web search engine queries. In:
Proceedings of the 16th international conference on World Wide Web. ACM, May, pp 1149–1150.
https://doi.org/10.1145/1242572.1242739

Kammerer Y, Gerjets P (2014) The role of search result position and source trustworthiness in the
selection of web search results when using a list or a grid interface. Int J Hum Comput Interact
30(3):177–191

Karanam S, van Oostendorp H (2016) Age-related differences in the content of search queries
when reformulating. In: Proceedings of the 2016 CHI conference on human factors in computing
systems. ACM, May, pp 5720–5730

Kawashima T, Matsumoto E (2018) Negative cues lead to more inefficient search than positive cues
even at later stages of visual search. Acta Physiol (Oxf) 190:85–94. https://doi.org/10.1016/j.
actpsy.2018.07.003

Kelly D, Arguello J, Edwards A, Wu W-C (2015) Development and evaluation of search tasks for
IIR experiments using a cognitive complexity framework. In: Proceeding of the international
conference on the theory of information retrieval. ACM, New York, NY, pp 101–110

Kroustallaki D, Kokkinaki T, Sideridis GD, Simos PG (2015) Exploring students' affect and achievement goals in the context of an intervention to improve web searching skills. Comput Hum Behav
49:156–170. https://doi.org/10.1016/j.chb.2015.02.060

Lazonder AW, Biemans HJ, Wopereis IG (2000) Differences between novice and experienced users
in searching information on the World Wide Web. J Am Soc for Inf Sci 51(6):576–581. https://
doi.org/10.1002/(SICI)1097-4571(2000)51:6%3c576:AID-ASI9%3e3.0.CO;2-7

Lei PL, Lin SS, Sun CT (2013) Effect of reading ability and internet experience on keyword-based
image search. Educ Technol Soc 16(2):151–162

Lindow S, Betsch T (2019) Children's adaptive decision making and the costs of information search.
J Appl Dev Psychol 60:24–34. https://doi.org/10.1016/j.appdev.2018.09.006

Moher J, Lakshmanan BM, Egeth HE, Ewen JB (2014) Inhibition drives early feature-based
attention. Psychol Sci 25:315–324. https://doi.org/10.1177/0956797613511257

Monchaux S, Amadieu F, Chevalier A, Mariné C (2015) Query strategies during information searching: effects of prior domain knowledge and complexity of the information problems to be solved.
Inf Process Manag 51(5):557–569. https://doi.org/10.1016/j.ipm.2015.05.004

Morris N, Jones DM (1990) Memory updating in working memory: the role of the central executive.
Br J Psychol 81(2):111–121

Oulasvirta A, Kärkkäinen L, Laarni J (2005) Expectations and memory in link search. Comput
Hum Behav 21(5):773–789. https://doi.org/10.1016/j.chb.2004.02.018

Pak R, Price MM (2008) Designing an information search interface for younger and older adults.
Hum Factors 50(4):614–628

Park DC (2000) The basic mechanisms accounting for age-related decline in cognitive function. Cogn Aging Primer 11(1):3–19

Park DC, Smith AD, Lautenschlager G, Earles JL, Frieske D, Zwahr M, Gaines CL (1996) Mediators of long-term memory performance across the life span. Psychol Aging 11(4):621

Phan N, Bailey P, Wilkinson R (2007) Understanding the relationship of information need specificity to search query length. In: Proceedings of the 30th annual international ACM SIGIR conference on research and development in information retrieval. ACM, July, pp 709–710

Pirolli P, Card S (1999) Information foraging. Psychol Rev 106(4):643

Salthouse TA, Atkinson TM, Berish DE (2003) Executive functioning as a potential mediator of age-related cognitive decline in normal adults. J Exp Psychol Gen 132(4):566. https://doi.org/10.1037/0096-3445.132.4.566

Sanchiz M, Chin J, Chevalier A, Fu WT, Amadieu F, He J (2017a) Searching for information on the web: impact of cognitive aging, prior domain knowledge and complexity of the search problems. Inf Process Manag 53(1):281–294. https://doi.org/10.1016/j.ipm.2016.09.003

Sanchiz M, Chevalier A, Amadieu F (2017b) How do older and young adults start searching for information? Impact of age, domain knowledge and problem complexity on the different steps of information searching. Comput Hum Behav 72:67–78. https://doi.org/10.1016/j.chb.2017.02.038

Sanchiz M, Amadieu F, Fu WT, Chevalier A (2019a) Does pre-activating domain knowledge foster elaborated online information search strategies? Comparisons between young and old web user adults. Appl Ergon 75:201–213. https://doi.org/10.1016/j.apergo.2018.10.010

Sanchiz M, Amadieu F, Paubel P-V, Chevalier A (2019b) Older user-friendly search interface: supporting search goal refreshing in working memory to improve search strategies. Behav Inf Technol 31(8):1–16. https://doi.org/10.1080/0144929X.2019.1642384

Scholer F, Kelly D, Wu WC, Lee HS, Webber W (2013) The effect of threshold priming and need for cognition on relevance calibration and assessment. In: Proceedings of the 36th international ACM SIGIR conference on research and development in information retrieval. ACM, July, pp 623–632. https://doi.org/10.1145/2484028.2484090

Sharit J, Hernández MA, Czaja SJ, Pirolli P (2008) Investigating the roles of knowledge and cognitive abilities in older adult information seeking on the web. ACM Trans Comput Hum Interact (TOCHI) 15(1):3. https://doi.org/10.1145/1352782.1352785

Sharit J, Taha J, Berkowsky RW, Profita H, Czaja SJ (2015) Online information search performance and search strategies in a health problem-solving scenario. J Cogn Eng Decis Mak 9(3):211–228. https://doi.org/10.1177/1555343415583747

Sihvonen A, Vakkari P (2004) Subject knowledge improves interactive query expansion assisted by a thesaurus. J Doc 60(6):673–690. https://doi.org/10.1108/00220410410568151

Slegers K, Van Boxtel MP, Jolles J (2012) Computer use in older adults: determinants and the relationship with cognitive change over a 6 year episode. Comput Hum Behav 28(1):1–10. https://doi.org/10.1016/j.chb.2011.08.003

Smith CL (2015) Domain-independent search expertise: a description of procedural knowledge gained during guided instruction. J Assoc Inf Sci Technol 66(7):1388–1405. https://doi.org/10.1002/asi.23272

Tabatabai D, Shore BM (2005) How experts and novices search the web. Libr Inf Sci Res 27(2):222–248. https://doi.org/10.1016/j.lisr.2005.01.005

Thatcher A (2006) Information-seeking behaviours and cognitive search strategies in different search tasks on the WWW. Int J Ind Ergon 36:1055–1068

Vakkari P (2001) Changes in search tactics and relevance judgements when preparing a research proposal a summary of the findings of a longitudinal study. Inf Retrieval 4(3–4):295–310. https://doi.org/10.1023/A:1016089224008

Vakkari P, Pennanen M, Serola S (2003) Changes of search terms and tactics while writing a research proposal: a longitudinal case study. Inf Process Manag 39(3):445–463. https://doi.org/10.1016/S0306-4573(02)00031-6

Van Deursen AJ, van Dijk JA (2009) Improving digital skills for the use of online public information and services. Gov Inf Quart 26(2):333–340. https://doi.org/10.1016/j.giq.2008.11.002

van Oostendorp H, Karanam S, Indurkhya B (2012) CoLiDeS + Pic: a cognitive model of web-navigation based on semantic information from pictures. Behav Inf Technol 31(1):17–30. https://doi.org/10.1080/0144929X.2011.603358

Vanderschantz N, Hinze A (2017) A study of children's search query formulation habits. In: Proceedings of the 31st British computer society human computer interaction conference. BCS Learning and Development Ltd., July, p 7. https://doi.org/10.14236/ewic/hci2017.7

Verhaeghen P, Cerella J (2002) Aging, executive control, and attention: a review of meta-analyses. Neurosci Biobehav Rev 26(7):849–857. https://doi.org/10.1016/S0149-7634(02)00071-4

Wagner N, Hassanein K, Head M (2010) Computer use by older adults: a multi-disciplinary review. Comput Hum Behav 26(5):870–882. https://doi.org/10.1016/j.chb.2010.03.029

Wildemuth BM (2004) The effects of domain knowledge on search tactic formulation. J Am Soc Inf Sci Technol 55(3):246–258. https://doi.org/10.1002/asi.10367

Wildemuth BM, Kelly D, Boettcher E, Moore E, Dimitrova G (2018) Examining the impact of domain and cognitive complexity on query formulation and reformulation. Inf Process Manag 54(3):433–450. https://doi.org/10.1016/j.ipm.2018.01.009

Zhang X, Anghelescu HG, Yuan X (2005) Domain knowledge, search behaviour, and search effectiveness of engineering and science students: an exploratory study. Inf Res Int Electron J 10(2):n2

Chapter 6
Semantic Relevance Feedback on Queries and Search Results for Younger and Older Adults

Herre van Oostendorp and Saraschandra Karanam

Abstract In this chapter, we describe research in which the influence of providing feedback on the semantic relevance of queries and search results is examined with younger and older adults when they reformulate their search queries. Providing feedback on the semantic relevance of search queries and search results increased the semantic relevance of future search queries as they reformulated both for younger and older adults. This applies especially to more difficult search problems. For younger adults, in addition to the semantic relevance of search queries, also an improvement in their search performance (in terms of the amount of time and the number of clicks needed to solve the task) was observed. No such difference in search performance was found for older adults. A possible explanation could be that, older adults need more time to adjust to the new search interface in order to find effects not only in the semantic relevance of queries but also in their search performance.

Keywords Search queries · Reformulations · Semantic relevance · Feedback · Aging

6.1 Introduction

Searching for information on the Internet can be challenging and involves cognitive processes such as attention, comprehension, memory, problem solving and decision making (Wildemuth et al. 2014). These cognitive processes are known to be affected by aging-related declines in cognitive abilities. It is for instance known that older

Saraschandra Karanam: User Experience Group, The MathWorks—This work was carried out by the author when he was working as a postdoctoral researcher at Utrecht University.

H. van Oostendorp (✉)
Department of Information and Computing Sciences, Utrecht University, Princetonplein 5, Utrecht 3584CC, The Netherlands
e-mail: h.vanoostendorp@uu.nl

S. Karanam
User Experience Group, The MathWorks, Bangalore, India
e-mail: skaranam@mathworks.com

adults generate less queries when using a search engine, use less keywords per query, reformulate less, spend more time evaluating the search results, spend more time evaluating the content of websites opened from search engine results pages (SERPs), and switch less between SERPs and websites (Chin et al. 2015; Dommes et al. 2011; Pak and Price 2008; Queen et al. 2012). Information problem solving tasks frequently require users to issue more than one query. Older adults find it often difficult to reformulate their previous unsuccessful query, leading to suboptimal search performance (Chevalier et al. 2015).

In well-known Information Search models like that of Vakkari (2001) or Kuhlthau (2004) it is acknowledged that solving complex information problems needs a successive series of attempts. See also Huurdeman and Kamps (2020). They focus on the temporal aspects of information search behavior at various stages of information search during solving complex tasks. However, in empirical literature, there has not been much attention to semantic, knowledge-related aspects of reformulations, in contrast to studies focused on structural transformations (like generalization, specification, etc.; see e.g. Wildemuth et al. 2018) and that is the focus of the current chapter. It could be that users, particularly older adults, not only lack the means to make an informed decision whether to reformulate or not but also lack the means to evaluate easily the relevance of search results.

In the next section, we will first discuss some studies on the effect of aging on the semantics of query reformulations. In the third section, we present briefly two experimental user studies that address the research question whether providing support in terms of the semantic relevance of their query and search results enhances the semantic relevance of their subsequent queries. This is examined for both older as well as younger adults. In the last section, we conclude and discuss limitations of the two studies and opportunities for future research.

6.2   Related Work on Semantics of Query Reformulations

Research on search strategies has so far overlooked analysis of the semantic aspects of query reformulations and age-related differences in the actual content of search queries during reformulations. We briefly describe two studies that examined the effects of age and task difficulty on semantic relevance of search queries during reformulations. The focus in these studies (Karanam and van Oostendorp 2016, 2017) was whether the semantic relevance of the reformulated queries increased compared to the preceding queries. The basic idea is that, in an ideal scenario, as one reformulates, one moves semantically closer to the desired target information. This should also be reflected in the semantic relevance of search queries. That is, as one reformulates, the semantic relevance of search queries should gradually increase. They could contain more keywords that are relevant for the target information.

Search engines usually rely on external assessors or use implicit user interaction patterns to estimate relevance of a search result. However, both these methods are not always accurate from a user's perspective as illustrated in studies by Mao et al.

(2016, 2017) and Jiang et al. (2017). Concerning the concept "relevance", the papers by Mao et al., and Jiang et al. are trying to define a "usefulness" metric from a user's perspective. What they actually mean is the subjective, contextual estimation of relevance as computed by the user during the course of the entire search session taking into account queries issued and documents viewed in the past (in that search session). The measure (Semantic Relevance of Queries-(SRQ, see below)) we will use, has similarities with these user-perceived measures. It has also direct connection with the concept of Information Scent (Pirolli and Card 1999). See also Karanam and Van Oostendorp (2020). Briefly, Information Scent is defined as the estimation by the user of the usefulness of a hyperlink to get closer to target information during navigation and it has been found as driving factor of steering web navigation. The main idea is that in their CoLiDeS+ model SERP results for each query are evaluated in working memory, on the basis of semantic characteristics, and that when the evaluated semantic relationship is high enough a result is selected (and e.g. the respective link opened), or a new query started when the semantic relationship is too low. Semantic relevance of queries (SRQ) is computed using Latent Semantic Analysis (LSA) (Landauer and Dumais 1997). LSA is a mathematical technique that provides a vector representation for each word (or text) in a high dimensional semantic space and provides a similarity measure between any two words (or texts) in that space using the cosine between the vectors (McNamara et al. 2007; see Landauer et al. [1998] for an introduction to LSA and semantic similarity). Karanam and van Oostendorp (2016, 2017) used a corpus of 70,000 Dutch documents (consisting of 60% newspaper articles and 40% medical and health related articles) to create a semantic space in Dutch, using Gallito (Jorge-Botana et al. 2013) and we made use of this semantic space. The semantic space represents the background knowledge of participants. The SRQ metric based on LSA estimates how close in semantic similarity the queries generated by the participants are to the target information by computing the cosine value between vectors of the query and the target information, respectively.

A high LSA value indicates a high semantic overlap between the query and the target information. Therefore, in general, the higher the SRQ is, the more relevant the query is, as demonstrated in Karanam and van Oostendorp (2016, 2017).

It also appeared in these studies that the semantic relevance of queries (SRQ) generated by younger adults remained constant across reformulations, or even increased, while that of the queries generated by older adults showed a decreasing trend as they reformulated (see further Karanam and van Oostendorp 2016, 2017). Older adults were here participants older than 63 years (mean age 75,72 year), and young participants were between 18 and 24 years (mean age 21,08 year). The discrepancy in mean SRQ over cycles was particularly the case with difficult tasks (Fig. 6.1b). Difficult tasks were tasks that could not directly be answered by looking at the search results on the SERP but needed some further examination of search results and reasoning. One of the possible explanations could be that older adults, due to their higher crystallized intelligence, are able to utilize the higher contextual information present in the simple tasks much better than younger adults (see also Sanchiz et al. 2020). But,

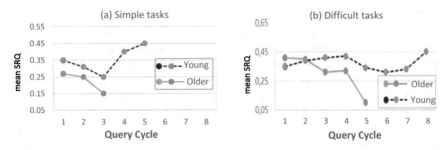

Fig. 6.1 Mean semantic relevance of queries (SRQ) for each reformulation cycle for **a** simple and **b** difficult tasks. The first cycle corresponds to the 1st query for a specific task, and the 2nd cycle stands for the 2nd reformulated query in that task and so forth

when it comes to difficult tasks, which demand generating own queries using one's own knowledge and understanding of the task, older adults perform poorly compared to younger adults.

One example to illustrate a sequence of search terms with increasing LSA values, given a difficult task (translated from Dutch) is *"Fieke, 6 year old, wants to drink a lot of water and has to urinate frequently. Often very exhausted. The physician diagnoses a high glucose value. What could be the problem, be specific, and what treatment would the physician start?"* A participant issued as first search terms "child of 6, thirsty, urinates frequently" (LSA = 0.11), 2nd cycle of search terms "6 year old, exhausted, high glucose value" (LSA = 0.57) and finally as third series of search terms "Type 1 diabetes of 6 years old, treatment?" (LSA = 0.95). The correct answer was here Diabetes Type 1 and treatment with insulin.

A second example concerns the following task *"Joost (15 years old) often helps his father in the bakery with baking bread. After the summer holidays, during which Joost assisted his father fulltime, he has troubles with stuffiness. Besides that, you hear him squeaking with exhaling. Which disease has Joost probably, and what is probably the provoking factor?"*. First query of a participant was "bakery, disease" (LSA = 0), the second query was "problems with respiration" (LSA = 0.28), the third query "causes, COPD" (LSA = 0.52), and the fourth query "cause, Asthma" (LSA = 0.87) and the correct answer was COPD and dust particles (flour).

A number of interfaces have been developed recently to assist users during various stages of the information search process, such as formulating and evaluating queries in beginning stages, and evaluating and selecting search results on the SERPS in later stages. For example, Peltonen et al. (2017) developed a Topic-Relevance Map to aid rapid comprehension of search results. A topic-relevance map organizes keywords representing the search results onto a radial layout. The radius, i.e. the distance from the centre of the circle represents relevance estimated for a keyword. The angle between keywords represents their projected topical similarity. ProjSnippet, developed by Gomez-Nieto et al. (2014), helps users gain a more comprehensive view of the search results, highlighting related documents and web pages while still retaining, as much as possible, the good properties of the conventional list-based paradigm, namely, the rank information and the summary content provided by the snippets. Umemoto et al. (2016) developed a query suggestion interface called ScentBar, for visualizing the amount of missed relevant information for intrinsically diverse search (information search tasks that demand collection of information about a topic covering different aspects). ScentBar visualizes, for both the search query and suggestion queries, the amount of missed information important to the current search topic in the form of a stacked bar chart so that users can grasp their search progress visually. See Umemoto et al. (2020), also for other examples.

While the first two studies are not concerned with queries but rather with evaluating search results, the third study comes very close to what we intend to do. However, these interfaces do not directly examine the phase of issuing a query and its reformulation. In this respect an exception is Scentbar (Umemoto et al. 2016). Scentbar does focus on the queries by visualizing the amount of missed, relevant information. However, it does not provide an estimate of how semantically relevant a user's query is, which is exactly what our proposed interface plans to do. Furthermore, we also want the interface to enable users to assess easily the semantic relevance of search results, whereas with Scentbar users still must spend time and efforts analyzing these.

6.3   Two Studies on Semantic Relevance Feedback

Based on the above studies and their outcomes we examined whether we can improve reformulations of older and younger adults by giving feedback based on the semantic relevance of the query (SRQ). Reducing problems with monitoring semantic relevance of the query and warning them when the semantic relevance of a query and search results fall below a threshold could be helpful to users, especially for older adults.

There is evidence that formulating queries, monitoring their appropriateness and reformulating them is difficult for older users, at least with more difficult search problems, probably because of their decline in fluid abilities (Chevalier et al. 2015; Chin et al. 2015; and see Sanchiz et al. 2020). Also evaluating (many) search results on SERPS can be problematic because of the same declining fluid abilities. In view of this, we performed two experimental user studies with a new and modified interface for the SERPs, one study with younger adults and the other with older adults. The new interface visually displays the semantic relevance of a query and search results (see Fig. 6.2), in contrast to Scentbar (Umemoto et al. 2016). In Fig. 6.2a (1), at the top of the SERP, semantic relevance feedback on the query, using semantic overlap between query *and* target information, based on LSA is presented. Below that (in Fig. 6.2a (2)), relevance feedback of the search results, using overlap between title plus snippet *and* target information, based on LSA, is presented. It is worthwhile to note that semantic relevance feedback is generated automatically by applying online the LSA computation. Having available this information could be helpful in generating a

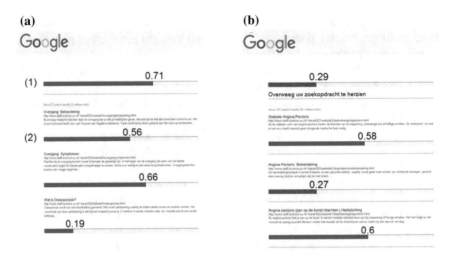

Fig. 6.2 (**a**) Visualizing semantic relevance feedback on the interface (originally in Dutch): (1) the relevance value corresponding to the search query and (2) the relevance values of the search results. In the right image (**b**), the bars become red when they fall below the pre-defined threshold value

new query and evaluating search results. As we saw above older participants have difficulties especially with difficult tasks in generating semantically relevant queries during reformulations. A possible reason could be that they do not have information available to evaluate easily the relevance of a query or search results. The central idea of current studies is to keep users informed about the relevance of their queries and search results, which might help in formulating better new queries. We hypothesize that providing a mechanism to monitor the relevance of search queries and search results and warn when the semantic relevance falls below a pre-defined threshold would help them in information search.

Two LSA thresholds were examined: a *lenient* criterion, i.e. the LSA threshold was set on 0.3 and a *strict* one, i.e. the threshold at 0.5, that is, if the LSA values are below these values, participants were given an indication that their query was not relevant enough (the color changed to red, as shown in Fig. 6.2b). So many more search results will become red when the strict criterion is applied. Participants were free to either ignore the indication and continue using the same query or reformulate and come up with a semantically more relevant query. The idea is that providing the indication pushes the user in the direction of reformulation. Because the LSA threshold values can vary between 0 and 1, they have to be predefined and we will examine the optimal value for two values empirically. Based on previous research (Karanam and van Oostendorp 2016) we took the mean LSA value of SRQ of successful tasks and not-successful tasks resp., and that provided the values of 0.5 and 0.3 used in current studies.

Note that both support aspects (feedback on the semantic relevance of the query and feedback on relevance of search results) are simultaneously examined. In the first study, we tested 48 university students (mean age 23 years) and in the second study, we tested 48 older adults without any cognitive or physical problems (mean age 72). We used 5 mock up websites (ranging 37–194 pages each) with Dutch medical and health information. For details, see Karanam and Van Oostendorp (2017).

We used simulated information search tasks (Borlund and Ingwersen 1997) from the domain of health, divided into low precise (= difficult) tasks and high precise (= easy) tasks. See Appendix 1 for the complete list of tasks. Task preciseness is based on the semantic similarity between the task description and the content of the target page(s) containing the answer to the task. LSA was used to compute task preciseness. Tasks with a high LSA value of task preciseness provide accurate contextual information directly pointing to the target information, while low precise tasks require users to engage in higher-level cognitive activities. As an example of a high precise task (originally presented in Dutch) "*Patient Jansen has probably a cerebral hemorrhage because of bleeding in and around the brain. A CT scan shows a malformed blood vessel. What options for a surgical procedure does a neurosurgeon have?*" The underlined words are present on the target page. This task has high semantic overlap with its target page, LSA = 0.75. The semantic similarity values obtained for low and high precise tasks showed a significant difference. Compared to the previous difficulty index, this measure provides an objective and empirical way of calculating overlap in meaning and to distinguish easy *versus* difficult tasks (Karanam and van Oostendorp 2016, 2017).

We analysed the mean semantic relevance of the queries (SRQ) with the target information at a *granular* level by looking at each reformulation cycle separately, first for younger adults (study 1). The resulting graph is shown in Fig. 6.3. The first cycle corresponds to the first query, the second cycle corresponds to the second query, and the third cycle corresponds to the third query and so on. The mean semantic relevance was computed for all the queries of all the tasks of a particular type (high precise and low precise separately), generated by participants in the three experimental conditions in each reformulation cycle. To achieve higher reliability, only those cycles were considered for which there were at least 4 queries (per reformulation cycle) available (the maximum number of queries per condition and cycle is 16). By doing so, only 5.1% of data was excluded from the analysis. We do this only for low precise tasks as previous research has shown that the age-related differences in information

Fig. 6.3 Mean semantic relevance of queries at each reformulation cycle for low precise tasks for younger adults

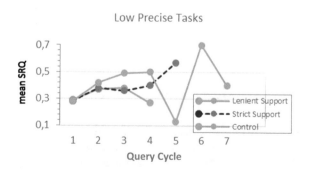

Fig. 6.4 Mean semantic relevance of queries at each reformulation cycle for low precise tasks for older adults

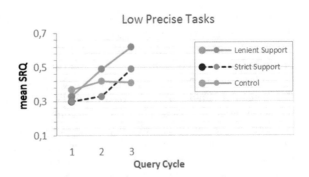

search performance are more prominent only for difficult tasks (Karanam and Van Oostendorp 2016, 2017; Sanchiz et al. 2017).

6.3.1   Study 1: Younger Adults

We can observe from Fig. 6.3 for younger adults and low precise tasks in the strict support condition, the mean SRQ of an ending query was higher than that of the starting query, but not in the lenient support or the control condition. For these low precise tasks, there is a significant increasing linear trend in the strict support condition. Other effects were not significant. See Fig. 6.3.

6.3.2   Study 2: Older Adults

Next, we studied the older adults. Regarding the older adults we found significant effects again only for low precise tasks: for the lenient support condition as well as for the strict support condition, there is a significant increasing linear trend. See Fig. 6.4.

All in all, these patterns of semantic relevance of queries of younger and older adults indicate, thus, that as participants reformulated, they produced queries whose semantic relevance was significantly increasing, at least for difficult tasks when they were supported. For both age groups a strict LSA criterion appeared to be effective.

6.4   Conclusions and Discussion

The most important results of the empirical work discussed here concern the effects on semantic relevance of queries. For both older adults and younger adults an increasing trend was found in semantic relevance of the queries when they received semantic relevance feedback which was the case for difficult tasks. We assume that providing feedback on the semantic relevance of a search query and the search results enables participants to make an informed decision to reformulate or not, as well as on the semantic direction of the reformulation. We analyzed also search performance itself, that is, we looked at the time needed to solve the task and the number of clicks needed (these results were not presented here, see Karanam and van Oostendorp 2017). We found that younger adults who got feedback were significantly faster in their search and clicked significantly less, while for older adults no such difference in search performance was found. Therefore, even though the feedback does indeed help both groups to formulate better queries, we don't see a difference in search performance (in time or clicks) of older adults. One possible explanation could be that older adults need more time and practice to adjust to the new search interface before they could improve their search performance, whereas younger adults easily adapt to the new interface, and thus we do see with younger adults already an improvement also in their search performance.

We also examined the difference in increase of semantic relevance of queries (SRQ) between the two support conditions in order to check what degree of feedback or LSA criterion (lenient or strict) should be employed. For younger adults we found an increase in SRQ only in the strict support condition, for older adults we found no significant difference in increase between both support conditions, though both conditions increased significantly compared to the control condition; so overall it seems best to use the *strict* criterion, that is, providing a high degree of negative feedback because compared to the lenient criterion more results are flagged.

These results are encouraging and present evidence to the influence of providing feedback on the semantic relevance of query reformulations. We think that the feedback influences mainly the following two cognitive processes underlying information search: first, 'comprehension' by fostering understanding of the search results provided by a search engine, and secondly, 'decision making' by facilitating to choose a relevant search result, enabling to reformulate unfruitful queries. By providing feedback on semantic relevance of each search result, the interface enables users to easily select the search result with the highest relevance value. Similarly, by providing feedback on semantic relevance of a search query, the interface enables users to make an informed decision whether to reformulate a query or not. The mental resources that a user invests in performing these two kinds of activities are thus, as we assume, freed up considerably, thereby reducing the cognitive load. This might explain the observed enhancement of search performance, at least for the younger adults. It is interesting to note that with older adults, providing relevance feedback had a positive effect on the semantic relevance of their query reformulations. The reason could be that cognitive load and cognitive flexibility which are well known problems for older adults (Chin et al. 2015; see also Sanchiz et al. 2020) are alleviated.

We also conducted semi-structured post-experiment interviews with randomly chosen participants. Many participants had very positive reviews and comments about the interface such as *"very useful to know that my search query is not relevant"*, *"interesting way of presenting search relevance"* etc. Some participants also had some very interesting suggestions. We did not change the ordering of search results that the search engine generated (in terms of LSA rank order). One of the participants wondered, what would happen if we reorder the search results based on their relevance values. We think that this is an interesting suggestion that needs to be empirically tested in a next study.

We also want to address some limitations of current studies. In both studies the means of support (feedback on the relevance of the query and relevance of search results) were presented simultaneously, so it is impossible based on the current data, to make a difference in effectiveness of the two support means. Furthermore, we fixed the LSA threshold value and the user had no option to modify it. How would the behavior change if the user was given the option to modify the LSA threshold value? Further empirical research is needed to clarify these issues.

One of the main limitations of our work so far is that the semantic relevance of queries measurement can only be used for those types of tasks for which there is a known target answer page(s). It is necessary to know the target page(s) in advance to be able to compute the semantic relevance of the query (or search results) with respect to the target information. Though this limits the applicability of the metric in real environments where neither the user intent nor the target answer are known beforehand, it can be very useful in providing training and support to users with low information search skills such as, for instance, older adults. To avoid this limitation, we suggest to use the task description as an alternative to the target answer, in real environments, at least in those situations where a clear task description is available. Whether the semantic similarity values computed using the task description (instead of the target answer) give the same outcomes as in this study or not, has to be empirically verified. Another reason why we are not really impressed by the indicated limitation—maybe disappointing to some (applied) researchers—is that we are not primarily interested in building the best interface. Our primary aim is more theoretically-oriented: does the principle of semantic relevance judgment and accompanying feedback influence the process of information search and the quality of search results. And this is what we demonstrated.

Next, further studies could explore the comparative effectiveness of different ways of visualizing the feedback or reordering of search results, but even before such work to optimize the interface, the results of this work show that providing feedback on, and making users aware of, semantic relevance fosters formulation of better queries.

Finally, we showed how results from previous modeling work (see e.g. Karanam and van Oostendorp 2020) can be applied to design of interface features that help younger and older adults search for information. In fact, most applications do not take into account how semantic relevance can help to generate reformulations of queries, and the proposed application is one of the first theoretically driven tools that provide the necessary feedback to guide query reformulation. The other interesting implication is how this approach can be potentially more useful for older users, who likely will need more help from intelligent interfaces than their younger counterparts.

Acknowledgements We thank Tijs Ditvoorst and Justin van Doorn for their valuable input to this study. This research was supported by the Netherlands Organization for Scientific Research (NWO) Open Research Area Plus project MISSION (464-13-043).

Appendix 1 List of the (12) Tasks Used (Originally in Dutch)

No	Website	Task	Topic	Level	PRE
1	1	Miss Oostvogels is acquainted with angina pectoris. For this problem she receives next to nitrates also two other types of medicines. Mention these two types	Angina pectoris	1	H
2	1	Boudewijn has now three days troubles with atrial fibrillation. The doctor wants to proceed with the treatment to repair his heart rhythm. Ablation is no option for Boudewijn. The doctor can now make the choice out two treatment options. Mention these two treatment options. Indicate which of the two treatment options the doctor will choose and why	Cardio-version	4	L
3	1	Patient Jansen has probably a cerebral hemorrhage because there seems to have occurred a bleeding in and around the brain. On a CT scan one can see a malformed blood vessel. Which options for treatment does the doctor have?	Cerebral hemorrhage	3	H

(continued)

(continued)

No	Website	Task	Topic	Level	PRE
4	2	Joris (68 years old) did one year ago go to the optician. He wanted to get measured new glasses. With his old glasses he had bad eyesight. Half a year later Joris is again back. The optician measures his eyes again and notices that his eyes had deteriorated considerably. Joris tells that car driving at night is less pleasant, because the head-lights of oncoming cars do shine. What will the optician diagnose based on this story?	Cataract	2	L
5	2	Fieke, 6 years old, was troubled by a dry mouth, and had to urinate very frequently, especially at night. Also she is very tired. The doctor determines that her blood sugar is much too high. What is a plausible diagnosis, be specific. What treatment will the doctor apply?	Diabetes Type 1	3	L
6	2	Maria (65 years) has joint complaints on her knees. They become thick, warm and stiff. And they give a lot of pain. The doctor suspects rheumatism. What type of examination to be sure, should be performed?	Rheumatism	3	H
7	3	Joost (15 years old) often helps his father in the bakery with baking bread. After the summer holidays, during which Joost assisted his father fulltime, he has troubles with stuffiness. Besides that, you hear him squeaking with exhaling. Which disease has Joost probably, and what is probably the provoking factor?	Asthma	3	L

(continued)

(continued)

No	Website	Task	Topic	Level	PRE
8	3	One patient had troubles with thick, red, warm and painful joints. Happily it is now under control, but the patient gets still allopurinol prescribed. For what is allopurinol specifically used?	Gout	2	H
9	4	Marleen has many troubles with itching on her stomach. The doctor also detects vesicles on her skin. He suspects that the disease is shingles. What means he will prescribe?	Shingles	1	L
10	4	A mother visits the doctor with her son of 10 years old. The son has colds with high fever and red eyes. Inside of his cheeks white spots with red dots are visible. This rash seems to spread out over his face and neck. What diagnosis is here very probable	Measles	2	H
11	5	Mary is a women (38 years old) and has complaints to her doctor about menopausal symptoms: hot flashes, violently perspire and fatigue. Her doctor thinks that it is appropriate to do further examination, in spite her young age, especially because Mary's period has already stopped. He decides also to check the bone decalcification. Which hormone plays in this a role?	Period	3	H
12	5	Martijn is a man of 65 years old, and has trouble with his back. He feels pain form his lower back into a leg. This pain becomes worse when he has to cough. Which treatment will his doctor follow in first instance in order to lessen the complaints and the pain?	Back hernia	2	L

References

Borlund P, Ingwersen P (1997) The development of a method for the evaluation of interactive information retrieval systems. J Doc 53(3):225–250

Chevalier A, Dommes A, Marquié JC (2015) Strategy and accuracy during information search on the Web: effects of age and complexity of the search questions. Comput Hum Behav 53:305–315

Chin J, Anderson E, Chin C, Fu W-T (2015) Age differences in information search: an exploration-exploitation tradeoff model. In: Proceedings of the human factors and ergonomic society (HFES 2015), pp 85–89

Dommes A, Chevalier A, Liao S (2011) The role of cognitive flexibility and vocabulary abilities of younger and older users in searching for information on the Web. Appl Cogn Psychol 25(5):717–726

Gomez-Nieto E, San Roman F, Pagliosa P, Casaca W, Helou ES, de Oliveira MCF, Nonato LG (2014) Similarity preserving snippet-based visualization of Web search results. IEEE Trans Visual Comput Graphics 20(3):457–470

Huurdeman HC, Kamps J (2020) Designing multistage search systems to support the information seeking process. In: Fu W-T, van Oostendorp H (eds) Understanding and improving information search: a cognitive approach. Springer, Cham, Switzerland, pp 113–137

Jiang J, He D, Kelly D, Allan J (2017) Understanding ephemeral state of relevance. In: Proceedings CHIIR'17 conference. ACM, Oslo, Norway, pp 137–146, 7–11 March 2017

Jorge-Botana G, Olmos R, Barroso A (2013) Gallito 2.0: a natural language processing tool to support research on discourse. In: Proceedings of the 13th annual meeting of the society for text and discourse. University of Valencia, Spain

Karanam S, van Oostendorp H (2016) Age-related differences in the content of search queries when reformulating. In: Proceedings of the 2016 CHI conference on human factors in computing systems. ACM, pp 5720–5730

Karanam S, van Oostendorp H (2017) Age-related effects of task difficulty on the semantic relevance of query reformulations. In: Proceedings of the 16th IFIP TC 13 international conference on human-computer interaction INTERACT 2017

Karanam S, van Oostendorp H (2020) Cognitive modeling of age and domain knowledge differences in information search. In: Fu W-T, van Oostendorp H (eds) Understanding and improving information search: a cognitive approach. Springer, Cham, Switzerland, pp 47–68

Kuhlthau CC (2004) Seeking meaning: a process approach to library and information services. Libraries Unlimited, Westport, CT

Landauer TK, Dumais ST (1997) A solution to Plato's problem: the latent semantic analysis theory of acquisition, induction, and representation of knowledge. Psychol Rev 104:211–240

Landauer TK, Foltz PW, Laham D (1998) An introduction to latent semantic analysis. Discourse Process 25(2–3):259–284

Mao J, Liu Y, Luan H, Zhang M, Ma S, Luo H, Zhang Y (2017) Understanding and predicting usefulness judgment in Web search. In: Proceedings of SIGIR'17 conference. ACM, Shinjuku, Japan, pp 1169–1172, 7–11 August 2017

Mao J, Liu Y, Zhou K, Nie J-Y, Song J, Zhang M, Ma S, Sun J, Luo H (2016) When does relevance mean usefulness and user satisfaction in Web search. In: Proceedings SIGIR'16 conference. ACM, Pisa, Italy, 10 pp, 17–21 July 2016

McNamara DS, Cai Z, Louwerse MM (2007) Optimizing LSA measures of cohesion. In: Landauer TK, McNamara DS, Dennis S, Kintsch W (eds) Latent semantic analysis. Erlbaum Ass, Mahwah, pp 379–400

Pak R, Price M (2008) Designing an information search interface for younger and older adults. Hum Factors: J Hum Factors Ergon Soc 50(4):614–628

Peltonen J, Belorustceva K, Ruotsalo T (2017) Topic-relevance map: visualization for improving search result comprehension. In: Proceedings of the 22nd international conference on intelligent user interfaces. ACM, New York, pp 611–622

Pirolli P, Card S (1999) Information foraging. Psychol Rev 106(4):643–675

Queen TL, Hess TM, Ennis GE, Dowd K, Gruhn D (2012) Information search and decision making: effects of age and complexity on strategy use. Psychol Aging 27(4):817–824

Sanchiz M, Amadieu F, Chevalier A (2020). An evolving perspective to capture individual differences related to fluid and crystallized abilities in information searching with a search engine. In: Fu W-T, van Oostendorp H (eds) Understanding and improving information search: a cognitive approach. Springer, Cham, Switzerland

Sanchiz M, Chin J, Chevalier A, Fu WT, Amadieu F, He J (2017) Searching for information on the Web: Impact of cognitive aging, prior domain knowledge and complexity of the search problems. Inf Process Manage 53(1):281–294

Umemoto K, Yamamoto T, Tanaka K (2016) Scentbar: a query suggestion interface visualizing the amount of missed relevant information for intrinsically diverse search. In: 39th international ACM SIGIR conference, SIGIR'16. ACM, New York, USA, pp 405–414

Umemoto K, Yamamoto T, Tanaka K (2020) Search support tools. In: Fu W-T, van Oostendorp H (eds) Understanding and improving information search: a cognitive approach. Springer, Cham, Switzerland, pp 139–160

Vakkari P (2001) A theory of the task-based information retrieval process: a summary and generalisation of a longitudinal study. J Doc 57(1):44–60

Wildemuth B, Freund L, Toms EG (2014) Untangling search task complexity and difficulty in the context of interactive information retrieval studies. J Doc 70(6):1118–1140

Wildemuth BM, Kelly D, Boettcher E, Moore E, Dimitrova G (2018) Examining the impact of domain and cognitive complexity on query formulation and reformulation. Inf Process Manage 54:433–450

Chapter 7
Designing Multistage Search Systems to Support the Information Seeking Process

Hugo C. Huurdeman and Jaap Kamps

Abstract Due to the advances in information retrieval in the past decades, search engines have become extremely efficient at acquiring useful sources in response to a user's query. However, for more prolonged and complex information seeking tasks, these search engines are not as well suited. During complex information seeking tasks, various *stages* may occur, which imply varying support needs for users. However, the implications of theoretical information seeking models for concrete search user interfaces (SUI) design are unclear, both at the level of the individual features and of the whole interface. Guidelines and design patterns for concrete SUIs, on the other hand, provide recommendations for feature design, but these are separated from their role in the information seeking process. This chapter addresses the question of how to design SUIs with enhanced support for the macro-level process, first by reviewing previous research. Subsequently, we outline a framework for complex task support, which explicitly connects the temporal development of complex tasks with different levels of support by SUI features. This is followed by a discussion of concrete system examples which include elements of the three dimensions of our framework in an exploratory search and sensemaking context. Moreover, we discuss the connection of navigation with the search-oriented framework. In our final discussion and conclusion, we provide recommendations for designing more holistic SUIs which potentially evolve along with a user's information seeking process.

7.1 Introduction

Revolutionary advances in information retrieval technology have occurred during the past decades. We have arrived at the point where systems may actually *solve* problems for users. For instance, search engines on the Web provide us with "instant

H. C. Huurdeman (✉) · J. Kamps
University of Amsterdam, Amsterdam, The Netherlands
e-mail: h.c.huurdeman@uva.nl

J. Kamps
e-mail: kamps@uva.nl

© Springer Nature Switzerland AG 2020
W. T. Fu and H. van Oostendorp (eds.), *Understanding and Improving Information Search*, Human–Computer Interaction Series,
https://doi.org/10.1007/978-3-030-38825-6_7

answers" for factual questions ranging from the weather in the next weekend to the birthdate of the current prime minister. Information seeking in the context of more complex tasks, however, is still not as straightforward because such tasks cannot be fully articulated with a single query, nor directly answered by a succinct snippet of information. For instance, gaining novel ideas for research or finding the appropriate sources for writing an essay requires intensive interaction with search engines as well as information sources. These types of complex tasks typically involve "sustained interaction and engagement with information" (Kelly et al. 2013), thus involving more lengthy information interactions. Associated search episodes can include multiple subtasks (Wildemuth et al. 2014), and these types of tasks feature learning and construction, understanding and problem formulation (Byström and Järvelin 1995). During the process of information seeking and use, as occurring in complex research-based tasks, the needs and understanding of a user may evolve, moving from broad conceptualizations to a focused perspective (Kuhlthau 2004). Therefore, to create supportive systems for complex tasks featuring sustained information interaction, current ad-hoc approaches to search-based interaction should be rethought. Instead of optimizing the results display of singular queries, there is a need for a fundamentally different approach that would provide dynamic support for a user's information seeking *process*.

The non-trivial question which follows is how to concretely achieve this enhanced process support. This chapter focuses on the presentation of results from search engines via their constituent search user interface (SUI) features, representing the key information interaction components of the system. Creating compositions of interface features with high *usability* is no easy task. Thus, as Oddy already argued in 1977, the "art" of information system design is to "find the form and timing of information presentation which will best aid the system user" in whichever task at hand. In this chapter, we focus on the timing and form of SUI features, assessing how they fit in different stages of the information seeking process, and how they can potentially be recombined in dynamic ways. This book chapter truly stands on the shoulders of giants, incorporating findings from decades of research in library and information science and interactive information retrieval (e.g., Bennett 1972; Bates 1990; Ingwersen 1992; Marchionini 1995; Golovchinsky and Belkin 1999; Ruthven 2008; Hearst 2009; Wilson et al. 2010). It also builds on our own earlier work in recent years (e.g., Kamps 2011; Huurdeman and Kamps 2014; Huurdeman et al. 2016), and extends Huurdeman (2017, 2018). Earlier findings are further integrated into a framework for complex task support in search systems.

To this end, we first present background literature related to process support for complex tasks (Sect. 7.2). Based on previous research, we then outline our framework for complex task support and its relation to SUI features (Sect. 7.3). Then, we introduce examples in relation to the proposed framework (Sect. 7.4). In Sect. 7.5, we discuss the relationship between navigation and search. Finally, we provide a discussion of our findings and our conclusions (Sect. 7.6).

7.2 Background

This section reviews relevant concepts and literature on search and work tasks, information seeking models, and user interface components of information search systems.

7.2.1 Conceptualizations of Tasks

This chapter focuses on information seeking models, search user interfaces and the underlying information retrieval systems. The "*raison-d'être* of information retrieval systems is to deliver task-specific information that leads to problem resolution," as Toms (2011) has suggested. This also points to the importance of the *task* itself, which is pivotal in relation to this chapter. A variety of conceptualizations of task exists, but we take the general view as "an activity to be performed in order to accomplish a goal." (Vakkari 2003). In particular, we focus on cognitively complex tasks. Unlike simple lookup tasks, complex tasks (Wildemuth et al. 2014) may involve learning and construction, understanding and problem formulation (Byström and Järvelin 1995). They might be performed by topic novices but also by more experienced actors. For instance, a student may perform a task involving a topic she knows little about, but this knowledge advances over time, or a researcher may start with a loose research question, which becomes more focused after interaction with a set of information. Besides their obvious occurrence in work and study contexts, complex tasks are also performed in leisure settings, for instance shopping for products which are inherently complex.

In this chapter, we look at *work tasks*, which might consist of various *search tasks*, within a particular *environment* (Toms 2011). Work task has been defined as a "job-related task or non-job associated daily-life task or interest to be fulfilled by cognitive actor(s)." These tasks can be "natural, real-life tasks," assigned requests or assigned simulated work task situations (Ingwersen and Järvelin 2005, p. 20). Work tasks, in their turn, may lead to one or more search tasks, defined as "the task to be carried out by a cognitive seeking actor(s) as a means to obtain information associated with fulfilling a work task" (Ingwersen and Järvelin 2005, p. 20). The complexity of information seeking and searching has been captured in a wide variety of models, discussed in the next section.

7.2.2 Information Behavior, Seeking and Searching

We now describe the concept of information behavior and the macro-level, cognitive models of information seeking and search.

Information behavior has been defined by Wilson (1999) as "the totality of human behavior in relation to sources and channels of information, including both active and passive information seeking, and information use." In Wilson (1999)'s nested model of information seeking and searching, a subset of information behavior is *information seeking*, which is "human information behavior dealing with searching or seeking information by means of information sources and (interactive) information retrieval systems" (Ingwersen and Järvelin 2005, p. 21). Finally, the *information searching* subset in Wilson (1999)'s nested model focuses specifically on the interaction between information user and information system.

7.2.2.1   Information Seeking

We first discuss information *seeking*: In the field of library and information science, a large variety of models has been conceived, describing information seeking from a macroperspective. These include temporally based models, such as the Information Search Process model by Kuhlthau (1991, 2004); non-sequential models, such as Ellis (1989)' behavioral model, and nonlinear models (e.g., Foster 2005). Furthermore, some models focused on problem solving, such as Wilson (1999)'s problem-solving model. In this chapter, our focal point is the temporally based models defined by Kuhlthau (1991, 2004) and Vakkari (2001).[1]

Kuhlthau (1991, 2004)'s *Information Search Process* (ISP) model, which focuses on a temporal progression of stages based on several longitudinal studies, has been influential and is one of the most cited models in the library and information science field (Beheshti et al. 2014). A key aspect of the model is that it looks at information seeking as a process of knowledge construction across six broad stages (summarized in Table 7.1), during which a user's uncertainty fluctuates. These include early stages of *initiation* and *topic selection*, as well as *exploration*. At a certain point, a *focus* is formulated, after which information seeking in itself becomes more focused, and stages of *collection* and *presentation* follow. The ISP model focuses on the evolution of users' thoughts, feelings and actions (see Fig. 7.1).

Based on other longitudinal studies, Vakkari (2001) introduced a theory of the task-based information retrieval process. He refined Kuhlthau's stages into three categories: *pre-focus*, *focus formulation* and *post-focus*. Vakkari focused in particular on the pivotal aspect of finding a focus within the search process. Within the initial pre-focus stage, fragmented, vague and general thoughts occur, and there is a difficulty for a searcher to specify the information needed. When a focus is formulated, more directed searches follow, and the final post-focus stage involves specific searches and potential rechecks for additional information. While Kuhlthau (1991, 2004)'s ISP model does not focus on the effects of the stages on search system use directly, Vakkari (2001)'s theory "is more specific in the domain of information retrieval," and documents the effects of stages in the context of IR system use. He observed

[1] An extensive further overview of information seeking models can for instance be found in Case (2012), Fisher et al. (2005).

Table 7.1   Kuhlthau's search stages, adapted from Kuhlthau (2005)

Stage	Description
1. Initiation	Becoming aware of a lack of knowledge or understanding, often causing uncertainty
2. Selection	Identifying and selecting general area, topic or problem, sense of optimism replaces uncertainty
3. Exploration	Exploring and seeking information on the general topic, inconsistent info can cause uncertainty
4. Formulation	Focused perspective is formed, uncertainty is reducing, while confidence increases
5. Collection	Gathering pertinent information to focused topic, less uncertainty, more interest/involvement
6. Presentation	Completing the search, reporting and using results

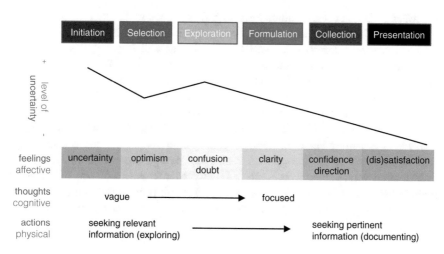

Fig. 7.1   ISP Model documenting stages in tasks involving construction; Figure adapted from Kuhlthau (2004, p. 206)

implications for information sought, assessed relevance and search tactics, terms and operators (see Fig. 7.2). Information sought converges from general background information to specific information, while assessment of relevance becomes easier over time. The number of search terms increases, in particular narrower terms and synonyms, while broader terms gradually decrease over time.

7.2.2.2   Information Searching

As in the case of the information seeking models, a wide range of information *searching* models exists (Wilson 1999), focusing on the direct interaction between user and system. For instance, Spink (1997)'s model of the IR interaction process

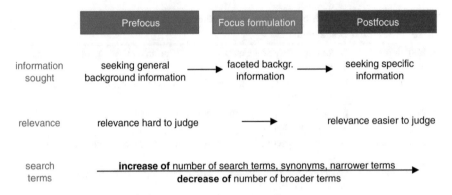

Fig. 7.2 Effects of search stages—diagram summarizes findings (Vakkari 2001)

describes specific cycles of interaction with IR systems, including user judgments, search strategies, tactics and moves. Saracevic (1997)' Stratified model of Information Retrieval Interaction views IR interaction as a dialogue between user and computer and includes different levels (strata) of interactions. Belkin et al. (1995) have modeled the behavior "people engage in while searching for information in some knowledge resource" as information seeking strategies (ISS). These may be seen as interactions between user and IR system components, and an "episode" may consist of a sequence of ISSs. ISSs can be described using four dimensions: *method of interaction* (scanning versus searching), *goal of interaction* (learning versus selecting), *mode of retrieval* (recognizing versus specifying) and *considered resources* (information versus meta-information). Finally, Marchionini's (1995) Information seeking Process Model describes various specific sub-processes and their relationships (including "define problem," "select source," "formulate query," "execute query").

7.2.3   Search User Interfaces

We now describe the micro-level search system features and UI design considerations to actively support user search behavior in the context of complex tasks.

Search user interfaces (SUIs) play the role of intermediary between a user and information available in a system and thus facilitate information searching. Hearst (2009) has characterized their role as aiding "users in the expression of their information needs, in the formulation of their queries, in the understanding of their search results, and in keeping track of the progress of their information seeking efforts." As this multifaceted role implies, designing effective and user-friendly SUIs can be a severe challenge, and "creating an environment in which tasks are carried out almost effortlessly and users are "in the flow" requires a great deal of hard work by the designer" (Shneiderman and Pleasant 2005). SUI design involves a variety of trade-offs, including the tension between simplicity and offered functionality.

The view of SUI design as a challenge is not necessarily new: already in the 1970s, researchers looked at challenges in designing interfaces for (bibliographic) search systems (Bennett 1971, 1972). This includes the characteristics of searchers, the search environment and feedback to searchers. More recent research related to information retrieval and search interfaces has proposed a wide variety of potential features, including facets (Tunkelang 2009), personal result spaces (Donato et al. 2010) and visual keyword suggestions (such as Google's discontinued "Wonder Wheel"[2]). However, the majority of these types of features are not integrated in current general Web search user interfaces.

Current IR systems, such as online search engines, are usually streamlined and focus on query formulation and result inspection. As Hearst (2009) has suggested, reasons underlying the simple appearance of current general-purpose search engines might include that search engines need to be understandable and accessible for audiences with a wide variation of search and system experience. Other motivations behind the simple design are related to different cognitive aspects: search tasks are usually part of larger work tasks, and the interface should distract as little as possible (Hearst 2009). This issue has also been illustrated by Diriye et al. (2010), who found that excessive SUI features with respect to the complexity of the task at hand might actually impede information searching. We can connect these cognitive aspects to *cognitive load theory*, which describes cognitive load as the load on working memory (Sweller et al. 1998). The working memory has a limited capacity for processing information, as opposed to the "effectively unlimited" long-term memory, in which knowledge schemas can be stored. The act of processing and incorporating information in knowledge schemas that may be part of information-intensive work tasks is already demanding, i.e., has a high *intrinsic* cognitive load. Overly complex search interfaces may further increase *extraneous* cognitive load and thus leave less cognitive resources available for the core task.

Notwithstanding the deceivingly simple appearance of current search interfaces, the "art" of designing them is still complex. Over the years, however, a number of frameworks, guidelines and design pattern libraries have been created (Shneiderman and Pleasant 2005). Despite the immediate value of those frameworks for creating appropriate search user interfaces, they mainly focus on designing the functionality of SUI elements in the best way.[3] In that sense, it is unclear at which moments of complex tasks these features are most useful, and how they can be combined to support (and not impede) complex searches—thus, how these features fit in the macro-level information seeking process.

In the context of this chapter, we make use of two specific frameworks. First, with respect to the concrete features of SUIs, Wilson (2011) has proposed a taxonomy for thinking about SUI designs. It divides the features of SUIs into four main groups: *input features* allow searchers to express their input to the search engine, *control*

---

[2]Google's Wonder Wheel provided "an interactive way of exploring related searches" (Wilson 2011).

[3]For instance, how to design a "pagination control" feature for a search engine, http://web.archive.org/web/20150406100824/developer.yahoo.com/ypatterns/navigation/pagination/search.html.

Table 7.2 Wilson (2011) taxonomy of SUI features, with examples (adapted from Huurdeman and Kamps (2014))

Group	Feature example
Input	Search box, categories, clusters, faceted metadata, social metadata
Control	Related searches, corrections, sorting, filters, grouping
Informational	Results display, text snippets, deep links, thumbnails, immediate feedback, visualizations
Personalizable	Recent searches, item tray

features make it possible to modify or restrict input, *informational features* provide results or information about them, and *personalizable features* are tailored to the specific experience of a searcher (see Table 7.2). This framework can aid the creation and analysis of search user interfaces.

Second, a potentially helpful higher-level system perspective has been provided by Bates (1990). The "degree of user vs. system involvement in the search" encompasses a continuum, ranging from fully manual search activities to fully automated searches. Also, she distinguishes various levels of search activities. The lower-level activities are *moves* and *tactics*. Moves are simple actions, for example, entering a search term, and serve as the basic units of search activities. Tactics consist of one or more moves to further a search and have strategic considerations. For instance, reformulating an entered search term to a broader (superordinate) term. Higher-level activities include *stratagems*, and *strategies*. A stratagem is a complex set of tactics and moves and generally includes a specific information domain and a mode of tackling the file organization of that domain—for instance performing author searches in bibliographic databases to find other materials written on the same subject. Finally, a strategy is a plan for the entire information search and may include all previous types of search activity.[4] Bates' search activities may provide inspiration for a better understanding of levels of system support across stages.

7.2.4 Search Interface Features for Different Information Seeking Stages

From the previous sections, we can observe that there are issues in the translation from the rich stages described in information seeking literature to concrete support in terms of search system features and vice versa. Information seeking models such as Kuhlthau (2004) and Vakkari (2001) thoroughly studied the *macro-level* multistage nature of the information seeking process but do not provide immediate handles for

---

[4]Although, as Bates (1990) notes, it is difficult to list a search strategy in advance "in any but the simplest searches, because most real-life searches are influenced by the information gathered along the way in the search.".

implementing search system and user interface features at the specific *micro-level*. Conversely, also the exact role of specific *micro-level* user interface features at different stages of the *macro-level* information seeking process is fuzzy (Huurdeman and Kamps 2014). Only a limited number of studies have combined these perspectives.

Most of these studies have looked at feature use over time, often based on system log data. For instance, White et al. (2005) looked at implicit and explicit relevance feedback functionality and concluded that implicit RF was used more in the beginning of search sessions and explicit RF near the end. Query suggestions, according to Niu and Kelly (2014), were used for more difficult tasks and in later phases of search, suggesting their use as Bates (1979) "idea tactics." Some studies using eye tracking, including Kules et al. (2009), showed that users' main focus moved over time from looking at facets, query and results to looking mainly at results during the search sessions. According to Kules and Capra (2012), feature use varied over time, and they indicated that facets were especially used in cognitively demanding stages. Diriye et al. (2013) distinguish between search stage-specific features (e.g., query box and "starter pages" containing basic information) useful in the beginning of a search, and search stage agnostic features useful across stages (in their case, e.g., facets). Finally, Huurdeman and Kamps (2014) included a small-scale quantitative analysis of data from a user study involving eye tracking with 12 participants and provided further indications that some types of search system features are search stage-sensitive, while other features are useful in all stages.

Many of these studies use a temporal division of search sessions to derive search stages, which could be better characterized as "phases of search" according to Niu and Kelly (2014)—since they might not include the same level of learning and construction as indicated in information seeking models such as Kuhlthau (2004)'s and Vakkari (2001)'s. Therefore, Huurdeman et al. (2016) looked further into exactly how the usefulness of specific types of search functionality evolves, via a user study with 26 participants with a novel multistage simulated task approach.[5] Participants used the experimental search engine *SearchAssist* to perform three distinct tasks, representing Vakkari (2001)'s *pre-focus*, *focus* and *post-focus* stages. Using extensive logging and tracking, insights were gained into the active and passive use of features, grouped via Wilson (2011)'s taxonomy of interface features. Questionnaires and interviews provided indications of how useful the users perceived the features to be over time, allowing for triangulation of findings. The main finding was that within a multistage task involving knowledge construction, the active, passive and perceived usefulness of SUI features differ per information seeking stage. *Informational features* were naturally useful in all information seeking stages. *Input* and *control features*, to express needs and modify input, could be categorized as search stage-sensitive features. The value of these features was highest in the initial pre-focus stage and decreased over time. This reflects a user's increasing understanding of a topic, during which the value of features to help formulating a query and delimiting a resultset may decrease. Contrary to input and control features, *personalizable*

---

[5]The task approach has been further described in Huurdeman et al. (2019).

features became more useful over time, as they may "grow" hand-in-hand with a user's understanding during the information journey.

7.2.5 Summary

In this section, we started with an overview of tasks and information behavior and gradually zoomed in to information seeking, information searching, as well as concrete search user interfaces and concluded that the ways in which they support the inherent cognitive aspects of macro-level information seeking stages is rather opaque. Therefore, in the next section, we introduce a framework which aims to provide more direct connections between macro-level stage and (categories) of micro-level SUI features.

7.3 Toward a Framework for Complex Task Support

This section outlines a framework for complex task support and its relation to user interface features of information search systems.

The information seeking models discussed in the previous section have illustrated that a searcher's conceptual framework about a topic may evolve over time during cognitively complex tasks. For instance, during a novice user's information journey, knowledge structures evolve, just as during a scholars' research process, conceptualizations of a topic may undergo changes.

Keeping this evolution in mind, the system should constitute a "helpful framework within which the user can make problem-solving decisions" (Oddy 1977). However, current search interfaces typically do not evolve with a user's knowledge—to become truly "helpful," a system should ideally support the information seeking *process* of a user, moving from exploratory *pre-focus*, to *focus formulation* and final *post-focus* stages. As indicated in the previous section, existing information seeking models, such as Vakkari (2001), Kuhlthau (2004), do not contain explicit references to actual search system and search user interface design.

Therefore, we introduce our framework for supporting complex tasks involving learning and construction, which explicitly connect the temporal development of complex tasks with different levels of support by SUI features. The framework combines the temporal stages proposed by Vakkari (2001), the findings from Huurdeman and Kamps (2014), Huurdeman et al. (2016), and Bates (1990)' notion of search activities—in particular moves, tactics, strategems and strategies.

Our proposed framework is visualized by Fig. 7.3. The framework consists of three dimensions. As context, we use SUI features listed in Wilson (2011)'s taxonomy of SUI features, augmented with more recently introduced features. The dimensions are distinguished based on associated features' level of support for the process and the relative importance in different stages of a complex task.

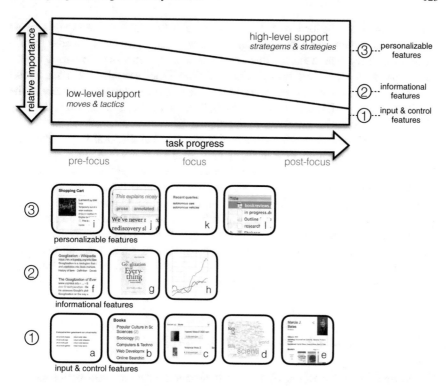

Fig. 7.3 Schematic overview our framework for complex task support: low-level support for moves and tactics gradually gives way to higher-level support for stratagems and strategies

The *first dimension* of the framework focuses on low-level support (Sect. 7.3.1). The *second dimension* consists of the general seeking support offered by informational features, i.e., the actual search results and information about those results (Sect. 7.3.2). These features might provide low- and high-level support. The focal point of the *third dimension* is on specific high-level support (Sect. 7.3.3). During complex information seeking tasks, the relative importance of low-level support gradually decreases, while conversely the relative importance for high-level support is gradually increasing. The mid-point is formed by informational features, which have the same level of relative importance over time. Next, we will discuss each of the three dimensions in more detail.

7.3.1   First Dimension: Input and Control Features

The first dimension of our framework consists of features offering automatically generated suggestions to users. This support typically takes place at Bates (1990)'s search activity level of the "move" (e.g., entering search terms) and "tactic" (e.g., choosing a broader term). For instance, a word cloud feature may suggest keywords for a query, or a query suggestion feature may propose a broader formulation of a query. The need for this *low-level* support, embodied in various *input* and *control* features, generally decreases over time. When a user's conceptualization of a topic grows, she becomes increasingly able to express herself precisely in the context of that topic (Huurdeman et al. 2016; Kuhlthau 2004) and support at the level of moves and tactics becomes more superfluous.

An SUI designer has a wide variety of features at her disposal to provide low-level support for searching. First of all, at the level of the query (see Fig. 7.3, part ①), **Query Corrections**, **Query Autocomplete** and **Query Suggestions (a)** can provide help in formulating the right query and suggesting alternative queries. Especially in initial stages, **Facets and Filters (b)** can be useful to delineate resultsets, and adapting **Results Ordering (c)** may initially help to find the right items. **Word Clouds (d)**, even though their effectiveness in information searching has shown fluctuating results, may also provide inspiration. Finally, current search interfaces often contain **Entity cards (e)**, an information panel with brief information and related entities for an intended query target.

7.3.2 Second Dimension: Informational Features

The second dimension of our framework is formed by general information seeking support. This constitutes *informational* features, which provide the actual results, or information about encountered result items. For instance, a search system may show the title of a document, a short snippet and basic metadata. As evidenced in previous experiments (i.e., Huurdeman et al. 2016), these features may be useful throughout the process. They provide low-level support at the move and tactic level, for instance selecting and opening information sources, but also higher-level support (e.g., offered by visualizations of result sets).

Thus, informational features may provide both low and high-level support (see Fig. 7.3, part ②). These features contain the **Search Results (f)** themselves, commonly shown by their title and a short textual snippet. Especially in e-commerce systems, also **Thumbnails (g)** might visually depict resultset items. **Visualizations (h)** can provide more insights into retrieved resultsets. These may initially be useful for a researcher to explore a set of data but also to visualize a gathered set of focused results for analysis.

7.3.3 Third Dimension: Personalizable Features

The third dimension of a "helpful framework" consists of features which can support seeking at a higher level. While these types of features may include automated functionality, the main aim is to provide insights into a user's process *through her*

actions. As Kuhlthau's model has indicated, activities including hypothesis generation, data collection, information organization and the preparation of a personalized
synthesis of a topic take place during processes of knowledge construction (Kuhlthau
2004, p. 194). This reflects the highly personalized nature of such complex activities,
meaning that automated support may not suffice. Instead, the aim of *personalizable*
features should be to aid users in performing their task. In different experiments, the
usefulness of annotation, saving and organization features by both students and grad-
uate researchers has been evidenced (e.g., Morris et al. 2008; Huurdeman et al. 2016;
Hearst and Degler 2013). As opposed to low-level features, these higher-level features may support Bates' "stratagems" and "strategies" (i.e., planning in the context
of an entire search). On the one hand, through logging user's actions and potentially
gathering data about the actors' domain knowledge or task at hand, they provide
a trail of activities, which may (passively) aid users in locating where they are in
the process. On the other hand, they also allow a user to "work with results" and
thus encourage reflection on encountered results. As such, they become increasingly
useful throughout a task.

More high-level support throughout the process (see Fig. 7.3, part ③) may be
offered by **Results Saving (i)** features, alternatively embodied in, e.g., shopping
carts and wishlists. Interfaces may also offer **Personal Results Organization** opportunities. Furthermore, especially in a research context, **Annotations (j)** are used at
different points in the process (Melgar et al. 2017). Other tools which may be useful,
sometimes only in passive ways (Huurdeman et al. 2016), are **Query History (k)**
features. Finally, **External tools (l)** may provide high-level support, such as word
and data processing, as well as reference management.

7.3.4 Concrete Example: SearchAssist

In the previously described study by Huurdeman et al. (2016), the three dimensions of
our framework for complex task support were included in an adaptable open-source
search user system, using generally available search APIs and Web frameworks. This
interface shown in Fig. 7.4 serves to illustrate the three dimensions of our framework.
Its first dimension is reflected by the input and control features in the left-hand side
panel, which make it possible to use low-level support in user's searches, with ①
category filters, ② word clouds, ③ query suggestions and ④ a query box, including query corrections. The framework's second dimension is reflected by ⑤, and
the search results feature displayed in the middle. Finally, the right-hand side panel
originates from the third dimension of our framework: ⑥ recent queries, ⑦ catego-
rizable saved results and ⑧ a task bar. Besides its use in an experimental context, this
interface was meant as a reusable component for information seeking studies, also
reflected in the rich logging possibilities. Adaptive support for users can be catered
for by gradually turning on and off features in this interface depending on the user's
search stage. Further information on this search system and interface can be found
in Huurdeman et al. (2019).

Fig. 7.4 Screenshot SearchAssist: *input and control features* (first dimension) in ①–④; *informational features* (second dimension) in ⑤ and *personalizable features* (third dimension) in ⑥–⑧

7.3.5 Summary

More dynamic support for complex research-based tasks may be achieved by differentiating SUI feature categories and their levels of support. In particular, functionality providing low-level support (i.e., *input* and *control features*), is useful in the initial stages of a complex research-based task. Searchers with low domain knowledge but also researchers exploring a new topic and collection may utilize this functionality to bootstrap their searches. Features providing high-level support (in particular *personalizable* features) may invite searchers to explicitly reflect and interact with results, as well as seeing how these results fit in their process and strategy.

Our supportive framework for complex task support provides practical pointers to the use of features over time and thus makes it possible to design SUIs pinpointed to the task at hand. On the one hand, this can be by customizing the interface on the basis of expected user activities, for instance, low-level activities or more high-level activities. On the other hand, our framework might be useful for creating more adaptive, stage-aware interfaces. This adaptation can be done by the system by automatically adapting features but could also be done by the user herself. A concrete example is the user-selectable interface panels as evaluated in Gäde et al. (2016), which include a *Browse view*, a *Search view* and a *Book-bag* view, aiming to support pre-focus, focus formulation and post-focus stages.

These types of interfaces might contribute to creating more holistic systems for complex tasks where tasks can be carried out "in the flow." Our framework can also help understand and explain the design considerations of existing systems used in the context of complex tasks, which we discuss in the following section.

7.4   Systems Integrating Complex Task Support

This section connects the complex task support framework to examples of concrete systems within a research context, in particular the emphasis is on exploratory search and sensemaking systems.

7.4.1   Exploratory Search Systems and Features

As indicated by Marchionini (2006), traditional search is often focused on lookup searches, while *exploratory search* also includes learning and investigation. White and Roth (2009b) characterize it as a complex form of information seeking, which is multifaceted and open-ended—complex information problems are involved, as well as a poor understanding of terminology and information space structure. Also, exploratory searchers often exhibit a desire to learn.

As argued by Huurdeman and Kamps (2014), there are similarities between exploratory search and the initial parts of Kuhlthau's multistage model. White and Roth (2009a) indicate that searchers might initially experience uncertainty, and this uncertainty might decrease when exploratory searching transitions to focused searching—this has similarities with Kuhlthau's model as depicted in Fig. 7.1. As such, the concept of exploratory search fits well in the first dimension of our framework since these SUI features are especially useful in the initial stages of a search.

A variety of exploratory search features has been presented in White and Roth (2009a) and summarized in Huurdeman and Kamps (2014). Many of the discussed features fit in the first dimension of our framework (Fig. 7.3, part ①). FilmFinder (Ahlberg and Shneiderman 1994) facilitated rapid query refinement in visual ways (thus representing an input and control feature). Flamenco (Yee et al. 2003) allowed for rich metadata-based filtering and facets and thus also allows users for input and control. Other features are characterized as supporting exploratory search but more specifically can be classified as personalizable features which fit in the high-level support outlined by the framework (Fig. 7.3, part ③). For instance, SearchBar allows for "search task management, a system for proactively and persistently storing query histories, browsing histories and users' notes and ratings in an interrelated fashion" (Morris et al. 2008).

7.4.2   Sensemaking Systems and Features

In the context of human–computer interaction, the combined process of information seeking, analysis and synthesis, has been described as *sensemaking*, which relates to the framework discussed in the previous section. Hearst (2009) has described sensemaking as "the iterative process of formulating a conceptual representation from a large volume of information."

The concept of sensemaking is commonly used in the context of complex and information-intensive tasks, and comparable to Kuhlthau's and Vakkari's models, albeit sensemaking is more often described in a professional, as opposed to the more educational context of Kuhlthau (2004) and Vakkari (2001). For information analysts, Pirolli and Card (2005) describe two main loops in sensemaking: the information foraging loop ("processes aimed at seeking information, searching and filtering it"), and the sensemaking loop ("iterative development of a mental model that best fits the evidence"). There are explicit relations with Kuhlthau's model as she indicates that the latter stages in her model (i.e., formulation, collection, presentation) include processes related to hypothesis generation, data collection, information organization and personalized syntheses of topics (Kuhlthau 2004).

As such, sensemaking has a relation with the third dimension of our framework (Fig. 7.3, part ③), i.e., support at a higher-level, and features supporting sensemaking become increasingly important over the course of an information seeking process. Ample practical examples of sensemaking in previous literature exist. Hearst (2009) discusses the main elements which constitute sensemaking interfaces, including flexible grouping of information, notetaking and sketching, hypothesis formulation, as well as collaborative search. Some of these, mostly personalizable, features are included in CoSen, which organizes retrieved information in a tree structure (Qu and Furnas 2008). Sandbox has been described as a "thinking environment." It allowed for visual organization of results and makes hypothesis generation possible (Wright et al. 2006). Hearst and Degler (2013) describes the process of designing and evaluating "a user interface at the seam between searching and saving and organizing search results." CoSense (Paul and Morris 2009), on the other hand, focuses on sensemaking in the context of collaborative tasks.

7.4.3   Summary

The search systems and interfaces discussed in this section have outlined the relationship between on the one hand exploratory search and sensemaking features and on the other hand our framework for complex task support. In particular, many features allow for organization of retrieved results and task management. However, most of these features do not take into account the support for navigating found Web sites and their structures, which we discuss in the following section.

7.5   Connecting Search and Navigation

This section discusses how the complex task support framework naturally integrates search and navigation features across search stages, and to what extent this both supports "search by navigation" and "search by query."

7.5.1   Navigation Support and Informational Features

Thus far, this chapter has mainly focused on *information seeking*, concerning inter-action with information sources, and *information searching*, specifically focusing on the interaction between information user and information system. In a search context, Jul and Furnas (1997) also have distinguished between "search by query" tasks, i.e., those tasks conducted within a search system and "search by navigation" tasks. While we have covered the former type of task in detail, we have focused less on search by navigation: users might navigate beyond the actual search interface by clicking on resultset items, examine resources linked from the result list (e.g., web-pages) and navigate further from the encountered resource (e.g., to other Webpages in the found Web site). While visiting various pages, users might learn about their topic from contextual information encountered along the way (Karanam et al. 2016; Karanam and van Oostendorp 2020; van Oostendorp and Karanam 2020).

Our framework suggests a holistic approach, where further interaction with the search results (the second dimension with informational features, Fig. 7.3, part ②) is conceptually regarded as part of the system. It is an open question how visible the system should be when interacting with results outside the system itself: it could be always present as a task bar, or minimized and available upon request, or remain hidden until the user navigates back to the search support system. Other than the search results themselves, including ways of deep linking, and aggregated results already mentioned in Sect. 7.3, there seem no additional informational features to support navigation. But there are further connections between navigation support and the search-based aspects of the first and third dimension of our framework.

7.5.2   Navigation and Input and Control Features

In the first dimension of our framework (Fig. 7.3, part ①), we listed various input and control features which offer automatically generated suggestions to users at Bates (1990)' move and tactic level. In terms of navigation support, these types of features offer a continuum, ranging from a focus on navigating the search result space, to pure navigational support for found resources.

First, the discussed facets and filters make it possible to better judge the types of information retrieved so far, both by their grouping and by their labeling. These labels may provide a more analytical view on content and can be considered as *suggestions* for navigation. Using facets and filters, it is possible to navigate the result space without reformulating a query, and get a basic idea of what is being found—even before visiting the actual pages. Other initial topical information and ideas for basic navigation might be given by the query suggestions, entity cards, as well as result space visualizations (e.g., Ruotsalo et al. 2014).

Second, we might combine search and navigation, inspired by additional features discussed in previous literature. Capra et al. (2015) describe search assistance in the form of a 'Search Guide,' which allowed users to view previous search trails from three other users. Search trails "provide an interactive display with information about how another person searched and may include the queries issued, results clicked, pages viewed, pages bookmarked and annotations made by the original searcher." This way, a searcher might get more information on likely successful browsing paths, aiding in navigation, and these types of features might provide "information scents" to users (Pirolli and Card 1999).

Third, an approach more specifically focused on navigation has been described by Dehghani et al. (2017), involving browsing path recommendation. Their approach includes a path recommendation engine, which based on a text query, "ranks different browsing paths in the hierarchy based on their likelihood of covering relevant documents." An SUI feature which offers this approach might help users to more quickly understand the structure of important retrieved Web sites, especially in the context of complex information structures.

Thus, we may extend the feature set specified in the first dimension of our framework (Sect. 7.3) with additional features tailored to assisting navigation, for instance by showing search trails by other users and by means of a browsing path recommendation feature.

7.5.3 Navigation and Personalizable Features

The third dimension of our framework (Fig. 7.3, part ③) contains features which can support seeking at a higher level—the discussed personalizable features provide insights into a user's process through her actions. Examples of these kind of personalizable features included lists of recent queries and previously visited pages.

As indicated by users utilizing the SearchAssist system depicted in Fig. 7.4, its previous searches feature became increasingly useful over the search episode because it indicated what searchers did before, thus providing handles to monitor their process (Huurdeman et al. 2016). This notion of task management can be extended further. For instance, Jia and Niu (2014) present a "history preview" feature, meant to "assist searchers to review what they have done within a search session in order to help them define the next steps during the search process." The visualized "search trajectory" includes previous queries, and per query, list actions such as clicked results, saved results and pagination use—thus showing the trail of activities and previous navigation done by a user. This provides similar functionality as the search trail feature by

Capra et al. (2015) but focused on a user's own process and by nature personalized. An extensive search trajectory SUI feature could support Bates (1990)' notion of a search strategy, i.e., documenting a plan for the entire search, potentially consisting of moves, tactics and stratagems. These types of features could also show conducted navigation steps beyond Webpages directly found in the search system. Insights into the structure of found information could be for instance visualized using tree structures (e.g., Qu and Furnas 2008).

Thus, in the light of supporting navigation, the feature set mentioned in the third dimension of our framework (Sect. 7.3) can be extended with history features showing a user's own search trail, including previous queries and actions.

7.5.4 Summary

Our inquiry into supporting both "search by query" and "search by navigation" resulted in two new insights: the potential for integrating navigation-related features in our framework, as well as the potential for supporting users in their navigation steps outside of the search system within longer sessions.

First, our framework naturally supports the integration of novel navigation-oriented features within the discussed first and third dimension and within the associated early and late stages of search. More specifically, the idea of search trails might aid users in both early (pre-focus) stages and late (post-focus) stages of the information seeking process. First, in early stages by recommending potentially viable search and navigation trails using input and control features. For these kinds of recommendations for instance previous user data but also computational cognitive models of Web navigation might be of value (Karanam et al. 2016), as well as further path recommendation techniques (Dehghani et al. 2017). Second, in late stages, users might be able to view their *own* search trails using personalizable features. The concepts of search trails can be connected to both Bates (1989)' Berrypicking model and Pirolli and Card (1999)'s information foraging theory. By providing search as well as navigation support, these types of features might potentially further aid users in complex task performance.

Second, we touched upon the support for showing search and navigation trajectories including navigation steps beyond Webpages directly found in the search system. Such a feature could register navigation behavior outside of the search system and show this in the SUI interface. For instance, this could be implemented by showing a "minimized" version of the SUI in further navigation ventures (for instance in a frame) or by including a browser extension capturing navigation steps across the overall search episode.

7.6 Discussion and Conclusions

This chapter was inspired by a paradox: On the one hand, search engines on the Web provide a world of information at our fingertips, and the answers to many of our common questions are just a simple click away. On the other hand, many of our tasks are complex and multifaceted and involve a process of knowledge construction: various information seeking models describe a complex set of cognitive stages, influencing the interplay of users' feelings, thoughts and actions (Kuhlthau 2004; Vakkari 2001). Despite the evidence of the models, the functionality of search engines, nowadays the prime intermediaries between information and user, has converged to a streamlined set. Even though the past years have embodied rapid advances in contextualization and personalization, our complex information environment is still reduced to a set of ten 'relevant' blue links. This may not be beneficial for supporting complex tasks involving ill-formulated or exploratory needs (White and Roth 2009a), for tasks requiring sustained interaction with information and for ventures involving the formulation of a deep understanding on a topic (Kelly et al. 2013; Smith and Rieh 2019). This suggests that the currently dominating lookup search approach falls short of the rich interaction needed for task-sharing between user and system (Beaulieu 2000).

The main reason for the current lack of complex task support is that designing optimal search user interfaces is highly non-trivial. Real-world applications vary dramatically over use-cases, work tasks, available information and encoding, available systems and searcher competencies—making every application highly unique. Properly supporting them requires significant advances in our general understanding of how generic search components support information interaction at a higher level of abstraction. Indeed, the design of SUIs can be seen as an "art" (Oddy 1977; Smith and Mosier 1986), involving numerous thorny issues and trade-offs in usability. For instance, combining excessive sets of features may overload the user, while a streamlined approach can be too limiting for supporting user needs in different stages of complex tasks. At each stage of a task, an optimal combination of features may exist. This paper provides handles to determine the **relative importance** of features when designing SUIs, thus connecting theoretical information seeking models and more concrete search user interface design.

At the level of the whole SUI, various approaches for the provision of dynamic support for information seeking stages can be suggested. First of all, a totally open approach is possible: Searchers are free to choose a custom set of SUI features at any point of the process ("build your own SUI"). Second, predefined interface panels combining features can be offered to a user (e.g., for exploration and focused search). This way, a user can choose a panel she needs at any stage or indicate their current information seeking stage (for instance, via a selector or slider). Third, a totally adaptive approach may be followed: Using evidence from usage data, interface features are automatically offered or disabled. Hence, the potential adaptation of interfaces for complex tasks spans a continuum, ranging from fully manual to entirely automatic approaches. Albeit we focus on the SUI level, this is reminiscent of Bates (1990)' degree of user and system involvement in the search process.

In the CLEF Interactive Book Search Track, users were able to select interface panels for pre-focus, focus and post-focus search stages, and positive effects on user engagement were found (Gäde et al. 2015). It would be valuable to gain further insights into the influence of dynamic presentation of search stage-sensitive SUI features on user satisfaction, i.e., the features within the first and third dimension of the framework discussed in Sect. 7.3. Future studies should further look at the impact of dynamic and adaptive presentation of SUI elements, especially since this influences the consistency of an interface. This may be tested by adaptively enabling and disabling SUI features in experimental systems with rich functionality in a (simulated) complex work task setting. Multistage systems may provide new ways to reduce unnecessary *extraneous* cognitive load (as defined by Sweller et al. (1998)) by hiding superfluous interface elements and increase *germane* cognitive load, focused on the stage of the learning task at hand. Furthermore, providing further navigation support for resources linked from search engines might provide value.

At the level of atomic SUI features, this paper briefly outlined feature utility during the information seeking process, based on Bates (1990) levels of search activities discussed in Sect. 7.2.3 (i.e., *moves, tactics, strategies* and *strategems*). Further research is needed to allow for making more conscious choices of which features to include in an interface, based on the purpose they serve in the process. For instance, we may use Bates' levels of search activities as a "lens" for analyzing existing SUI features. Furthermore, as suggested in Huurdeman et al. (2016), individual features could be improved by taking previous user interactions as a basis and thus becoming more *personalizable*. For instance, query suggestions can lose their value over time due to a user's increased domain knowledge but may provide more "intelligent" suggestions by taking into account previous user interactions.

Previous literature in the area of cognitive modeling and devised computational cognitive models such as SNIF-ACT (Fu and Pirolli 2007), CoLiDeS (Kitajima et al. 2005) and CoLiDeS+ (Karanam et al. 2016) can inspire further improvements of SUIs supporting a user's process, especially in early search stages. First of all, by utilizing the models, we might derive the optimal formulation of category and link labels, for instance within the category filters feature of the Search Assist interface described in Sect. 7.3.4, thus providing optimal information scents (Pirolli 2009). Second, cognitive models might provide further browsing path recommendations in the context of search systems, as shown in, e.g., Dehghani et al. (2017) and provide ongoing assistance in selecting useful links and paths. Third, we might use cognitive models and associated cognitive architectures as an inspiration to improve design. Further work is necessary, however, to utilize predictive models at broader, macro-level scales—potentially needing "layers of models at different bands" (Pirolli 2009; see also Pirolli 2019). Challenges might occur: Such models should be able to capture the dynamics of the information seeking process documented by Kuhlthau (2004) and ought to be able to "handle the complexities in realistic environments," such as real websites (Karanam et al. 2016).

The other way around, our research can inspire future development of cognitive models in an SUI context. Multifaceted data were collected in the context of Huurdeman et al. (2016), including eye tracking, detailed usage logs, questionnaires and interviews, and these rich kinds of data might be used to build up computational cognitive models.

The presented framework is a first step toward a more holistic approach for SUI design. Further research on the utility of SUI features, as well as more high-level SUI functionality in search systems, is needed (see also Umemoto et al. 2020). For instance, explicit support for Bates' strategems and strategies is still rare, almost 30 years after her seminal paper. However, the ubiquitous presence of search engines in diverse manifestations may allow for more inclusive views on user activities in consecutive stages of complex search processes. By adapting low- and high-level support, thus creating dynamic SUI compositions, we may be able to arrive at a more "intellectual symbiosis" between user and system as envisioned by Bates (1990).

Our main general conclusion is that there are many relatively unexplored ways to better support the search process, in ways that empower users to control complex information search tasks. This holds the promise to lead to better and more transparent search results and work task outcomes. And all this with the system adapting to the user's needs, rather than have the user adapt their entire search process to the system's functionality and (in)abilities.

Acknowledgements The authors wish to thank Max Wilson for collaboration and discussion leading to the work reported in this chapter. Earlier research was funded by the Netherlands Organization for Scientific Research (NWO CATCH program, # 640.005.001). Subsequent work on this chapter was made possible by NWO project # 314.99.302.

References

Ahlberg C, Shneiderman, B (1994) Visual information seeking: tight coupling of dynamic query filters with starfield displays. In: Proceedings of the CHI. ACM, pp 313–317

Bates MJ (1979) Idea tactics. J Am Soc Inform Sci 30(5):280–289

Bates MJ (1989) The design of browsing and berrypicking techniques for the online search interface. Online Rev 13(5):407–424

Bates MJ (1990) Where should the person stop and the information search interface start? Inf Proc Man 26(5):575–591 Jan

Beaulieu M (2000) Interaction in information searching and retrieval. J Doc 56(4):431–439 Aug

Beheshti J, Cole C, Abuhimed D, Lamoureux I (2014) Tracking middle school students' information behavior via Kuhlthau's ISP Model: temporality. J Am Soc Inform Sci Technol

Belkin NJ, Cool C, Stein A, Thiel U (1995) Cases, scripts, and information-seeking strategies: on the design of interactive information retrieval systems. Expert Syst Appl 9(3):379–395 Jan

Bennett JL (1972) The user interface in interactive systems. Annu Rev Inf Sci Technol 7:159–196

Bennett JL (1971) Interactive bibliographic search as a challenge to interface design. In: Interactive bibliographic search: the user/computer interface. AFIPS Press, pp 1–16

Byström K, Järvelin K (1995) Task complexity affects information seeking and use. Inf Proc Man 31(2):191–213

Capra R, Arguello J, Crescenzi A, Vardell E (2015) Differences in the use of search assistance for tasks of varying complexity. In: Proceeding of the SIGIR, SIGIR 2015. ACM, pp 23–32

Case DO (2012) Looking for information: a survey of research on information seeking, needs, and behavior. Emerald

Dehghani M, Jagfeld G, Azarbonyad H, Olieman A, Kamps J, Marx M (2017) Telling How to narrow it down: browsing path recommendation for exploratory search. In: Proceedings of the CHIIR 2017. ACM Press, pp 369–372

Diriye A, Blandford A, Tombros A (2010) When is system support effective? In: Proceedings of the IIiX. ACM, pp 55–64

Diriye A, Blandford A, Tombros A, Vakkari P (2013) The role of search interface features during information seeking. In Proceedings of the TPDL 2013. LNCS, vol 8092. Springer, pp 235–240

Donato D, Bonchi F, Chi T, Y. Maarek (2010) Do you want to take notes?: identifying research missions in yahoo! search pad. In: Proceedings of the WWW 2010. ACM, pp 321–330

Ellis D (1989) A behavioural approach to information retrieval system design. J Doc 45:171–212

Fisher KE, Erdelez S, McKechnie L (eds) (2005) Theories of information behavior. Information Today

Foster A (2005) Nonlinear information seeking. In Fisher et al. (2005)

Fu W-T, Pirolli P (2007) SNIF-ACT: a cognitive model of user navigation on the World Wide Web. Hum-Comput Interact 22(4):355–412 Nov

Gäde M, Hall M, Huurdeman H, Kamps J, Koolen M, Skov M, Toms E, Walsh D (2015) Overview of the interactive social book search track. In: Working notes of CLEF 2015-conference and labs of the evaluation forum, vol 1391. CEUR-WS

Gäde M, Hall M, Huurdeman H, Kamps J, Koolen M, Skov M, Toms E, Walsh D (2016) Overview of the INEX 2016 interactive social book search track. In: Working notes of CLEF 2016-conference and labs of the evaluation forum. CEUR-WS

Golovchinsky G, Belkin NJ (1999) Innovation and evaluation of information: a CHI98 workshop. SIGCHI Bull 31(1):22–25

Hearst M (2009) Search user interfaces. Cambridge University Press

Hearst MA, Degler D (2013) Sewing the seams of sensemaking: a practical interface for tagging and organizing saved search results. In: Proceedings of the HCIR 2013. ACM

Huurdeman HC (2018) Supporting the complex dynamics of the information seeking process. PhD thesis, University of Amsterdam

Huurdeman HC (2017) Dynamic compositions: recombining search user interface features for supporting complex work tasks. In: Proceedings of the second workshop on supporting complex search tasks co-located with the acm sigir conference on human information interaction & retrieval (CHIIR 2017), vol 1798. CEUR-WS, pp 21–24

Huurdeman HC, Kamps J (2014) From multistage information-seeking models to multistage search systems. In: Proceedings of the IIiX 2014. ACM, pp 145–154

Huurdeman HC, Wilson ML, Kamps J (2016) Active and passive utility of search interface features in different information seeking task stages. In: Proceedings of the CHIIR, CHIIR 2016. ACM, pp 3–12

Huurdeman HC, Kamps J, Wilson ML (2019) The multi-stage experience: the simulated work task approach to studying information seeking task stages. In: Proceedings of the BIIRRR workshop at CHIIR 2019, vol 2337. CEUR-WS

Ingwersen P (1992) Information retrieval interaction. Taylor Graham

Ingwersen P, Järvelin K (2005) The turn-integration of information seeking and retrieval in context. Springer, Dordrecht

Jia Y, Niu X (2014) Should i stay or should i go: two features to help people stop an exploratory search wisely. In: Proceedings of the CHI EA 2014. ACM Press, pp 1357–1362

Jul S, Furnas GW (1997) Navigation in electronic worlds: a CHI 97 workshop. ACM SIGCHI Bull 29(4):44–49

Kamps J (2011) Toward a model of interaction for complex search tasks. In: ESAIR. ACM, pp 7–8

Karanam S, van Oostendorp H (2020) Cognitive modeling of age & domain knowledge differences in information search. In: Fu W-T, van Oostendorp H (Eds) Understanding and improving information search: a cognitive approach. Springer, Cham, Switzerland, pp 47–68

Karanam S, van Oostendorp H, Tat Fu W (2016) Performance of computational cognitive models of web-navigation on real websites. J Inf Sci 42(1):94–113

Kelly D, Arguello J, Capra R (2013) NSF workshop on task-based information search systems. SIGIR Forum 47(2):116–127

Kitajima M, Blackmon MH, Polson PG (2005) Cognitive architecture for website design and usability evaluation: comprehension and information scent in performing by exploration. In: Proceedings of the HCI international 2005, vol 4. L. Erlbaum Associates

Kuhlthau CC (1991) Inside the search process: information seeking from the user's perspective. J Am Soc Inform Sci 42:361–371

Kuhlthau CC (2004) Seeking meaning: a process approach to library and information services. Libraries Unlimited, Westport, CT

Kuhlthau CC (2005) Kuhlthau's information search process. In: Fisher et al. (2005)

Kules B, Capra R (2012) Influence of training and stage of search on gaze behavior in a library catalog faceted search interface. J Am Soc Inform Sci Technol 63:114–138

Kules B, Capra R, Banta M, Sierra T (2009) What do exploratory searchers look at in a faceted search interface? In: Proceedings of the JCDL. ACM, pp 313–322

Marchionini G (1995) Information seeking in electronic environments. Cambridge University Press, Cambridge

Marchionini G (2006) Exploratory search: from finding to understanding. Commun ACM 49(4):41–46

Melgar LM, Koolen M, Huurdeman HC, Blom J (2017) A process model of scholarly media annotation. In: Proceedings of the CHIIR, CHIIR 2017. ACM

Morris D, Ringel Morris M, Venolia G (2008) Searchbar: a search-centric web history for task resumption and information re-finding. In: Proceedings of the CHI 2008. ACM, pp 1207–1216

Niu X, Kelly D (2014) The use of query suggestions during information search. Inf Process Manage 50:218–234

Oddy RN (1977) Information retrieval through man-machine dialogue. J Doc 33(1):1–14

Paul SA, Morris MR (2009) Cosense: enhancing sensemaking for collaborative web search. In: Proceedings of the CHI 2009. ACM, pp 1771–1780

Pirolli P (2009) Powers of 10: modeling complex information-seeking systems at multiple scales. IEEE Comput 42:33–40

Pirolli P (2019) Challenges for a computational cognitive psychology for the new digital ecosystem. In: Understanding and improving information search: a cognitive approach, chapter 2, This volume. Springer

Pirolli P, Card S (1999) Information foraging. Psychol Rev 106(4):643

Pirolli P, Card S (2005) The sensemaking process and leverage points for analyst technology as identified through cognitive task analysis. In: Intelligence analysis, pp 2–4

Qu Y, Furnas GW (2008) Model-driven formative evaluation of exploratory search: a study under a sensemaking framework. Inf Process Manage 44:534–555

Ruotsalo T, Jacucci G, Myllymäki P, Kaski S (2014) Interactive intent modeling: information discovery beyond search. Commun ACM 58(1):86–92

Ruthven I (2008) Interactive information retrieval. Annu Rev Inf Sci Technol 42:43–91

Saracevic T (1997) The stratified model of information retrieval interaction: extension and applications. In: Proceedings of the ASIS annual meeting, vol 34. Learned Information (Europe) Ltd., pp 313–327

Shneiderman B, Pleasant C (2005) Designing the user interface: strategies for effective human-computer interaction. Pearson Education

Smith CL, Rieh SY (2019) Knowledge-context in search systems: toward information-literate actions. In: Proceedings of the CHIIR 2019, CHIIR 2019. ACM, pp 55–62

Smith SL, Mosier JN (1986) Guidelines for designing user interface software. Technical report, MITRE

Spink A (1997) Study of interactive feedback during mediated information retrieval. J Am Soc Inform Sci 48(5):382–394

Sweller J, Merrienboer JJGV, Paas FGWC (1998) Cognitive architecture and instructional design. Educ Psychol Rev 10(3):251–296

Toms EG (2011) Task-based information searching and retrieval. In: Interactive information seeking, behaviour and retrieval. Facet

Tunkelang D (2009) Faceted search. Synth Lect Inf Concepts Retr Serv 1(1):1–80

Umemoto K, Yamamoto T, Tanaka K (2020) Search support tools. In: Fu W-T, van Oostendorp H (Eds) Understanding and improving information search: a cognitive approach. Springer, Cham, Switzerland, pp 139–160

Vakkari P (2003) Task-based information searching. ARIST 37:413–464

Vakkari P (2001) A theory of the task-based information retrieval process: a summary and generalisation of a longitudinal study. J Doc 57(1):44–60

van Oostendorp H and Karanam S (2020) Semantic relevance feedback on queries and search results for younger and older adults. In: Fu W-T, van Oostendorp H (Eds) Understanding and improving information search: a cognitive approach. Springer, Cham, Switzerland, pp 97–111

White RW, Roth RA (2009a) Exploratory search: beyond the query-response paradigm. Synth Lect Inf Concepts Retr Serv 1:1–98

White RW, Roth RA (2009b) Exploratory search: beyond the query-response paradigm. Synthesis lectures on information concepts, retrieval, and services. Morgan & Claypool Publishers

White RW, Ruthven I, Jose JM (2005) A study of factors affecting the utility of implicit relevance feedback. In: Proceedings of the SIGIR. ACM, pp 35–42

Wildemuth B, Freund L, Toms EG (2014) Untangling search task complexity and difficulty in the context of interactive information retrieval studies. J Doc 70(6):1118–1140

Wilson ML (2011) Search user interface design. Synth Lect Inf Concepts Retr Serv 3(3):1–143

Wilson ML, Kules B, Schraefel MC, Shneiderman B (2010) From keyword search to exploration: designing future search interfaces for the web. Found Trends Web Sci 2(1):1–97

Wilson TD (1999) Models in information behaviour research. J Doc 55:249–270

Wright W, Schroh D, Proulx P, Skaburskis A, Cort B (2006) The sandbox for analysis: concepts and methods. In: Proceedings of the CHI, CHI 2006. ACM, pp 801–810

Yee K-P, Swearingen K, Li K, Hearst MA (2003) Faceted metadata for image search and browsing. In: Proceeding of the CHI, CHI 2003. ACM, pp 401–408

Chapter 8
Search Support Tools

Kazutoshi Umemoto, Takehiro Yamamoto and Katsumi Tanaka

Abstract This chapter presents in-depth reviews of search tools for supporting information search. With the brief introduction of cutting-edge search support tools, we describe the key ideas behind the tools and implications for design. We also discuss the limitations of conventional search interfaces to explore directions for future research on search support tools.

8.1 Introduction

Providing the right information at the right time and place in the right manner is essential for information retrieval (IR) systems to satisfy users. Among many IR applications, Web search engines are the best known and most frequently used ones. Therefore, developing support tools for Web search is of great practical importance. What makes it challenging is that, unlike many domain-specific IR applications (e.g., enterprise search and legal search), Web search is used by a variety of people to obtain relevant information on any topics. A system requiring excessive search skills and/or domain knowledge would not be able to support general users. As another example, if a system presents search results and provides interaction mechanisms in a way totally different from conventional Web search engines, users would find it difficult to master how to use the system. To make a search support tool successful, it should not only integrate functions effective for target tasks into a search system seamlessly but also keep its interface simple and easy to use.

K. Umemoto (✉)
NICT/The University of Tokyo, Tokyo, Japan
e-mail: umemoto@tkl.iis.u-tokyo.ac.jp

T. Yamamoto
University of Hyogo, Kobe, Japan
e-mail: t.yamamoto@sis.u-hyogo.ac.jp

K. Tanaka
Kyoto University, Kyoto, Japan
e-mail: tanaka.katsumi.85e@st.kyoto-u.ac.jp

© Springer Nature Switzerland AG 2020
W. T. Fu and H. van Oostendorp (eds.), *Understanding and Improving Information Search*, Human–Computer Interaction Series,
https://doi.org/10.1007/978-3-030-38825-6_8

139

The difficulty in developing better tools for Web search is partly explained by the fact that the fundamental framework of commercial Web search engines remains largely unchanged for the last dozen years. A user formulates a search query with a few keywords (Bailey et al. 2010), and then a system returns a search engine results page (SERP) containing the textual summaries of retrieved documents (so-called ten blue links). However, the interface of Web search did improve slightly over time, and we can now observe different elements in SERPs depending on queries. When a query like `weather Tokyo` is issued, recent Web search engines often include in SERPs *answers* that can directly meet searchers' information needs (a weather forecast for the example query) (Chilton and Teevan 2011). When a query is related to an entity (e.g., celebrities and movies), the *structured summary* of the entity (e.g., main properties, related entities) is shown alongside organic search results to improve information accessibility and help searchers navigate related searches (Bota et al. 2016). To help searchers judge the correctness of information, a mechanism with which Web site owners can include in SERPs *fact checks* for claims in their documents has been established recently (Wang et al. 2018).

How can we develop good search support tools? Hearst (2009, Chap. 1) describes eight guidelines that should be considered when designing search user interfaces. These can be summarized as follows.

- **Feedback**. To show the status of the system so that searchers can understand how they can interact with it (e.g., query term highlighting; dynamic ranking with user-specified criteria; query suggestion and auto-completion).
- **Controllability**. To take a balance between the system control, which is powerful yet opaque, and the user control, which is less effective yet comprehensible (e.g., transparency in result ranking and query transformation).
- **Memory Load**. Not to force searchers remember everything about their search process so that they can focus more on achieving the goals behind their search (e.g., showing recently issued queries and recently accessed documents; integrating navigation into search to leverage recognition, which often puts less cognitive load on searchers than recall).
- **Shortcut**. To provide (experienced) users with alternative ways that can complete tasks more efficiently (e.g., shortcut pages, or so-called sitelinks; answers described above).
- **Error**. To reduce errors that searchers make with the system (e.g., spell correction, query expansion, and result previews to mitigate mismatch in vocabulary between searchers and document collections).
- **Detail**. To be meticulous about small details (e.g., the use of a wide search bar to promote long queries; the change in position and wording to improve searchers' awareness for spelling suggestions).
- **Aesthetics**. To make the interface more visually appealing as the graphical design is known to affect both subjective and objective outcomes (e.g., the quality of the interface; user engagement and satisfaction; task completion time).

Now that about ten years have passed since the publication of Hearst's book (2009) on search interfaces, this chapter explores what have been studied for this decade to make search tools better, with a primary focus on Web search. More specifically, we introduce cutting-edge search tools developed for supporting the following four trending topics in the field of information search:

Relevance Judgment (Section 8.2). Information seeking comprises a number of cognitive processes, including defining an information problem, formulating search queries, and examining search results (Marchionini 1995). For searchers, judging whether given information is relevant to their information needs is a fundamental information seeking activity that occurs not only when finding search results to click on but also when reading landing documents and selecting the next query from query suggestions, etc. The past work on neuroscience has associated brain areas with cognitive functions important for relevance judgment (Eugster et al. 2014). Thus, reducing searchers' cognitive load during relevance judgment is crucial to search systems.

Information Credibility (Section 8.3). Topically relevant documents are not always sufficient for searchers to satisfy their information needs. The quality of information plays an important role especially when searchers make critical decisions through their search activities. If search systems provide users with misinformation, the resulting decisions would not be satisfactory to them (what is worse, they might misrecognize the provided information as credible). To support such search scenarios, search systems need to offer features with which searchers can judge the credibility of information.

Exploratory Search (Section 8.4). People use search engines in very diverse ways. While looking up known items can be done with a few interactions, some other tasks may require searchers to issue many queries and browse many documents to complete. Learning and/or investigating new topics are typical scenarios of the latter tasks. In addition to relevance judgment, these tasks often require more intellectual activities, such as comparing, aggregating, and evaluating information, putting more cognitive load to searchers. The conventional support for individual search actions is insufficient to avoid searchers being overloaded, which calls for tools that support the whole search session.

Search Skill (Section 8.5). The past studies have revealed the difference in search performance between general users and experts (Hölscher and Strube 2000; White et al. 2009). While most support tools focus on providing useful features with which general users can improve the performance of the current search, it is also possible to consider training them so that they can perform better in future search without getting any support from those tools.

Later, we take *biases* in search systems and users as open problems we should address to design better search support tools and discuss how the key ideas behind the existing tools could be leveraged to solve these problems (Sect. 8.6). Finally, we conclude this chapter with a brief summary of common techniques that can be used to develop search support tools across different topics (Sect. 8.7).

8.2   Relevance Judgment

Both *relevance* and *information needs* are two of the big three issues in information search (Croft et al. 2009). Searchers judge whether information they find is relevant to their information needs at every step of their search process. Due to this reason, much effort has been devoted to developing tools for supporting searchers' relevance judgment.

Assessing search results is the most typical case where relevance judgment is made. When ambiguous and/or underspecified queries (Clarke et al. 2009) consisting of a few keywords are issued, recent search engines diversify search results so that they can cover as many searchers with different intents as possible with a single SERP (Agrawal et al. 2009; Clarke et al. 2008; Dou et al. 2011; Santos et al. 2010). With the aim of helping searchers locate relevant information covering their desired aspects of underspecified queries, Iwata et al. (2012) developed a SERP interface, called AspecTiles (Fig. 8.1). Given a underspecified query with multiple aspects, AspecTiles presents a SERP where per-aspect document relevance is visualized with colored squares (or tiles) to the left of each search result. The presence of a non-white color in a tile indicates the relevance to the corresponding aspect, while a darker color indicates a higher degree of relevance. As mentioned by the authors, AspecTiles is inspired by TileBar (Hearst 1995) and its simpler interface HotMap (Hoeber and Yang 2006), both of which visualize the frequency (not relevance) of each query term (not aspect) in documents with similar widgets, and is tailored for aspect-aware search tasks. A user study involving 32 participants revealed the effectiveness and efficiency of AspecTiles in search tasks requiring them to collect answers relevant to several aspects of the topic: AspecTiles significantly outperformed a conventional SERP interface in terms of the recall of found answers, the time taken to find the first answer, the average number of clicks between finding two answers, etc. Another

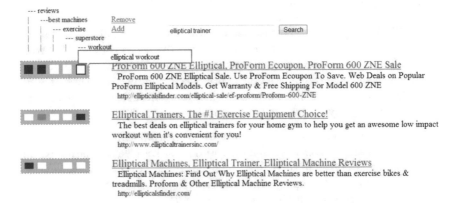

Fig. 8.1 AspecTiles (Iwata et al. 2012) is a SERP interface for underspecified queries. It visualizes per-aspect document relevance alongside each search result to help searchers find documents covering their desired aspects. Copyright © 2012 ACM (www.acm.org). Used with permission

interesting finding is that AspecTiles users tended to reformulate queries fewer times and examined the SERP deeper instead.

Formulating appropriate queries is necessary to find relevant documents in SERPs. While the query suggestion feature is effective to refine their queries, searchers with a limited vocabulary on the search topic cannot gain much insight from the suggested queries about which one would retrieve better results. To address this issue, Zha et al. (2009) proposed an image search interface that provides query suggestions each of which is accompanied by representative images. When a user selects one of the query suggestions, their interface first retrieves candidate images by expanding the original query with the selected keywords and then refines the search results on the basis of the similarity to the selected images. The authors conducted a user study in which 40 participants used 25 queries to compare the proposed interface with two existing image search engines that provide conventional query suggestions. All participants preferred the proposed interface over the conventional ones and answered that visual query suggestions were useful for eliciting their true search intent. The authors also demonstrated through an experiment that refining search results with visual query suggestions improved the search performance compared with both the original query and the reformulated query with the keyword suggestion.

When a search result looks relevant, searchers typically click its URL to read the details of the landing document. Relevance judgement is also made within the document: searchers scan through its content to find relevance pieces of information. Feild et al. (2013) proposed clickable snippets, which orient searchers on the SERP toward landing document content. A snippet extracted from the text (not the metadata) of the landing document is underlined to indicate its affordance (i.e., clickable). When the searcher clicks this snippet, he/she is navigated to the part of the landing document containing the clicked snippet text through a gradual transition. A user study was conducted in which each of 48 participants worked on 12 tasks using either of clickable snippets and five other systems (i.e., conventional SERPs with no orientation support; SERPs with the thumbnail previews of landing documents, which used to be available in Google search; landing documents with query term highlighting; landing documents with snippet text highlighting; a variant of clickable snippets that performs transition immediately, not gradually[1]). Findings from the study include the following: (1) 56% of participants had tried to locate snippet text on landing documents over half of their searches (none reported never doing this), indicating the demand of the proposed system; (2) participants completed the tasks with the proposed system more effectively and efficiently; (3) clickable snippets with the gradual transition were preferred to the other systems.

It has been reported that queries for *re-finding* (i.e., searching for documents that the searcher has browsed before) account for a significant fraction of the total search volume (e.g., 21.9% (Tyler and Teevan 2010) and 38.8% (Teevan et al. 2007)). For this kind of search, searchers make relevance judgment on the basis of their memory. Teevan et al. (2009) studied compact document representation that supports the iden-

---

[1] While the gradual mode performs the transition as a seamless animation over the course of a second or two, the immediate mode shows the destination promptly with no animation.

tification of both unseen, relevant documents and seen, relevant ones. Inspired by the high-quality document representation created by a graphic designer, the authors designed visual snippets that consist of the title, salient image, and logo of documents and proposed a method for the automatic visual snippet generation. The authors conducted a user study comprising two phases: The first is collecting documents relevant to given tasks, and the second is finding documents collected in the first phase the day before. In the study, 197 participants completed four of 12 tasks with each of three search result representations: text snippets, visual snippets, and thumbnails. Results for the re-finding phase revealed that (1) the visual representations outperformed the textual one and (2) visual snippets were effective even when participants were interacted with different representations in the first phase.

Summary. This section has reviewed the tools that help searchers judge relevance. Relevance judgment is the fundamental cognitive process made on every step of search activities, including query (re)formulation, SERP examination, landing document orientation, and information re-finding. A technique common to these tools is enhancing the presentation of information (e.g., queries, SERPs, and documents) in visually intuitive and appealing manners so that searchers' cognitive load during relevance judgment can be reduced. In Chapter 6, some ideas about the use of modeling predictions to indicate relevance and how they help search are also discussed.

While this section has focused mostly on *topical* relevance (i.e., whether the topic of information is relevant to the searcher's intent), it is, however, just one of various relevance types (the others include *cognitive*, *situational*, and *motivational* relevance) (Saracevic 1996). For example, cognitive search intent can be characterized by exhaustiveness, comprehensibility, subjectivity and objectivity, and concreteness and abstractness (Kato et al. 2014). Topically relevant documents are not necessarily relevant to the searcher's cognitive search intent. To support users with these other types of search intents, different functionality would need to be established. Other research directions include (1) better understanding the relationship between relevance judgment and user behavior, (2) supporting relevance judgment for more fine-grained information (e.g., sentences and passages) rather than documents and for multi-modal information (e.g., texts, images, and videos) as the unit of search results, and (3) exploring device-specific search interfaces and interactions to support relevance judgment (e.g., for smartphones and smart speakers).

8.3 Information Credibility

On the Web, as opposed to other mass media such as newspapers and television, anyone can publish unchecked information, which may be inaccurate and/or misleading. Due to this nature, the *credibility* of information should be taken into consideration especially when users make critical decisions through their search activities. Ranking high-quality documents (e.g., those containing accurate information) at top positions is not the only challenge here. Indeed, in the fields of communication and

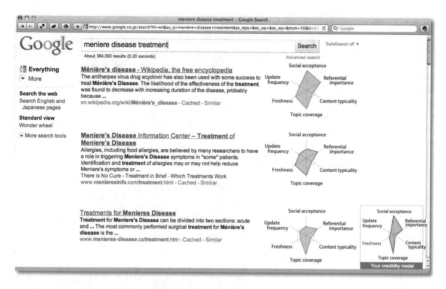

Fig. 8.2 CowSearch (Yamamoto and Tanaka 2011) shows the scores of six credibility dimensions for each search result. It also leverages the searcher's feedbacks to predict his/her credibility judgment model, which is used to update the ranking to put search results that he/she thinks are more credible at higher positions. Copyright © 2011 ACM (www.acm.org). Used with permission

social psychology, credibility is thought to be a subjective quality perceived by the information receiver and to have two key components, namely trustworthiness and expertise (Flanagin and Metzger 2008; Fogg and Tseng 1999). In this section, we introduce tools developed for helping searchers judge the information credibility and encouraging them to have careful thought while searching.

Yamamoto and Tanaka (2011) developed a SERP interface for helping the credibility judgment based on multiple aspects. As shown in Fig. 8.2, their interface, named CowSearch, shows a radar chart indicating the scores of the following six dimensions (taken from five credibility aspects) for each search result: referential importance (accuracy), social acceptance (authority), content typicality (objectivity), topic coverage (coverage), and freshness and update frequency (currency). As well as assessing the credibility of each search result, searchers can give CowSearch their feedback on (subjectively) important credibility dimensions. When the searcher double-clicks the chart of a search result that he/she thinks is credible, CowSearch updates his/her credibility judgment model (shown at the bottom right of the figure) to reflect the scores of the selected result and changes the ranking so that results whose charts are similar to his/her judgment model are ranked at higher positions. The authors conducted both online and laboratory studies (involving 960 and ten participants, respectively) and reported that CowSearch helped users (with knowledge about search topics, in particular) more efficiently find credible documents than a conventional SERP interface.

Fig. 8.3 Dispute
Finder (Ennals et al. 2010)
alerts the searcher when a
document that he/she is
reading contains disputed
claims. Clicking on a
highlighted disputed claim
triggers this tool to open a
popup window containing
supporting and opposing
articles for the claim.
Copyright © 2010 IW3C2
(www.iw3c2.org). Used with
permission

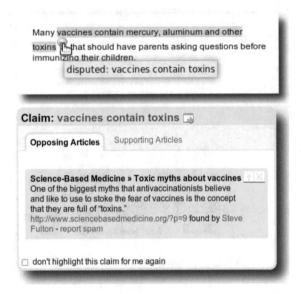

Providing an alert has been studied as an approach to promoting careful information seeking for disputed search topics (Ennals et al. 2010; Yamamoto and Shimada
2016). Dispute Finder is a browser extension developed by Ennals et al. (2010). As
shown in the top of Fig. 8.3, this tool highlights disputed claims in documents that the
searcher is reading. When the searcher clicks on a highlighted claim, a popup window containing supporting and opposing articles for the claim is shown to him/her
(the bottom of Fig. 8.3). The authors performed three qualitative user studies to collect feedback on Dispute Finder from participants (24 in total). Most participants
reported that they would want to use the tool when searching for disputed topics.
The studies also revealed the low performance of the tool, which frustrated users.
Yamamoto and Shimada (2016) also investigated the effect of a similar highlighting
tool on searchers' attitudes and behavior through a crowdsourced study involving 92
participants. They reported that highlights in SERPs encouraged searchers to seek
information carefully, while highlights in landing pages were used as complementary
information for their decision making.

Liao and Fu (2014) investigated how the expertise of information source affected
searchers' behavior on controversial social–political topics. To this end, they conducted a user study where 76 participants were instructed to write their own posts
after browsing the search results of comments on controversial issues in an online
discussion forum. The search interface was controlled based on two between-subject
variables: whether to present four-level position indicators (strong pro, moderate
pro, moderate con, and strong con) and randomly assigned five-level expertise indicators (from 1-star to 5-star) to each comment. As a result, the expertise indicators
were found to increase the participants' selection of information with high expertise.
Interestingly, presenting both the position and expertise indicators encouraged the

Fig. 8.4 Balancer (Munson et al. 2013) is a browser extension that shows the degree of the searcher's political lean based on his/her past browsing history. Copyright © 2019 AAAI (www.aaai.org). Used with permission

participants to select information whose attitudes were inconsistent with their own ones.

As an alternative approach to nudging searchers to explore information with diverse opinions, Munson et al. (2013) developed a browser extension, which they call Balancer. As shown in Fig. 8.4, Balancer visualizes the numbers of liberal documents (the right blue bar) and conservative documents (the left red bar) that the search has browsed for the week to date. The authors conducted a two-month field study where 1,145 participants installed the extension to their browsers. For comparison, two conditions were designed: participants in the treatment condition used Balancer from the beginning while those in the control condition had no access to the visualization during the first month. A small improvement toward more balanced reading was observed (e.g., four new monthly visits to a right-leaning site for the median liberal user).

Summary. This section has reviewed the tools for supporting credibility judgment of users. Their approaches included providing the additional information that is useful for credibility judgment and nudging searchers to be aware of different opinions. As the dissemination of the inaccurate information on the Web has been a crucial problem in our society, the importance of such tools becomes prominent.

One important concern when supporting credibility judgment is how to encourage users having little *motivation* to judge the credibility of Web information. The dual processing model of Web site credibility assessment (Metzger 2007) explains that a user is required to have enough motivation to evaluate the credibility before demonstrating their ability to judge the credibility. The model suggests that the tools should not only support users' credibility judgment ability but also motivate them to obtain credible information. In this direction, Yamamoto and Yamamoto have proposed a query suggestion interface called query priming to activate users' attitude to be critical (Yamamoto and Yamamoto 2018). Query priming displays terms such as "evidence," "comparison," and "validation," all of which are associated with high critical thinking attitude. The authors observed through a user study that participants who used the query priming interface tended to issue more queries and select more documents containing evidence during search tasks. As illustrated by their work, motivating users to obtain credible information would be one promising direction to explore.

8.4 Exploratory Search

Recent Web search engines are more than tools for lookup search (e.g., finding facts and visiting specific sites). People also address more complex search, called *exploratory search* (Marchionini 2006; White and Roth 2009), to learn and/or investigate topics. Exploratory search is open-ended, ill-structured, and multi-faceted, involves uncertainty and evolves dynamically (Wildemuth and Freund 2012). Due to these properties, exploratory search often requires searchers to issue multiple queries. Thus, the whole-session support needs to be taken into consideration for exploratory search.

As searchers often issue multiple queries in a single session of exploratory search, the same documents may be retrieved multiple times with distinct queries. To provide a better insight into effective query (re)formulation, Querium developed by Qvarfordt et al. (2013) presents a widget that enables searchers to preview search results when they are typing queries. The preview widget consists of ten bars each summarizing the state of ten consecutive documents in the search results (e.g., the leftmost bar represents the top ten documents). More specifically, each bar visualizes the numbers of the documents that have not yet been retrieved in the past searches, have been retrieved but not clicked, and have already been clicked. The authors carried out a user study in which 13 participants performed six recall-oriented search tasks to collect academic papers relevant to given patent applications. Results of the study showed the effect of the preview widget on search behavior and performance. Compared with participants who used the baseline interface without the preview widget, those who used the proposed interface issued fewer queries, saved more documents, browsed more lower-ranked documents, and achieved better precision and recall. In addition, analyzing eye-tracking data revealed that, during the query formulation process, users of the proposed interface paid more attention to the query area (including the preview widget) than others.

Some exploratory search tasks require users to collect extensive information covering different aspects. To support users conducting such intrinsically diverse search tasks (Raman et al. 2013), Umemoto et al. (2016) proposed a query suggestion interface, called ScentBar. Unlike Querium (Qvarfordt et al. 2013), which visualizes the *number* of documents that have not yet investigated, ScentBar visualizes the *amount* of relevant information that a user misses collecting from the search results (or missed information) of individual queries. In Fig. 8.5, the length of the dark-colored bar of each query represents the amount of the missed information of that query, while the length of the light-colored one represents its initial value (i.e., the total amount of relevant information available from the search results). The amount of missed information is estimated with an aspect-aware algorithm (Tsukuda et al. 2013) for subtopic

Fig. 8.5 ScentBar (Umemoto et al. 2016) is a query suggestion interface that visualizes (1) how much relevant information is available from the search results of individual queries and (2) of which how much is still left unexplored. Copyright © 2016 held by the authors

mining and search result diversification so that it should be high when the search results contain many relevant documents covering important aspects that the searcher has not explored much. Results of a user study where 24 participants worked on four tasks showed that, when the estimation algorithm worked reasonably, (1) ScentBar users stopped examining search results after collecting a greater amount of relevant information; (2) they issued more promising queries whose search results contained more missed information; (3) they obtained higher gain particularly at the late stage of their sessions; and (4) they obtained higher gain per unit time, compared with searchers who used a conventional query suggestion interface.

Searchers need to read multiple documents when addressing exploratory tasks, which results in their browsers being filled with many tabs. To support searchers' efficient task management, Liu and Tajima (2010) developed WildThumb, a new browsing interface that shows the visual snippets of opened tabs at the both sides of the currently focused document. Compared with conventional tabs displaying document titles, visual snippets helps users find documents to which they want to switch their focus, even when many documents are opened. To improve the recognizability, WildThumb overlays notable elements in documents (e.g., site logos) onto the corresponding snippets, similarly to Teevan et al.'s work (2009) introduced in Sect. 8.2. It also enlarges the visual snippets of documents that are highly relevant to the currently focused document, where the relevance between opened documents is calculated based on the user's switching history. The authors conducted a user study where nine participants were asked to iteratively select a specified document from opened documents. WildThumb was shown to significantly save the switching time compared with two baselines (tabs and thumbnails). Results of an exit questionnaire also revealed the participants' strong preference to visual snippets over ordinary thumbnails.

The many-tab problem gets serious in mobile devices due to the limited screen size, frequent interruption, difficulties in organizing information, etc. To overcome the limitations of tabs, Hahn et al. (2018) proposed a novel mobile browser, called Bento Browser. Their key idea is to separate the task management and workspace functions served by conventional tabs into two distinct interfaces. In Bento Browser, queries issued from the top search box initiate new tasks, while those from the middle box are added as subtasks of the current task. Tasks are organized into cards, which allow searchers to focus on the current task in a separate workspace and to easily switch between tasks just by swiping cards. When the searcher taps a subtask, Bento Browser shows the list of search results for the corresponding query. This workspace is mutable and looks similar to the inbox presentation of emails offered by recent mobile apps: the searcher can read documents, put them some labels (e.g., unread and stars), and move them to a trash box with simple interactions. This helps searchers track the progress of the current tasks and resume the previous tasks. The authors conducted three studies (a laboratory evaluation, a qualitative real-world deployment, and an expanded quantitative deployment), all of which revealed participants' stronger preference to Bento Browser over Safari (a mobile browser) in terms of information organization and task resumption.

To make decisions through exploratory tasks, searchers may need to compare and aggregate relevant pieces of information scattered in different documents. Aiming at supporting information organization across multiple documents, Yahoo! integrated a note-taking tool, called Search Pad (Donato et al. 2010), into their search system (Fig. 8.6). Search Pad presents searchers with an editable note containing the titles, URLs, and thumbnails of documents that they have visited in the current task. Searchers can type and/or paste text in the note, reopen it later, and share it with oth-

(a) Complex task detection   (b) Editable note integration

Fig. 8.6 Yahoo! Search Pad (Donato et al. 2010) **a** automatically detects whether the current task is complex and, if so, **b** presents the searcher with an editable note containing the summary of documents they have visited. Copyright © 2010 IW3C2 (www.iw3c2.org). Used with permission

ers. A notable feature of Search Pad is that the note-taking tool is enabled only when the current task is detected as complex. Donato et al. (2010) conducted experiments over a fraction of the Yahoo! search traffic. Experimental results revealed that (1) the time required for Search Pad to trigger is less than 12 ms, which would be acceptable for searchers; and (2) Search Pad achieved detection performance scores greater than 0.6 in terms of both precision and recall. Note, however, that search outcomes and experience that users can gain from Search Pad are unclear.

While this section has so far introduced the past studies that help searchers understand and evaluate their own behavior, they may also gain insight from the behavior of others who have approached the same or a similar exploratory search task. In this context, mining and presenting the *search trails* of related users draw increasing attention (Bilenko and White 2008; Singla et al. 2010; White et al. 2007; White and Huang 2010; Yuan and White 2012). SearchGuide developed by Capra et al. (2015) is one of the most recent tools that aim at guiding searchers by presenting related search trails in SERPs. SearchGuide shows in separate tabs the search trails of three searchers who conducted the same search task previously. Each tab displays the list of queries issued by a previous searcher. Clicking on a query expands an accordion control[2] that contains his/her clicked search results and bookmarked documents for the query. Users can interact with SearchGuide by issuing previous queries, visiting clicked or bookmarked documents, and confirming reasons for bookmarks. The authors conducted a user study in which 48 participants completed four tasks of varying levels of cognitive complexity (from fact-finding to decision making). Findings from their study include the following: (1) searchers interacted greatly with SearchGuide for complex tasks; (2) they used SearchGuide for verification and assurance in simple tasks and for finding new information or search strategies in complex tasks; and (3) SearchGuide degraded user experience when it failed to provide good documents worth bookmarking.

Summary. This section has reviewed the literature on tools for exploratory search. Those tools were designed to support a variety of aspects of exploratory search, ranging from employing search strategies (e.g., query formulation, document selection, search stopping, and wayfinding) to managing search workspace (e.g., switching tabs and subtasks) to organizing search outcomes (annotating relevant information found so far). See also Chapter 7 for a framework that supports the multistage nature of exploratory search. The fact that more and more people use Web search engines for not only lookup tasks but also more complex tasks calls for an increasing need to develop better tools for exploratory search.

The ideal functionality of support tools may depend on topics or domains that searchers explore. For example, educational support could help students learn new concepts efficiently and effectively, while such support would be useless for those examining which products to purchase. As we have seen in this section, the existing tools mostly provide the general assistance for the process of exploratory search. One direction worth exploring in future is developing tools that provide task-specific

---

[2]The accordion control is a user interface widget that uses collapsible content panels for presenting information in limited space.

assistance by understanding underlying goals that cause exploratory search. In fact, *search as learning* (Collins-Thompson et al. 2017), which focuses on human learning during the search process, attracts rising attention recently although tools and interfaces specific to this purpose have not well established.

As exploratory search tasks are complex in nature, tools for supporting these tasks also tend to get complicated. As described in Sect. 8.1, however, difficult tools tend to put an extra cognitive load and in the worse case would not be used by general users. Thus, for developing better tools, it is also important to better understand the tradeoff between the complexity of support functionality and its usability, which can be divided into effectiveness, efficiency, and satisfaction (Kelly 2009, Sect. 10), in the context of exploratory search (Diriye et al. 2010).

8.5 Search Skill

The tools that we have seen so far are mostly designed to support searchers in finding relevant information and completing their tasks. As another research direction, educational tools for *upskilling searchers* (Allan et al. 2012) have also been studied.

Bateman et al. (2012) proposed an interface, called Search Dashboard, for reflection on personal search behavior. Search Dashboard presents an individual's search history aggregated into 12 specific elements in three data types: techniques (e.g., the use of advanced query operators), tendencies (e.g., the number of search terms; the number of clicks per query), and topics (e.g., popular search categories; salient search terms). To help the searcher get an idea to improve his/her search, Search Dashboard also shows others' search behavior aggregated based on three user archetypes: typical users, search experts, and topic experts. The authors conducted a five-week user study involving 90 participants, where they controlled which data type to show and whether to show others' statistics for comparison. Findings from the study include the following: participants perceived less search skill at the end of the study, suggesting that they noticed their search behavior has room to improve through the use of Search Dashboard, showing the comparison data, of search experts in particular, increased the participants' insights and changed their behavior (on the techniques and tendencies types).

Harvey et al. (2015) aimed to train searchers by providing high-quality query suggestions. To this end, three studies were carried out in their work. First, the authors investigated the characteristics of high-performing queries through a crowdsourced study, in which workers judged queries that achieve high average precision. A key finding from this study is that participants did not recognize many of presented queries as being effective. Second, as a pilot study, 22 participants interacted with a search interface that suggests high-quality queries. This interface also presents how effective the current query is. When searching with suggested queries, participants were asked to describe why they think those queries perform better than their own queries. A qualitative analysis of this feedback suggested that participants were able to notice properties that high-quality queries have. Finally, the authors conducted a main study involving 91 participants. Each participant was randomly assigned to one of three conditions: (a) presenting high-quality query suggestions recognized as effective in the first study; (b) presenting those recognized as ineffective; and (c) presenting no query suggestions. In the conditions (a) and (b), query suggestions were presented for the first four topics (i.e., training) and not for the rest two topics (i.e., test). Main findings from this study are as follows: participants exposed to high-quality query suggestions during the training phase were able to formulate effective queries by themselves during the test phase; queries submitted by those participants look similar to expert queries; and the recognizability of query suggestions did not have a significant effect on improving participants' query formulations.

Suggesting search tactics and strategies is another attempt to improve the skill of searchers. Moraveji et al. (2011) focused on tactical search tips, which explain how to use the functionality offered by search systems (e.g., advanced search operators and search result filters). In their initial study, participants in the experiment group were shown search tips when working on six specified tasks, while those in the control group had no access to search tips. As a result, participants shown search tips completed their tasks substantially faster than those who were not shown any tips. About one week later, the authors carried out a follow-up study, in which the same participants were instructed to complete similar tasks without search tips. Again, participants in the experiment group completed most of their tasks faster than those in the control group, suggesting that the performance gains obtained from search tips were retained. Savenkov and Agichtein (2014) proposed an interface suggesting strategic search hints to guide searchers in completing complex tasks. A search hint comprises a set of steps (based on the divide-and-conquer strategy) required to complete a given task. The authors conducted a user study, in which each participant was asked to find answers to complex factual questions under one of three conditions: with task-specific hints; with generic hints; and without any hint. Overall, participants shown task-specific hints achieved higher task success rates than those in other conditions. Interestingly, general hints decreased the search performance of participants. Note, however, that it remains unclear whether the gain from task-specific hints persisted after the study.

Summary. This section has reviewed the recent attempt to improve the skill of searchers so that they can perform better in future search. The techniques used for this aim can be summarized as (1) informing searchers about the difference in search behavior between themselves and others (including experts), (2) training searchers by showing good examples that improve search performance, and (3) teaching searchers how to use functionality provided by search systems and to decompose complex tasks into doable search actions. Compared to the tools we have introduced in the previous sections, the approach to improving search skill plays a complementary role in bridging the gap in search performance between general users and experts.

One open question is how long the reported effect would be sustained. More longitudinal studies need to be carried out to answer this question. Future topics in this direction include predicting when the effect will diminish and making intervention to reactivate it. Theories and findings from psychology such as *forgetting curve* and *habituation* might be leveraged for this purpose.

8.6 Toward Combating Biases

This section describes open problems we should address to design better search support tools. We focus here on *biases* as a general topic that are valid for all search systems and users. Emerging topics in information search are also covered in other chapters of this book. For example, see Chapter 13 for conversational search.

Search systems are used for knowledge acquisition and decision making in various domains. Biases in the search process could result in undesired outcomes both for individuals (e.g., cyberchondria (White and Horvitz 2009)) and societies (e.g., election control (Epstein and Robertson 2015)). To combat biases, developing search systems that are fair, accountable, confidential, and transparent, which are collectively called FACT (Culpepper et al. 2018), is attracting attentions from the IR community (Biega et al. 2018; Castillo 2019; Singh and Joachims 2018; Zhang et al. 2019), as with other research areas such as machine learning and artificial intelligence. In what follows, we discuss two types of search biases and open problems to be addressed to combat these biases.

System Bias. The first type of biases exists in search systems. For example, document collections, from which search results are retrieved, may cover different amounts of information for different items (e.g., people, products, and opinions). This could result in more SERPs containing particular items more often than other ones. Biases in ranking models (learned from biased user feedback such as clicks with position bias (Craswell et al. 2008)) exacerbate the unfairness of the items being searched. Past studies demonstrated that search results for yes–no questions tended to be skewed toward particular answers (usually positive), irrespective of the truth (White 2013), and search results biased toward incorrect information led users to make more incorrect decisions (Pogacar et al. 2017). Although new algorithms (e.g., unbiased learning for document ranking (Joachims et al. 2017) and for query suggestion) may help mitigate the problems, there are many other research questions that we need to study toward developing support tools for FACT search. Are there any result presentation better than ranking in terms of fairness? What information should be appended to each search result to improve the explainability and provenance? How should it be presented? For these questions, some ideas behind the search support tools we have introduced so far might be reused (e.g., the tile-based visualization (Iwata et al. 2012) and the position and expertise indicators (Liao and Fu 2014)). How much additional information is acceptable to retain explainability while avoiding cognitive overload? Should we change the explanation depending on the knowledge and/or expertise of searchers? Carefully designed user studies would be necessary to answer these questions.

User Bias. The second are biases that searchers have. In the era of filter bubble and echo chamber, users tend to be immersed in affirmative information that they believe. How to resolve polarization on social media is being studied intensively (Garimella et al. 2017; Gillani et al. 2018). Result diversification (based not on different topics but on different attitudes, claims, opinions, and/or sentiments (Aktolga and Allan 2013) on a single topic) would be one of approaches that search systems can take to combat biases in searchers. However, presenting contradictory information without reason could have little effect on searchers with strong beliefs and, what is worse, decrease user experience (White 2014). This calls for designing mechanisms that can encourage searchers to willingly investigate diverse information. Techniques adopted in the aforementioned tools (e.g., providing alerts (Ennals et al. 2010; Yamamoto and Shimada 2016) and visualizing searchers' leaning (Munson et al. 2013) and missed information (Umemoto et al. 2016)) would be worth revisiting for this purpose. Another approach is to make a change in the attitude and behavior of searchers without making them conscious about it. Such examples include adding terms that can stimulate critical thinking to query suggestions (Yamamoto and Yamamoto 2018) and substituting meals with similar, healthier dishes in recommender systems (Elsweiler et al. 2017). Collaboration with other research fields studying human factors, including psychology, cognitive science, and social science, would be essential for better interaction design and interface development to combat biases in searchers.

8.7   Conclusions

This chapter has reviewed search support tools developed in the past decade. While it covers the diverse research topics in information search (i.e., relevance judgment, information credibility, exploratory search, and search skill), there exist common techniques that can be applied to different tools and topics as summarized below.

- Enhancing the presentation of search queries and query suggestions for recall-oriented search (Qvarfordt et al. 2013), intrinsically diverse search (Umemoto et al. 2016), critical thinking (Yamamoto and Yamamoto 2018), and visual awareness (Zha et al. 2009);
- Enhancing the presentation of search results for judging per-aspect relevance (Iwata et al. 2012) and credibility (Liao and Fu 2014; Yamamoto and Tanaka 2011);
- Visually representing documents with salient features for task management (Liu and Tajima 2010) and re-finding (Teevan et al. 2009);
- Presenting the behavior of other searchers for search guide (Capra et al. 2015) and upskilling (Bateman et al. 2012).

These techniques offer important information that guides searchers to choose the right actions (e.g., judging the relevance and/or credibility of queries and documents, reflecting on search strategies, etc.), which are otherwise easily neglected. By doing so, searchers are *nudged* to better use the functionality of search systems. Reducing the load of taking search actions in this way would eventually support people in conducting the broader set of cognitive tasks that encompass search tasks.

While some progress has been made in each of these topics, the current tools still have room to improve. For example, the following challenges would be worth tackling: supporting the judgment of non-topical relevance, motivating searchers to assess the credibility of information, developing task-specific support functionality for exploratory search, and understanding the sustained effect of tools for improving search skill (and making it longer).

As a future topic, we have also discussed biases in both search systems and users. While the aforementioned techniques could be used to address some specific challenges, this topic has many open, multidisciplinary research problems. Thus, enhancing collaboration with other research areas would play a key role in developing better search support tools for combatting biases (e.g., machine learning for system biases; psychology, cognitive science, and social science for user biases).

References

Agrawal R, Gollapudi S, Halverson A, Ieong S (2009) Diversifying search results. In: Proceedings of the second ACM international conference on web search and data mining, WSDM 2009. ACM, pp 5–14

Aktolga E, Allan J (2013) Sentiment diversification with different biases. In: Proceedings of the 36th international ACM SIGIR conference on research and development in information retrieval, SIGIR 2013. ACM, pp 593–602

Allan J, Croft B, Moffat A, Sanderson M (2012) Frontiers, challenges, and opportunities for information retrieval: report from SWIRL 2012 the second strategic workshop on information retrieval in Lorne. SIGIR Forum 46(1):2–32

Bailey P, White RW, Liu H, Kumaran G (2010) Mining historic query trails to label long and rare search engine queries. ACM Trans Web 4(4):15:1–15:27

Bateman S, Teevan J, White RW (2012) The search dashboard: how reflection and comparison impact search behavior. In: Proceedings of the SIGCHI conference on human factors in computing systems, CHI 2012. ACM, pp 1785–1794

Biega AJ, Gummadi KP, Weikum G (2018) Equity of attention: amortizing individual fairness in rankings. In: The 41st international ACM SIGIR conference on research and development in information retrieval, SIGIR 2018. ACM, pp 405–414

Bilenko M, White RW (2008) Mining the search trails of surfing crowds: identifying relevant websites from user activity. In: Proceedings of the 17th international conference on World Wide Web, WWW 2008. ACM, pp 51–60

Bota H, Zhou K, Jose JM (2016) Playing your cards right: the effect of entity cards on search behaviour and workload. In: Proceedings of the 2016 ACM on conference on human information interaction and retrieval, CHIIR 2016. ACM, pp 131–140

Capra R, Arguello J, Crescenzi A, Vardell E (2015) Differences in the use of search assistance for tasks of varying complexity. In: Proceedings of the 38th international ACM SIGIR conference on research and development in information retrieval, SIGIR 2015. ACM, pp 23–32

Castillo C (2019) Fairness and transparency in ranking. SIGIR Forum 52(2):64–71

Chilton LB, Teevan J (2011) Addressing people's information needs directly in a web search result page. In: Proceedings of the 20th international conference on World Wide Web, WWW 2011. ACM, pp 27–36

Clarke CL, Kolla M, Cormack GV, Vechtomova O, Ashkan A, Büttcher S, MacKinnon I (2008) Novelty and diversity in information retrieval evaluation. In: Proceedings of the 31st annual international ACM SIGIR conference on research and development in information retrieval, SIGIR 2008. ACM, pp 659–666

Clarke CL, Kolla M, Vechtomova O (2009) An effectiveness measure for ambiguous and underspecified queries. In: Proceedings of the 2nd international conference on theory of information retrieval: advances in information retrieval theory, ICTIR 2009. Springer, pp 188–199

Collins-Thompson K, Hansen P, Hauff C (2017) Search as learning (Dagstuhl Seminar 17092). Dagstuhl Rep 7(2):135–162

Craswell N, Zoeter O, Taylor M, Ramsey B (2008) An experimental comparison of click position-bias models. In: Proceedings of the 2008 international conference on web search and data mining, WSDM 2008. ACM, pp 87–94

Croft B, Metzler D, Strohman T (2009) Search engines: information retrieval in practice, 1st edn. Addison-Wesley Publishing Company

Culpepper JS, Diaz F, Smucker MD (2018) Research frontiers in information retrieval: report from the third strategic workshop on information retrieval in Lorne (SWIRL 2018). SIGIR Forum 52(1):34–90

Diriye A, Blandford A, Tombros A (2010) When is system support effective? In: Proceedings of the third symposium on information interaction in context, IIiX 2010. ACM, pp 55–64

Donato D, Bonchi F, Chi T, Maarek Y (2010) Do you want to take notes?: identifying research missions in Yahoo! search pad. In: Proceedings of the 19th international conference on World Wide Web, WWW 2010. ACM, pp 321–330

Dou Z, Hu S, Chen K, Song R, Wen JR (2011) Multi-dimensional search result diversification. In: Proceedings of the fourth ACM international conference on web search and data mining, WSDM 2011. ACM, pp 475–484

Elsweiler D, Trattner C, Harvey M (2017) Exploiting food choice biases for healthier recipe recommendation. In: Proceedings of the 40th international ACM SIGIR conference on research and development in information retrieval, SIGIR 2017. ACM, pp 575–584

Ennals R, Trushkowsky B, Agosta JM (2010) Highlighting disputed claims on the web. In: Proceedings of the 19th international conference on World Wide Web, WWW 2010. ACM, pp 341–350

Epstein R, Robertson RE (2015) The search engine manipulation effect (seme) and its possible impact on the outcomes of elections. Proc Natl Acad Sci 112(33):E4512–E4521

Eugster MJ, Ruotsalo T, Spapé MM, Kosunen I, Barral O, Ravaja N, Jacucci G, Kaski S (2014) Predicting term-relevance from brain signals. In: Proceedings of the 37th international ACM SIGIR conference on research and development in information retrieval, SIGIR 2014. ACM, pp 425–434

Feild H, White RW, Fu X (2013) Supporting orientation during search result examination. In: Proceedings of the SIGCHI conference on human factors in computing systems, CHI 2013. ACM, pp 2999–3008

Flanagin AJ, Metzger MJ (2008) The credibility of volunteered geographic information. GeoJournal 72(3–4):137–148

Fogg BJ, Tseng H (1999) The elements of computer credibility. In: Proceedings of the SIGCHI conference on human factors in computing systems, CHI 1999. ACM, pp 80–87

Garimella K, De Francisci Morales G, Gionis A, Mathioudakis M (2017) Reducing controversy by connecting opposing views. In: Proceedings of the tenth ACM international conference on web search and data mining, WSDM 2017. ACM, pp 81–90

Gillani N, Yuan A, Saveski M, Vosoughi S, Roy D (2018) Me, my echo chamber, and I: introspection on social media polarization. In: Proceedings of the 2018 World Wide Web conference, international World Wide Web conferences steering committee, WWW 2018, pp 823–831

Hahn N, Chang JC, Kittur A (2018) Bento browser: complex mobile search without tabs. In: Proceedings of the 2018 CHI conference on human factors in computing systems, CHI 2018. ACM, pp 251:1–251:12

Harvey M, Hauff C, Elsweiler D (2015) Learning by example: training users with high-quality query suggestions. In: Proceedings of the 38th international ACM SIGIR conference on research and development in information retrieval, SIGIR 2015. ACM, pp 133–142

Hearst MA (1995) TileBars: visualization of term distribution information in full text information access. In: Proceedings of the SIGCHI conference on human factors in computing systems, CHI 1995. ACM Press/Addison-Wesley Publishing Co., pp 59–66

Hearst MA (2009) Search user interfaces, 1st edn. Cambridge University Press

Hoeber O, Yang XD (2006) A comparative user study of web search interfaces: Hotmap, concept highlighter, and google. In: Proceedings of the 2006 IEEE/WIC/ACM international conference on web intelligence, WI 2006. IEEE Computer Society, pp 866–874

Hölscher C, Strube G (2000) Web search behavior of internet experts and newbies. Comput Netw 33(1–6):337–346

Iwata M, Sakai T, Yamamoto T, Chen Y, Liu Y, Wen JR, Nishio S (2012) AspecTiles: tile-based visualization of diversified web search results. In: Proceedings of the 35th international ACM SIGIR conference on research and development in information retrieval, SIGIR 2012. ACM, pp 85–94

Joachims T, Swaminathan A, Schnabel T (2017) Unbiased learning-to-rank with biased feedback. In: Proceedings of the tenth ACM international conference on web search and data mining, WSDM 2017. ACM, pp 781–789

Kato MP, Yamamoto T, Ohshima H, Tanaka K (2014) Investigating users' query formulations for cognitive search intents. In: Proceedings of the 37th international ACM SIGIR conference on research and development in information retrieval, SIGIR 2014. ACM, pp 577–586

Kelly D (2009) Methods for evaluating interactive information retrieval systems with users. Found Trends Inf Retr 3(1–2):1–224

Liao QV, Fu WT (2014) Expert voices in echo chambers: effects of source expertise indicators on exposure to diverse opinions. In: Proceedings of the 32nd annual ACM conference on human factors in computing systems, CHI 2014. ACM, pp 2745–2754

Liu S, Tajima K (2010) WildThumb: a web browser supporting efficient task management on wide displays. In: Proceedings of the 15th international conference on intelligent user interfaces, IUI 2010. ACM, pp 159–168

Marchionini G (1995) Information seeking in electronic environments. Cambridge University Press

Marchionini G (2006) Exploratory search: from finding to understanding. Commun ACM 49(4):41–46

Metzger MJ (2007) Making sense of credibility on the web: models for evaluating online information and recommendations for future research. J Am Soc Inf Sci Technol 58(13):2078–2091

Moraveji N, Russell D, Bien J, Mease D (2011) Measuring improvement in user search performance resulting from optimal search tips. In: Proceedings of the 34th international ACM SIGIR conference on research and development in information retrieval, SIGIR 2011. ACM, pp 355–364

Munson SA, Lee SY, Resnick P (2013) Encouraging reading of diverse political viewpoints with a browser widget. In: Proceedings of the seventh international AAAI conference on weblogs and social media, ICWSM 2013, pp 419–428

Pogacar FA, Ghenai A, Smucker MD, Clarke CL (2017) The positive and negative influence of search results on people's decisions about the efficacy of medical treatments. In: Proceedings of the ACM SIGIR international conference on theory of information retrieval, ICTIR 2017. ACM, pp 209–216

Qvarfordt P, Golovchinsky G, Dunnigan T, Agapie E (2013) Looking ahead: query preview in exploratory search. In: Proceedings of the 36th international ACM SIGIR conference on research and development in information retrieval, SIGIR 2013. ACM, pp 243–252

Raman K, Bennett PN, Collins-Thompson K (2013) Toward whole-session relevance: exploring intrinsic diversity in web search. In: Proceedings of the 36th international ACM SIGIR conference on research and development in information retrieval, SIGIR 2013. ACM, pp 463–472

Santos RL, Macdonald C, Ounis I (2010) Exploiting query reformulations for web search result diversification. In: Proceedings of the 19th international conference on World Wide Web, WWW 2010. ACM, pp 881–890

Saracevic T (1996) Relevance reconsidered. In: Proceedings of the second conference on conceptions of library and information science, pp 201–218

Savenkov D, Agichtein E (2014) To hint or not: exploring the effectiveness of search hints for complex informational tasks. In: Proceedings of the 37th international ACM SIGIR conference on research and development in information retrieval, SIGIR 2014. ACM, pp 1115–1118

Singh A, Joachims T (2018) Fairness of exposure in rankings. In: Proceedings of the 24th ACM SIGKDD international conference on knowledge discovery and data mining, KDD 2018. ACM, pp 2219–2228

Singla A, White R, Huang J (2010) Studying trailfinding algorithms for enhanced web search. In: Proceedings of the 33rd international ACM SIGIR conference on research and development in information retrieval, SIGIR 2010. ACM, pp 443–450

Teevan J, Adar E, Jones R, Potts MAS (2007) Information re-retrieval: repeat queries in Yahoo's logs. In: Proceedings of the 30th annual international ACM SIGIR conference on research and development in information retrieval, SIGIR 2007. ACM, pp 151–158

Teevan J, Cutrell E, Fisher D, Drucker SM, Ramos G, André P, Hu C (2009) Visual snippets: summarizing web pages for search and revisitation. In: Proceedings of the SIGCHI conference on human factors in computing systems, CHI 2009. ACM, pp 2023–2032

Tsukuda K, Sakai T, Dou Z, Tanaka K (2013) Estimating intent types for search result diversification. In: Proceedings of the 9th Asia information retrieval societies conference, AIRS 2013. Springer, pp 25–37

Tyler SK, Teevan J (2010) Large scale query log analysis of re-finding. In: Proceedings of the third ACM international conference on web search and data mining, WSDM 2010. ACM, pp 191–200

Umemoto K, Yamamoto T, Tanaka K (2016) ScentBar: a query suggestion interface visualizing the amount of missed relevant information for intrinsically diverse search. In: Proceedings of the 39th international ACM SIGIR conference on research and development in information retrieval, SIGIR 2016. ACM, pp 405–414

Wang X, Yu C, Baumgartner S, Korn F (2018) Relevant document discovery for fact-checking articles. In: Companion proceedings of the the the web conference 2018, international World Wide Web conferences steering committee, WWW 2018, pp 525–533

White R (2013) Beliefs and biases in web search. In: Proceedings of the 36th international ACM SIGIR conference on research and development in information retrieval, SIGIR 2013. ACM, pp 3–12

White RW (2014) Belief dynamics in web search. J Assoc Inf Sci Technol 65(11):2165–2178

White RW, Horvitz E (2009) Cyberchondria: studies of the escalation of medical concerns in web search. ACM Trans Inf Syst 27(4):23:1–23:37

White RW, Huang J (2010) Assessing the scenic route: measuring the value of search trails in web logs. In: Proceedings of the 33rd international ACM SIGIR conference on research and development in information retrieval, SIGIR 2010. ACM, pp 587–594

White RW, Roth RA (2009) Exploratory search: beyond the query-response paradigm. Synthesis lectures on information concepts, retrieval, and services. Morgan & Claypool Publishers

White RW, Bilenko M, Cucerzan S (2007) Studying the use of popular destinations to enhance web search interaction. In: Proceedings of the 30th annual international ACM SIGIR conference on research and development in information retrieval, SIGIR 2007. ACM, pp 159–166

White RW, Dumais ST, Teevan J (2009) Characterizing the influence of domain expertise on web search behavior. In: Proceedings of the second ACM international conference on web search and data mining, WSDM 2009. ACM, pp 132–141

Wildemuth BM, Freund L (2012) Assigning search tasks designed to elicit exploratory search behaviors. In: Proceedings of the symposium on human-computer interaction and information retrieval, HCIR 2012. ACM, pp 4:1–4:10

Yamamoto Y, Shimada S (2016) Can disputed topic suggestion enhance user consideration of information credibility in web search? In: Proceedings of the 27th ACM conference on hypertext and social media, HT 2016. ACM, pp 169–177

Yamamoto Y, Tanaka K (2011) Enhancing credibility judgment of web search results. In: Proceedings of the SIGCHI conference on human factors in computing systems, CHI 2011. ACM, pp 1235–1244

Yamamoto Y, Yamamoto T (2018) Query priming for promoting critical thinking in web search. In: Proceedings of the 2018 conference on human information interaction & retrieval, CHIIR 2018. ACM, pp 12–21

Yuan X, White R (2012) Building the trail best traveled: effects of domain knowledge on web search trailblazing. In: Proceedings of the SIGCHI conference on human factors in computing systems, CHI 2012. ACM, pp 1795–1804

Zha ZJ, Yang L, Mei T, Wang M, Wang Z (2009) Visual query suggestion. In: Proceedings of the 17th ACM international conference on multimedia, MM 2009. ACM, pp 15–24

Zhang Y, Zhang Y, Zhang M (2019) Report on EARS'18: 1st international workshop on explainable recommendation and search. SIGIR Forum 52(2):125–131

Chapter 9
Eye-Tracking as a Method for Enhancing Research on Information Search

Jacek Gwizdka and Andrew Dillon

Abstract The human eye plays an essential role in information acquisition from external world, and much of our contemporary information technology relies on visual processing. The eye-mind hypothesis suggests that human attention is connected to where our eyes are looking (Just and Carpenter 1980). Taken together with the continual movement of our eyes and the limited area of high-acuity human vision, eye-tracking methods are considered to offer theoretically reliable measures of visual attention and search task activities. We first briefly review cognitive factors of interest to information search and the "traditional" methods of their measurement. We then present examples of eye tracking tools and how they capture data before examining how eye-tracking data has been used to assess select cognitive factors in information search.

9.1 Introduction

While the term 'information search' (IS) is often used to convey the fast 'term generation and results judgement' cycle of interaction, the actual nature of searching in cognitive terms is complex and extends beyond simple input-output loops of search engines. Rather, searching involves the recognition of an information need, the translation of this need into an exploratory act involving physical, perceptual and cognitive co-ordination as appropriate screen locations are found and suitable query terms are generated, entered and interpreted. The definition of a search task is complicated by the extended nature of many people's information activities. Outputs from a search might not mark the end but only be a partial step toward completing the initial search goal. As search results are selected, partially read and comprehended, these can lead to further refined query terms as this sub-task is repeated, sometimes multiple times, with the user narrowing or broadening expressions, reacting and

J. Gwizdka (✉) · A. Dillon
Information eXperience Lab, School of Information, University of Texas at Austin,
1616 Guadalupe St., Ste. 5.202, Austin, TX 78701, USA
e-mail: jacekg@ischool.utexas.edu

© Springer Nature Switzerland AG 2020
W. T. Fu and H. van Oostendorp (eds.), *Understanding and Improving Information Search*, Human–Computer Interaction Series,
https://doi.org/10.1007/978-3-030-38825-6_9

attempting to incorporate the results into their model of their own information need at that time and assessing when sufficient information has been obtained. While some tasks might be relatively quick and easy (e.g., searching for a factual item such as the latest local weather forecast or the identification of the capital city of a nation), other tasks might be extensive, spread over minutes, hours and perhaps longer (e.g., seeking relevant literature on a topic for a research paper) which might or might not be considered one or more search interactions depending on context.

Viewed this way, we can appreciate that information search involves the complete set of human cognitive processes including perception, comprehension, decision making, attention allocation, and knowledge integration. In many ways information search is a particular form of reading activity, mixing rapid scanning and extended engagement with text and images, and the commensurate interplay of all the underlying components and processes we associate with this skilled act.

When considering the cognitive characteristics that are of most interest to IS research, it is worth drawing a distinction between stable (or fixed) and dynamic (or fluid) attributes of human processing. By definition, stable characteristics do not change over extended periods of time, and can be assumed to remain constant during an information search session. The most pertinent stable cognitive characteristics studied in information search typically include specific abilities or cognitive styles (Arguello and Choi 2019; Brennan et al. 2014; Chen et al. 2005; Ford et al. 2005; Frias-Martinez et al. 2009; Goodale et al. 2014; Gwizdka 2009, 2017; Karanam and van Oostendorp 2016a; for example, Palmquist and Kim 2000) but might also include the searcher's level of education, prior knowledge in the task domain (Cole et al. 2013; Dinet et al. 2010; Guo et al. 2014; Karanam et al. 2017a; Liu et al. 2012; Wildemuth 2004), personality (Heinstrőm 2003), or even age (Karanam et al. 2017b; Karanam and van Oostendorp 2016b, 2017), where the focus is on the different processing characteristics of people across the human lifespan.

In contrast, dynamic or fluid attributes can change quickly, typically in the time range of milliseconds to minutes (Pirolli 2009), and result from internal thought processes, external or contextual factors, or perhaps from their interaction. Since cognition is a dynamic process, we conceive of searching as involving an ongoing series of judgements, decision making, mental model construction (Tang and Solomon 1998), even mood changes, which can shift across task completion and varyingly reflect attentional load and allocation (Arapakis et al. 2010; Lopatovska 2011; Irene Lopatovska 2014).

In traditional information search studies, stable characteristics are frequently assessed by questionnaires or survey tools, or, where the acquisition of new information or knowledge is of interest, by pre- and post-task assessments. As such, there are multiple tools and techniques available to researchers interested in measuring stable cognitive characteristics in the search task environment. In assessing the more fluid aspects of cognition while searching, researchers have relied traditionally on process measures such as mouse movements and clicks, concurrent verbal protocols, navigation path selection and people's articulated or observed relevance judgements (see Dillon 2004 for a summary). Researchers have also employed secondary task measures to identify attentional focus and cognitive load (Gwizdka 2010). Such methods have provided useful insights into the processes searchers go through in completing a task but are comparatively gross, in analytical terms, compared to the data it is possible to capture with eye-tracking tools which can offer a more fine-grained and objective set of measures concerning eye-location and duration of fixations throughout the process. With these finer-grained measures, we can not only begin to determine the focus and progression of searcher attention in real-time, but also compare these data with the verbal reports and even post-task recollections and explanations offered by participants in typical studies to determine accurate correlates between methods. Furthermore, many modern eye-tracking tools are comparatively non-invasive, allowing for a more natural and perhaps even ecologically valid form of data capture than methods such as secondary tasks and concurrent verbal protocols.

In the following sections we explore specific examples of eye-tracking technologies and outline how they operate. Then we explain how a typical eye-tracking experimental session is organized before highlighting how eye-tracking methods have been applied in information search studies. In conclusion we argue that this technique of data capture is beneficial in both methodological and theoretical terms.

9.2 Eye-Tracking

Eye-tracking (ET) equipment aims to provide real-time information on where a person is looking. At any point in time, the human eye is capable of seeing with high acuity only a tiny fraction of the surrounding world, approximately 1.5–2° of visual angle—so called foveal vision. Outside this small area our peripheral vision reaches approximately 90° in each direction but the perceived image becomes progressively blurred and we can perceive movement but not the detail (visual acuity drops sharply from 100% in foveal view to 25% at around 6–7° of visual angle [Rayner et al. 2011]). Therefore, in order to perceive the surrounding world, our eyes need to oscillate or move continually. Normal eye movements consist of periods when the eyes are (relatively) still and periods of rapid jumps in-between. The former are called *fixations*, the latter *saccades*. Both are examples of what are termed *eye events*. Another eye event of interest is the *blink* (Holmqvist et al. 2011), a normal physical movement of the eyelids which keeps the eyes moist and free of irritants.

Visual information is acquired by humans only when our eyes fixate. Visual details essential for reading are captured only in the foveal view, in which we can see approximately 4–6 characters. It has been experimentally established that when reading an alphabetic language, such as English, we can see up to around 14 characters to the right (in the direction of reading) and four characters to the left (Rayner et al. 2011). Eye movements (in particular those movements involved in reading) are controlled by cognition (what we term as a top-down process) and by perception (a bottom-up process) (Findlay and Gilchrist 2003; Rayner et al. 2011). In other words, the act involves the dual engagement of perceptual and cognitive activities. According to some contemporary reading models the eyes fixate until cognitive processing is completed (Rayner 1998; Rayner et al. 2011) and then proceed to jump forward using cues from para-foveal vision (approximately six degrees of visual angle [Rayner 1975; Schotter et al. 2011]) to guide movements. Eyes can also move backward during reading. These movements are called *regressions* and occur approximately 10–15% of the time in skilled readers (Rayner 2009; Reichle et al. 2003). On texts at the appropriate difficulty level for skilled readers, regressions are typically to the immediately preceding word. When the text is difficult for the reader, regressions are often more long-range and occur to earlier words in the text.

Taken together, we can say that attention is where our eyes are looking—this is frequently referred to as the *eye-mind hypothesis* (Just and Carpenter 1980). While this is an oversimplification and covert attention phenomena are known (Findlay 2003), we can safely assume for our purposes that in the context of information search (where information is largely textual) the eye-mind hypothesis generally holds.

9.2.1   Types of Eye-Trackers

The first devices to track eye movement were built towards the end of XIX c. These original eye-trackers were comparatively crude and mechanical (Delabarre 1898; Huey 1898) and required subjects to be restrained to maintain posture or to use bite-bars to keep their heads still. It is interesting to note that the first experimental use of eye tracking was to investigate reading processes, and as noted by Dillon (2016), the findings of early research on eye-movements proved to be remarkably accurate in terms of later discoveries and data captured with more advanced technologies. A major later development involved camera-based eye-trackers which became the dominant technology in later years. To avoid interference with visible light, modern eye-trackers use near-infrared light sources and cameras. They come in three main flavors, remote eye-trackers (fixed under or above a display, see Figs. 9.1 and 9.2), wearable eye-trackers (built into specialized eye-glasses, see Fig. 9.3), and eye-tracker add-ons for virtual and augmented reality headsets (see Fig. 9.4). These eye-trackers capture images of reflections from the cornea (the outer part of eye) and eye pupil and employ geometry to calculate in real-time where each eye is looking, in case of remote eye-trackers on computer screen in screen coordinates, and in case of wearable eye-trackers, in external world in degrees of visual angle.

One of the most important parameters of an eye-tracker is its frequency of operation. This reflects the speed of image capture and thus acquisition speed of eye positions. Typical speeds are 50 or 60 Hz (tied to alternating current power supply frequency in a given area of the world), which correspond to recording eye gaze position every 20 ms and 16.67 ms respectively. Some low-end eye-trackers operate at 30 Hz while the frequency of fast, while higher-end eye-tracker speeds range from 250 to 2000 Hz.

The raw data from eye-tracking devices contains information about eye gaze points but not eye events. To obtain eye events the raw data needs to be further processed with dedicated software which typically applies off-line algorithms to identify fixations and saccades. Two frequently used fixation detection methods are

Fig. 9.1 Example high-end remote eye-tracker built into a display (Tobii TX-300) (*Image credit* Tobii AB. Used with permission)

Fig. 9.2 Example low-end remote eye-tracker built into a display (Gazepoint GP3 60 Hz) (*Image source* https://www.gazept.com/product/gazepoint-gp3-eye-tracker/ Used with permission)

dispersion-threshold identification (I-DT) and velocity threshold identification (I-VT). I-DT is based on the fact that during fixations gaze points tend to cluster closely together because of the slow speed of eye movement. I-VT is a velocity-based method which uses moment-to-moment velocities between gaze points to identify fixations and saccades (Salvucci and Goldberg 2000). Of most interest to IS research are eye fixations. Remote eye-tracking devices provide fixation data that consists of sequence of triplets $<x, y, t>$, where: (x, y) are the screen coordinates (in pixels) and t is the timestamp (in milliseconds).

An additional measure typically captured by eye-trackers is pupil diameter, which is also of interest to researchers examining information search. Pupil dilation is controlled by the autonomic nervous system (Onorati et al. 2013), and under constant illumination, pupil dilation has been associated with a number of cognitive functions,

Fig. 9.3 Example wearable
middle-end eye-tracking
glasses (Pupil Labs Glasses)
(*Image source* https://pupil-
labs.com/store/ Used with
permission)

Fig. 9.4 Example
middle-end eye-tracker
add-on for virtual reality
(Pupil Labs) (*Image source*
https://pupil-labs.com/store/
Used with permission)

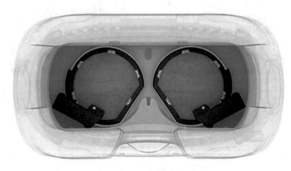

including mental workload (Kahneman and Beatty 1966), interest (Krugman 1964),
surprise (Preuschoff et al. 2011), and decision making (Preuschoff et al. 2011). Given
the tools and the range of measures possible, in the next section we outline how a
typical eye-tracking session is set up and run.

9.2.2 A Typical Eye-Tracking Procedure

Collecting eye-tracking data starts with a calibration procedure that needs to be performed for each study participant. For remote eye-trackers, the participant should be seated approximately 50–70 cm away from the monitor (this distance varies slightly with eye-tracker model). Calibration requires participants to look at a moving dot displayed on screen. The participant is asked to follow the dot with their eyes only and fixate on it whenever it pauses. For wearable eye-trackers, the procedure is similar and involves participant looking at specified points in the surrounding environment. Data recorded during calibration is used to map the points on which the participant looked at with the appearance of their eyes at these locations. After calibration is successfully completed, data recording starts. Calibration is not always assured however for every participant. This may be the case when eyesight correction or eye features interfere with the tracker's operation. For example, corrective glasses may cause tracking issues if the lenses are too small, multi-focal or have thick frames. Contact lenses are generally easier to work with, but may pose problems when air bubbles under the lenses create additional reflections. Participants with drooping eyelids, long eye-lashes or heavy use of make-up such as mascara may also cause interference with detection of pupils, therefore participants should be instructed not to wear any make-up for an eye-tracking study. Nonetheless, it is always the case that use of eye-tracking tools involves a necessary set-up process to ensure individual participant's data capture can proceed effectively.

For remote eye-trackers, tracking conditions should match the calibration conditions. The ambient light should not be changed (best results are obtained in windowless rooms with fluorescent lights) and the participant position in relation to the eye-tracker should remain the same. That is, participants are not allowed to move the chair or to change their posture. However, head movement is allowed within small head box the size of which depends on the eye-tracker model and ranges from 25 × 11 cm (for smaller, low-end eye-trackers) to 50 × 36 or even 40 × 90 cm (for higher-end eye-trackers). If tracking conditions change, the participant needs to be recalibrated.

Another consideration is the eye-tracker's accuracy. Typical accuracy ranges from 0.4–1 degree of visual angle (depending on the model) at the typical distance from monitor (approximately 65 cm). This corresponds to about half an inch or 1.2 cm. The manufacturer's accuracy specification is provided for ideal conditions, in real life the difference between measured and actual gaze locations will be larger for participants with corrective lenses or if they move during the test window. The eye-trackers calibration typically outputs the average accuracy measured for a person being calibrated. Depending on the research goals, some researchers do not proceed with eye-tracking data collection unless calibration accuracy is less than 0.5° (Tatler 2007), while others accept worse calibration accuracy (e.g., Komogortsev and Khan 2008 accepted accuracy up to 1.7°). In reading studies the height of words (the distance between the ascender and descender lines) should be greater than the measured accuracy.

After data collection is completed and before moving into analysis, the data needs to be cleansed. Three main considerations in cleansing eye-tracking data are the quality of calibration, missing data samples, and offsets. If calibration was poor or unsuccessful then the eye-tracking data cannot be used, but other types of interaction data, if collected, may still be useful. Eye-tracking data may be missing for several reasons. If participants blink, look down, or away from screen their eye gaze will not be captured. This is acceptable as we routinely expect people to do this occasionally in normal contexts. Researchers can minimize the need to look away by minimizing the need to consult printed instructions and instead provide all instructions on the same computer screen (on demand). Missing data samples can also be caused by corrective lenses or eye features as described above. Researchers should set a threshold for acceptable level of missing data. Typically, these levels are set between 10–30%. After good calibration, the offset, that is the difference between the actual and the measured gaze location, is expected to be small. However, given the multiplicity of factors influencing eye-tracking data collection the offset may increase or fluctuate. One way to discover when it happens is by monitoring in real-time on secondary monitor the content of participant screen and their eye movements and checking for discrepancies. It should be noted when occurring, and, if possible, corrective action taken. For example, the researcher may need to prompt the participant to sit straight.

After cleansing data, only then can researchers proceed to data analysis. Presenting full scope of eye-tracking data analysis and how it can be combined with other supplementary data sources is beyond the scope of the current chapter. Basically, both qualitative and quantitative analyses are employed by researchers. The former involves reviewing and annotating a video replay of screen states with superimposed eye movement or data visualizations presented. The latter involves exporting eye-event data and working with it in spreadsheet, statistical analysis or data mining software to determine specific measures of key variables of interest to the researcher e.g., fixation durations and locations and to examine their spatial and temporal patterns. One particular eye-movement pattern of interest reflects reading. We describe modeling reading using eye-tracking data in the next subsection.

9.2.3   Using Eye-Tracking Data to Model Reading

Information search is a particular form of reading activity which includes eye fixations on text and rapid text scanning. Not surprisingly researchers frequently use eye-tracking data to model reading in information search (Biedert et al. 2012; Campbell and Maglio 2001; Cole et al. 2011). The exported and cleansed eye-tracking data is processed by algorithms (e.g., classification) to detect the reading states a searcher goes through. Here we describe one approach based on our own work.

We model eye movements in reading using our approach described in (Cole et al. 2011), which we briefly summarize. Our approach is influenced by the EZ Reader

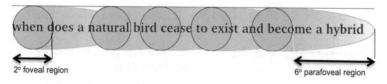

2° foveal region   6° parafoveal region

Fig. 9.5 Sequence of reading fixations

model (Rayner et al. 2011; Reichle et al. 2006). EZ Reader proposes a cognitively-controlled, serial-attention model of eye movements in reading. It takes word iden-tification, visual processing, attention, and control of the oculomotor system as joint determinants of eye movement in the reading process. It posits that the saccade to the next word is programmed while the text in the current fixation is being cognitively processed. Assumptions of that model that are pertinent to our work are as follows: (1) reading is serial and words are processed one at a time in the order of their appear-ance in text, (2) more than one word can be processed on single fixation when the next word in the reading direction is identified in para-foveal view (Rayner 1975; Schotter et al. 2011), and (3) there is a minimum fixation time required for acqui-sition of a word's meaning (Fig. 9.5). In practice, the fixation duration threshold is dependent on the speed of eye-tracker and the algorithm used to identify fixations. In our work we have used 110 ms for a faster eye-tracker (300 Hz) and I-VT algorithm, while 150 ms for a slower eye-tracker (60 Hz) and I-DT algorithm.

We refer to fixations above this threshold as lexical fixations. We use temporal as well as spatial features of lexical fixations and classify them into two reading states: reading and scanning. A scanning state represents isolated lexical fixations. A reading state represents reading in one line, if reading continues to the subsequent line it is currently represented as a new reading state. Output from this computa-tional model labels fixations as reading or scanning and calculates probabilities of transitions between the reading and scanning states (Fig. 9.6). The resulting reading characterization can then be related to differences in documents, search tasks, or cog-nitive factors. This approach to modeling reading is relatively robust as it does not rely on identifying fixations on individual words, and, instead, uses features of the human visual system engaged in reading, such as the size of foveal and para-foveal view calculated in the linear dimensions of the computer screen.

Fig. 9.6 Two-state modeling of reading p and q are probabilities of transitions between states

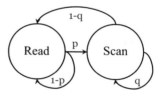

9.3 Contributions Made by Eye-Tracking to IS Research

In our view eye-tracking contributes to IS research in two main ways, by improving the measurement of cognitive factors compared to traditional methods, and by offering unique insights into traditionally-not-measurable or difficult to measure cognitive factors. In this section we illustrate how research on selected cognitive factors has been informed by studies involving the eye-tracking method.

9.3.1 Domain Knowledge

The effects of domain knowledge on information search behavior are well established in IS research (Dinet et al. 2010; Guo et al. 2014; Karanam et al. 2017a; Liu et al. 2012; Wildemuth 2004). One can ask if differences in domain knowledge are reflected in eye-tracking measures. From research in reading psychology we know that in constrained experimental reading paradigms (e.g., reading one word at a time) fixation durations are longer on less familiar words (Rayner et al. 2011; Reichle et al. 2003). Thus, it is reasonable to expect differences in more open ended experimental paradigms such as in information search tasks, and we can ask how eye movements and eye fixations on information search tasks are affected by the differences in domain knowledge?

To investigate this question Cole and colleagues captured eye-tracking data on five genomics-related search tasks from 40 participants who differed in their knowledge of genomics (Cole et al. 2013). They evaluated participant knowledge using self-ratings of knowledge of 409 genomics-related terms and calculated cognitive effort measures associated with reading eye movements (such as reading speed and length, spacing of fixations, median, maximum, and total fixation durations) during the search tasks. They found that these content-independent measures were all good predictors of searchers' level of genomics domain knowledge.

Other researchers investigated this research question in different knowledge domains and information search paradigms. For example, Lu et al. (2018) conducted eye-tracking study with 24 participants who were asked to find and read information on statistics topic in three types of tasks (fact finding task, partial understanding task, and full-text understanding task) performed on a hierarchically structured and navigable document. They found that the total fixation duration on text area was significantly longer for novices than for experts, and did not find differences on any other eye-tracking measures.

These results suggest there is a possibility of real-time detection of differences in domain knowledge using this method too, raising interesting potential questions about the underlying perceptual and cognitive processes associated with more knowledgeable performance.

9.3.2 Search as Learning

In recent years the view of *search as learning* has gained increased interest among some scholars (Eickhoff et al. 2017; Freund et al. 2014; Gwizdka et al. 2016; Rieh et al. 2016). The view of *search as learning* is highly variable (Hansen and Rieh 2016; Rieh et al. 2016), but one aspect relevant to information search processes is the examination of learning processes in the evaluation of search systems (Freund et al. 2013).

If we consider learning as an integral part of information search process, one challenge then is how to measure human learning. Search provides an opportunity for learning on multiple levels (Anderson et al. 2001). For example, Bhattacharya and Gwizdka (2019) measured changes in verbal knowledge level (Anderson et al. 2001) of health search topics before and after two multi-aspectual health information search tasks. Eye-tracking measures related to acquiring information use (task duration, total length of backward regressions in reading, mean and total duration of reading fixations) were found to differ significantly between two groups ($n = 30$), those who learned fewer words and those who learned more words. Such work gives us suggestive insights into what is happening when users learn and leads us to consider how we might instruct people or design displays that encourage deeper information processing so as to increase knowledge in a domain.

9.3.3 Cognitive Load

Assessing cognitive load or mental effort experienced by a user during information search is important for understanding cognitive demands imposed by search tasks, search interfaces, and information displays, and for identifying where, and possibly how, to lower the mental effort required for effective interaction with information. Cognitive load has related to and explained by the load on working memory (Sweller et al. 2011). More broadly cognitive load can be understood as arising from the relation between the demands on mental resources imposed by a task and an information system, and the person's ability to supply those (Moray 1979). For a long time eye-tracking measures have been considered as possible indicators of cognitive load. Three classes of complementary eye-tracking measures are of interest, (1) eye-movement-related (e.g., fixation duration, fixation rate, saccade length and duration), (2) pupil diameter, and (3) blinks (rate and duration). As early as in the 1960s Kahneman and Beatty (1966) showed that pupil dilates with increased mental load (for a review of a more recent work see: van der Wel and van Steenbergen 2018). Fixation duration was also shown to be related with mental effort. In particular, it was shown to be longer on infrequent and more difficult words, which require more mental processing (Rayner et al. 2011; Reichle et al. 2003). Further, eye blinks were demonstrated to correlate with mental effort (Veltman and Gaillard 1998).

In one of the first studies in this area Marshall (2002) created index of cognitive activity (ICA) which was computed in real-time from abrupt discontinuities in pupil diameter. More recently (Buettner et al. 2015) demonstrated the feasibility of using low-cost eye-trackers to obtain real-time pupil measurements to assess user performance on communication and information tasks. (Greef et al. 2009) found significant differences in pupil dilation and fixation duration between information surveillance and reconnaissance tasks performed on military naval ships.

Chen et al. (2011) combined three classes of eye-tracking measures (eye-movement, pupil diameter, and blinks) and applied them to assessing mental effort on sports training video viewing tasks. They reported differences in all eye-tracking measures and showed improvements in discriminating different effort levels that can be made by combining multiple eye-tracking features.

9.3.4 Cognitive Abilities—Working Memory

One of the most widely applied theories of cognitive abilities is Carroll's three-stratum model (Carroll 1993). At the most detailed and lowest level, the model contains over 70 specific abilities that can be assessed. Selected abilities from this large set have been studied in terms of their impact on information search, an incomplete list would include, for example, examinations of associative memory (Brennan et al. 2014), perceptual speed (Arguello and Choi 2019; Brennan et al. 2014), spatial ability (Karanam and van Oostendorp 2016a), visualization abilities (Brennan et al. 2014), verbal closure (Gwizdka 2009), and working memory (Arguello and Choi 2019; Gwizdka 2009, 2013a). Gwizdka, for example, found that on more demanding search tasks low and high WM searchers behaved differently. High-WM searchers tended to perform more actions to find more information, while low-WM users changed their behavior on more difficult search tasks by significantly decreasing the number of documents they visited (Gwizdka 2013a, b). This difference in behavior between the two searcher groups could potentially be explained by satisficing (Simon 1956).

More recently, Arguello and Choi (2019) found that high-WM searchers experienced lower workload than low-WM searchers on the same tasks. Further, they observed that high-WM participants worked at a faster pace and seemed to perform more search actions (e.g., bookmarked more web pages) than low-WM participants (Arguello and Choi 2019). Such results, in combination, suggest that high-WM searchers can perform more actions even in more demanding conditions, indicating WM capacity and speed might be significant cognitive predictors of performance. Where employed, eye-tracking data sheds specific light on search task performance related to the differences in WM. For example, Gwizdka found that searchers with high-WM tended to read more (Gwizdka 2017). This difference was particularly apparent on search engine result pages (SERPs). The absolute reading time and time relative to the search task time were statistically significantly longer for high-WM than for low-WM. In this analysis, dividing search tasks into three phases, the results indicated that in the last phase of search tasks, low-WM searchers tended to read less on opened document pages, but at the same time they seemed to increase their reading time on SERPs. This could, again, be a searcher's satisficing strategy (Simon 1956), similar to the one observed in Gwizdka (2013a, b).

Such observed behavior can be framed using concepts from information foraging theory (Pirolli and Card 1999). *Exploration* of information patches corresponds to the time spend on SERPs entering queries and reading search results, while *exploitation* of information patches corresponds to visiting and reading results pages. Select findings from (Gwizdka 2017) for low- and high-WM searchers in the last task phase bear some similarity to findings from (Chin et al. 2015) where, in tasks with lower availability of information, older adults did less exploitation than younger adults by reducing the number of visited document pages. Instead, older adults did more exploration by spending more time on SERPs. Thus the pattern of differences between older and younger adults resembles that between low- and high-WM searchers observed in (Gwizdka 2017). A more thorough comparison between these two studies is difficult because thanks to the use of eye-tracking the latter study contains not only the record of searcher query entry, web page opening along with associated dwell times, but also finer-grain record level of human behavior (such as reading). In the context of the present chapter the study by Gwizdka (2017) exemplifies how eye-tracking data can help us understand how an WM ability might manifest itself in key aspects of task performance.

9.3.5 Relevance Judgements

A particular construct of interest to IS research is information *relevance*. Typical usage of relevance refers to "the quality or state of being closely connected or appropriate".[1] In information science, relevance is a fundamental concept, and the concern with better understanding the human perception or interpretation of relevance continues to be important (Saracevic 2007, 2016; Sonnenwald 2016, Chapter 8, page 152). IS scholars generally agree on five manifestations of relevance: system or algorithmic relevance, subject or topical relevance, pertinence or cognitive relevance, usefulness or situational relevance, and affective relevance (Belkin 2016; Borlund 2003; Cole et al. 2009; Cosijn and Ingwersen 2000; Saracevic 1996, 2007, 2016). For eye-tracking-based relevance assessment the most pertinent manifestation is the *situational relevance*. Situational relevance reflects the relation between searcher's situation, task, or problem at hand and information, and it is assessed by considering the usefulness of information in decision making, and its appropriateness in satisfying a searcher's information need (Saracevic 2016; Sonnenwald 2016). This relevance manifestation reflects the user-centered perspective in which relevance arises from interactions between searcher's information need and information objects (Borlund 2003) and while there are still debates about the best definition or operationalization

---

[1]Oxford dictionary, https://www.lexico.com/en/definition/relevance.

of the construct, the importance of relevance to the process of human information search is self-evident.

Eye tracking offers a particularly unique approach to the study of relevance. Whereby typical studies extract relevance judgements from users or from domain experts who examine a pool of results, with eye-tracking we can correlate measurable differences in user behavior with judgements, thereby adding objective processing and performance indices to ratings. This approach has utilized measures derived from fixations (e.g., duration), saccades (e.g., duration, distance, speed), and pupil dilation. For example, Buscher et al. (2012) found the strongest indicator in text passage relevance was length of text read, though fixation duration was uncorrelated.

Gwizdka (2014) used a broader set of measures derived from eye-tracking including the output from the reading model (see Sect. 9.2.3). He observed the highest probability of reading for relevant documents, while the highest probability of scanning occurred for irrelevant documents. Judging the relevance of topical (but not relevant) documents required greater mental effort, while judging irrelevant (off-topic) documents was the easiest. Reading speed in screen-pixels was higher for topical and relevant documents, while it was lower for irrelevant documents. However, there was no difference in reading speed measured by number of words between the different types of documents. Total number of fixations and reading duration normalized per word, were significantly higher for the relevant than for irrelevant documents.

Gwizdka et al. (2017) re-analyzed eye-tracking data set that was reported in Gwizdka (2014) using the data limited to one second before the relevance decision. They found reading distance, total duration of reading and scanning fixations, and variability of these measures differed significantly and were the best predictors of judgements of relevant and irrelevant documents. On relevant documents participants seemed to do more reading, less scanning, and had more variability in fixation duration and reading distance.

Other work has treated relevance judgements as a form of decision making that should affect pupil dilation (Preuschoff et al. 2011). As expected, changes in searchers' pupil diameter have been demonstrated in response to differing levels of information relevance. For example, Oliveria and colleagues (Oliveira et al. 2009) first reported that readers' pupils dilated for higher relevance text and image stimuli and since then Gwizdka and colleagues have shown significant pupil dilation on relevant documents, in particular, during the one-to-two second period preceding the relevance decision. This effect is consistent for short text documents (Gwizdka 2014; Gwizdka et al. 2017) and for web pages (Gwizdka 2018; Gwizdka and Zhang 2015) which suggests that there are physiological correlates of relevance that users might provide which do not rely on, and which even precede, verbal reports. This opens up a very different line of research on how humans determine relevance, and the speed with which this decision can be taken. In sum, processing relevant documents compared with irrelevant documents tends to require more reading and more mental effort, which is typically reflected in eye movement patterns, increased fixation durations, and pupil dilation.

New developments in machine learning algorithms and eye-tracking (often in combination with electroencephalography (EEG)) data offer intriguing possibilities in building systems which adapt to users by incorporating implicit relevance feedback into information retrieval. One difficulty in dealing with eye-tracking (and, more generally, neurophysiological) signals in real-time systems is noise, potential incompleteness, and idiosyncrasy. Obtaining calibration data for each person, and possibly each task type, in naturalistic settings may prove difficult. Nonetheless, successful attempts have been reported in the literature. First, Ajanki et al. (2009) used eye-movement-based features to select additional query terms in an implicit relevance feedback system. Eye-movement features that significantly contributed to their model included regressions from following words and relative duration of the first fixation on a word. This work showed a modest improvement in mean average precision (MAP) on the document retrieval tasks when the eye-based features were used to select additional query terms.

More recently, Jacucci et al. (2019) described the first fully integrated information retrieval system that makes use of real-time implicit relevance feedback generated from brain signals (measured using EEG), and eye movements. They were able to compute information relevance in real-time with performance significantly better than chance for the majority of study participants (80%). For some of these participants the achieved classification accuracy was over 70% (the specific classification measure reported in this work was the area under receiver operating characteristic curve (AUROC) > 70%). Low performance for the remaining 20% participants was likely due to fact that EEG feedback does not typically work well for approximately 15–30% people. Although experimental measures of task performance did not allow the authors to demonstrate how the classification outcomes translated into search task performance, this work points to a future where dynamic engagement of users with information spaces may be possible.

9.4 Conclusions and Outlook

Information search is a routine human activity we all increasingly engage in as part of our work and leisure. Research on information search has shown that the process is complex and involves a wide range of perceptual and cognitive processes that vary across tasks and individuals. Traditionally, researchers interested in studying these processes have relied heavily on verbal or outcome-based measures to establish choices, paths and decisions made by searchers, and have correlated these with various individual differences in cognitive abilities or preference. This work has yielded many interesting findings but has lacked precision in helping us identify important psychological determinants of search behavior.

Eye tracking data now offers us the ability to examine where user attention is focused, how different user types explore an information display, and what perceptual behaviors precede or correlate with performance and judgements of relevance. Such fine-grained data capture serves to complement existing methods by extending our insights into the underlying processes involved in the act of searching. On its own, eye tracking provides a very rich data stream which delivers a clear window into where attention is focused, but in combination with more established methods of human task performance gives us the opportunity to correlate attention and behavior with expressed choices and outcomes.

There is a further benefit to be gained from the precision of eye-tracking methods in terms of design. While typical tests of interface usability might compare two designs in terms of task performance or user preference, eye-tracking can help us determine which features of an information space are really important to user performance (that is, users allocate attention to their presence) rather than reported as important based on post-task comments or ratings. Over time, the body of research obtained this way can better inform interface designers of what features are not just liked or remembered but actually enhance or detract from performance.

More recent projects employ eye-tracking data in a feedback loop which creates a new intriguing possibility for building adaptive systems with human in the loop. Such work points to a time when information systems might infer relevance directly from eye-tracking data (possibly together with other neurophysiological signals) and combine it with explicit user interactions, where they exist, to effectively improve information search processes without requiring users to invest significant explicit effort.

Eye-tracking tools have developed sufficiently now to be affordable and usable by most trained researchers, and this should be welcomed. However, in closing, it is important to reiterate that use of the method and interpretation of the resulting data are not equivalent. To gain value from the results of eye-tracking techniques, researchers should understand human information processing and the underlying perceptual and cognitive architecture of our minds so as to best interpret this rich but complex data type.

Acknowledgements The authors wish to thank the research support from the 2011 Google Faculty Research Award to Jacek Gwizdka, Institute for Museum and Library Studies (IMLS) Career Development Grant to Jacek Gwizdka #RE-04-11-0062-11A, and the Portuguese Foundation for Science and Technology and the Digital Media Program at University of Texas at Austin. Andrew Dillon wishes to thank the V.M. Daniel Professorship for research support.

References

Ajanki A, Hardoon DR, Kaski S, Puolamäki K, Shawe-Taylor J (2009) Can eyes reveal interest? implicit queries from gaze patterns. User Model User-Adap Inter 19(4):307–339. https://doi.org/10.1007/s11257-009-9066-4

Anderson LW, Krathwohl DR, Bloom BS. (2001) A taxonomy for learning, teaching, and assessing: a revision of Bloom's taxonomy of educational objectives. Longman

Arapakis I, Athanasakos K, Jose JM (2010) A comparison of general vs personalised affective models for the prediction of topical relevance. In: Proceedings of the 33rd international ACM SIGIR conference on research and development in information retrieval. ACM, New York, NY, USA, pp 371–378. https://doi.org/10.1145/1835449.1835512

Arguello J, Choi B (2019) The effects of working memory, perceptual speed, and inhibition in aggregated search. ACM Trans Inf Syst 37(3):36:1–36:34. https://doi.org/10.1145/3322128

Belkin NJ (2016) People, interacting with information. SIGIR Forum 49(2):13–27. https://doi.org/10.1145/2888422.2888424

Bhattacharya N, Gwizdka J (2019) Measuring learning during search: differences in interactions, eye-gaze, and semantic similarity to expert knowledge. In: Proceedings of the 2019 conference on human information interaction and retrieval. ACM, New York, NY, USA, pp 63–71. https://doi.org/10.1145/3295750.3298926

Biedert R, Hees J, Dengel A, Buscher G (2012) A robust realtime reading-skimming classifier. In: Proceedings of the symposium on eye tracking research and applications. ACM, New York, NY, USA, pp 123–130. https://doi.org/10.1145/2168556.2168575

Borlund P (2003) The concept of relevance in IR. J Am Soc Inform Sci Technol 54(10):913–925. https://doi.org/10.1002/asi.10286

Brennan K, Kelly D, Arguello J (2014) The effect of cognitive abilities on information search for tasks of varying levels of complexity. In: Proceedings of the 5th information interaction in context symposium. ACM, New York, NY, USA, pp 165–174. https://doi.org/10.1145/2637002.2637022

Buettner R, Sauer S, Maier C, Eckhardt A (2015) Towards ex ante prediction of user performance: a novel NeuroIS methodology based on real-time measurement of mental effort. In: 2015 48th Hawaii international conference on system sciences. Presented at the 2015 48th Hawaii international conference on system sciences, pp 533–542. https://doi.org/10.1109/HICSS.2015.70

Buscher G, Dengel A, Biedert R, Elst LV (2012) Attentive documents: eye tracking as implicit feedback for information retrieval and beyond. ACM Trans Interact Intell Syst 1(2):9:1–9:30. https://doi.org/10.1145/2070719.2070722

Campbell CS, Maglio PP (2001) A robust algorithm for reading detection. In: Proceedings of the 2001 workshop on perceptive user interfaces. ACM, New York, NY, USA, pp 1–7. https://doi.org/10.1145/971478.971503

Carroll JB (1993) Human cognitive abilities: a survey of factor analytic studies. Cambridge University Press, Cambridge

Chen S, Epps J, Ruiz N, Chen F (2011) Eye activity as a measure of human mental effort in HCI. In: Proceedings of the 15th international conference on intelligent user interfaces. ACM, New York, NY, USA, pp 315–318. https://doi.org/10.1145/1943403.1943454

Chen SY, Magoulas GD, Dimakopoulos D (2005) A flexible interface design for web directories to accommodate different cognitive styles. J Am Soc Inf Sci Technol 56(1):70–83. https://doi.org/10.1002/asi.20103

Chin J, Anderson E, Chin C-L, Fu W-T (2015) Age differences in information search: an exploration-exploitation tradeoff model. Proc Hum Factors Ergon Soc Annu Meet 59(1):85–89. https://doi.org/10.1177/1541931215591018

Cole MJ, Gwizdka J, Liu C, Belkin NJ, Zhang X (2013) Inferring user knowledge level from eye movement patterns. Inf Process Manag 49(5):1075–1091. https://doi.org/10.1016/j.ipm.2012.08.004

Cole MJ, Gwizdka J, Liu C, Bierig R, Belkin NJ, Zhang X (2011) Task and user effects on reading patterns in information search. Interact Comput 23(4):346–362. https://doi.org/10.1016/j.intcom.2011.04.007

Cole M, Liu J, Belkin N, Bierig R, Gwizdka J, Liu C et al (2009) Usefulness as the criterion for evaluation of interactive information retrieval. In: Third workshop on human computer interaction and information retrieval (HCIR '09). Presented at the HCIR'09, pp 1–4

Cosijn E, Ingwersen P (2000) Dimensions of relevance. Inf Process Manag 36(4):533–550. https://doi.org/10.1016/S0306-4573(99)00072-2

Delabarre EB (1898) A method of recording eye-movements. Am J Psychol 9(4):572–574. https://doi.org/10.2307/1412191

Dillon A (2004) Designing usable electronic text. 2nd edition, Boca Raton: CRC Press

Dillon A (2016) Theory for design: the case of reading. In: Sonnenwald DH (ed) Theory development in the information sciences. University of Texas Press, Austin, TX, USA, pp 222–238

Dinet J, Bastien JMC, Kitajima M (2010) What, where and how are young people looking for in a search engine results page?: impact of typographical cues and prior domain knowledge. In: Proceedings of the 22nd conference on L'Interaction Homme-Machine. ACM, New York, NY, USA, pp 105–112. https://doi.org/10.1145/1941007.1941022

Eickhoff C, Gwizdka J, Hauff C, He J (2017) Introduction to the special issue on search as learning. Inf Retr J 20(5):399–402. https://doi.org/10.1007/s10791-017-9315-9

Findlay JM (2003) Visual selection, covert attention and eye movements. In: Active vision: the psychology of looking and seeing. Oxford University Press. Accessed 6 Feb 2019

Findlay JJM, Gilchrist ID (2003) Active vision: the psychology of looking and seeing. Oxford University Press, Incorporated

Ford N, Miller D, Moss N (2005) Web search strategies and human individual differences: cognitive and demographic factors, Internet attitudes, and approaches. J Am Soc Inf Sci Technol 56(7):741–756. https://doi.org/10.1002/asi.20168

Freund L, Gwizdka J, Hansen P, Kando N, Rieh SY (2013) From searching to learning. In: Agosti M, Fuhr N, Toms E, Vakkari P (eds) Evaluation methodologies in information retrieval, vol 13441, pp 102–105. http://drops.dagstuhl.de/opus/volltexte/2014/4433

Freund L, He J, Gwizdka J, Kando N, Hansen P, Rieh SY (2014) Searching As Learning (SAL) workshop 2014. In: Proceedings of the 5th information interaction in context symposium. ACM, New York, NY, USA, pp 7–7. https://doi.org/10.1145/2637002.2643203

Frias-Martinez E, Chen SY, Liu X (2009) Evaluation of a personalized digital library based on cognitive styles: adaptivity vs. adaptability. Int J Inf Manage 29(1):48–56. https://doi.org/10.1016/j.ijinfomgt.2008.01.012

Goodale P, David Clough P, Fernando S, Ford N, Stevenson M (2014) Cognitive styles within an exploratory search system for digital libraries. J Doc 70(6):970–996. https://doi.org/10.1108/JD-03-2014-0045

de Greef T, Lafeber H, van Oostendorp H, Lindenberg J (2009) Eye movement as indicators of mental workload to trigger adaptive automation. In: Schmorrow DD, Estabrooke IV Grootjen M (eds) Foundations of augmented cognition. Neuroergonomics and operational neuroscience. Springer, Berlin, Heidelberg, pp 219–228. http://link.springer.com.ezproxy.lib.utexas.edu/chapter/10.1007/978-3-642-02812-0_26. Accessed 16 Dec 2013

Guo X, Li R, Alm C, Yu Q, Pelz J, Shi P, Haake A (2014) Infusing perceptual expertise and domain knowledge into a human-centered image retrieval system: a prototype application. In: Proceedings of the symposium on eye tracking research and applications. ACM, New York, NY, USA, pp 275–278. https://doi.org/10.1145/2578153.2578196

Gwizdka J (2009) What a difference a tag cloud makes: effects of tasks and cognitive abilities on search results interface use. Inf Res 14(4). http://informationr.net/ir/14-4/paper414.html. Accessed 15 Sept 2013

Gwizdka J (2010) Distribution of cognitive load in web search. J Am Soc Inf Sci Technol 61(11):2167–2187. https://doi.org/10.1002/asi.21385

Gwizdka J (2013a) Effects of working memory capacity on users' search effort. In: Proceedings of the international conference on multimedia, interaction, design and innovation. ACM, New York, NY, USA, pp 11:1–11:8. https://doi.org/10.1145/2500342.2500358

Gwizdka J (2013b) Searchers switch tactics under increased mental load. In: Proceedings of the 76th ASIS&T annual meeting: beyond the cloud: rethinking information boundaries, vol 50. American Society for Information Science, Silver Springs, MD, USA, pp 146:1–146:3. http://dl.acm.org/citation.cfm?id=2655780.2655926. Accessed 15 Dec 2017

Gwizdka J (2014) Characterizing relevance with eye-tracking measures. In: Proceedings of the 5th information interaction in context symposium. ACM, New York, NY, USA, pp 58–67. https://doi.org/10.1145/2637002.2637011

Gwizdka J (2017) I can and so I search more: effects of memory span on search behavior. In: Proceedings of the 2017 conference on conference human information interaction and retrieval. ACM, New York, NY, USA, pp 341–344. https://doi.org/10.1145/3020165.3022148

Gwizdka J (2018) Inferring web page relevance using pupillometry and single channel EEG. In: Davis FD, Riedl R, vom Brocke J, Léger P-M, Randolph AB (eds) Information systems and neuroscience. Presented at the NeuroIS 2017. Springer, Cham, Switzerland, pp 175–183. https://doi.org/10.1007/978-3-319-67431-5_20

Gwizdka J, Hansen P, Hauff C, He J, Kando N (2016) Search As Learning (SAL) workshop 2016. In: Proceedings of the 39th international ACM SIGIR conference on research and development in information retrieval. ACM, New York, NY, USA, pp 1249–1250. https://doi.org/10.1145/2911451.2917766

Gwizdka J, Hosseini R, Cole M, Wang S (2017) Temporal dynamics of eye-tracking and EEG during reading and relevance decisions. J Assoc Inf Sci Technol 68(10):2299–2312. https://doi.org/10.1002/asi.23904

Gwizdka J, Zhang Y (2015) Differences in eye-tracking measures between visits and revisits to relevant and irrelevant web pages. In: Proceedings of the 38th international ACM SIGIR conference on research and development in information retrieval. ACM, New York, NY, USA, pp 811–814. https://doi.org/10.1145/2766462.2767795

Hansen P, Rieh SY (2016) Editorial recent advances on searching as learning: an introduction to the special issue. J Inf Sci 42(1):3–6. https://doi.org/10.1177/0165551515614473

Heinström J (2003) Five personality dimensions and their influence on information behaviour. Inf Res 9(1):05.2.2008

Holmqvist K, Nyström M, Andersson R, Dewhurst R, Jarodzka H, van de Weijer J (2011) Eye tracking: a comprehensive guide to methods and measures. Oxford University Press, Oxford, UK

Huey EB (1898) Preliminary experiments in the physiology and psychology of reading. Am J Psychol 9(4):575–586. https://doi.org/10.2307/1412192

Jacucci G, Barral O, Daee P, Wenzel M, Serim B, Ruotsalo T et al (2019) Integrating neurophysiologic relevance feedback in intent modeling for information retrieval. J Assoc Inf Sci Technol 70(9):917–930. https://doi.org/10.1002/asi.24161

Just MA, Carpenter PA (1980) A theory of reading: from eye fixations to comprehension. Psychol Rev 87(4):329–354. https://doi.org/10.1037/0033-295X.87.4.329

Kahneman D, Beatty J (1966) Pupil diameter and load on memory. Science 154(3756):1583–1585. https://doi.org/10.1126/science.154.3756.1583

Karanam S, Jorge-Botana G, Olmos R, van Oostendorp H (2017a) The role of domain knowledge in cognitive modeling of information search. Inf Retr J:1–24. https://doi.org/10.1007/s10791-017-9308-8

Karanam S, van Oostendorp H, Sanchiz M, Chevalier A, Chin J, Fu W-T (2017b) Cognitive modeling of age-related differences in information search behavior. J Assoc Inf Sci Technol 68(10):2328–2337. https://doi.org/10.1002/asi.23893

Karanam S, van Oostendorp H (2016a) Modeling individual differences in information search. In: Proceedings of the 8th Indian conference on human computer interaction. ACM, New York, NY, USA, pp 12–23. https://doi.org/10.1145/3014362.3014363

Karanam S, van Oostendorp H (2016b) Age-related differences in the content of search queries when reformulating. In: Proceedings of the 2016 CHI conference on human factors in computing systems. ACM, New York, NY, USA, pp 5720–5730. https://doi.org/10.1145/2858036.2858444

Karanam S, van Oostendorp H (2017) Age-related effects of task difficulty on the semantic relevance of query reformulations. In: Bernhaupt R, Dalvi G, Joshi A, Balkrishan DK, O'Neill J, Winckler M (eds) Human-computer interaction—INTERACT 2017. Springer, pp 77–96

Komogortsev OV, Khan JI (2008) Eye movement prediction by Kalman filter with integrated linear horizontal oculomotor plant mechanical model. In: Proceedings of the 2008 symposium on eye tracking research & applications. ACM, New York, NY, USA, pp 229–236. https://doi.org/10.1145/1344471.1344525

Krugman HE (1964) Some applications of pupil measurement. JMR, J Mark Res (pre-1986) 1(000004):15

Liu C, Liu J, Cole M, Belkin NJ, Zhang X (2012) Task difficulty and domain knowledge effects on information search behaviors. Proc Am Soc Inf Sci Technol 49:1–10. https://doi.org/10.1002/meet.14504901142

Lopatovska I (2011) Emotional correlates of information retrieval behaviors. In: 2011 IEEE Workshop on Affective Computational Intelligence (WACI). Presented at the 2011 IEEE Workshop on Affective Computational Intelligence (WACI), pp 1–7. https://doi.org/10.1109/WACI.2011.5953145

Lopatovska I (2014) Toward a model of emotions and mood in the online information search process. J Assoc Inf Sci Technol 65(9):1775–1793. https://doi.org/10.1002/asi.23078

Lu Q, Zhang J, Chen J, Li J (2018) Predicting readers' domain knowledge based on eye-tracking measures. Electron Libr 36(6):1027–1042. https://doi.org/10.1108/EL-05-2017-0108

Marshall SP (2002) The Index of Cognitive Activity: measuring cognitive workload. In: Proceedings of the 2002 IEEE 7th conference on human factors and power plants, 2002. Presented at the Proceedings of the 2002 IEEE 7th conference on human factors and power plants, 2002, IEEE, pp 7-5-7–9. https://doi.org/10.1109/HFPP.2002.1042860

Moray N (1979) Models and measures of mental workload. In Moray N (ed) Mental workload: its theory and measurement. Springer US, Boston, MA, pp 13–21. https://doi.org/10.1007/978-1-4757-0884-4_2

Oliveira FTP, Aula A, Russell DM (2009) Discriminating the relevance of web search results with measures of pupil size. In: Proceedings of the SIGCHI conference on human factors in computing systems. ACM, New York, NY, USA, pp 2209–2212. https://doi.org/10.1145/1518701.1519038

Onorati F, Barbieri R, Mauri M, Russo V, Mainardi L (2013) Characterization of affective states by pupillary dynamics and autonomic correlates. Front Neuroeng 6:9. https://doi.org/10.3389/fneng.2013.00009

Palmquist RA, Kim K-S (2000) Cognitive style and on-line database search experience as predictors of web search performance. J Am Soc Inf Sci 51(6):558–566. https://doi.org/10.1002/(SICI)1097-4571(2000)51:6%3c558:AID-ASI7%3e3.0.CO;2-9

Pirolli P (2009) Powers of 10: modeling complex information-seeking systems at multiple scales. Computer 42(3):33–40. https://doi.org/10.1109/MC.2009.94

Pirolli P, Card S (1999) Information foraging. Psychol Rev 106(4):643–675

Preuschoff K, Hart BM, Einhäuser W (2011) Pupil dilation signals surprise: evidence for noradrenaline's role in decision making. Front Decis Neurosci 5:115. https://doi.org/10.3389/fnins.2011.00115

Rayner K (1975) Parafoveal identification during a fixation in reading. Acta Psychol 39(4):271–281. https://doi.org/10.1016/0001-6918(75)90011-6

Rayner K (1998) Eye movements in reading and information processing: 20 years of research. Psychol Bull 124(3):372–422. https://doi.org/10.1037/0033-2909.124.3.372

Rayner K (2009) Eye movements and attention in reading, scene perception, and visual search. Q J Exp Psychol 62(8):1457–1506. https://doi.org/10.1080/17470210902816461

Rayner K, Pollatsek A, Ashby J, Clifton C Jr (2011) Psychology of reading, 2nd edn. Psychology Press

Reichle ED, Pollatsek A, Rayner K (2006) EZ Reader: a cognitive-control, serial-attention model of eye-movement behavior during reading. Model Eye-Mov Control Read 7(1):4–22

Reichle ED, Rayner K, Pollatsek A (2003) The E-Z Reader model of eye-movement control in reading: comparisons to other models. Behav Brain Sci 26(04):445–476. https://doi.org/10.1017/S0140525X03000104

Rieh SY, Collins-Thompson K, Hansen P, Lee H-J (2016) Towards searching as a learning process: a review of current perspectives and future directions. J Inf Sci 42(1):19–34. https://doi.org/10.1177/0165551515615841

Salvucci DD, Goldberg JH (2000) Identifying fixations and saccades in eye-tracking protocols. In: Proceedings of the 2000 symposium on eye tracking research & applications. ACM, New York, NY, USA, pp 71–78. https://doi.org/10.1145/355017.355028

Saracevic T (1996) Relevance reconsidered. Information science: integration in perspectives. In: Proceedings of the second conference on conceptions of library and information science, Copenhagen, Denmark, pp 201–218

Saracevic T (2007) Relevance: a review of the literature and a framework for thinking on the notion in information science. Part II: nature and manifestations of relevance. J Am Soc Inf Sci Technol 58(13):1915–1933. https://doi.org/10.1002/asi.20682

Saracevic T (2016) The notion of relevance in information science: everybody knows what relevance is. But, what is it really? Morgan & Claypool Publishers

Schotter ER, Angele B, Rayner K (2011) Parafoveal processing in reading. Atten Percept Psychophys 74(1):5–35. https://doi.org/10.3758/s13414-011-0219-2

Simon HA (1956) Rational choice and the structure of the environment. Psychol Rev 63(2):129–138. https://doi.org/10.1037/h0042769

Sonnenwald DH (2016) Theory development in the information sciences. University of Texas Press, Austin, TX, USA

Sweller J, Ayres P, Kalyuga S (2011) Measuring cognitive load. In: Cognitive load theory. Springer New York, New York, NY, pp 71–85. http://www.springerlink.com/content/h7221p68q5658303/. Accessed 23 Jan 2012

Tang R, Solomon P (1998) Toward an understanding of the dynamics of relevance judgment: an analysis of one person's search behavior. Inf Process Manag 34(2):237–256. https://doi.org/10.1016/S0306-4573(97)00081-2

Tatler BW (2007) The central fixation bias in scene viewing: selecting an optimal viewing position independently of motor biases and image feature distributions. J Vis 7(14):4–4. https://doi.org/10.1167/7.14.4

Veltman JA, Gaillard AWK (1998) Physiological workload reactions to increasing levels of task difficulty. Ergonomics 41(5):656–669. https://doi.org/10.1080/001401398186829

van der Wel P, van Steenbergen H (2018) Pupil dilation as an index of effort in cognitive control tasks: a review. Psychon Bull Rev 25(6):2005–2015. https://doi.org/10.3758/s13423-018-1432-y

Wildemuth BM (2004) The effects of domain knowledge on search tactic formulation. J Am Soc Inf Sci Technol 55(3):246–258

Part III
Areas of Applications

Chapter 10
Children's Acquisition of Text Search Strategies: The Role of Task Models and Relevance Processes

Jean-François Rouet, Julie Ayroles, Mônica Macedo-Rouet, and Anna Potocki

Abstract Searching texts both online and in print has become an essential skill for twenty-first-century students. Although most children can read fluently and comprehend short texts by the age of 10, research suggests that older students and even adults experience difficulties when searching for information inside texts. This chapter synthesizes various theoretical models of the processes involved in information search, drawing from information science as well as cognitive psychology. We identify three key processes that may represent specific challenges for young students: constructing a task model, selectively scanning and assessing the relevance of information. We review the evidence regarding children's ability to search for information, and we stress the importance of the task model on subsequent search processes. In the last part of the paper, we review attempts to foster children's information search skills and we highlight some preconditions for skill acquisition. Finally, we discuss the implications of research on children's search skills for future research in this domain.

Keywords Acquisition · Comprehension · Instruction · Memory · Reading · Search · Self-regulation · Strategies

Information search is a prevalent mode of interaction with printed and digital texts. From the elementary grades on, teachers assign tasks that require students to use texts in order to locate information of interest (Armbruster and Armstrong 1993). Adults most often engage with texts in order to locate information as part of purposeful activities such as locating factual information, finding solutions for a problem or making informed decisions (Britt et al. 2018; White et al. 2010). Although pervasive, information search is a challenging activity not only for children but also for older students and adults (Macedo-Rouet et al. 2012). Extensively documented difficulties range from not knowing exactly what or how to search, to selecting inadequate

J.-F. Rouet (✉) · J. Ayroles · A. Potocki
Centre National de la Recherche Scientifique (CNRS) and Université de Poitiers, Poitiers, France
e-mail: jean-francois.rouet@univ-poitiers.fr

M. Macedo-Rouet
University of Paris 8, Saint-Denis, France

© Springer Nature Switzerland AG 2020
W. T. Fu and H. van Oostendorp (eds.), *Understanding and Improving Information Search*, Human–Computer Interaction Series,
https://doi.org/10.1007/978-3-030-38825-6_10

documents or portions of documents, to not finding the target information even though it is actually there, to making ineffective use of the information. Effective search skills are arguably the outcome of students' experiences with purposeful reading in and out of school, during primary and secondary education (for the more advanced search skills that may come as an outcome of higher education and domain specialization, see e.g., Khosrowjerdi and Iranshahi 2011; Vibert et al. 2009). Therefore, in order to understand adult users' challenges when searching for information, it is important to understand how search skills develop throughout childhood and how they may be influenced by education.

The cognitive processes underlying information search have been examined from various perspectives. Information scientists have described the processes and stages that are generally involved in an information search situation (Belkin 1993; Kuhlthau 1991; Marchionini 1995). Behavioral research has examined the cognitive processes actually brought to bear by individuals as they search. Studies have documented how these processes may change as a function of individual development and learning, but also as a function of the demands of particular contexts and tasks (Britt et al. 2018; Rouet 2006; Wellman 1985). Nevertheless, research into children's acquisition of information search skills has been relatively scarce.

The present chapter seeks to contribute to a multidisciplinary approach to information search by focusing on children's acquisition of information search skills and how these skills relate to cognitive development and educational practice. More specifically, our goal is to propose a framework for understanding the challenges children face when searching printed or digital texts, and how these challenges can be addressed. We believe that such an understanding can provide insights into the design of effective instructional situations and computer tools. Our definition of information search encompasses any situation in which the person engages with printed or digital texts based on a specific need, purpose or goal in mind. We focus on searching information within texts, as opposed to other types of information resources or media, in order to highlight the specific challenges that come with reading in the context of search tasks, especially for children. We also focus on studies conducted with children between the ages of 7 and 12 (see Hahnel et al. 2018, or Salmerón et al. 2018a, for examples of studies involving older students; see also Salmerón et al. 2018b, for a more general review of online reading).

The chapter is organized into three main sections. In the first section, we review various theoretical approaches to information search, and we propose a unifying framework to identify the critical stages and processes that may represent particular challenges for children. This framework emphasizes the role of the "task model," or the person's understanding of their task and goals. The framework serves as a structuring scheme for the following two sections. The second section reviews the extant research devoted to children's challenges when searching information in texts. The third section examines some attempts to foster search skills through either general or specific interventions. We conclude with some directions for future research in this area, both from a cognitive and an information science standpoint.

10.1   Information Search as a Complex Skill

Searching for information is a pervasive but complex kind of behavior. Information searchers need to know what they are searching for (i.e., their goal); they need to be aware of the available information sources and of the means available to access information (i.e., a query tool); they need to make decisions as regards source(s) they encounter; they need to actually query or browse through the source and to decide when the information found matches their needs. Finally, searchers need to decide when the information gathered is sufficient to satisfy their goal, considering available time, subjective importance of the task, other potential sources available and likelihood of obtaining better outcomes. Over the past three decades, scholars from various academic disciplines (e.g., information science, psychology, computer science) have attempted to describe these processes. In this section, we review a few of these attempts in an effort to identify the core overlapping constructs and to organize them into a unifying framework. Note that our ambition is not to provide an exhaustive review of information search theories but rather to show how different theories converge toward a common set of key constructs.

10.1.1   A Brief Review of Information Search Models

Early works rooted in the library and information sciences have proposed broad descriptions of information seeking considered from the point of view of the "user" (e.g., Belkin 1993; Kuhlthau 1991; see Savolainen 2018, for a recent discussion). Kuhlthau's (1991) seminal model of the Information Search Process (or ISP) identi-fied the cognitive and affective states that users generally experience as they engage in information activities. According to Kuhlthau, information search involves six stages: initiation (or acknowledging one's information need), selection (defining a topic or an approach), exploration (broad examination of the resources based on an ill-defined goal), formulation (defining a more focused perspective on the topic of interest), collection (acquisition of information on the focal topic) and presentation (or making use of the search outcomes). Kuhlthau proposed to link specific affective states to each of these stages, with for instance exploration being associated with frustration or doubt, whereas formulation would come with a sense of "clarity." Like Kuhlthau, Belkin (1993) challenged a dominant approach at the time, which assumed that the information need of users querying an information system was relatively static and accurately represented in their queries. Belkin's "berrypicking" model assumed that searchers gather information one piece after the other and refine their information needs *en route* as they hit (un)satisfactory results. She also pointed out that people use a broad range of strategies when searching information, with querying being only one of them. For instance, information searchers may direct themselves to particular areas in a library, look for particular authors, or scrutinize particular sections of a document in order to find references. These strategies are based on people's experience with some search domains but also information environments and tools (Marchionini 1995). The opportunistic, iterative nature of information search was further stressed in later works such as the "information foraging" theory (Pirolli and Card 1999). Information foraging sees the "optimal" searcher as a person who "seeks to maximize the rate of information gained per unit cost" (p. 5), given the constraints of the task environment. Their ACT-IF model assumed that information searchers are guided by signals (such as headers or summaries) that provide cues as to where the information of interest may be located and how to get it. They provided support to the model through a series of case studies of adult, rather well-educated users interacting with specialized information repositories. More recently, Agarwal (2018) proposed a model that stresses the role of "context" in information searching, with the view that information behavior depends on a number of circumstantial variables. He builds on the previous conceptualizations of context (e.g., Rieh 2004), to stress the need to identify specific contextual factors that influence searchers during the information search process. Similarly, Savolainen (2018) reviewed key models of information seeking as temporal developments and proposes a new model that reconciles the perspectives of stage-based and cyclic models of information seeking.

Meanwhile, research stemming from cognitive and developmental psychology has also attempted to understand the processes involved in text and document search, although with a different perspective. Information search was considered a specific reading strategy, to be contrasted with the sustained reading of continuous texts for comprehension. Thus, early research in that area has attempted to account for the selective reading of texts under specific task contexts. Guthrie and his colleagues proposed that locating information in text involves processes that are cognitively distinct from reading for comprehension. Guthrie (1988) described five core processes involved in text search, namely (a) form a goal, (b) inspect categories of information in the text, (c) detect and extract relevant details from each category, (d) integrate the information with prior knowledge and the goal and (e) recycle steps 1–4 until the goal is achieved. Although processes (a), (d) and (e) may also be found in other reading activities, processes (b) and (c) did not match any of the cognitive models of reading comprehension available at the time. Guthrie and Kirsch (1987) found that comprehending technical articles and locating information in articles or in schematics constituted two independent proficiency factors in a group of electrical technicians and engineers. Guthrie and Mosenthal (1987) listed a number of features that distinguished locating information from other constructs such as problem solving, reading comprehension or studying. For instance, contrary to reading comprehension, locating information in a text does not require the reader to memorize the contents read. It does, however, require the reader to make decisions regarding which parts of the documents to inspect (and which to ignore). Guthrie and Mosenthal further conjectured that locating information may not depend so much on readers' prior content schemata but rather on their acquisition of "procedural" schemata regarding the typical organization of information in documents.

Although Guthrie and his colleagues' early work was primarily designed to account for the specific task of locating information in printed documents, their theoretical insights resonate in more recent descriptions of students' interactions with complex information systems, such as Brand-Gruwel et al.'s (2009) model of information problem-solving on the Internet (IPS-I) or Goldman et al.'s (2010) model of multiple-source comprehension. Brand-Gruwel et al.'s (2009) IPS-I model includes five core processes, namely define the information problem, search, scan and process information, and organize and present information. These processes are assumed to rest on three types of foundational skills: reading, evaluating and computer skills. Finally, the IPS-I model also considers the cognitive regulation mechanisms that control the "flow" of search processes. Regulation involves planning (i.e., setting goals and anticipating the actions to be carried out), monitoring, steering and evaluating the outcomes of one's actions. A distinctive feature of the IPS-I model is that it acknowledges the flexibility of reading processes by contrasting scanning vs. deeper (integrative) processing of a page content. In addition, the model stresses the importance of both lower-level processes (e.g., literal comprehension) and higher-order, metacognitive processes (monitoring, evaluating). Other researchers have emphasized the links between the search and comprehension of information, on the one hand, and the transformation and communication of that information, on the other hand. Goldman and her colleagues (2010) proposed a framework for analyzing students' multiple-source comprehension, in which they defined a source as "any form of information that a person is able to process or use" (p. 261). They postulated a process model with five main components: interpret the task; search for or gather resources; use information about the source to inform the selection process; analyze and synthesize the resources and apply the resources (with the latter involving a decision about which resource is most appropriate for the task at hand). The latter process emphasizes the fact that comprehension often involves making use of information to address the demands of the tasks. Application may require the reader to transform information found in a source and/or to combine it with information found in another source. In their perspective, texts are not the "building blocks" of comprehension but rather resources from which readers may draw as a function of their adequacy to the task at hand. Leu and his colleagues (2013) similarly highlight the importance of transforming information as they list four core skills that are focused on in their ORCA assessment of Internet literacies. These skills include locating and evaluating information but also synthesizing and communicating the outcomes of one's research. The generalization of online reading has prompted further efforts to bridge general and more analytic approaches. For instance, Salmerón et al. (2018b) proposed three core competencies specifically involved in Internet reading, namely navigation (i.e., which sources to access and in which order), integration (i.e., comprehending information within and across Web pages) and evaluation (i.e., assessing the relevance and trustworthiness of information).

Both the early models of locating information and more recent models of complex information activities stress the importance of tasks and goals. Vakkari (2003) noted that meaning acquired from text is mostly a function of readers' information goals and needs, combined with their prior knowledge. McCrudden and Schraw (2007) examined the demands of various types of instructions that students may receive prior to engaging with text. Based on a review of research into the role of reading standards and goals, they proposed that "relevance instructions" drive readers' attention to relevant parts of texts and determine the appropriate level of processing of content information. It is important to note that in McCrudden and Schraw's perspective, relevance instructions do not necessarily involve the search and extraction of specific information from text. Instead, their framework encompasses specific and general types of instructions, which they argue call for specific types of reading strategies. Rouet (2006) and Rouet and Britt (2011) further specified the processes whereby the reading task context may influence reading decisions and processes. The Multiple-document task-based relevance assessment and content extraction model (MD-TRACE; Rouet and Britt 2011) posits that readers interpret task instructions and other features from the context in order to set reading goals. Thus, given a context and a set of instructions, readers' search behavior is likely to vary as a function of their individual understanding of the context. More recently, Britt et al. (2018) suggested that readers' relevance decisions are driven by their understanding of the context including, but not limited to, task instructions. Thus, readers may make different decisions based on, for instance, how much time is available or whether the task involves high or low stakes. Readers' individual task model also determines readers' extraction of information from texts and their actual use of the information in their task product (Rouet et al. 2017).

10.1.2   Three Specific Cognitive Demands of Information Search

Put together, the works reviewed above consistently emphasize three critical demands of information search: (a) the need to information users to understand their task and to generate and update their search goals accordingly; (b) the need to use proximal and distal cues in order to access information of interest while minimizing the time spent processing irrelevant information; (c) the need to assess the adequacy and sufficiency of information with respect to the end goal and/or product. Table 10.1 provides a summary of how these demands match some of the descriptions reviewed above. Table 10.1 also briefly specifies how these demands differ in search tasks compared to plain reading comprehension task. The reference to reading comprehension is helpful to identify potential gaps in the current educational programs and methodologies, which are clearly centered in the latter construct.

As shown in Table 10.1, the processes of forming a task model, selecting information of interest and assessing the information with respect to the task goal or product were identified in most earlier models of information search under various but consistent wordings. In addition, they emphasize the sharp contrast between reading for comprehension, on the one hand, and using texts (or information systems) for specific

Table 10.1 Three core demands of information search and how they differ from reading comprehension

	Correspondence with past frameworks	Contrasts between search and reading comprehension tasks
Form a task model	"Initiation", "Formulation" (Kuhlthau 1991) "Form a goal" (Guthrie 1988) "Define the information problem" (Brand-Gruwel et al. 2009) "Interpret the task" (Goldman et al. 2010) "Form a task model" (Rouet and Britt 2011)	Text comprehension may be considered a generic task whereby the reader seeks to construct a mental model of the situation described in the text (Kintsch 1998; but see van den Broek et al. 2011). In contrast, each search task calls for a specific task model based on the external specifications of the task and/or on self-generated goals
Select information of interest	"Selection", "Exploration", "Collection" (Kuhlthau 1991). "Inspect categories of information" (Guthrie 1988) "Search, Scan" (Brand-Gruwel et al. 2009) "Search for/gather resources" (Goldman et al. 2004) "Locate and evaluate" (Leu et al. 2013) "Selection, Extraction, Integration" (Rouet and Britt 2011)	In a typical text comprehension setting, information is read in the text order of presentation. The position of information in readers' mental model reflects a hierarchy of structural importance in the text; in a search task, the reader focuses on portions of the text(s) that are relevant to the task, disregarding any other information irrespective of their structural importance (see e.g., McCrudden and Schraw 2007)
Assess information with respect to task product	"Presentation" (Kuhlthau 1991) "Apply the resources" (Goldman et al. 2004) "Synthesize and communicate" (Leu et al. 2013) "Create/Update a task product" (Rouet and Britt 2011)	As a product, text comprehension is achieved when the reader has processed the text entirely. In a search setting, the reader has to decide whether to use the information and whether additional texts are required

purposes, on the other. Finally, this synthesis stresses the importance of construct-ing and revising goals (e.g., forming an adequate task model). Neither the selection nor the assessment of information acquired may be achieved without an adequate representation of the task. We believe that this prominence of the task model may explain some of the difficulties observed in children and teenagers as they engage in information search as part of learning activities.

In the rest of this chapter, we examine children's acquisition and use of these processes. In the next section, we review the existing research on children's chal-lenges when searching information in texts. Then, we examine researchers' attempts to design interventions that may support children's acquisition of better search skills.

10.2 Children's Challenges with Information Search: Task Model Construction, Selective Access, and Relevance Assessment

A child is broadly defined by the World Heath Organization as a person 19 years or younger (WHO, n.d.). For the purposes of this chapter, we will focus on studies conducted with children between the ages of 7 and 12. As stated earlier, children experience the need to read texts selectively in order to identify specific pieces of information very early in school curricula (Armbruster and Armstrong 1993; Rouet and Potocki 2018). Early research has evidenced that reading in order to locate spe-cific information is a challenge for students in the elementary grades (Armbruster and Armstrong 1993; Kobasigawa 1983; Kobasigawa et al. 1980; Raphael 1984). More recently, international large-scale studies such as PIRLS have found that search-ing in a text is not any simpler for fourth-grade students compared to, for instance, identifying the main idea of a passage (Mullis et al. 2017). The PISA study has pro-vided additional evidence that searching and integrating information from different paragraphs are challenges even for fifteen-year-old students (OCDE 2013).

The challenges of searching texts, both in print and online, may be examined in light of the broad conceptual framework outlined in the first section of this chapter. The first challenge is to *gain an adequate understanding of the task demands* (form a task model); the second challenge is to *make decisions regarding which information to focus on* and which information to skip or ignore (Select information of interest) and the third challenge is to *determine the adequacy and sufficiency of information given the task objectives.* The latter challenge amounts to being able to decide when one may quit reading vs. recycle through earlier steps in the search process (see Guthrie 1988). It thus requires some monitoring of one's progress toward the end goal.

In the rest of this section, we review extent research into children's performance and challenges related to these three core components of search.

10.2.1   Challenges in Understanding and Remembering the Search Task

A task model is a mental representation that includes one's interpretation of the task statement (e.g., a search question) but also the expected outcome of the search (i.e., the expected task product) and some initial action to be performed (i.e., an initial subgoal; Rouet and Britt 2011; Britt et al. 2018). To illustrate the challenge of forming a task model, imagine a middle school student who is studying the spread of epidemics and how to prevent them. This student is asked to find out *"When should a traveler start taking medication in order to prevent malaria?"* Constructing a task model involves understanding what the question is asking. According to Graesser and Franklin's (1990) QUEST model, understanding a question involves categorizing it (in this case, a "when" question) and identifying what the question is about (in this case, taking a medication in order to prevent malaria). Identifying the question focus amounts to constructing a mental model of a situation. The situation may range from a simple object, character or fact, to a complex causal explanation. The task model also involves generating an initial action to be performed, for instance, *locate information that looks like it is a date or a period*. Researchers have acknowledged the importance of building an accurate mental model of the task in functional reading (Goldman and Durán 1988; McCrudden and Schraw 2007; McCrudden et al. 2010). Indeed, the chain of decisions and processes that unfold during search depends on the searcher's understanding of what the search is about. Moreover, readers have to keep their task model in mind throughout the search, as they examine various texts and sections within texts. Some studies have already pointed the complexity of such construction for readers (Rouet 2003; Vidal-Abarca et al. 2010). However, most of these studies have focused on teenagers (i.e., 13–19 years of age) and young adults (i.e., older than 19 years of age; WHO, n.d.)

Among the few studies targeting younger students, Vidal-Abarca et al. (2010) analyzed the self-regulation processes present in task-oriented reading activities of skilled and less-skilled comprehenders at the seventh and eighth grades (13–15 years of age). Using an error detection paradigm (Hannon and Daneman 2004), they introduced inconsistencies within questions (e.g., *When should treatment begin to cause malaria? NB. Emphasis added*) and asked participants whether the questions could be answered using text information. The probability for a reader to say that the question could not be properly answered was higher for skilled than for less-skilled readers. The authors speculated that skilled readers are more able to integrate several ideas contained in the question and, thus, to detect a potential contradiction (e.g., between *treatment* and *causes of malaria*). Similar results were obtained by Cerdán et al. (2013). They asked 40 ninth graders to explain search questions by rewriting them with their own words. Skilled comprehenders included a higher number of bridging inferences, and less-skilled comprehenders included a greater number of incomplete and wrong ideas in their answers. These results indicated that less-skilled comprehenders had built an incorrect and incomplete representation of task demands, which in turn deteriorated their comprehension performance.

Developing readers may also have difficulty remembering the demands of a search task as they selectively scan documents. Potocki et al. (2017), found that fifth graders' (9–10 years of age) performance depends on the cognitive demands of the search question. Questions that required the comparison of several paragraphs (i.e., integration questions) generated longer search times and more errors than location questions. Also, integration questions generated more incomplete answers, which suggest that children sometimes partially forgot the question during their search. This hypothesis is consistent with Rouet and Coutelet (2008) who observed that many third graders tended to forget the question during a search task involving an encyclopedia. Finally, Potocki et al. (2017) noticed that the participants in their experiment sometimes answered a different but related question instead of the one they had been asked. In those cases, the initial question was often simplified (e.g., "*What is the highest mountain?*" instead of "*Which are the two highest mountains?*"). Thus, it is also possible that children's memory for the question gets distorted during the search.

In sum, cognitive and developmental research has found that one of the core difficulties children experience when searching for information is the construction and maintenance of an accurate task model. This line of research fully corroborates early researchers' claims that a person's goal when searching should not be equated with the task they were assigned or the query they articulate (Belkin 1993; Kuhlthau 1991). Instead, search goals are the outcome of a constructive process whereby individuals examine cues from the context and the task instructions (when available) and derive a representation of the task product and the means needed to generate that product (Britt et al. 2018).

10.2.2 Challenges in Selectively Accessing Content Information

Another challenge of information searching in texts is the requirement to access relevant information rapidly and efficiently, without wasting processing effort and time with irrelevant pages or paragraphs. Contrary to text comprehension, information search does not always demand the construction of a broad representation of the text's meaning. Instead, the aim is to gather the information needed to answer a question (Kaakinen et al. 2015). To this aim, the use of metatextual cues such as titles or links in a menu is an effective strategy for finding information. The problem is that until the end of elementary school, children's knowledge of metatextual cues seems to be rather limited (Garner et al. 1986; Eme and Rouet 2001).

Garner et al. (1986) probed children's metatextual knowledge by asking third, fifth and seventh graders to complete a series of paragraph construction tasks. Almost all of the participants were able to identify paragraphs in the text and group topically related sentences together to make short texts. However, only the seventh graders were able to describe what makes a paragraph, and none of the participants could appropriately formulate the main idea of a paragraph through a formal title. These results were partly replicated by Eme and Rouet (2001). In their study, participants demonstrated good knowledge of what a title or a paragraph is, but only a few students could tell the purpose of such devices. Hence, the children had knowledge of the "structural" aspects of texts but not of the "functional" aspects of metatextual cues. These results suggest that the acquisition of metatextual knowledge is a prerequisite for locating relevant information in texts (Potocki et al. 2017).

Even though they may possess some knowledge of metatextual cues, children may be challenged by the use of such cues during information searching. For instance, for the question *"What do marine crocodiles eat?,"* it is highly likely that the answer may be found in a paragraph titled *"What marine crocodiles eat"* or even *"Feeding in marine crocodiles."* Most readers are able to identify such paragraphs thanks to a literal matching between the keywords *marine crocodiles* and *eat/feeding*. However, when the link between the question and the title is not explicit, inferential matching is necessary. In this situation, readers need to infer the relevance of a paragraph by comparing mentally implicit title content with their understanding of the question, that is, their task model. A study by Kobasigawa (1983) illustrated how this task is challenging for children. In response to the search question *"I want to find out why China cannot produce enough food even when many people are working on farms,"* fourth graders restricted their keywords to *farming* and *food*, while eighth graders provided additional keywords (e.g., *population, climate* and *soil*).

Dinet et al. (1998) examined the use of metatextual cues by 8–10 year olds and adults in a simulated Internet environment. Participants had to select five titles that seemed relevant for a search on "the role of peasants in the French Revolution," from a list of 24 items. Relevance was manipulated through the semantic adequacy of the reference (i.e., adequate/inadequate), typographic marking (i.e., keywords in regular typeset or in capitals) and the number of relevant keywords in the reference. Children were more prone to selecting inadequate references than adults. In addition, the probability for children to choose an irrelevant reference increased when the reference contained two descriptors and/or if this reference included capitalized keywords. Dinet and colleagues concluded that younger learners tend to assign relevance based on visual cues (e.g., capitals, boldface type…) rather than on the semantic relation between the reference and the topic. These results are consistent with Rouet et al. (2011) study showing that fifth and seventh graders' Web menu selection strategies were strongly influenced by superficial relevance cues. In a subsequent study, Dinet et al. (2010) recorded fifth graders' eye movements while they were exploring a list of Web links. They identified four visual strategies: (1) a F-shaped scanning pattern whereby information at the top and/or to the left of the page was more likely to be fixated; (2) the visual scanning of whole Web pages (or "exhaustive" strategy); (3) a simple visual detection strategy (i.e., skimming from keyword to keyword); (4) a reversed F-shaped strategy (i.e., similar to the F-shape but with a deeper examination of the bottom of the page). In echo with evidence regarding the influence of superficial cues on children's search, the results also show that children use mostly a simple visual detection strategy, especially if the words are typographically marked (here, in bold). Hence, using metatextual cues efficiently is more complex than just knowing their definitions and functions and may represent a serious barrier for children until the end of elementary school.

Some studies have highlighted the effect of comprehension skills on students' ability to inhibit distracting information from the text. In a study by Cerdán et al. (2011), 14-year-old students had to read two texts and answer questions. Half of the questions had been manipulated to create a misleading matching between the wording of the question and distracting pieces of information in the text. Participants were characterized as skilled or less-skilled based on standardized test of reading comprehension. Skilled comprehenders were more able to discard the distracting information compared to less-skilled comprehenders.

Taken together, these results suggest that younger or less-skilled comprehenders tend to consider superficial cues in their task model as valid, whereas older readers or skilled comprehenders tend to match the search question and the text contents based on deeper semantic processing. Indeed, Cataldo and Cornoldi (1998, experiment 2) highlighted the importance of children's reading comprehension strategies, including when selectively scanning texts. They compared the ability of sixth–seventh grade poor and good comprehenders to use strategies in order to answer comprehension questions. Contrary to the control group, the experimental group was explicitly invited to search through the text and to underline with different colors the sentences necessary to answer each question. This manipulation resulted in an increase in search performance. Therefore, children's difficulties seemed to be due to a lack of effective use of strategies rather than an inability to search for relevant information in a text per se. A related study by Kobasigawa et al. (1980) explored the spontaneous use of skimming strategies by fourth, sixth and eighth graders. They found that children were able to skim but only when explicitly asked of do so. These results are in line with Dreher and Sammons' (1994) study exploring the use of structure indicators (e.g., index, table of content) by fifth graders in an information search task. Most of their participants were able to define the structure indicators but did not use it unless they were prompted to do so (through guiding questions before and during the task). Indeed, prompting increased the likelihood that a child would use the index, and index use greatly improved the chances of locating the answer. Moreover, several studies reveal that spontaneous use of content cues as a strategy to locate specific information develops gradually with age. For example, Kobasigawa et al. (1988) compared the use of titles in an information search task for fourth, sixth and eighth graders. The results showed that the spontaneous use of the titles does appear in half of the fourth and sixth graders and in all the eighth graders. However, even in the eighth graders, this spontaneous use does not intervene at the beginning of the task but is set up little by little during the search for information.

More recently, Rouet and Coutelet (2008) also showed that information retrieval strategies evolved according to grade level (third, fifth and seventh). Indeed, third graders ran the text from top to bottom, not seeming to use text organizers, contrary to older students who were the ones who used the most textual cues (table of contents, index) while searching for information. Thus, top-down strategies, based on the examination of headings and keywords appeared only at grades five and seven. However, even for the older ones, searching the relevant information to answer a question in a text was still a difficult activity. These developmental trends are consistent with Dreher and Guthrie's (1990) study showing that more efficient 11th graders were quicker than less efficient ones thanks to their use of content cues, especially when task complexity increases. Indeed, they spent more time, in the first phase, to select relevant units through the index, glossary, table of content of a chapter (presented on a computer screen) allowing them, in the second phase, to localize and extract faster the information needed. Moreover, Rouet and Coutelet (2008) examined the relationships between search performance and strategy use and found that the acquisition of efficient search strategies is linked to students' awareness and use of text organizers. Finally, Potocki et al. (2017) examined children's use of headings when scanning a document to answer a specific question. Twenty-six French fifth graders were asked to search relevant information in a text in order to respond to questions while their eye movements were recorded. Potocki et al. (2017) analyzed their visual scanning patterns based on the type of transition between areas of interest: title-to-title transitions or paragraph-to-paragraph transitions. They assumed that title-to-title transitions reflect a top-down strategy, whereas paragraph-to-paragraph transitions reflect linear reading. The use of a top-down strategy resulted in shorter response time than linear reading. However, Potocki et al. observed strong differences between children. Some fixated titles systematically, while others never used them. Interestingly, and in line with the results of Rouet and Coutelet (2008), these differences were more strongly related to participants' knowledge of text features reading strategies than to their reading comprehension abilities. Hence, good decoding and understanding are not enough to mobilize effective strategies but seem to be more related to the metaknowledge as well as the quality of the task model.

In sum, children who learn to search of information need to generate search criteria and match them with the information available in the environment. This is best done by focusing on content organizers and other metatextual cues that will yield the strongest "scent" with respect to one's task model (Pirolli and Card 1999). Until the end of primary education, however, students have limited metatextual knowledge and do not seem to know how to use it effectively. From grade five on, readers seem to gradually acquire knowledge about the functions and uses of metatextual cues (e.g., titles, menus, links). It would therefore be interesting to examine more closely the spontaneous use of these content cues during an information search task. Even if metatextual knowledge increases with age and education, most seventh or eighth graders do not seem to use it spontaneously in the service of information search. Moreover, students tend to use the available cues in a superficial way, perhaps due to their inadequate representation of the task demands.

10.2.3 Challenges in Assessing the Relevance and Quality of Information

Based on the construction and the maintenance of a task model, as well as on the use of search strategies (i.e., use of content cues), readers have to determine whether the information is adequate and sufficient to achieve the reading goal.

Examining the adequacy of information is not a trivial task for children when they search for information in a text. Cataldo and Cornoldi (1998) found that six and seventh graders with poor comprehension could acknowledge when their answers to comprehension questions were inadequate (through confidence ratings after each question). However, such an acknowledgement did not improve their performance. Thus, poor comprehenders did not use spontaneously reading comprehension strategies, but raising their awareness was insufficient to promote their use of more efficient strategies. Hence, poor comprehenders were able to monitor their comprehension and identify the inadequacy of their answer but could not overcome that difficulty. In the study by Kobasigawa (1983), the participants (fourth and eighth graders) had to read another student's research report and evaluate how well it answered three specific questions. In general, the younger children were not sensitive to the need to evaluate the adequacy and sufficiency of the answer according to the question. However, when the experimenter explicitly asked if the information reported answered to a specific question, the fourth graders were able to state correctly if the report did not include all required information. Therefore, fourth graders appear to have the ability to recognize what constitutes appropriate solutions to search tasks, but they often fail to use it spontaneously to evaluate the quality of answers. More recently, Potocki et al. (2017) proposed that the difficulties of children could be linked to their low level of monitoring while searching the text. In their experiment, even though participants were given the possibility to ask the question again while searching for an answer in the document, few of them did use this opportunity. The authors suggested that readers who have a better task model might know what they are looking for and can ask the question just to make sure they answer it correctly (Rouet and Britt 2011).

Children might also lack self-regulation strategies that are necessary to the assessment of sufficiency of information. Vidal-Abarca et al. (2010) examined seventh and eighth graders' self-regulation of the search process by calculating (a) the percentage of time spent reading relevant information during the question-answering process over the total time spent reading all information and (b) the number of times a student answered the question immediately after reading a relevant piece of text. In two-thirds of the cases, when skilled readers decided to search, they found a segment with relevant information, and they then immediately gave an answer based on the relevant information just read. In contrast, less-skilled readers adopted the same search behavior less than half of the time. Vidal-Abarca et al. did not find significant differences between skilled and less-skilled readers in the distribution of search time, but the observed differences were in the predicted direction.

Finally, children may also be challenged by other dimensions of information evaluation such as the assessment of source reliability. Coiro et al. (2015) asked seventh graders to locate and evaluate reliable Web sites in a Web-like database. Although most students correctly identified source information, such as the author's name, only 31% provided a clear yes/no answer to whether the author was an expert, and 51% failed to cite any specific criteria for expertise. Thus, one's ability to locate information does not necessarily mean that one can interpret that information properly. Similarly, Paul et al. (2018) found that fourth graders could successfully identify source information and evaluate informants' expertise and intentions in simple search tasks but failed to apply this ability to more complex and implicit tasks. Moreover, Dreher and Guthrie (1990) showed that monitoring and determining the adequacy and sufficiency of information are challenging even for older students. In their study, high school students had to locate information in a textbook chapter in order to answer questions. The results showed that 14 of 31 participants answered incorrectly. Among those, eight went to at least some of the correct pages but failed to extract the relevant information. Such results illustrate that less efficient text searchers struggle to assess adequacy of information with respect to the task demands.

Put together, the studies reviewed in this section illustrate the difficulties of children and adolescents in addressing the challenges of information search. Research suggests that many children struggle to construct and maintain a detailed and effective task model in memory. A poor task model may impact their ability to select information adequately and to monitor their attainment of the reading goal. Additionally, the studies point out the critical importance of self-regulation in initiating, monitoring and regulating the search activity (Brand-Gruwel et al. 2009). Finally, although several studies highlight the improvement of search strategies with age and schooling, the same studies point to the uneven acquisition of these strategies among children at any given grade level. Thus, it would seem important to implement some explicit teaching of functional reading skills as soon as students have acquired basic reading skills, that is, to say from grades three–four on (Macedo-Rouet et al. 2013).

10.3 Fostering Readers' Search Skills

A large number of studies have attempted to teach reading strategies using various instructional approaches (e.g., National Reading Panel 2000; Palincsar and Brown 1984; Paris et al. 1984). However, as Ng and Graham (2017) have quite rightly pointed out, these interventions have generally been conducted within the framework of single text comprehension (e.g., one reader reading one text for the general purpose of comprehension). On the contrary, very few studies have focused on functional reading situations, such as searching for specific information in texts or critically assessing the reliability of information. In the more recent period, researchers have begun to address these more advanced literacy skills. Consistent with the scope of this chapter, we will focus here on studies conducted with children.

Using the same framework as in the previous sections, we discuss (1) interventions proposing pre-search activities in order to enhance students' task model (understanding the task and implementing an adequate strategy); (2) interventions focused on the purposeful reading of documents and in particular, on <u>relevance or reliability</u> <u>evaluations</u>; and (3) interventions <u>combining different stages</u> of the information search processes. We then discuss some perspectives these studies afford for the development of efficient programs to foster children's functional reading skills.

10.3.1 Interventions Using Pre-Search Activities to Enhance Readers' Task Models

As discussed earlier in this chapter, models of information search emphasize the importance of having an adequate mental model of the task. For example, students need to develop an accurate understanding of what the question is asking for and to anticipate the target information they have to find in the document(s). A few studies have tried to develop interventions focusing on students' construction of a task model prior to their engagement in the actual search process.

Coutelet and Rouet (2004) proposed an intervention to enhance third- and fifth-grade students' search skills by means of a series of guided training tasks following a three-stage model called Evaluation-Selection-Processing (Rouet and Tricot 1996). Their training tasks focused on making the children reflect on (a) their objective when searching, and (b) ways for them to locate relevant information in relation to this objective, in particular by taking into account metatextual cues such as headers and introductions. The participants took part in small group activities 30 min per week over a five-week period. Their performance on a criterion search task was evaluated before and after the training sessions and was compared to that of a control group (performing only reading tasks during the training sessions). A medium-term effect was also tested with a delayed posttest administered one month after the end of the intervention. The intervention had no overall effect on participants' search speed nor correct responses (but the authors reported a ceiling effect in terms of correct response with an error rate of just 1%). However, by distinguishing different types of strategies used by the children when searching (Cataldo and Oakhill 2000), they observed that in the delayed posttest, third-grade children from the experimental group no longer used low-level strategies (i.e., linear reading of the whole text from top to bottom), whereas 20% of the control group children still used them. Conversely, trained children used more elaborated strategies (i.e., use of titles and subtitle to access the relevant information) than the control group children (43,75% versus 15%, respectively) after the intervention. Such effects were not observed in older readers in grade five for whom the authors reported no differences between the experimental and the control group.

De Vries et al. (2008) examined the influence of pre-search activities as a means to promote "reflective" Web search in fifth and sixth graders. More specifically, they conducted a study in which they trained children to use an experimental portal and a worksheet when they were searching information on Internet. The portal consisted in a preselection of Web sites for biology topics (e.g., design of bees' or ants' communities) presented in a structured way. They also provided the students with a worksheet inciting them to write down their search questions and to note their results. In this worksheet, the authors also provided (in Experiment 2) a specific space inviting the children to explicate their prior knowledge on the topic and the potential answer to the question that can be derived from their previous knowledge before carrying out the actual search. Qualitative analysis of worksheet contents and other qualitative observations indicated that the method was actually beneficial. First, the portal seems to have helped children to locate relevant information more efficiently, suggesting that narrowing the search space and categorizing information might be beneficial for them. Second, the worksheet used in this study seemed to help children to stick to their question, to pre-activate relevant knowledge on the topic and, in doing so, was beneficial in terms of information search outcomes. This study however did not include any control condition making it difficult to conclude about the specific impact of this intervention.

Using a different procedure, Rouet et al. (2011, Experiment 2) attempted to foster students' selection of items in a simulated search engine menu by proposing a pre-search activity to students in grades five and seven. In this study, the authors examined the influence of prior elaboration on the search topic on children's Web site selection. Eighty-eight students were randomly assigned to two conditions. In an "Elaboration" condition, the children had to first read a text elaborating on the search topic and to answer a comprehension about this text before actually start searching. In the control condition, children directly engaged in the search task. In each condition, the authors also distinguished between good and poor readers based on a reading fluency test. The search task was composed of 10 search topics presented on a computer screen. Each topic included a search phrase (e.g., "The highest mountains of the world") and a simplified search engine list displaying 16 Web site titles. Each Web site title contained two or three keywords from the search phrase with half of the titles being semantically relevant (e.g., "All the highest mountains") and half being not (e.g., "Highest cathedrals in the world"). The children were asked to select the four most relevant Web sites for each search topic. A trial was considered successful if the participants indeed correctly select the four relevant Web sites. The "Elaboration" condition indeed improved good readers' selections of relevant Web sites but had no significant impact on poor readers' selections. In sum, the pre-search elaboration task, which itself was based on reading, was only effective for children with a higher level of reading fluency.

Based on the previous studies conducted by Llorens and Cerdán (2012) or Cerdán et al. (2013) with older readers, Ayroles et al. (2018) recently proposed a short intervention study to enhance fifth graders' task model construction and to investigate whether a better task model indeed enhances children's ability to locate information in texts. In this study, 37 participants had to answer a series of questions by searching on a one-page, six-paragraph document displayed on the screen of an eyetracker. All questions involved the location of a specific piece of information within a single paragraph (see also Potocki et al. 2017 for a similar methodology). The children were randomly assigned to one of two conditions. In an "enhanced task model" condition, after reading each search question but prior to engaging in search, the participants were asked "what do you have to search to answer this question?" In a control condition, the children were asked "Is the word xxx present in this question?" The impact of this manipulation was examined in terms of children's correct responses, response time and search strategies (by analyzing eyetracking data). Participants in the "task model" condition obtained higher scores than those in the control condition. However—and unexpectedly—the authors observed no differences between "task model" and control conditions in terms of response time nor reading strategies (i.e., time to explore relevant vs irrelevant paragraphs, first fixation on relevant paragraph, etc.). Thus, making children elaborate the question demands had positive effects on their performance but did not lead them to search more rapidly nor to modify their actual search strategies.

Finally, other studies, not specifically focused on interventions per se, bring nonetheless interesting elements as regards the way "pre-search" activities could improve children's search skills. For example, Raphael and McKinney (1983) made fifth- and eighth-grade children reflect on whether the answer to the question posed to them was "right there; think and search; or on my own" (i.e., awareness about the fact that the answer was either explicitly stated in text, implied by text or can be found in the individual's knowledge base). The authors did not test however the impact of such intervention on children's search skills but found relatively positive effects on more classical reading comprehension measure (i.e., correct responses to questions presented after the reading of the texts). An exploratory study conducted by Kammerer and Bohnacker (2012) also provides interesting insights into interventions that could focus on improving children's use of relevant keywords in search engines. The authors asked eight- and 10-year-old students to conduct a set of search tasks using a search engine. For each task, they analyzed the queries typed into the search box, the time taken to complete the task and also recorded browser activities (i.e., typing, clicking, scrolling, etc.) as well as children's eye movements during the search. In general, the use of keyword lists was not beneficial for the participants, as they found more relevant information and did so more efficiently by typing the entire question in the search box. The authors therefore concluded that "children succeed better using their own strategies than trying to apply adult strategies" (p. 187). This result has important implications in terms of knowing what prerequisites are needed for children to enhance their search queries. An example is readers' awareness of text structure. Meyer and Ray (2017; see also Williams et al. 2004) recently reviewed empirical studies on text structure interventions for elementary school students. They showed that such interventions were beneficial to improve expository text comprehension and knowledge of text structure. However, we do not know so far whether such training on structure strategy could indeed lead to better information search strategies in children. Such an investigation could be explored in future works.

In sum, interventions using pre-search activities may improve the quality of children's search outcomes. However, these interventions do not result in better research strategies per se (Ayroles et al. 2018) and seem only beneficial for some readers (Coutelet and Rouet 2004; Rouet et al. 2011). Other studies have therefore also developed interventions focused on later steps of information search activity such as processing of the documents and an evaluation about their relevance and reliability.

10.3.2   Interventions Focused on Selecting and Evaluating Document Information

Studies focused on the training of information selection have mostly focused in issues of information quality and reliability. In contrast with studies targeting older readers (adolescents, or young adults; see for example, Brante and Strømsø 2018), research focusing on elementary school children is still scarce. One study by Macedo-Rouet et al. (2013) attempted to raise fourth- and fifth-grade students' (9–10 years of age) awareness of source attributes and information evaluation based on these attributes. Ninety-six students were either assigned to an experimental group or a control group. The experimental group attended a one-session intervention (30 min) consisting of mediated discussion in small groups. After making children think and discuss the reasons to accept or reject someone's advice or opinion, the session involved the reading of a small text containing two characters which had opposing views about a specific topic. The characters were introduced through their professional occupation (e.g., veterinarian) or personal traits (e.g., young lady who loves dogs as pets). The professional occupation implied that the character was a specialist on the domain, whereas the personal trait suggested an interest but no specific qualification or expertise in the topic. The general goal of this session was to encourage children 1/ to identify source parameters in texts ("who is Louise?"), 2/ to establish links between sources and content (i.e., "who said what?") and 3/ to assess the knowledgeability of each source as regards the topic at stake in the text (i.e., "who is the more knowledgeable on this topic?"). A discussion about the notion of knowledgeability, differences between non-expert and expert authors, the necessity to take into account different perspectives and to refer to the source of information was led by the experimenter with the children. In the control condition, children performed a series of reading comprehension tasks (i.e., reading of short texts followed by comprehension questions). To examine the effect of this intervention, participants had to complete before and after the intervention a source evaluation task in which they have to remember, after the reading of four short texts, the source of an information and to identify "the more knowledgeable" character of each text. By contrasting the performance of good versus less-skilled comprehenders, Macedo-Rouet et al. found that the intervention was beneficial for less-skilled readers only. This result contrasts with Rouet et al.'s (2011) intervention (based on the reading of a short text) whose benefits were observed for better readers only. Macedo-Rouet et al. therefore argued that the specific format of the intervention provided (i.e., spoken modality, small groups and interactive discussion) may have been particularly beneficial for less-skilled comprehenders.

In sum, studies focusing on the processing of documents and their evaluation in terms of reliability bring promising results in enhancing children's evaluation skills. Such processes have also been targeted in studies conducting more "comprehensive" interventions encompassing different stages of functional reading and information search.

10.3.3 Interventions Combining Several Stages of the Information Search Processes

Most instructional interventions published thus far have combined activities targeting different steps of information search processes in order to foster children's functional reading abilities (Table 10.2).

Kuiper et al. (2008) evaluated the impact of an educational program conducted by four 5th grade teachers that aimed at fostering Web search skills. The program

Table 10.2 Instructional objectives identified in a set of intervention studies and correspondence with the three core challenges of information search (see Table 10.1)

Study	Building a task model	Accessing information	Assessing adequacy and sufficiency
Kuiper et al. (2008)	Not explicitly addressed in training plan	Search for Web information Read and interpret Web information	Assess and evaluate Web information
Zhang and Duke (2011)	Have a plan, write a to-do list	Know how Web site is organized	Check source (who, why, when written) Check whether information helps meet search needs
Kingsley et al. (2015)	Not explicitly addressed in training plan[a]	Locate information	Evaluate and synthesize information
Gerjets and Hellenthal-schorr (2008)	General knowledge of information problems (Module 2) Break complex problem into subproblems (Module 6)	Know the Web as an information environment (Module 1) Localize Web site (Module 4) and information within Web site (Module 3) Select an information provider (Module 5)	Not explicitly addressed in training plan

[a]Kingsley et al. did stress the importance of generating questions as part of the goal of locating information

was composed of eight weekly sessions (1.5–2 h each) and tapped different aspects of functional literacy such as locating information and evaluating document information (see Table 10.2). All activities were based on the single topic of healthy food. The authors collected a variety of data, mostly qualitative (e.g., lesson observations, interviews with teachers and students, teacher diaries, student questionnaires) and also examined the impact of this intervention on children's Web search skills. The results were promising as regards the possibility of making usual classroom-teachers implement this type of interventions in their educational program. However, the study remained inconclusive as regards its impact on children's functional reading skills. For instance, the intervention did not influence children's search behavior in a non-supervised Web search activity, and only two of the four participating classes showed progress in their evaluation skills. Zhang and Duke (2011) proposed a longer intervention (4 times 30 min) in which fourth and fifth graders were trained on information evaluation using a framework called WWWDOT. This framework was designed to enhance children's critical evaluation of information by encouraging them to reflect about at least six aspects about a document (see Table 10.2). Paired randomization was used to assign the 242 participants of the study to either an experimental or a control group. The children in the experimental group attended four sessions of 30 min in which they were taught the WWWDOT lessons in their classroom. The control children followed their usual teaching program. Different tasks assessing source evaluation skills were administered before and after the interventions to all the children: a questionnaire, a single Web site evaluation task and a Web site ranking task. The results obtained in the questionnaire showed that the WWWDOT framework made children more aware of the need to evaluate information for credibility on the Internet, for example, by making them more aware of the existence of untrustworthy information. As regards the two Web site evaluation tasks, children in the experimental group were not better in the reliability judgment scales but justified their reliability scoring using more source-based reasons.

Kingsley et al. (2015) conducted a quasi-experimental study with 418 fifth graders and obtained more conclusive results as regards the ability to enhance elementary students' online research skills. In this study, they compared an eight-week intervention to a control condition and made use of several quantitative indicators of potential benefits of their intervention (Online Research and Comprehension Assessment—ORCA—Elementary-Revised performance, Leu et al. 2009). The instructional framework selected in this study was the Internet Reciprocal Teaching (IRT) model (Leu et al. 2005; Leu and Reinking 2010). The intervention program is comprised of 13 lessons spread over 8 weeks and were conducted within the classrooms using laptops. These lessons addressed three major aspects of information search: 1/ locating information (e.g., navigate within Web sites, internet-specific vocabulary, self-generated questioning, effective keywording, etc.); 2/ critical evaluation (questioning the author, checking information accuracy, bias detection, etc.) and 3/ synthesizing (e.g., synthesize information from inquiry research, use of online concept mapping, etc.). Following the Reciprocal Teaching framework (Palincsar and Brown 1984), the training sessions alternate between lesson, practice (guided or not) and discussion times. Children in the control condition continue to follow their typical instructional activities. After controlling for children's "traditional" reading skills, the results demonstrated that the intervention group showed significantly higher gains from pretest to posttest on the online research measures. More precisely, by distinguishing between three subscales of the ORCA test, the authors reported that these differences concerned the online skills of locating and synthesizing, but no significant group differences were observed for growth in the domain of critical evaluation skills. Authors also observed that the children with higher skills in traditional reading activities demonstrated greater gains after the intervention on the online research tasks.

Finally, Gerjets and Hellenthal-Schorr (2008) developed a Web-based training for children (CIS-WEB, Competent Information Search in the World-Wide WEB, see also Schorr 2005) which aims at fostering knowledge and skills necessary for efficient information search on the Web. Interestingly, they compared its effectiveness over a conventional technically oriented Internet training ("Surfcheck- Online") or an unguided exploration of the Web. The CIS-WEB program consisted of six training modules (12 sessions of 45 min each) that combined direct instruction and individual and/or dyad practice and used a problem-solving training approach. The training modules addressed issues from basic knowledge about the WWW to more complex strategies to locate relevant information on a Web site or evaluate information with regard to its credibility and actuality. The results showed that neither the conventional Internet training nor an unguided exploration of the Web was helpful to improve children's search performance. In contrast, the CIS-WEB training substantially improved participants' declarative knowledge as regards search-irrelevant versus search relevant information and also increased their performance in information problem solving using the Internet. The authors noticed that such positive effects were visible from the end of the first training module (i.e., after three training sessions only), whereas further improvements seem to depend on children's investment in the worksheets and exercises embedded in the training.

10.3.4   Summary and Perspectives for Future Intervention Studies

In conclusion, the studies presented in this section provide promising evidence as regards the possibility to foster children's information search skills through adequate interventions. The studies conducted so far have either targeted specific processes at work in information search or offered interventions aimed at fostering simultaneously several processes and steps of information search.

Specific interventions aimed at having the children develop a better task model (e.g., "what am I looking for?"; "how can I access effectively relevant information depending on what I am looking for?") or assessing the relevance of information (e.g., "is the information found relevant and reliable?"). Although the evidence is still scarce, it seems that these interventions may have positive effects: Trained students showed better mastery of the targeted processes. However, we also noticed that the effects of these interventions were sometimes confined to certain types of readers (e.g., good readers, Rouet et al. 2011, or younger readers, Coutelet and Rouet 2004) or concerned only some measures but not others (e.g., Ayroles et al. 2018). The promising point here is that these studies usually consisted in relatively short interventions (sometimes a single 30-min session, Macedo-Rouet et al. 2013 or even a specific prompt given at the time of the search, Ayroles et al. 2018). It remains to be found whether more substantial interventions would expand these benefits.

The latter studies have attempted to develop more comprehensive interventions aimed at fostering simultaneously different information search processes. These studies combined an instruction both at the level of relevant information localization, its evaluation in terms of reliability or credibility and the synthesis of information found in different documents (or Web sites). These studies, which involved longer intervention times (generally spread over several sessions), also yield overall positive conclusions. In addition, such interventions, based on the majority on didactical principles already used for the teaching of "traditional" reading comprehension skills (e.g., reciprocal teaching, Palincsar and Brown 1984), seem to be more effective than a simple use of the Internet or than interventions centered on more "technical" aspects of online reading (Gerjets and Hellenthal-Schorr 2008).

Some of the aforementioned studies also showed that this type of interventions could well be implemented in classrooms by regular teachers (Kuiper et al. 2008). This point is of particular interest given that most countries have now such expectations about information search skills in their school curricula (e.g., in France, with issues relating to media education). Nevertheless, teachers often lack definite content on how to teach functional reading skills to children, and we believe the studies presented in this chapter could provide some interesting insights into both the processes that can be targeted in such instructional sessions and the activities that could be proposed to children in order to enhance the use of these processes.

10.4   Conclusions

In this chapter, we have examined children's acquisition of information search skills as they apply to printed and digital texts. Text search is a complex form of reading that involves a series of cognitive and metacognitive processes. Based on a review of theories stemming from information science and psychology, we have highlighted three core processes that may pose specific challenges to developing readers: forming and maintaining and adequate mental model of the task, accessing relevant information and assessing the quality and sufficiency of information with respect to the task goal (or product). We have reviewed evidence that children between the ages of 7 and 12 indeed experience difficulties with these processes. Finally, we have reviewed the literature regarding instructional interventions focusing on search skills.

Despite a sustained interest dating back from the 1980s, information search as a complex skill is still an under-researched area. Furthermore, the domain itself has evolved dramatically with the advent and widespread dissemination of digital reading environments. Different perspectives can be identified and could be explored in future works, in reference to the three core processes elicited in this chapter. For instance, few studies have been conducted to improve children's ability to construct and handle search task models (Rouet and Britt 2011). Beyond studies prompting students to think about the question (Ayroles et al. 2018), one could consider interventions targeting the different dimensions of the task model such who is asking and why? In what context do I perform this task? for which purpose? (see Britt et al. 2018); the type of response that can be expected (a "single" response located in a specific part of the text, such as a specific date or a single word, or an answer that will require searching for more information located in several parts of the text or even, in several documents) or the potential location of the searched information within the documents. Interventions could also focus on document structure and in particular the use of organization and content cues in Web sites to access more efficiently the searched information.

Systematic work aimed at training students' information search can and should also be undertaken with elementary and secondary school students. Research conducted so far does provide interesting hints, but studies carried out with older readers (e.g., Brante and Strømsø 2018; Pérez et al. 2018) could also serve as a basis for the development of future interventions with younger students. However, as the aforementioned study by Kammerer and Bohnacker (2012) pointed out, caution is needed in applying adult search strategies to children. Interventions designed for children should take into account their actual potential and limitations (e.g., by favoring oral discussion over the reading of written explanations; see Macedo-Rouet et al. 2013). Learning to effectively search information is also related to other dimensions of children's language and cognitive development. For instance, children's acquisition of vocabulary is critical for their use of search engines, as querying rests on an ability to flexibly generate and refine verbal expressions in relation to a search need. Finally, strategies for reading multiple documents and integrating integration from multiple documents (including how to handle inconsistencies and contradictions) must be an important point to work with young students. This type of situation is indeed very common in the reading activities children carry out on a daily basis, whether in the school context or in their daily life. Generally speaking, the acquisition of effective functional reading strategies cannot be reached without going through an explicit teaching of such strategies. In order to benefit all students—whatever is, for example, their level in "traditional" reading comprehension—such interventions would ideally be adapted to the student's initial level and knowledge.

Acknowledgements This research was supported in part through grant ANR-17-CE28-0016 from the Agence Nationale pour la Recherche.

References

Agarwal NK (2018) Exploring context in information behavior: seeker, situation, surroundings, and shared identities. Morgan & Claypool

Armbruster BB, Armstrong JO (1993) Locating information in text: a focus on children in the elementary grades. Contemp Educ Psychol 18:139–161

Ayroles J, Potocki A, Ros C, Salin M, Guérineau M, Cerdán R, Britt A, Rouet JF (2018) Do you know what you are reading for? supporting task model construction enhances 5th graders' purposeful reading. Paper presented at the 28th annual meeting of the society for text and discourse, Brighton, United Kingdom, 17–19 July

Belkin NJ (1993) Interaction with texts: information retrieval as information seeking behavior. Inf Retrieval 93:55–66

Brand-Gruwel S, Wopereis I, Walraven A (2009) A descriptive model of information problem solving while using internet. Comput Educ 53:1207–1217

Brante EW, Strømsø HI (2018) Sourcing in text comprehension: a review of interventions targeting sourcing skills. Educ Psychol Rev 30(3):773–799

Britt MA, Rouet J-F, Durik A (2018) Literacy beyond text comprehension: a theory of purposeful reading. Taylor & Francis

Cataldo MG, Cornoldi C (1998) Self-monitoring in poor and good reading comprehenders and their use of strategy. Br J Dev Psychol 16:155–165

Cataldo MG, Oakhill J (2000) Why are poor comprehenders inefficient searchers? an investigation into the effects of text representation and spatial memory on the ability to locate information in text. J Educ Psychol 92(4):791–799

Cerdán R, Gilabert R, Vidal-Abarca E (2011) Selecting information to answer questions: strategic individual differences when searching texts. Learn Individ Differ 21:201–205

Cerdán R, Gilabert R, Vidal-Abarca E (2013) Self-generated explanations on the question demands are not always helpful. Span J Psychol, 16

Coiro J, Coscarelli C, Maykel C, Forzani E (2015) Investigating criteria that seventh graders use to evaluate the quality of online information. J Adolesc Adult Lit 59(3):287–297. https://doi.org/10.1002/jaal.448

Coutelet B, Rouet JF (2004) Apprendre à chercher dans un texte: effets d'un entraînement à 8 et 10 ans (Learning to search in a text: effects of a training intervention at 8 and 10 years of age). Enfance 56(4):357–386

De Vries B, van der Meij H, Lazonder AW (2008) Supporting reflective web searching in elementary schools. Comput Hum Behav 24(3):649–665

Dinet J, de Cara B, Thérouanne P, Chanquoy L, Rouet J-F, Tricot A, … Dumercy L (2010) L'utilisation des moteurs de recherche par les jeunes : Impact des connaissances du domaine et des connaissances procédurales sur les stratégies d'exploration visuelle (The use of search engines by young people: impact of domain and procedural knowledge on visual scanning strategies). Paper presented at the 7ème Colloque International TICE'2010, France

Dinet J, Passerault J-M, Rouet J-F (1998) Les «nouveaux outils» de recherche documentaire sont-ils compatibles avec les stratégies cognitives des élèves ? (Are the "new document search tools" compatible with students cognitive strategies?). Paper presented to the Quatrième colloque hypermédias et apprentissages, Paris, France

Dreher MJ, Guthrie JT (1990) Cognitive processes in textbook chapter search tasks. Read Res Q 25(4):323–339

Dreher MJ, Sammons RB (1994) Fifth graders' search for information in a textbook. J Read Behav 26(3):301–314

Eme E, Rouet J-F (2001) Les connaissances métacognitives en lecture-compréhension chez l'enfant et l'adulte (Metacognitive knowledge in children and adults). Enfance 53:309–328

Garner R, Alexander P, Slater W, Hare VC (1986) Children's knowledge of structural properties of expository text. J Educ Psychol 78(6):411–416

Gerjets P, Hellenthal-Schorr T (2008) Competent information search in the World Wide Web: development and evaluation of a web training for pupils. Comput Hum Behav 24(3):693–715

Goldman SR (2004) Cognitive aspects of constructing meaning through and across multiple texts. In: Shuart-Ferris N, Bloome DM (eds) Uses of intertextuality in classroom and educational research. Information Age Publishing, Greenwich, CT, pp 313–347

Goldman SR, Durán RP (1988) Answering questions from oceanography texts: learner, task, and text characteristics. Discourse Process 11(4):373–412

Goldman SR, Lawless KA, Gomez KW, Braasch J, McLeod S, Manning S (2010) Literacy in the digital world. In: McKeown M, Kucan L (eds) Bringing reading research to life. Guilford Press, New-York, pp 257–284

Graesser AC, Franklin SP (1990) QUEST: a cognitive model of question answering. Discourse Process 13(3):279–303

Guthrie JT (1988) Locating information in documents: examination of a cognitive model. Read Res Q 23:178–199

Guthrie JT, Kirsch I (1987) Distinctions between reading comprehension and locating information in text. J Educ Psychol 79:210–228

Guthrie JT, Mosenthal P (1987) Literacy as multidimentional: locating information and reading comprehension. Educ Psychol 22:279–297

Hahnel C, Goldhammer F, Kröhne U, Naumann J (2018) The role of reading skills in the evaluation of online information gathered from search engine environments. Comput Hum Behav 78:223–234

Hannon B, Daneman M (2004) Shallow semantic processing of text: an individual-differences account. Discourse Process 37(3):187–204

Kaakinen JK, Lehtola A, Paattilammi S (2015) The influence of a reading task on children's eye movements during reading. J Cogn Psychol 27(5):640–656

Kammerer Y, Bohnacker M (2012, June). Children's web search with Google: the effectiveness of natural language queries. In: Proceedings of the 11th international conference on interaction design and children, ACM, pp 184–187

Khosrowjerdi M, Iranshahi M (2011) Prior knowledge and information-seeking behavior of PhD and MA students. Libr Inf Sci Res 33(4):331–335

Kingsley TL, Cassady JC, Tancock SM (2015) Successfully promoting 21st century online research skills: interventions in 5th-grade classrooms. Read Horiz 54(2):5

Kobasigawa A (1983) Children's retrieval skills for school learning. Alta J Educ Res 29(4):259–271

Kobasigawa A, Lacasse MA, Macdonald VA (1988) Use of headings by children for text search. Can J Behav Sci 20:50–63

Kobasigawa A, Ransom CC, Holland CJ (1980) Children's knowledge about skimming. Alta J Educ Res 26:169–182

Kintsch W (1998) Comprehension: a paradigm for cognition. Cambridge University Press, Cambridge, MA

Kuiper E, Volman M, Terwel J (2008) Integrating critical Web skills and content knowledge: development and evaluation of a 5th grade educational program. Comput Hum Behav 24(3):666–692

Kuhlthau CC (1991) Inside the search process: information seeking from the user's perspective. J Am Soc Inf Sci 42(5):361

Leu DJ, Castek J, Hartman D, Coiro J, Henry L, Kulikowich J, Lyver, S. (2005) Evaluating the development of scientific knowledge and new forms of reading comprehension during online learning. In: Final report presented to the North Central Regional Educational Laboratory/Learning Point Associates. Retrieved May, 15, 2006

Leu DJ, Kulikowich J, Sedransk N, Coiro J (2009) Assessing online reading comprehension: the ORCA project. Research grant funded by the US Department of Education, Institute of Education Sciences

Leu DJ, Reinking D (2010) Final report: developing Internet comprehension strategies among adolescent students at risk to become dropouts. U.S. Department of Education's Institute for Educational Science Research Grant

Leu DJ, Forzani E, Burlingame C, Kulikowich J, Sedransk N, Coiro J, Kennedy C (2013) The new literacies of online research and comprehension: assessing and preparing students for the 21st century with common core state standards. In: Quality reading instruction in the age of common core standards, pp 219–236

Llorens AC, Cerdán R (2012) Assessing the comprehension of questions in task-oriented reading. Revista de Psicodidáctica 17(2):233–252

Macedo-Rouet M, Rouet J-F, Ros C, Vibert N (2012) How do scientists select articles in the PubMed database? an empirical study of criteria and strategies. Rev Eur Psychol Appliquée/Eur Rev Appl Psychol 62(2):63–72

Macedo-Rouet M, Braasch JL, Britt MA, Rouet JF (2013) Teaching fourth and fifth graders to evaluate information sources during text comprehension. Cogn Instr 31(2):204–226

Marchionini G (1995) Information seeking in electronic environments. Cambridge University Press

McCrudden MT, Magliano JP, Schraw G (2010) Exploring how relevance instructions affect personal reading intentions, reading goals and text processing: a mixed methods study. Contemp Educ Psychol 35(4):229–241

McCrudden MT, Schraw G (2007) Relevance and goal-focusing in text processing. Educ Psychol Rev 19:113–139

Meyer BJ, Ray MN (2017) Structure strategy interventions: increasing reading comprehension of expository text. Int Electron J ElemTary Educ 4(1):127–152

Mullis IVS., Martin MO, Foy P, Hooper M (2017) PIRLS 2016 international results in reading. International Association for the Evaluation of Educational Achievement (IEA)

National Reading Panel (US), National Institute of Child Health & Human Development (US) (2000) Teaching children to read: an evidence-based assessment of the scientific research literature on reading and its implications for reading instruction. National Institute of Child Health and Human Development, National Institutes of Health

Ng C, Graham S (2017) Engaging readers in the twenty-first century: what we know and need to know more. In: Ng C, Bartlett B (eds) Improving reading and reading engagement in the 21st century. Springer, Singapore, pp 17–46

Organisation for Economic Co-operation and Development (OECD) (2013) PISA 2012 assessment and analytical framework

Palincsar AS, Brown AL (1984) Reciprocal teaching of comprehension-fostering and comprehension-monitoring activities. Cogn Instr 1(2):117–175

Paris SG, Cross DR, Lipson MY (1984) Informed strategies for learning: a program to improve children's reading awareness and comprehension. J Educ Psychol 76:1239–1252

Paul J, Cerdán R, Rouet JF, Stadtler M (2018) Exploring fourth graders' sourcing skills/Un análisis de la capacidad de escrutinio sobre las fuentes de información de los estudiantes de cuarto grado. Infanc Y Aprendiz 41(3):536–580

Pérez A, Potocki A, Stadtler M, Macedo-Rouet M, Paul J, Salmerón L, Rouet JF (2018) Fostering teenagers' assessment of information reliability: effects of a classroom intervention focused on critical source dimensions. Learn Instr 58:53–64

Pirolli P, Card SK (1999) Information foraging. Psychol Rev 106:643–675

Potocki A, Ros C, Vibert N, Rouet J-F (2017) Children's visual scanning of textual documents: effects of document organization, search goals and metatextual knowledge. Sci Stud Read 21(6):480–497

Raphael TE (1984) Teaching learners about sources of information for answering comprehension questions. J Read (January):303–311

Raphael TE, McKinney J (1983) An examination of fifth-and eighth-grade children's question-answering behavior: an instructional study in metacognition. J Read Behav 15(3):67–86

Rieh SY (2004) On the Web at home: information seeking and Web searching in the home environment. J Am Soc Inform Sci Technol 55(8):743–753

Rouet J-F (2003) "What was I looking for?" the influence of task specificity and prior knowledge on students' search strategies in hypertext. Interact Comput 15:409–428

Rouet J-F (2006) The skills of document use: from text comprehension to Web-based learning. Erlbaum, Mahwah, NJ

Rouet J-F, Britt MA (2011) Relevance processes in multiple document comprehension. In: Text relevance and learning from text, p 19–52

Rouet JF, Britt MA, Durik AM (2017) RESOLV: readers' representation of reading contexts and tasks. Educ Psychol 52(3):200–215

Rouet J-F, Coutelet B (2008) The acquisition of document search strategies in grade school students. Appl Cogn Psychol 22:389–406

Rouet J-F, Tricot A (1996) Task and activity models in hypertext usage. In: van Oostendorp H, de Mul S (eds) Cognitive aspects of electronic text processing. Ablex, Norwood, NJ, pp 239–264

Rouet J-F, Potocki A (2018) From reading comprehension to document literacy: learning to search, evaluate, and integrate information across texts. Infanc Y Aprendiz 41(3):415–446

Rouet JF, Ros C, Goumi A, Macedo-Rouet M, Dinet J (2011) The influence of surface and deep cues on primary and secondary school students' assessment of relevance in Web menus. Learn Instr 21(2):205–219

Rouet J-F, Vidal-Abarca E, Bert-Erboul A, Millogo V (2001) Effects of information search tasks on the comprehension of instructional text. Discourse Process 31(2):163–186

Salmerón L, García A, Vidal-Abarca E (2018a) The development of adolescents' comprehension-based Internet reading activities. Learn Individ Differ 61:31–39

Salmerón L, Strømsø HI, Kammerer K, Stadtler M, van den Broek P (2018b) Comprehension processes in digital reading. In: Thomson J, Barzilai M, Schroeder S, van den Broek P (eds) Learning to read in a digital world. John Benjamins, Amsterdam, pp 91–120

Savolainen R (2018) Information-seeking processes as temporal developments: comparison of stage-based and cyclic approaches. J Assoc Inf Sci Technol 69(6):787–797

Schorr T (2005) Kompetente Informationssuche im World Wide Web: Entwicklung und Evaluation eines Webtrainings für Schüler (Competent information search in the World Wide Web: development and evaluation of a Web training for pupils). University of Tuebingen, Tuebingen

Vakkari P (2003) Task-based information searching. Ann Rev Inf Sci Technol 37(1):413–464

van den Broek P, Bohn-Gettler CM, Kendeou P, Carlson S, White MJ (2011) When a reader meets a text: the role of standards of coherence in reading comprehension. In: McCrudden MT, Magliano JP, Schraw G (eds) Text relevance and learning from text. Information Age Publishing, Greenwich, CT, pp 123–140

van Dijk TA, Kintsch W (1983) Strategies of discourse comprehension. Lawrence Erlbaum Associates, Hillsdale, NJ

Vibert N, Ros C, Le Bigot L, Ramond M, Gatefin J, Rouet J-F (2009) Effects of domain knowledge on reference search with the PubMed database: an experimental study. J Am Soc Inform Sci Technol 60:1423–1447

Vidal-Abarca E, Maña A, Gil L (2010) Individual differences for self-regulating task-oriented reading activities. J Educ Psychol 102:817

Wellman HM (ed) (1985) Children's searching: the development of search skill and spatial representation. Erlbaum, Hillsdale, NJ

White S, Chen J, Forsyth B (2010) Reading-related literacy activities of American adults: time spent, task types, and cognitive skills used. J Lit Res 42:276–307

Williams JP, Hall KM, Lauer KD (2004) Teaching expository text structure to young at-risk learners: building the basics of comprehension instruction. Exceptionality 12(3):129–144

World Health Organization (n.d.) Definitions of key terms. Retrieved from https://www.who.int/hiv/pub/guidelines/arv2013/intro/keyterms/en/

Zhang S, Duke NK (2011) The impact of instruction in the WWWDOT framework on students' disposition and ability to evaluate web sites as sources of information. ElemTary Sch J 112(1):132–154

Chapter 11
Trainings and Tools to Foster Source Credibility Evaluation During Web Search

Yvonne Kammerer and Saskia Brand-Gruwel

Abstract On the Web, anyone can publish information without review by professional gatekeepers. Thus, in order to avoid obtaining incomplete or inaccurate information, Web searchers need to critically evaluate the credibility of online information or its source, respectively. However, previous research has indicated that Web users of all ages infrequently engage in credibility evaluation spontaneously during Web search. Therefore, in recent years, various interventions have been developed and tested that aim at fostering individuals' credibility evaluation during Web search. The present chapter provides an overview of these interventions. Specifically, the chapter distinguishes between three different types of interventions or support tools, respectively. These are comprehensive long-term training programs that teach students the whole process of conducting Web searches (of which credibility evaluation is only one aspect among many), short-term trainings that focus explicitly on aspects of credibility evaluation during Web search, and last but not least computer-based applications or search results interfaces that provide prompts or cues that help evaluate the credibility of online information during Web search. The different types of approaches will be compared and critically discussed in terms of both their effectiveness and limitations.

11.1   Introduction

During the last two decades, the World Wide Web (or shortly: the Web) has become an essential knowledge resource in our digital society, with search engines, such as Google, providing easy access to billions of websites on just about any conceivable topic. Thus, for many people searching on the Web has become an everyday activity to gain information on or learn about a certain topic, that is, to solve a particular

Y. Kammerer (✉)
Leibniz-Institut für Wissensmedien, Tübingen, Germany
e-mail: y.kammerer@iwm-tuebingen.de

Y. Kammerer · S. Brand-Gruwel
Open University of the Netherlands, Heerlen, The Netherlands

© Springer Nature Switzerland AG 2020
W. T. Fu and H. van Oostendorp (eds.), *Understanding and Improving Information Search*, Human–Computer Interaction Series,
https://doi.org/10.1007/978-3-030-38825-6_11

information problem at hand (e.g., Brand-Gruwel et al. 2009). As long as 30 years ago, Marchionini (1989) has pointed out that 'Information-seeking is a special case of problem solving, [that …] includes recognizing and interpreting the information problem, establishing a plan of search, conducting the search, evaluating the results, and if necessary, iterating through the process again' (p. 54). Information problems can be well-structured or ill-structured (cf. Jonassen 1997). Well-structured information problems possess one correct answer or a set of convergent answers, such as when searching for facts or definitions. Ill-structured information problems are characterized by having multiple solutions for which fragile and conflicting evidence and competing perspectives and arguments exist, such as when learning about controversial scientific or health-related issues. Because on the Web anyone can publish information without review by professional gatekeepers, particularly when using the Web to learn about ill-structured problems, Web users should critically evaluate the accuracy of the encountered information. If individuals cannot directly evaluate the accuracy of information themselves because they lack prior knowledge about the subject matter (which is often the case when acquiring new knowledge), assessing the credibility of the sources that provide the information (i.e., the Web authors or website providers) is a valuable alternative (Stadtler and Bromme 2014). Two key dimensions to evaluate a source's credibility are its expertise and trustworthiness (Hovland et al. 1953; Hovland and Weiss 1951). Specifically, expertise and trustworthiness refer to an individual's perceptions about whether a source is competent (expertise) and willing (trustworthiness) to provide information both accurate and valid (Danielson 2006; Metzger 2007). A related concept to source credibility is that of information quality, which according to Tate (2010) consists of five dimensions: (1) authority, that is, the degree to which the author of the information can be identified as having knowledge of the respective subject area; (2) objectivity, that is, the purpose of a website and the degree to which information is presented without distortion by personal feelings or other biases (e.g., commercial interests); (3) currency, that is, whether the information provided by a website is up-to-date; (4) accuracy, that is, the degree to which a website is free of errors; and (5) coverage, that is, the comprehensiveness or depth of information provided by a website (also see Kammerer and Gerjets 2012a). Furthermore, source credibility evaluation can be considered as a sub-component of 'sourcing,' which comprises processes of attending to and evaluating available or accessible information about the sources of documents, such as, who authored them and for what reason, as well as of remembering or recalling such information, and referencing sources in own task products (Bråten et al. 2018). But which role does source credibility evaluation play in the process of information problem solving on the Web?

Following Marchionini (1989), during the last three decades several models from the fields of information science, human–computer interaction, and educational psychology have described the process of information problem solving by segmenting it into several sub-processes (i.e., steps or stages). A prominent model from information science on the process of information problem solving is Kuhlthau's (1991) *Information Search Process (ISP)* model (also see e.g., Kuhlthau et al. 2008). The ISP model describes the process of information search, which can span over several search sessions, consisting of the following six stages: (1) initiation of the process by recognizing an information need, (2) selection of an appropriate topic or approach, (3) exploration of information on the general topic, (4) formulation of a focused perspective of the topic, (5) collection of information relevant to the focused perspective, and (6) presentation of the findings based on a own synthesis of the topic or problem. For each stage, the model considers cognitive, affective, and behavioral dimensions of the search process. That is, the model addresses changes in searchers' thoughts (cognitive), feelings (affective), and actions (behavioral) across the different stages, with thoughts shifting from general or vague to focused, feelings changing from uncertainty over confusion or clarity to relief, satisfaction, or disappointment, and actions ranging from seeking background information to seeking relevant and focused information. Extending Kuhlthau's (1991) model, Vakkari's theory of the *Task-Based Information Retrieval Process* (2001) describes more specifically how the extent and quality of individuals search terms, search tactics, and relevance judgments change across different stages of the search process. Similarly, Sharit et al. (2008) from the field of human–computer interaction have also proposed a model of *Search Engine Information-Seeking Behavior*. They distinguish three iterative (cognitive or metacognitive) sub-processes of information problem-solving activity: (a) creating a mental representation of the problem statement, (b) planning the process, that is, defining operations or strategies to solve the problem, and (c) executing the operations that were developed during the planning process, such as formulating or refining search queries and judging the relevance of search results and websites. Moreover, they focus on how these cognitive processes are affected by individuals' domain and technical knowledge and cognitive abilities (e.g., verbal ability, visuo-spatial ability, working memory capacity; Sharit et al. 2008, 2015).

However, none of these models has specifically focused on credibility evaluation during Web search. By contrast, the *Information Problem Solving on the Internet (IPS-I)* model by Brand-Gruwel and colleagues (Brand-Gruwel et al. 2005, 2009) from educational psychology, that distinguishes five iterative processing steps that unfold during Web search, considers aspects of credibility evaluation in several steps of the information problem-solving process (for similar models from educational psychology, also see e.g., Kiili et al. 2018; Rouet and Britt 2011). In Step 1 ('define information problem'), the searcher defines his or her information problem and formulates a concrete question based on the information needed. In Step 2 ('search information'), the searcher selects a search strategy (e.g., to use a search engine), transforms the question into search terms and types them into a search engine, and critically evaluates the search results provided on the search engine results page (SERP) to determine which information sources appear relevant and credible. In Step 3 ('scan information'), after having selected a website from the SERP, the searcher scans the website and critically evaluates it in light of its source. In Step 4 ('process information'), when deemed relevant and credible, the information provided by the website is processed more deeply and compared with and evaluated against own prior knowledge and information found on other websites. Finally, in Step 5 ('organize and present information') information from several websites is synthesized toward a solution of the information problem to prepare the task product (which can be in the individual's mind or an external task product such as an essay or presentation). In line with the IPS-I model, other researchers have distinguished three iterative phases of credibility evaluation during Web search (cf. Gerjets et al. 2011; Hilligoss and Rieh 2008): (1) when making predictive credibility judgments on the basis of the search results descriptions provided by a search engine (i.e., before accessing a website), (2) when making evaluative credibility judgments about an accessed website or the respective information provider or author (i.e., to assess whether the predictive judgments are met), and (3) when verifying or re-evaluating the credibility of a source after having accessed multiple websites, for instance, after having encountered discrepancies between documents.

From a cognitive perspective, previous research has indicated that the degree of critically evaluating the credibility of sources, while reading multiple online documents about complex science-related issues is positively related to individuals' learning and comprehension outcomes (Anmarkrud et al. 2014; Barzilai et al. 2015; Goldman et al. 2012; Wiley et al. 2009). This demonstrates the importance of credibility evaluation. However, according to the *Prominence-Interpretation Theory* by Fogg (2003) two constituent components for credibility assessments being made by individuals (also see Kammerer and Gerjets 2012a; Metzger 2007) are the prominence and the interpretation of credibility cues (e.g., author names, logos, website addresses, etc.) that are available in websites or search results descriptions. Prominence refers to the likelihood that such cues will be noticed by an individual, and interpretation refers to an individual's personal interpretation of a credibility cue that has been noticed. If a certain cue remains unnoticed, it will have no impact on an individual's credibility evaluation. Whether less prominent cues are noticed by a person might also depend on his or her personal involvement or credibility evaluation skills (Fogg 2003). On the basis of a cue that has been noticed, a person might draw inferences about the competence and motives of a source. The quality of such interpretation, however, again is likely to depend on a person's credibility evaluation skills as well as on his or her prior knowledge on the subject matter (Fogg 2003). Since credibility cues in search results descriptions or websites often lack prominence and/or individuals might lack the knowledge or skills to adequately evaluate these cues, and unsurprisingly, many studies have shown that Web users of all ages only infrequently evaluate the credibility of information sources spontaneously during Web search (for a recent review, see Bråten et al. 2018). Furthermore, many individuals predominantly select the first few search results presented by a search engine such as Google without evaluating the credibility of the sources by themselves (e.g., Hargittai et al. 2010). Yet, even websites listed among the top search results of a search engine results page (SERP) might turn out to be one-sided or commercially biased (Lewandowski 2011).

Therefore, in recent years, from an educational perspective, various interventions and support tools have been developed and tested that aim at fostering individuals' credibility evaluation during Web search. The purpose of this chapter is to provide a comprehensive overview on evaluation studies of such interventions and support tools that have been published until 2018. These comprise interventions and tools targeted at different user populations, that is, school students, university students, or other adults; some have been developed for classroom settings, others for non-academic settings.

11.2 Overview on Interventions and Support Tools for Source Credibility Evaluation

In the present chapter, we will distinguish between three different types of interventions or support tools: (1) comprehensive training programs that convey information problem-solving (IPS) skills (of which credibility evaluation is only one aspect among many) over a period of several weeks or months, (2) short-term trainings that last from 20 min to a few hours and that focus explicitly on aspects of credibility evaluation, and (3) computer-based applications or search results interfaces that provide prompts or cues that help evaluate the credibility of online information or its source. Whereas the first two types of interventions explicitly and directly *teach* individuals *how to* evaluate source credibility during Web search, the third type only *prompts* individuals either explicitly or implicitly to engage in source credibility evaluation.

In parts, we base our overview on recent systematic literature reviews by Brante and Strømsø (2018) and by Brand-Gruwel and Van Strien (2018), as well as on another comprehensive overview chapter by Bråten et al. (2018). Other than in the previous literature reviews, in the present chapter, however, we specifically focus on approaches that address the critical evaluation of information sources during Web search. Thus, we do not include interventions that teach credibility assessments in the context of reading a set of printed or Web-based documents without the necessity to search for or select documents from SERPs. Besides, we do not consider interventions that have not been empirically tested or interventions that focus on literature search in bibliographic databases rather than on Web searches. Moreover, in the present chapter we only focus on studies that have used at least one indicator of source credibility evaluation as a dependent variable. On the one hand, these can be measures of 'spontaneous' source credibility evaluation, such as verbal utterances reflecting credibility assessments of sources during Web search as measured by thinking-aloud methodology, the degree of credible or less credible websites being accessed during Web search, or the number of source references or credibility judgments included in essays or written justifications composed after Web search. On the other hand, these can be measures of 'prompted' source credibility evaluation, such as tasks that require rating or ranking search results or web pages according to their credibility, or tasks that require to mark credibility cues in search results or web pages.

Based on these inclusion criteria, the present chapter comprises 13 journal articles and one Cognitive Science Society proceedings paper that were also cited in at least one of the three previous reviews (also see the last column of Tables 11.1, 11.2 and 11.3). Furthermore, we have added two more recently published journal articles (Hagerman 2017; Pérez et al. 2018). Moreover, to find additional literature particularly from the field of human–computer interaction, we conducted a search

Table 11.1 Overview of comprehensive training programs and respective studies

Authors	Sample	Sample size	Implementation of intervention	Length of intervention	Search task used in evaluation study	Search environment in evaluation study	Dependent measures reflecting source credibility evaluation	Prior review(s) that included the study
Argelagós and Pifarré (2012)	7th and 8th grade students	40	Embedded into curriculum; teacher-led (Web-based)	60 h over two years	Complex and controversial socio-scientific issue	Open Web	Selection of different types of search results during search	Brand-Gruwel and Van Strien (2018) Brante and Strømsø (2018)
Brand-Gruwel and Wopereis (2006)	Students of teacher training college	16	Embedded into learning course on the topic of dyslexia; teacher-led	80 h over 10 weeks	Complex and controversial socio-scientific issue	Open Web	Source credibility evaluation utterances on SERPs and on websites	Bråten et al. (2018)
Hagerman (2017)	9th grade students	16 (8 dyads)	Embedded into science curriculum; researcher-led	Five sessions over several consecutive weeks	Complex and controversial socio-scientific issue	Open Web	Source credibility evaluation strategies coded based on audio, video, and navigation data	Not included in prior reviews
Kingsley et al. (2015)	5th grade students	418	Stand-alone; Web-based and self-paced	13 lessons over 12 consecutive weeks	Complex issues from the ORCA Elementary-Revised test	Test environment with preselected sources	ORCA Elementary-Revised test	Brante and Strømsø (2018)

(continued)

Table 11.1 (continued)

Authors	Sample	Sample size	Implementation of intervention	Length of intervention	Search task used in evaluation study	Search environment in evaluation study	Dependent measures reflecting source credibility evaluation	Prior review(s) that included the study
Kroustallaki et al. (2015)	5th and 6th grade students	96	Stand-alone classroom based; researcher-led	Three sessions of 45 min over three consecutive weeks	Complex (topic of recycling)	Open Web	Worksheets coded according to 4-point scale	Brand-Gruwel and Van Strien (2018)
Walraven et al. (2010)	9th grade students	84	Embedded into a history curriculum; teacher-led	15 lessons of 50 min	No concrete Web search	Printed SERP and websites; + 11 students with additional tasks on open Web	Selecting search results and marking source credibility cues in search results and in websites	Brand-Gruwel and Van Strien (2018)
Walraven et al. (2013)	9th grade students	101	Embedded into a history curriculum; teacher-led	15 lessons of 50 min	Complex	Printed SERP and websites	Selecting search results and marking source credibility cues in search results and in websites	Brante and Strømsø (2018) Brand-Gruwel and Van Strien (2018) Bråten et al. (2018)
Wopereis et al. (2008)	Psychology students of a distance education university	16	Embedded into a research methodology curriculum; teacher-led, Web-based	Complete course took 25 weeks	Complex and controversial socio-scientific issue	Open Web	Source credibility evaluation utterances on SERPs and on websites	Bråten et al. (2018)

Table 11.2 Overview of short-term, specific source credibility evaluation trainings and respective studies

Authors	Sample	Sample size	Implementation of intervention	Length of intervention	Search task(s) used in evaluation study	Search environment in evaluation study	Dependent measures reflecting source credibility evaluation	Prior review(s) that included the study
Graesser et al. (2007)	College students (psychology)	118	Stand-alone; a nutrition/health-related topic; self-paced, provided by researcher	Approx. 10 min (not explicitly reported)	Complex and controversial scientific issue	Predefined SERP linking to seven websites with several sub-web pages	Time spent on credible and less credible websites; number of pages accessed within sites; credibility rating and ranking task	Bråten et al. (2018)
Kammerer et al. (2015)	Adults without academic background	48	Stand-alone; medical and nutrition/health-related topics; self-paced, provided by researcher	20 min	Complex and controversial medical issue	Two predefined SERPs each linking to nine web pages	Time spent on different types of web pages	Bråten et al. (2018)

(continued)

Table 11.2 (continued)

Authors	Sample	Sample size	Implementation of intervention	Length of intervention	Search task(s) used in evaluation study	Search environment in evaluation study	Dependent measures reflecting source credibility evaluation	Prior review(s) that included the study
Mason et al. (2014)	9th grade students	134	Stand-alone; a health-related topic; researcher-led	Approx. 60 min (not explicitly reported)	Complex and controversial socio-scientific issue	Predefined SERP linking to nine web pages	Search results selections and time spent on credible and less credible websites; ranking task; written justifications	Brand-Gruwel and Van Strien (2018) Brante and Strømsø (2018)
Pérez et al. (2018)	9th grade students	137	Embedded; health-related, history, and societal topics; led by researchers and teacher	Three training sessions of 1 h	Complex and controversial scientific issues	Printed list of nine search results	Rating of search results on 5-point scale (degree to which they would consult the link)	Not included in prior reviews

(continued)

Table 11.2 (continued)

Authors	Sample	Sample size	Implementation of intervention	Length of intervention	Search task(s) used in evaluation study	Search environment in evaluation study	Dependent measures reflecting source credibility evaluation	Prior review(s) that included the study
Stadtler et al. (2015)	Middle school students ($M =$ 14.7 years)	112	Stand-alone; a nutrition/health-related topic; probably researcher-led	223 words	Complex and controversial socio-scientific issue	Predefined SERP linking to six web pages	Visits to and time spent on 'about us' pages; evaluative statements about sources in essays	Bråten et al. (2018)
Wiley et al. (2009)	Undergraduate students (psychology)	60	Stand-alone; a nutrition/health-related topic; self-paced, provided by researcher	1 h	Complex and controversial topic (volcanic eruptions)	Predefined SERP linking to seven websites with several sub-web pages	Time on and revisits to credible and less credible websites; credibility ranking task; written justifications	Brante and Strømsø (2018) Bråten et al. (2018)

Table 11.3 Overview of computer-based applications (providing prompts) and search results interfaces (providing cues) and respective studies

Authors	Sample	Sample size	Prompts or source cues provided	Search task(s) used in evaluation study	Search environment in evaluation study	Dependent measures reflecting source credibility evaluation	Prior review(s) that included the study
Graesser et al. (2007)	Undergraduate students (psychology)	33	Source credibility evaluation prompts provided by the SEEK Web tutor (on SERP and websites)	Complex and controversial scientific issue	Predefined SERP linking to seven websites with several sub-web pages	Time spent on credible and less credible websites; number of pages accessed within sites; credibility rating and ranking task	Bråten et al. (2018)
Kammerer and Gerjets (2012b)	University freshmen of different majors	58	Three source categories according to which search results were grouped	Complex and controversial medical issue	Two predefined SERPs each linking to nine web pages	Total fixation times on and selections of different types of search results	Bråten et al. (2018)
Schwarz and Morris (2011)	Middle school and high school students, and adults (ages 13–40 years)	26	Credibility cues provided for search results and web pages	Eight tasks (health, politics, finance)	No real search situation; only one preselected search result or web page shown at a time	Similarity of users' credibility ratings with expert credibility ratings; confidence in credibility ratings	Not included in prior reviews

(continued)

Table 11.3 (continued)

Authors	Sample	Sample size	Prompts or source cues provided	Search task(s) used in evaluation study	Search environment in evaluation study	Dependent measures reflecting source credibility evaluation	Prior review(s) that included the study
Stadtler and Bromme (2007)	Undergraduate students	79	Source credibility evaluation prompts on websites provided by the *met.a.ware* application	Complex and controversial medical issue	Predefined SERP linking to 15 web pages	Source references in essays; written justifications for selection of three most credible websites	Brante and Strømsø (2018)
Yamamoto and Shimada (2016)	Crowdworkers	92	Disputed information highlighted in search results (and on web pages)	Nine health-related search topics	The first 100 Google results were presented for each task	Selection of and time spent on disputed vs. undisputed web pages; total time on SERPs	Not included in prior reviews
Yamamoto and Tanaka (2011)	University students	10	Radar chart visualization next to each search result, indicating a web page's credibility	20 different topics (e.g., medical and health-related topics, economics)	The first 50 Google search results were presented for each task	Selection of credible search results	Not included in prior reviews

in the ACM (Association for Computing Machinery) Digital Library, which resulted in the inclusion of three additional ACM proceedings papers (Schwarz and Morris 2011; Yamamoto and Shimada 2016; Yamamoto and Tanaka 2011). Based on these 19 papers, in the remainder of this chapter 20 studies will be reviewed (one paper comprised two studies), of which eight studies evaluated the effectiveness of comprehensive training programs (Sect. 11.2.1), six studies the effectiveness of short-term trainings (Sect. 11.2.2), and another six studies the effectiveness of computer-based applications or search results interfaces (Sect. 11.2.3) on individuals' source credibility evaluation during Web search. In addition, Tables 11.1, 11.2, and 11.3 also give an overview regarding different aspects of these studies, such as the size and type of study sample, the search environment that was used (i.e., whether students searched on the open Web or whether they were provided with prefabricated SERPs), or the dependent variables that were used to assess source credibility evaluation (please note that dependent variables not related to source credibility evaluation are not listed though).

11.2.1 Comprehensive Training Programs Addressing the Whole IPS-I Process

The eight training programs reviewed in this section (also see Table 11.1) are characterized by using authentic learning tasks paired with scaffolds that guide the development of the whole IPS-I process on the Web. Thus, credibility evaluation is only one aspect among many in these trainings. Other aspects addressed in the trainings are, for instance, the definition of the information problem or the formulation of query terms (cf. Sharit et al. 2008, 2015). The trainings comprised multiple sessions and were run over a period of several weeks or months. All but one of the trainings have been embedded into the regular school or college curriculum.

Brand-Gruwel and Wopereis (2006) developed and tested an IPS training, in which all the steps of the IPS-I process were trained (Brand-Gruwel et al. 2005) and that over 10 weeks was embedded into a pre-service teacher curriculum. The training was built using the four-component instructional design (4C/ID) model of Van Merriën-boer (1997), which means using (1) authentic whole learning tasks and (2) part-task practices to train specific sub-processes, and providing (3) procedural information (i.e., how-to instructions), as well as (4) supportive information by including scaffolds and feedback. Students worked on four tasks and were for instance supported by process worksheets. In the worksheets, students were also prompted to evaluate the credibility of the sources and the respective information they presented. The training was evaluated with $N = 16$ students from two teacher training colleges for secondary language education, using a pretest–posttest control group design (with $n = 11$ students serving in the intervention group and $n = 5$ in the control group). Students' task was to conduct a Web search on a given scientific issue in order to subsequently write an outline about the issue. The effect of the intervention on students' IPS processes was measured using thinking-aloud methodology (cf. Ericsson and Simon 1993), and students' task outcome was measured by scoring students' written outlines. Results from thinking-aloud data revealed that students in the training group more frequently engaged in source credibility evaluation when scanning and processing web pages (i.e., Steps 3 and 4 of the IPS-I model), but not when evaluating and selecting search results (i.e., Step 2 of the IPS-I model). Moreover, intervention students scored higher on the quality of the outline than controls (i.e., Step 5 of the IPS-I model).

Wopereis, Brand-Gruwel, and Vermetten (2008) studied the effect of a similar IPS training (also designed according to the four components of the 4C/ID model) that over 25 weeks was embedded into a research methodology curriculum for distance education Psychology students, with $n = 8$ students serving in the intervention group and also $n = 8$ students in the control group. The effect of the intervention on students' IPS-I processes again was measured using thinking-aloud methodology. In the pre- and posttest, all students performed an authentic IPS Web search task (i.e., search for information and write an essay of 400–600 words) while thinking aloud. The thinking-aloud protocols showed (taken the results of the pretest into account) that students in the intervention group engaged in more source credibility evaluation while scanning and processing information in web pages (i.e., Steps 3 and 4 of the IPS-I model) than controls. However, during search result evaluation and selection (Step 2 of the IPS-I model) no differences were found between groups.

Walraven et al. (2010) evaluated two training programs for ninth grade students that both aimed at fostering students' IPS skills and particularly their source credibility evaluation skills. Both training programs (one using process worksheets and the other using group discussions and the joint construction of a mind map) comprised 15 lessons that were embedded into regular classroom activities (history class). To evaluate the effectiveness of the two training programs, students' source credibility evaluation skills on SERPs and on websites were measured during pre- and posttest using four different topics (two history topics and two biology topics, one during pretest and one during posttest). Specifically, for each topic students were provided with printed SERPs comprising 14 search results. Their task was to select three search results that they would click on and three search results that they would not click on, and to mark those parts of the search results that they based their decision on. They scored one point for each appropriate search result they selected and each inappropriate search results they did not select. Likewise, for each topic students were provided with eight printed websites and were asked to mark all features that served as indications for them to decide whether they would use the respective website. For each correctly marked criterion, they received one point. Results of the evaluation study, with $n = 39$ students receiving the training using process worksheets and $n = 45$ students undergoing the training using group discussions, showed that students' source credibility evaluation on websites increased to an equal extent from pre- to posttest in the two trainings (both for the history and the biology topics). However, again neither of the two trainings resulted in improvements in students' source credibility evaluation on SERPs.

A follow-up study by Walraven et al. (2013) using a pretest–posttest control group design tested another training program that used a combination of both previous training programs. Specifically, $n = 80$ ninth grade students of four different classes received a training of 15 lessons embedded into a history class curriculum. A fifth class ($n = 21$) served as control group. The goal of the first training lesson was confronting students with incorrect, false, and biased information and having them think about the importance of evaluating information. Students received a process worksheet with assignments for each lesson. The questions on the worksheets were linked to the five IPS-I phases. In the first three lessons, the focus was on defining information problems, the next three lessons focused on searching for information, and so on. Students worked on different tasks and filled out questions related to each phase of the IPS-I process. At the end of every lesson, teachers and students had a discussion on source credibility evaluation criteria. Students' source credibility evaluation was measured with the same printed materials as in Walraven et al. (2010). Results revealed that in the intervention group students' performance in source credibility evaluation on websites for the history topics increased from pre- to posttest, whereas in the control group performance decreased. Besides, however, students' performance in the other tasks (i.e., source credibility evaluation on SERPs for history and biology topics, and source credibility evaluation on websites for biology topics) did not increase from pre- to posttest. To conclude, the intervention was not successful in improving the evaluation of search results, neither was it successful in achieving transfer to another domain.

Argelagós and Pifarré (2012) also studied the effects of an IPS training for secondary school students that was embedded into regular, authentic classroom activities. Over two school years, the students (working collaboratively in pairs) were trained in a Web-based learning environment with activities belonging to the areas of technology, math, science, and social science. The training was presented as a WebQuest (cf. Dodge 1995) and included prompts, worksheets, and concept maps on different aspects of the whole IPS-I process. Concerning the process of searching for information, worksheets, for instance, requested to reflect on adequate search terms or on the evaluation of search results (i.e., Step 2 of the IPS-I model), and concerning the process of scanning and processing of information (i.e., Steps 3 and 4 of the IPS-I model), prompts, for instance, requested to assess a website's credibility (e.g., to identify the author and purpose of the website). The total training time was 60 h. The effect of the IPS training on source credibility evaluation as part of the whole IPS-I process was measured with $N = 40$ students of grades 7 and 8 in a pretest–posttest quasi-experimental control group design. Students' selection of sources was measured by analyzing their logfiles in an authentic IPS Web search task (searching information about the planet Mars) that they conducted on the open Web. From the logfiles, each selected site in a SERP was scored by the researchers as 'appropriate' or 'inappropriate,' The criteria taken into account to evaluate each search result were both usability and credibility. Each selected result was scored as 'appropriate' (1 point) when it was both usable and credible and as 'inappropriate' (0 points) when it was either not usable or not credible. The score was calculated as a percentage considering the number of total selected results and the number of appropriate ones. Results revealed that the students in the intervention group ($n = 20$) outperformed the students in the control group ($n = 20$) after the training, in that the former selected a higher percentage of appropriate (i.e., relevant and credible) search results.

Hagerman (2017) evaluated the LINKS (Learning to Integrate InterNet Knowledge Strategically) intervention for secondary school students, which—apart from reading and self-regulation strategies—taught strategies of source credibility evaluation on SERPs and on websites and strategies of comparing and contrasting information across multiple websites (comparable to Steps 2, 3, and 4 of the IPS-I model). The training consisted of five sessions, in which different instructional elements were used, such as discussion in dyads, direct instruction, modeling, and teacher-led questions. $N = 16$ ninth grade students worked in eight dyads (four intervention and four control dyads) performing several Web search tasks. Source credibility evaluation on SERPs and on websites was coded based on video and audio recordings. Results, however, did not show any differences between the intervention and control group in students' source credibility evaluation.

Kroustallaki et al. (2015) evaluated a stand-alone, classroom training that was developed for fifth and sixth grade students. The training consisted of three sessions using class discussion, modeling and explaining by the teacher, and practice tasks. The first session focused on the use of appropriate search terms. The goal of the second session was to be able to skim the text, identify various elements of text structure, and read selectively to locate relevant information. The third session focused on source credibility evaluation, in which students were first introduced to credibility evaluation criteria and then themselves created a checklist in the form of questions (e.g., Who wrote the page? Is information consistent with other sources? Does information agree with our prior knowledge?) regarding how to evaluate the credibility of websites (i.e., Steps 3 and 4 of the IPS-I model). Furthermore, students were introduced to a variety of websites and their genre and purpose of publishing information as well as were provided with a set of preselected websites, for which in pairs they evaluated their genre and purposes. In the evaluation study, $N = 96$ fifth and sixth grade students at four measurement points (one before and three during the intervention) were asked to complete four complex Web search tasks. Both in the intervention group ($n = 51$) and in the control group ($n = 45$) for each Web search task they had to fill out a process worksheet. Students' source credibility evaluation skills were evaluated based on the worksheets, by means of a 4-point scoring rubric (ranging from $1 =$ student does not apply credibility evaluation criteria to $4 =$ student uses a variety of criteria). Source credibility evaluation on SERPs, however, was neither trained nor measured in this study. Results revealed that students in the intervention group showed significant growth throughout the intervention in terms of the variety of credibility evaluation criteria that they used. In contrast, students in the control group did not show any improvement. The authors also tested students' general cognitive abilities (cf. Sharit et al. 2008, 2015), which, however, did not affect the rate of change in students' performance. In addition, they assessed students' positive and negative affect (cf. Kuhlthau 1991), which, however, also did not change across sessions, nor were there respective differences between intervention and control group.

Finally, Kingsley et al. (2015) investigated the effect of a stand-alone 12-week online training comprising 13 lessons, in which $n = 212$ fifth grade students learned to locate, evaluate, and synthesize information from different Web sources (i.e., addressing the whole IPS-I process). Five out of the 13 lessons (i.e., sessions 7–11) focused on source credibility evaluation (e.g., how to assess author credentials, check the accuracy of information, and detect whether a website has commercial intents). Students worked independently on a laptop or computer and received scripted lessons with PowerPoint materials, learning modules, and interactive materials. Explicit instruction, modeling, guided practice, and independent enquiry were used to train the skills. The tasks were designed from simple to complex and the principles of reciprocal teaching were used (Palinscar and Brown 1984). In addition, $n = 196$ students served in the control group. They also worked regularly on laptops or computers (approximately 60 min per week) as part of their standard curriculum. To measure the effects of the intervention on students' skills to locate, evaluate, and synthesize information, the ORCA (Online Research and Comprehension Assessment)-Elementary test including four information tasks incorporating a variety of Web sources was used. In three out of the four tasks, source credibility evaluation skills were assessed (e.g., evaluating an author's credential or identifying websites with commercial biases). However, no significant differences were found between the intervention group and control group regarding the part of the ORCA assessment measuring students' source credibility evaluation.

To conclude, the success of these comprehensive trainings of which the majority was designed for school students from grades 5 to 9 seems rather limited in terms of improving students' source credibility evaluation during Web search. One reason for the mixed findings and the limited effectiveness of some interventions might be that they typically addressed several different aspects of information problem solving on the Web. Thus, the focus of these training programs was not primarily on source credibility evaluation. It seems that more dedicated instruction and practice is needed to achieve that students will critically reflect on information sources' credibility spontaneously during Web search. Furthermore, because most of the interventions were embedded into a school or university curriculum, in which different activities and didactics were used, it is also difficult to disentangle which components, if any, had a positive effect on source credibility evaluation. Yet, from the studies of Walraven et al. (2010, 2013), Argelagós and Pifarré (2012), and Kroustallaki et al. (2015) it appears that working with process worksheets, which provide additional scaffolds or prompts, is beneficial (also see Sect. 11.2.3).

While several of the trainings fostered credibility assessments in websites, except for the intervention by Argelagós and Pifarré (2012) the trainings were not successful in fostering students' credibility assessments in SERPs. Argelagós and Pifarré (2012) were also the only ones who reported results from navigation logfiles, which can serve as implicit indicators for source credibility evaluation (e.g., how many credible vs. less credible search results students selected or how much time they spent on credible vs. less credible websites). The selection of search results from SERPs requires choosing between a large number of alternatives, for which only sparse information is provided (i.e., a title, a short description of the web page, and its URL). In such decision situations of high uncertainty, individuals typically aim at maximizing the outcome (i.e., gaining valuable information) while minimizing time and cognitive effort (Gigerenzer and Goldstein 1996; Pirolli 2007). Thus, individuals typically use a 'satisficing' strategy (cf. Simon 1955) when selecting search results from SERPs (Pirolli 2007). Moreover, search result descriptions predominantly comprise content information, whereas source credibility cues are sparse and of low prominence (e.g., hidden in the URLs of the search results), which according to the Prominence-Interpretation Theory makes credibility assessments rather unlikely (cf. Fogg 2003). To conclude, in order to notice and evaluate credibility cues in search results it might require the provision of prompts that explicitly ask for credibility assessments in SERPs during Web search or the presentation of more prominent credibility cues in search results (also see Sect. 11.2.3). Finally, it should be noted that sample sizes were quite low in some of the studies, which might have led to a large proportion of non-significant results, but also might have increased the likelihood for Type II errors.

11.2.2 Short-Term Trainings on Source Credibility Evaluation

Six trainings focused specifically on evaluating the credibility of information sources during Web search. As compared to the above-mentioned interventions, they were much shorter in length, typically lasting from 20 min to a few hours. In the following, we will provide an overview of these short-term trainings and their effectiveness to foster source credibility evaluation (also see Table 11.2).

The one-hour SEEK (Source, Evidence, Explanation, and Knowledge) intervention developed and tested by Wiley et al. (2009) consists of a combination of declarative information on source credibility evaluation and respective practical exercises with feedback. Specifically, in the first part of the intervention declarative information about different criteria to evaluate the credibility of websites was provided (i.e., focusing on Steps 3 and 4 of the IPS-I model). Central criteria addressed were the evaluation of the authors' or website providers' expertise and potential motives, the scientific evidence of the content, and the consistency of information across multiple credible websites and with one's one prior knowledge. In the second part of the intervention, individuals had to apply these criteria to a set of six websites (i.e., websites from official institutions or specialist media, commercial websites, and a personal homepage) that provided information on a health-related topic and that could be accessed via a SERP. For each website, the criteria had to be filled into a worksheet and the websites had to be ranked according to their credibility. In the third part of the intervention, the feedback was provided on how experts would rank these websites. For this purpose, individuals were again shown the SERP, and for each search result, their rank together with the expert rank was indicated. Individuals were asked to look at the differences between their rankings and the expert rankings, and think about why they might have evaluated the websites differently. Results of Wiley et al.'s (2009) experimental study showed that university students who had received the SEEK intervention ($n = 30$) outperformed controls ($n = 30$) in a transfer task on the topic of volcanic eruptions (conducted 2–7 days after the intervention) in differentiating between credible and less credible websites (as measured by a ranking task after the actual Web search). Moreover, intervention students were more likely to justify their rankings by referring to the sources and to the consistency of information across sites than controls. Students in the SEEK intervention group were also more likely to selectively re-read credible websites, whereas control students were more likely to re-read websites either non-selectively or with a bias for returning to less credible sites.

Mason et al. (2014), who tested a slightly adapted version of the first and the second part of the SEEK intervention in a study with $N = 134$ ninth grade students, found comparable results to Wiley et al. (2009). In a transfer task on genetically modified food that participants conducted one week after the intervention, students in the SEEK intervention group ($n = 69$) spent more time on credible websites, ranked the least credible websites lower (i.e., less credible), and were more likely to justify their ranking of credible websites by the presence of scientific evidence and consistency of information across sites than controls ($n = 65$).

In another experiment with $N = 118$ college students, Graesser et al. (2007) used only the declarative part of the SEEK intervention (together with one example website) and combined it with a SEEK Web tutor, that is, a computer-based application that prompted students during website reading to judge the credibility of each website as well as to fill in author information into an online form (for further details also see Sect. 11.2.3). In a 2×2 between-subject design, they varied the presence of the SEEK Web tutor and the provision of the declarative SEEK instruction prior to the Web search task (on volcanic eruptions). However, neither the provision of the SEEK declarative information nor the SEEK Web tutor had any significant effects on participants' time spent on credible as compared to less credible websites or on their credibility rankings. To conclude, only providing declarative information on source credibility evaluation might not be enough. However, both the use of the SEEK Web tutor and the provision of the declarative SEEK instruction-led students navigate to fewer sub-pages within a website. The authors argued that this might be an indication for both more thorough reading of and more deliberate navigation within websites.

Kammerer et al. (2015) tested the effectiveness of a self-paced online training (with a duration of approximately 20 min) in adults without academic background. Other than the SEEK intervention, this intervention included concrete examples of websites and search result descriptions and focused on Web searches on medical or health-related issues. Specifically, the intervention comprised three parts. The first part aimed at raising awareness of the importance of evaluating the credibility of information sources. The second part taught how to evaluate source credibility on the basis of information in search results and web pages regarding aspects such as the type of information source, expertise and potential motives of information providers, and the availability of source references. The third part addressed the comparison and corroboration of information across different websites. All parts of the intervention (mainly addressing Steps 2, 3, and 4 of the IPS-I model) contained a mix of declarative information, concrete examples, as well as several interactive exercises with feedback. All contents of the intervention were explained and illustrated by using examples of search results and web pages from a first Web search task on a complex medical topic that all participants had conducted prior to the intervention. Participants in the intervention group conducted this first Web search task, then underwent the intervention, and finally conducted a second Web search task on another complex health-and nutrition-related topic. Instead, control participants underwent the intervention only after having completed the two Web search tasks. Results of the pretest–posttest control group experiment showed that the intervention group ($n = 23$) in the second Web search task spent more time on websites from official institutions and less time on forum websites and commercial websites than the control group ($n = 25$). Moreover, in their post-search decision about the effectiveness of the nutritional supplement (i.e., was not effective) participants from the intervention group relied more on information from the official institutions and were also more certain of this decision than controls.

Pérez et al. (2018) tested an embedded classroom intervention for ninth grade students that consisted of three one-hour sessions. In each training session, declarative information on source credibility evaluation and respective practice tasks with concrete website materials on controversial topics were provided (i.e., focusing on Steps 3 and 4 of the IPS-I model). The first session addressed the evaluation of website authors' level of expertise about the topic. The second session was devoted to the evaluation of websites authors' potential biases (e.g., commercial interests). The third session focused on different types of media outlets. It was explained that in some types of websites (e.g., academic journals or magazines), information is validated before publication, whereas in other types of websites (e.g., blogs and forums), information at best is validated only after publication. In a pretest–posttest control group experiment, before the first intervention session (Pretest), one week after the last intervention session (Posttest 1) and three weeks after the last intervention session (Posttest 2), students' source credibility evaluation skills were assessed. For this purpose, they have presented a printed list of nine search results (on three complex topics from the domain of history, society, and health) and had to rate on a five-point Likert-scale the degree to which they would consult each of the links. Study results revealed that in Posttest 1, students from the control group ($n = 73$) indicated that they were more likely to consult less credible search results than those from the intervention group ($n = 64$). In Posttest 2 (using a different link list on a different topic), this was still the case for the least credible links, but for links of rather moderate credibility the difference had disappeared.

Finally, in an experimental study with $N = 112$ secondary school students, Stadtler et al. (2015) provided a short, written text (221 words) as instructional material. With this text, the intervention group was informed about the fact that on the Web not only experts can provide information on complex topics, but also people that hardly know anything about them. It was further explained that information providers can also provide biased or one-sided information and that, hence, in addition to understanding what the text says, readers would also need to consider who provides the information.

Finally, they were told to check for source information on every website they visited and to ask themselves whether the information providers have enough expertise about the topic. To conclude, the instruction addressed Steps 3 and 4 of the IPS-I model. Study results indicated that in a subsequent Web search task on a complex health-related issue the intervention group as compared to the control group paid more attention to source information in websites as indicated by more clicks on 'about us' links. Moreover, the intervention group was more likely to mention sources and evaluative comments about the sources in an argumentative essay written after the Web search than the control group.

To conclude, all but one study (the study by Graesser et al. 2007) revealed beneficial effects of the short trainings used to enhance school or university students' or other adults' source credibility evaluation during Web search for complex science-related issues. Other than the comprehensive training programs, which most of the times were embedded into a school or university curriculum, the majority of the short-term trainings and respective evaluation studies addressed Web searches on complex health-related topics. Of note is, however, that for the sake of experimental control, in all studies fabricated SERPs with a limited set of search results on given search topics were used. Except for the studies by Wiley et al. (2009) and Graesser et al. (2007), which used websites that contained several sub-web pages, the websites even were only single web pages (i.e., without further hyperlinks to sub-web pages). Thus, it is an open question of whether the interventions would also be effective when it comes to information searches (a) on the open Web, (b) outside the laboratory context, and (c) for self-chosen topics. In this vein, it is also an open question of whether and how the interventions might affect the formulation of search queries (cf. Sharit et al. 2008, 2015). It is conceivable, for instance, that individuals who have undergone an intervention on source credibility evaluation, will formulate more specific search queries (e.g., by specifying that they are looking for scientific studies or pros and cons of a controversial issue, respectively). Moreover, whereas several studies measured navigation logfiles as indicators for source credibility evaluation (i.e., the time spent on credible vs. less credible websites, or respective strategic revisits), the study by Pérez et al. (2018) was the only one that assessed the evaluation of search results with a paper printout. In this study, however, no Web search tasks had to be conducted by the students. Furthermore, like the comprehensive training programs, also most of the short-term interventions focused mainly on credibility assessments in websites. To the best of our knowledge, the short-term intervention by Kammerer et al. (2015) is the only one that explicitly addressed credibility assessments on SERPs. Future interventions should put a greater emphasis on critically evaluating search results.

11.2.3   Computer-Based Applications and Search Results Interfaces Using Prompts or Cues

Instead of teaching individuals how to evaluate the credibility of information sources *prior to* conducting Web searches, another approach is to provide them with prompts to engage in credibility assessments *during* their Web search. A central aim of prompting is to direct individuals' attention toward important aspects of their task processing and to reflect about them (Rosenshine et al. 1996). Therefore, prompts, which can vary from general unspecific questions to explicit execution instructions (Bannert 2009), should increase individuals' awareness of otherwise unconsidered mental activities (Bannert 2007). Similarly, the provision of additional (prominent and clear) credibility cues should also support credibility assessments during Web search (e.g., Fogg 2003). We identified six studies that evaluated computer-based applications or search results interfaces that provide prompts or cues, respectively, to support the evaluation of source credibility during Web search (also see Table 11.3).

Graesser et al. (2007), in addition to the experiment reported above, conducted another study in which they exclusively tested the effects of the SEEK Web tutor, with $n = 16$ undergraduate students serving in the intervention group and $n = 17$ in the control group. The SEEK Web tutor consisted of three main components. First, there was a 'hint' button on the Google SERP which contained suggestions on how to effectively guide students' search. When clicking on this button, spoken messages were provided that gave reminders of the goal of the task and suggestions on what to do next (e.g., reading websites with credible information). Messages were randomly selected from a fixed set of messages whenever the 'hint' button was clicked. That is, participants needed to proactively click on the button to receive the prompts. Graesser et al. (2007) did not provide any information about how often this feature was actually used by students. The second component consisted of ratings that were launched by a pop-up window that appeared on each website 20 s after it had been accessed. These ratings asked students to evaluate the credibility of the website on a 6-point scale and to provide a written rationale for their rating. The third component consisted of another pop-up window that appeared when leaving a website and that requested participants to fill out information about the author, the credibility and usefulness of the site, and the provided scientific evidence into text boxes. Results of the study by Graesser et al. (2007), however, indicated that the SEEK Web tutor did not have any significant effects on participants' credibility rankings of the websites. However, as in the combined study reviewed in Sect. 11.2.2, the use of the SEEK Web tutor resulted in the navigation of fewer sub-pages within a website. As mentioned above, the authors argued that this might be an indication for both more thorough reading of and more deliberate navigation within websites.

Stadtler and Bromme (2007) developed and tested the computer-based tool *met.a.ware*. The tool provided credibility evaluation prompts, such that before leaving a website, the application required to judge the website author's expertise and potential biases as well as one's own trust in the information provided by the websites, by means of three rating scales. Study results showed that the provision of credibility evaluation prompts increased the degree to which undergraduate students ($n = 40$) referred to sources in their essays compared to students who had not received such evaluation prompts ($n = 39$). Furthermore, when asked to select the three most credible websites, students with evaluation prompts tended to more often justify their selection according to the source than did students without evaluation prompts. However, the effects were quite small. Moreover, to the best of our knowledge, neither in the study by Stadtler and Bromme (2007) nor in the study by Graesser et al. (2007) it was assessed how helpful or annoying the prompts were perceived by participants (i.e., how these prompts affected individuals' emotions, cf. Kuhlthau 1991).

Instead of providing evaluation prompts, another possibility is to directly present additional source credibility cues in SERPs or web pages. Ideally, these cues should be easy to notice and understand (cf. Prominence-Interpretation Theory, Fogg 2003). Yamamoto and Tanaka (2011; see also Yamamoto 2017) have developed and evaluated a prototype search engine system that to the right of each search result presents a radar chart with scores for the authority, objectivity, currency, accuracy, and coverage of the respective web page (according to the five dimensions of information quality by Tate 2010). Authority has been defined as the number of social bookmarks for a web page; objectivity as the similarity of the content of a web page to other web pages; accuracy as the number of in-links to a web page (i.e., the PageRank, Brin and Page 1998), because accurate web pages are often linked to by other web pages as references; coverage as the number of technical terms about the topic provided in a web page; and currency by the last update of the web page as well as its update frequency. Yamamoto and Tanaka (2011) conducted a within-subject experiment with $N = 10$ participants who had to conduct 10 Web search tasks with a regular search engine and another 10 Web search tasks with the prototype. Specifically, their task was to select as many credible web pages as possible within three minutes (e.g., regarding a particular medical topic, such as Meniere's disease). Results revealed that with the radar chart visualizations available, participants selected more credible websites than with the regular Google interface. However, a second large user study with 960 participants indicated that the chart visualizations were rather complex and difficult to interpret for users with low topic knowledge.

In a similar approach, Schwarz and Morris (2011) augmented search results with visualizations that represented the PageRank of the web page (Brin and Page 1998), the number of bookmarks of the web page in del.icio.us (i.e., a previous social bookmarking service), the number of domain experts who had visited the page, and whether the web page had received any certifications such as HONcode (Health on the Net Foundation Code of Conduct) for credible health-related information. In a within-subject experiment, $N = 26$ participants (comprising both adolescents and adults) were presented with a set of search results and web pages with or without additional credibility visualizations available. It should be noted that, in each trial, participants were only presented a single search result or a single web page and had to rate its credibility. Thus, it was not a real search situation that was examined. Study results showed that for the augmented search results, participants' credibility ratings were significantly more accurate (i.e., more similar to experts' ratings) than for the regular search results. In contrast, however, the visualizations had no effect on the accuracy of participants' credibility ratings of web pages. In addition, survey data indicated that participants found the information about number of experts who had visited the page as most helpful for their credibility assessments.

Whereas search results are typically presented in a single list, Kammerer and Gerjets (2012b) tested a mockup of a SERP interface that presented search results in a tabular format, in which search results were grouped into three columns labeled as 'objective information,' 'subjective information,' and 'commercial information.' These genre categories were aimed to reflect the purpose on which the publication of a web page is based; that is, whether a web page's primary purpose is to provide factual information (i.e., objective information), to exchange opinions and experiences (i.e., subjective information), or to promote or sell products or services (i.e., commercial information). In a between-subject experiment with $N = 58$ undergraduate students, the tabular interface ($n = 29$) was compared to a standard Google-like list interface ($n = 29$). Results showed that in the tabular interface participants paid less attention to commercial search results than in the list interface. Likewise, while participants in the list interface paid an equal amount of attention to all kinds of search results, in the tabular interface objective search results were fixated for a longer time than search results of the two other categories. Moreover, in the tabular interface less commercial search results and more objective search results were accessed than in the list interface. Thus, the tabular interface was successful in guiding users' attention toward objective, that is, scholarly and neutral Internet resources. However, regarding participants' argumentative essays that they wrote after the Web search, the positive effect of the tabular interface on the number of arguments from objective web pages included was moderated by individuals' epistemic beliefs toward Internet information. Specifically, those students who believed that the Web contains correct knowledge listed more arguments from objective web pages in their argumentative summaries when having used a tabular interface than when having used a list interface. In contrast, for students who had doubts that the Web contains correct knowledge the interface had no effect. This might be an indirect indication that the latter students might have also doubted the classification provided by the tabular interface.

Finally, Yamamoto and Shimada (2016; see also Yamamoto 2017) have developed and evaluated a prototype search engine system, in which information that has been challenged by other (credible) sources is marked in search results or in web pages (for a similar idea, also see Ennals et al. 2010, who, however, did not assess effects on credibility evaluation in their study). That is, other than the rest of the alternative SERP designs reviewed in this section, this search results interface does not provide additional source information. However, the idea is that informing individuals that information is suspicious functions as indirect credibility warning. In an online between-subject experiment, $N = 92$ crowdworkers were asked to search the Web for health-related issues (i.e., to identify an effective method for a target health problem) by using one of three interfaces: a standard search interface, an interface in which suspicious information in search results was highlighted, or an interface in which suspicious information in web pages was highlighted. Results showed that participants in the condition with highlighted search results selected more search results without suspicious information and overall spent more time on SERPs than in the other two conditions. This indicates that they considered the highlighting cues in their selection decisions. Furthermore, while both participants who were using the interface with suspicious information being highlighted in the SERPs and participants who were using the interface with suspicious information being highlighted in the web pages selected fewer disputed information as their task answers than control participants, the highlights in the SERP were judged as more useful than the highlights in the web pages. To conclude, similar to the study by Schwarz and Morris (2011), cues seem more effective when they are provided on SERPs rather than on web pages. However, future research is needed to examine potential reasons for this finding. Furthermore, future research should investigate whether highlights of suspicious or disputed information might increase individuals' attention to source information, as previous research has indicated that encountering discrepancies between sources stimulates the attention to, evaluation of, and memory for source information (for an overview, see Braasch and Bråten 2017).

To conclude, of the two computer-based applications that provided source credibility evaluation prompts only one (i.e., the *met.a.ware* application but not the SEEK Web tutor) was successful in fostering source credibility evaluation in websites, even though the two systems used quite similar prompts to evaluate websites. In addition, the SEEK Web tutor (Graesser et al. 2007) also provided prompts on the SERP. Yet, as mentioned above, to receive these prompts, a 'hint' button needed to be clicked, which might have been too subtle for users. Thus, future studies should examine whether credibility evaluation prompts on SERPs might be more effective, when they are provided automatically. Instead of providing prompts, another possibility is to present additional information in SERPs or in websites that serves as credibility cues. The results of the experimental studies reviewed above indicate that the provision of such credibility cues in SERPs indeed has the potential to affect individuals' selection of search results, in that participants accessed more credible websites. Yet, the interfaces so far have only been tested in experimental environments with restricted tasks and for a limited number of websites provided and with the researchers being present or even explaining the meaning of the cues. Thus, it is an open question of whether source credibility cues would also be effective in more authentic Web search situations when searching on the open Web. According to the Prominence-Interpretation Theory (Fogg 2003), in order to be effective, users would need to notice the cues in the first place, second, they would need to correctly interpret them, and third, they would need to consider them in their selection decision.

11.3 Discussion

In this chapter, we reviewed studies that have tested different approaches to foster individuals' source credibility evaluation while solving information problems on the Web. Nowadays, with an ever-growing amount of information available on the Web that does not necessarily undergo any quality control, it is crucial to constantly evaluate the credibility of sources during Web search and to be critical toward one-sided, biased, or inaccurate information. From our review, it can be concluded that most of the reviewed short-term approaches, which were mainly under the control of the researchers, were successful in enhancing source credibility evaluation in websites. In contrast, this was the case for only some of the comprehensive training programs, of which most were carried out by teachers and embedded into the regular curriculum over a period of several weeks or months or even longer. Also only one of the two computer-based applications that provided source prompts resulted in better source credibility assessments in websites. With regard to source credibility evaluation on SERPs, apart from the studies that provided additional source credibility cues in the search results interface, only very few studies revealed beneficial effects. The majority of the intervention studies even did not examine this evaluation phase, neither did they address it as part of the intervention. Thus, both future interventions and respective evaluation studies should put more emphasis on this early evaluation phase, not least because search engines nowadays increasingly present answers to search queries directly on the SERPs, that is, without the need of accessing the actual website from which the information is derived. Providing users with additional credibility cues on SERPs based on tools that automatically assess the credibility of websites (e.g., Aggarwal et al. 2014) seems a promising approach to foster source credibility evaluation on SERPs. However, users might need training on how to interpret these cues (Yamamoto and Tanaka 2011).

Therefore, an important question is whether a combination of different approaches (e.g., training and prompts, or training and credibility cues) would be most beneficial to foster source credibility evaluation. To the best of our knowledge, the experiment by Graesser et al. (2007) has been the only one that examined the effectiveness of both training on source credibility evaluation and of respective evaluation prompts in a 2×2 factorial design. Unfortunately, in Graesser et al.'s (2007) study neither the training nor the prompts had an effect on source credibility evaluation. Nonetheless, we encourage future research to systematically examine whether or under which conditions, respectively, (a) the combination of both approaches is most effective or (b) prompts or cues provided in computer applications or search interfaces alone are sufficient to foster source credibility evaluation during Web search without any additional benefit of trainings. From a theoretical perspective, we argue that in case that individuals have an 'availability deficiency' (Veenman et al. 2000), that is, they do not possess sufficient knowledge and skills about *how to* evaluate source credibility during Web search, interventions that convey such knowledge and skills will be required in order to identify and correctly interpret credibility cues. Thus, in such cases the provision of source credibility evaluation prompts or source credibility cues alone might not be effective. On the contrary, for individuals with a 'production deficiency' (Veenman et al. 2000), that is, individuals who possess a certain level of knowledge and skills about how to evaluate source credibility, but do not use their knowledge and skills *spontaneously*, approaches that are limited to prompting or cueing source credibility evaluation during task performance might be sufficient. Furthermore, the correct interpretation of source credibility cues is likely to depend also on individuals' reading comprehension skills and general cognitive abilities. To conclude, when examining the effectiveness of approaches, future studies should also take individual difference factors into account, such as individuals' knowledge of source credibility evaluation, but also their reading comprehension skills and general cognitive abilities (Sharit et al. 2008, 2015). In addition, future research should also consider individuals' motivation to engage in source credibility assessments, which is likely to be higher when solving information problems of personal relevance (Metzger 2007)

From a methodological point of view, it should be mentioned that across the studies reviewed in this chapter, a large variety of dependent measures was used to assess source credibility evaluation; yet, each individual study used a rather limited or incomplete set of variables. Whereas in the context of the comprehensive training programs many studies used thinking-aloud methodology to get detailed insights into individuals' spontaneous source credibility evaluation, concurrent (or retrospective) verbal protocols were not used in any of the other studies. Moreover, not all studies assessed navigation data, that is, which kind of search results were selected or how much time was spent on different types of websites. To get a more complete picture of the effectiveness of a particular intervention, we therefore ask future research to use a comprehensive set of dependent measures that provide detailed insights into individuals' source credibility evaluation behavior and skills. Moreover, the success of both the short-term and the long-term interventions has been measured only directly after having terminated the intervention or, in a few cases, one to three weeks after the intervention at the latest (e.g., Pérez et al. 2018). Hence, in line with previous reviews (e.g., Brante and Strømsø 2018; Bråten et al. 2018) we argue that future research that examines long-term effects of such interventions is essentially needed. Furthermore, while most of the comprehensive training programs were evaluated by asking participants to conduct Web searches on the open Web, the studies that evaluated the short-term trainings, computer-based prompts, and search results interfaces were tested in rather restricted search environments with the researcher being present. Thus, it is an open question of whether these approaches would also be effective in more authentic Web search situations when searching on the open Web. Finally, all of the reviewed studies focused on source credibility evaluation in mostly text-based SERPs and websites. Yet, nowadays the Web is also a huge repository for multimedia materials such as pictures or videos, with video and image results also being provided as part of today's SERPs. As the credibility of YouTube videos on science issues also varies widely (e.g., Allgaier 2019), future interventions, for instance, should also train or prompt source credibility evaluation with regard to the selection and processing of video material.

In sum, we encourage educators and tool developers to jointly develop approaches that foster individuals' awareness for and engagement in source credibility evaluation both on SERPs and on websites in a long-lasting and profound way and thus help individuals to become critical citizens of today's knowledge society. At the same time, more research is clearly needed to understand the mechanisms by which interventions work as well as the characteristics of both the individual and the context that will enable the mechanism to work.

References

Aggarwal S., van Oostendorp H, Reddy YR, Indurkhya B (2014) Providing web credibility assessment support. In: Stary C, Neubauer M (eds) Proceedings of the 32nd European conference on cognitive ergonomics (ECCE 2014). ACM Press, New York

Allgaier J (2019) Science and environmental communication on YouTube: strategically distorted communications in online videos on climate change and climate engineering. Front Commun 4:36

Anmarkrud Ø, Bråten I, Strømsø HI (2014) Multiple-documents literacy: strategic processing, source awareness, and argumentation when reading multiple conflicting documents. Learn Individ Differ 30:64–76

Argelagós E, Pifarré M (2012) Improving information problem solving skills in secondary education through embedded instruction. Comput Hum Behav 28:515–526

Bannert M (2007) Beschreibung und Vermittlung wirksamer metakognitiver Lernstrategien und Regulationsaktivitäten [Metacognition in learning with hypermedia. Assessment, description, and mediation of effective metacognitive learning strategies and regulation activities]. Waxmann, Münster

Bannert M (2009) Promoting self-regulated learning through prompts: a discussion. Zeitschrift für Pädagogische Psychologie 23:139–145

Barzilai S, Tzadok E, Eshet-Alkalai Y (2015) Sourcing while reading divergent expert accounts: pathways from views of knowing to written argumentation. Instr Sci 43:737–766

Braasch JL, Bråten I (2017) The discrepancy-induced source comprehension (D-ISC) model: basic assumptions and preliminary evidence. Educ Psychol 53:167–182

Brand-Gruwel S, Van Strien JL (2018) Instruction to promote information problem solving on the Internet in primary and secondary education: a systematic literature review. In: Braasch JLG, Bråten I, McCrudden MT (eds) Handbook of multiple source use. Routledge, New York, pp 401–422

Brand-Gruwel S, Wopereis I (2006) Integration of the information problem-solving skill in an educational programme: the effects of learning with authentic tasks. Technol Instr Cogn Learn 4:243–263

Brand-Gruwel S, Wopereis I, Vermetten Y (2005) Information problem solving by experts and novices: analysis of a complex cognitive skill. Comput Hum Behav 21:487–508

Brand-Gruwel S, Wopereis I, Walraven A (2009) A descriptive model of information problem solving while using Internet. Comput Educ 53:1207–1217

Brante EW, Strømsø HI (2018) Sourcing in text comprehension: a review of interventions targeting sourcing skills. Educ Psychol Rev 30:773–799

Bråten I, Stadtler M, Salmerón L (2018) The role of sourcing in discourse comprehension. In: Schober M, Rapp DN, Britt MA (eds) Handbook of discourse processes. Taylor & Francis, New York, NY, pp 141–166

Brin S, Page L (1998) The anatomy of a large-scale hypertextual Web search engine. Comput Netw ISDN Syst 30:107–117

Danielson DR (2006) Web credibility. In: Ghaoui C (ed) Encyclopedia of human computer interaction. Idea Group, Hershey, PA, pp 713–721

Dodge B (1995) WebQuests: a technique for internet-based learning. Distance Educ 1:10–13

Ennals R, Trushkowsky B, Agosta JM (2010) Highlighting disputed claims on the web. In: Proceedings of WWW '10 proceedings of the 19th international conference on World wide web, pp 341–350

Ericsson KA, Simon HA (1993) Protocol analysis: verbal report as data. The MIT Press, Cambridge, MA; London, England

Fogg BJ (2003) Prominence-interpretation theory: explaining how people assess credibility online. In: Cockton G, Korhonen P (eds) Proceedings of CHI '03 extended abstracts on human factors in computing systems. ACM Press, New York, pp 722–723

Gerjets P, Kammerer Y, Werner B (2011) Measuring spontaneous and instructed evaluation processes during web search: integrating concurrent thinking-aloud protocols and eye-tracking data. Learn Instr 21:220–231

Gigerenzer G, Goldstein DG (1996) Reasoning the fast and frugal way: models of bounded rationality. Psychol Rev 103:650–669

Goldman SR, Braasch JLG, Wiley J, Graesser AC, Brodowinska K (2012) Comprehending and learning from Internet sources: processing patterns of better and poorer learners. Reading Res Q 47:356–381

Graesser AC, Wiley J, Goldman SR, O'Reilly T, Jeon M, McDaniel B (2007) SEEK Web tutor: fostering a critical stance while exploring the causes of volcanic eruption. Metacognition Learn 2:89–105

Hagerman MS (2017) Disrupting students' online reading and research habits: the LINKS intervention and its impact on multiple Internet text integration skills. J Literacy Technol 18:105–156

Hargittai E, Fullerton L, Menchen-Trevino E, Thomas KY (2010) Trust online: young adults' evaluation of Web content. Int J Commun 4:468–494

Hilligoss B, Rieh S (2008) Developing a unifying framework of credibility assessment: construct, heuristics, and interaction in context. Inf Process Manage 44:1467–1484

Hovland CI, Janis IL, Kelley HH (1953) Communication and persuasion; psychological studies of opinion change. Yale University Press, New Haven, CT, USA

Hovland CI, Weiss W (1951) The influence of source credibility on communication effectiveness. Public Opin Q 15:635–650

Jonassen DH (1997) Instructional design models for well-structured and ill-structured problem-solving learning outcomes. Educ Tech Res Dev 45:65–94

Kammerer Y, Amann D, Gerjets P (2015) When adults without university education search the Internet for health information: the roles of Internet-specific epistemic beliefs and a source evaluation intervention. Comput Hum Behav 48:297–309

Kammerer Y, Gerjets P (2012a) How search engine users evaluate and select Web search results: the impact of the search engine interface on credibility assessments. In: Lewandowski D (ed) Web search engine research. Emerald Group Publishing Limited, Bingley, pp 251–279

Kammerer Y, Gerjets P (2012b) Effects of search interface and Internet-specific epistemic beliefs on source evaluations during Web search for medical information: an eye-tracking study. Behav Inf Technol 31:83–97

Kiili C, Leu DJ, Utriainen J, Coiro J, Kanniainen L, Tolvanen A, Lohvansuu K, Leppänen PH (2018) Reading to learn from online information: modeling the factor structure. J Literacy Res 50:304–334

Kingsley TL, Cassady JC, Tancock SM (2015) Successfully promoting 21st century online research skills: interventions in 5th-grade classrooms. Reading Horizons 54:92–134

Kroustallaki D, Kokkinaki T, Sideridis GD, Simos PG (2015) Exploring students' affect and achievement goals in the context of an intervention to improve web searching skills. Comput Hum Behav 49:156–170

Kuhlthau C (1991) Inside the search process: information seeking from the user's perspective. J Am Soc Inf Sci 42:361–371

Kuhlthau CC, Heinström J, Todd RJ (2008) The 'information search process' revisited: is the model still useful. Inf Res 13:13–14

Lewandowski D (2011) The influence of commercial intent of search results on their perceived relevance. In: Proceedings of the 2011 iConference (iConference '11). ACM Press, New York, pp 452–458

Marchionini G (1989) Information-seeking strategies of novices using a full-text electronic encyclopedia. J Am Soc Inf Sci 40:54–66

Mason L, Junyent AA, Tornatora MC (2014) Epistemic evaluation and comprehension of web-source information on controversial science-related topics: effects of a short-term instructional intervention. Comput Educ 76:143–157

Metzger MJ (2007) Making sense of credibility on the Web: models for evaluating online information and recommendations for future research. J Am Soc Inform Sci Technol 58:2078–2091

Palinscar AS, Brown AL (1984) Reciprocal teaching of comprehension-fostering and comprehension-monitoring activities. Cognition and instruction 1:117–175

Pérez A, Potocki A, Stadtler M, Macedo-Rouet M, Paul J, Salmerón L, Rouet J-F (2018) Fostering teenagers' assessment of information reliability: effects of a classroom intervention focused on critical source dimensions. Learn Instr 58:53–64

Pirolli P (2007) Information foraging theory: adaptive interaction with information. Oxford University Press, Oxford, UK

Rosenshine B, Meister C, Chapman S (1996) Teaching students to generate questions: a review of the intervention studies. Rev Educ Res 66:181–221

Rouet J-F, Britt MA (2011) Relevance processes in multiple document comprehension. In: McCrudden MT, Magliano JP, Schraw G (eds) Text relevance and learning from text. Information Age Publishing, Greenwich, CT, pp 19–52

Schwarz J, Morris M (2011) Augmenting web pages and search results to support credibility assessment. In: Proceedings of the SIGCHI conference on human factors in computing systems. ACM Press, New York, pp 1245–1254

Sharit J, Hernández MA, Czaja SJ, Pirolli P (2008) Investigating the roles of knowledge and cognitive abilities in older adult information seeking on the web. ACM Trans Comput Hum Interact 15:1–25

Sharit J, Taha J, Berkowsky RW, Profita H, Czaja SJ (2015) Online information search performance and search strategies in a health problem-solving scenario. J Cogn Eng Decis Making 9:211–228

Simon HA (1955) A behavioral model of rational choice. Q J Econ 69:99–118

Stadtler M, Bromme R (2007) Dealing with multiple documents on the WWW: the role of metacognition in the formation of documents models. Comput Support Collaborative Learn 2:191–210

Stadtler M, Bromme R (2014) The content–source integration model: a taxonomic description of how readers comprehend conflicting scientific information. In: Rapp DN, Braasch JLG (eds) Processing inaccurate information: theoretical and applied perspectives from cognitive science and the educational sciences. MIT Press, Cambridge, MA, pp 379–402

Stadtler M, Paul J, Globoschütz S, Bromme R (2015) Watch out!—an instruction raising students' epistemic vigilance augments their sourcing activities. In: Noelle DC, Dale R, Warlaumont AS, Yoshimi J, Matlock T, Jennings CD, Maglio PP (eds) Proceedings of the 37th annual conference of the cognitive science society. Cognitive Science Society, Austin, TX, pp 2278–2283

Tate MA (2010) Web wisdom: how to evaluate and create information quality on the Web, 2nd edn. CRC Press, Boca Raton, FL

Vakkari P (2001) A theory of the task-based information retrieval process: a summary and generalisation of a longitudinal study. J Documentation 57:44–60

Van Merriënboer JJG (1997) Training complex cognitive skills: a four-component instructional design model for technical training. Educ Technol Publ, Englewood Cliffs, NJ

Veenman MV, Kerseboom L, Imthorn C (2000) Test anxiety and metacognitive skillfulness: availability versus production deficiencies. Anxiety Stress Coping 13:391–412

Walraven A, Brand-Gruwel S, Boshuizen HP (2010) Fostering transfer of web searchers' evaluation skills: a field test of two transfer theories. Comput Hum Behav 26:716–728

Walraven A, Brand-Gruwel S, Boshuizen HP (2013) Fostering students' evaluation behaviour while searching the internet. Instr Sci 41:125–146

Wiley J, Goldman SR, Graesser AC, Sanchez CA, Ash IK, Hemmerich JA (2009) Source evaluation, comprehension, and learning in Internet science inquiry tasks. Am Educ Res J 46:1060–1106

Wopereis I, Brand-Gruwel S, Vermetten Y (2008) The effect of embedded instruction on solving information problems. Comput Hum Behav 24:738–752

Yamamoto Y (2017) Supporting credibility judgment in web search. ACM SIGWEB Newsletter, (Spring), 3

Yamamoto Y, Shimada S (2016) Can disputed topic suggestion enhance user consideration of information credibility in Web search? In: Proceedings of the 27th ACM Conference on Hypertext and Social Media. ACM Press, New York, pp 169–177

Yamamoto Y, Tanaka K (2011) Enhancing credibility judgment of web search results. In: Tan D, Fitzpatrick G, Gutwin C, Begole B, Kellog W (eds) Proceedings of the 2011 annual conference on human factors in computing systems (CHI '11). ACM Press, New York, pp 1235–1244

Chapter 12
Computer-Supported Collaborative Information Search for Geopolitical Forecasting

Ion Juvina, Othalia Larue, Colin Widmer, Subhashini Ganapathy,
Srikanth Nadella, Brandon Minnery, Lance Ramshaw,
Emile Servan-Schreiber, Maurice Balick, and Ralph Weischedel

Abstract Geopolitical forecasting is the process of generating judgments of probability for a wide variety of future geopolitical events, such as political elections, international conflict, disease outbreaks, and macro-economic indicators. Governmental policy-makers, private organizations, and individuals use forecasting to aid their strategic decision-making. For example, a government agency may forecast the likelihood of a disease outbreak; business leaders may forecast how the market will respond if they launch a new product; individuals may employ forecasting to aid their decisions about what career to choose or how to invest for retirement. Recent research in geopolitical forecasting showed that instruction, practice, and peer interaction made a big difference in forecasting accuracy. In this chapter, we review relevant literature from the areas of decision-making, psychology, and human–machine interaction and suggest how findings from these areas could contribute to improvements in forecasters' performance. We also present data and insights gained from our experience as competitors in a government-funded forecasting tournament.

I. Juvina (✉) · O. Larue · S. Ganapathy
Wright State University, Dayton, OH, USA
e-mail: ion.juvina@wright.edu

C. Widmer · S. Nadella · B. Minnery
Kairos Research, 3640 Colonel Glenn Hwy, Dayton, OH 45435, USA

L. Ramshaw
Raytheon BBN Technologies, Cambridge, MA, USA

E. Servan-Schreiber · M. Balick
Hypermind, LLC, Paris, France

E. Servan-Schreiber
School of Collective Intelligence, Mohammed VI Polytechnic University,
Ben Guerir, Morocco

R. Weischedel
Information Sciences Institute, University of Southern California,
Los Angeles, CA, USA

© Springer Nature Switzerland AG 2020
W. T. Fu and H. van Oostendorp (eds.), *Understanding and Improving
Information Search*, Human–Computer Interaction Series,
https://doi.org/10.1007/978-3-030-38825-6_12

12.1 Introduction

We all are everyday forecasters. When choosing a career or investing for retirement, we predict how the future will unfold. More systematic forecasting takes place in public or private organizations. For example, intelligence analysts employ forecasting on a regular basis. They gather vast amounts of information from various sources and try to identify patterns or trends that allow them to predict future events. This complex activity is often done collaboratively and supported by information technology, particularly information search and sense-making tools.

Cognitive biases such as base rate neglect, confirmation bias, and hindsight bias (Kahneman and Egan 2011; Fischhoff 2011) affect how we search for relevant information and hinder our capacity to produce correct forecasts. For example, base rate neglect prevents us from searching for relevant historical information, while confirmation bias makes us search only for information that confirms our expectations. Biases are not limited to amateur forecasters; they are common among expert forecasters as well (Tetlock 2005; Fingar et al. 2011). Improving our ability to forecast, even by modest margins, would be highly desirable.

The Intelligence Advanced Research Projects Activity (IARPA) organized a series of tournaments aimed at scientifically studying geopolitical forecasting. The first tournament ran from 2011 to 2013 and resulted in significant progress in the scientific understanding of the individual and situational factors that determine human forecasting performance. For example, Mellers et al. (2015a) identified personality traits (being intelligent, open-minded, and analytical), behaviors (extensive information search and frequent updating of forecasts), and conditions (working in teams and being trained to overcome cognitive biases) that facilitated forecasting (see also Tetlock and Gardner 2015). However, it became clear that even the highest performing forecasters could be outperformed by aggregation algorithms that employed different methods of combining human forecasts (Ungar et al. 2012). In addition, human–machine teaming has been shown to greatly improve human performance in certain areas (Sankar 2012).

In 2018, IARPA organized the Hybrid Forecasting Competition (HFC), aimed at combining the strengths of human and machine forecasting. Participants had to provide a suite of hybrid, human–machine tools and demonstrate that they produce measurable improvements in forecasting performance. In this chapter, we present part of our efforts and results from the first year of this competition. The hybrid tools we proposed were intended to assist forecasters with searching for relevant information and generating and updating their forecasts. The assumption was that these tools would help forecasters deal with large amounts of information and improve both the accuracy of forecasts and the productivity of forecasters (i.e., the number of forecasts they were able to make given their time and effort limitations).

In Sect. 12.2, we present a brief review of the literature on information foraging, sense-making, psychology, and human–machine interaction that is potentially relevant to forecasting. In Sect. 12.3, we introduce the hybrid tools we implemented and tested in the HFC, the data we collected, and the hypotheses we tested. Section 12.4

presents the results of our studies, with a focus on the hybrid tools and their impact on forecasting performance. Finally, in Sect. 12.5, we discuss the results and lay out our plans for future work.

12.2 Background

In the previous tournament organized by IARPA (2010–2013), five university-based research groups competed to identify the best forecasting strategies, what were the limits to expertise in forecasting, and what kind of structure could elicit the best forecasts. Real-world events were used to evaluate the accuracy of the forecasts and select the best research team. Forecasters were not expert intelligence analysts; they were recruited from professional societies, research centers, alumni associations, science blogs, and word of mouth. Tetlock's research team was selected as the winning team (Tetlock and Gardner 2015). They identified traits that good forecasters shared and developed training modules to help forecasters avoid cognitive biases. In Sects. 12.2.1 and 12.2.2, we briefly review the literature on cognitive biases and personality traits that is relevant to forecasting. Then, in Sects. 12.2.3 and 12.2.4, we review the literature on information search, sense-making, and hybrid human–machine tools that is relevant to forecasting.

12.2.1 Cognitive Biases in Information Search and Decision-Making

Tetlock et al. (2015) distinguished two groups of participants: (1) the Big idea experts, "hedgehogs," pundits with one big idea that they applied to different domains without any proof that this knowledge would transfer across domains and (2) "foxes," eclectic experts who were open-minded, kept themselves informed, updated their knowledge, noticed when they were wrong, and were willing to correct their initial assumptions and forecasts. Furthermore, Mellers et al. (2015a) identified common cognitive biases that interfered with forecasting performance. For example, an explanatory urge could cause us to move too fast from an undefined and uncertain state to a clear and confident conclusion.

Dual process theories (Kahneman and Egan 2011; Evans and Stanovich 2013) postulate two types of cognitive processes. Type 1 processes help us deal with our limited cognitive capacities; they are designed to reach conclusions with little information; they help us act fast in our environment without involving costly cognitive processing (a characteristic of type 2 processes). However, different biases can occur during type 1 processing due to deciding based on insufficient relevant information. For example, born from our explanatory urge, the hindsight bias is the tendency to infer causal links between an event (e.g., a crisis) and the events that preceded it, when there might not be a strong causality or any causality at all (Fischhoff 2011). The hindsight bias will lead us in the future to overestimate the probability of an event happening when we observe what we wrongly identified as "precedents" of that event.

The availability heuristic (Tversky and Kahneman 1974) designates an evaluation process that is not guided by the quality of information but rather by how fast a first instance comes to mind. Recency and how easy it is to retrieve a piece of information from memory are going to be mistakenly equated to the relevance of the information to the problem at hand.

In the confirmation bias, one looks for and emphasizes information that confirms one's preexisting beliefs or hypotheses, ignoring or discrediting contradicting information. A complementary heuristic, Kahneman's "what you see is all there is" (WYSIATI) heuristic, leads us to focus on existing evidence and fail to search for additional information. Base rate neglect results from the tendency to overvalue the specific information and ignore the general information about an event. A bias toward an "inside view" may prevent the analyst from searching for relevant historical examples (i.e., taking an "outside view"). Overconfidence is the tendency one has to value one's own judgment more favorably than others' or as compared to the ground truth. Anchoring-and-adjustment (Tversky and Kahneman 1974) is a bias where an initial piece of information (i.e., the anchor) disproportionately influences decision-making and subsequent pieces of information insufficiently adjust the anchor. Finally, belief persistence is our tendency to stick with a first judgment and not revise it when presented with new contradicting information.

12.2.2 Traits and Behaviors Predicting Forecasting Performance

Dispositional variables (i.e., cognitive styles, cognitive abilities, and domain knowledge), situational variables (i.e., cognitive-debiasing exercises), and behavioral variables (i.e., revisiting and updating forecasts) have been shown to predict forecasting accuracy (Mellers et al. 2015a). Interestingly, results from the first IARPA forecasting tournament showed that intelligence had a stronger correlation with forecasting performance in the first year of the tournament than in later years, indicating that learning and skill development can offset the influence of dispositional variables. The actively open-minded thinking style significantly predicted forecasting accuracy. With regard to situational variables, two conditions improved performance: working in teams and training in probabilistic reasoning (which included cognitive debiasing). Teams outperformed even the best individuals, with the highest performing teams showing precise questioning, constructive confrontation, clearly defined goals, and plans for surprises and uncertainties. Finally, behavioral variables such as effort and engagement (measured with the number of predictions made per question as an indication of belief updating) and time spent before making a forecast (as an indication of deliberation time) also predicted forecasting accuracy.

Mellers et al. (2015b) assembled a psychological profile of the forecasters who consistently outperformed their peers, a cohort they deemed "superforecasters" (see also Tetlock and Gardner 2015). What set them apart from the rest were better numeracy and vocabulary capacities and a strong self-reported desire to be the best. They also had some specific skills other participants did not have (even the highest performing ones). They showed some resistance to scope insensitivity (Kahneman and Knetsch 1992) by identifying that the wider class of events should be judged as likelier than the subset (i.e., a dictator cannot be more likely to fall in 3 months than in 6 months). Additionally, superforecasters were more resistant to the anchoring bias. They also showed more granularity in their appreciation of uncertainty: the total number of unique probability estimates was higher for superforecasters. They showed more motivation and commitment. They did more research through the search tool provided and gathered more news and opinion pieces (Mellers et al. 2015b). Finally, superforecasters were likelier to share news stories with their teammates. They also probed the knowledge of their teammates more (i.e., they asked more questions and got more replies).

12.2.3 Information Search and Sense-Making Tools

Forecasting and other forms of intelligence analysis are information intensive tasks that rely heavily on information foraging and sense-making tools (Pirolli and Card 2005). A plethora of tools have been developed to support gathering, representation, and manipulation of information to facilitate insight and decision-making for individual users. For example, Sensemaker (Baldonado and Winograd 1997) supports searching and sense-making of heterogeneous sources of information in information exploration tasks. It helps users define and search within topics of interest. Entity Workspace (Billman and Bier 2007) provides an integrated work environment for searching within and across documents. It supports highlighting, annotating, and organizing information. InsightFinder and ScratchPad (Gotz 2007) are extensions to the standard browser interface that are designed to capture, organize, and exploit the information discovered while performing a sense-making task. They include context-aware algorithms that help connect user notes to relevant Web pages. The Sense-making-Supporting Information Gathering system (Qu 2003) provides tree structures to represent information found during Web search. Each folder in the tree corresponds to a topic or sub-topic that the user is interested in. Different features are provided to help the user search the Web, and construct, refine, and re-construct the tree representation.

In addition, given that sense-making is sometimes done collaboratively, tools have been proposed to support communities of users. They tend to offer two classes of support (Paul and Morris 2009): awareness features (e.g., sharing of group members' query histories, browsing histories, and/or comments on results) and division of labor features (e.g., chat systems, the ability to manually divide search results or URLs among group members, and/or algorithmic techniques for modifying group members' search results based on others' actions). For example, EWall (Keel 2007) helps remote collaborators navigate shared information and infers possible relationships among information items. CoSearch (Amershi and Morris 2008) supports division of labor by enabling group members to download distinct subsets of search results to their individual mobile phones. SearchTogether (Morris and Horvitz 2008) provides group query histories, comments, and ratings of Web pages; it also supports division of labor through chat and split result lists.

12.2.4   Hybrid Human–Machine Tools Supporting Forecasting

Forecasting is more challenging than other investigational search and sense-making tasks. In a typical investigational task, the answer exists somewhere and the users have to find their way to that answer or assemble an answer from pieces of information found in different locations. In forecasting tasks, the answers do not exist yet; they have to be constructed by the users. An element of novelty is always present in forecasting; no forecasting solution applies to more than one problem, even though general strategies may exist. Typically, real-world forecasting occurs over an extended time course, during which the world changes and potentially relevant but also irrelevant or misleading evidence accumulates. To make it even more complex, forecasters often engage in multiple forecasting tasks and each task may be attempted by a group of cooperating and/or competing forecasters.

The symbiosis between humans and machines (Licklider 1960) holds great promise to tackle the unparalleled complexity of the forecasting task. The science and practice of human–technology coordination have departed from the traditional function allocation methods (who-does-what or men-are-better-at/machines-are-better-at; Fitts 1951) and is currently moving toward a *human–technology teaming* approach in which the focus is on how machines can become effective team players (Dekker and Woods 2002) and how humans and technology co-evolve (Ackerman 2000). Teams of cooperating humans and machines have been shown in certain conditions to outperform even world-class experts working alone. For example, teams of amateur chess players equipped with chess-playing machines have surpassed both chess masters and machines alone in a free-style chess tournament (Sankar 2012).

The tools used in the HFC tournament are called *hybrid* because they are intended to combine human and machine capabilities (Rahwan et al. 2019) to improve the performance of the whole socio-technical system that generates forecasts. Using hybrid tools to assist forecasting serves three purposes: (1) correct for cognitive biases, (2) reduce the cognitive load of forecasters, and (3) increase the amount of relevant information available to the forecaster. These goals can be complementary and mutually reinforcing: providing humans with machine-made forecasts and making the relevant information easier to search and interpret may reduce cognitive load and cognitive biases, which in turn facilitates high-quality forecasts, which via various aggregation methods result in better "crowd" forecasts.

Cognitive workload and fatigue have been shown to affect judgment quality, with forecast quality decreasing as the number of forecasts made in a day increased. As they get fatigued, forecasters exhibit more herding behavior and less granularity in their forecasts (Hirshleifer et al. 2019). Task-offload tools can be used to delegate some task demands to automation (Kirlik 1993). However, externalizing too much task-related information can reduce the user's ability to meaningfully engage in high-level processes such as planning and reasoning and may harm motivation and performance (Van Nimwegen et al. 2006). Thus, the hybrid tool must strike a balance between offloading task demands and maintaining user engagement.

Lee et al. (2007) studied the situation in which human judgment is used to adjust statistical forecasts. These adjustments can improve accuracy under certain conditions, particularly when the human has information that is not available to the statistical method. They also give the forecaster a sense of ownership and may increase acceptability of the hybrid forecast relative to the machine-generated forecast. When making adjustments, forecasters often rely on analogies between past events and the future event to be forecasted. Reliance on analogies may be problematic for unaided forecasters because of memory errors, difficulty with similarity judgments, and difficulties with adapting the analogues cases to the specifics of the future event. Lee et al. (2007) designed a forecasting support system that provided a database of past cases ranked by their similarities with the future case. Similarity was automatically determined based on the number of matching attributes. Support for adaptation judgments was also provided; forecasters could interrogate the system about the effects of similar cases that differed in only one attribute at a time. Lee et al. (2007) found that forecasting performance and acceptability of the support system increased when all three types of support (i.e., memory, similarity, and adaptation) were provided.

Teams in the 2013 IARPA forecasting competition and other researchers worked on improving the way forecasts were aggregated. For instance, Turner et al. (2014) studied various methods of aggregating human-generated forecasts known to be more variable and sparser than machine-generated forecasts. They developed a number of models that first estimated and then corrected for the systematic biases humans made during forecasting, such as overconfidence. Models differed in terms of whether the recalibration (i.e., bias correction) was done before or after aggregation and whether individual differences between forecasters were accounted for. The model that applied recalibration before aggregation and captured individual differences via hierarchical modeling produced the best aggregated forecast. Budescu and Chen (2014) studied the wisdom of crowd (WOC) effect and developed a method to distinguish experts among forecasters. A forecaster's contribution was defined as the difference between the crowd's performance with and without that forecaster. Experts were defined as forecasters with positive average contributions, that is, those who consistently outperformed the crowd in a particular domain. Budescu and Chen (2014) showed significant improvements in crowd performance by excluding non-experts and weighting experts based on their contributions. This method of using aggregating weights based on relative performance is superior to methods that rely on absolute past performance (track-record) because it is robust to correlated judgments and group biases. Budescu and Chen (2014) also showed that identifying experts in a dynamic way, as evidence about forecasters' performance accumulates, further improves performance.

One of the teams from the IARPA 2018 competition (Beger and Ward 2018) implemented a system that automatically associated a forecasting question with relevant sources of information (databases). If related databases were found, the system displayed potentially relevant time series for the forecaster to consider. Additionally, the Auto ARIMA model (Hyndman and Khandakar 2007) was applied to the time series, and the resulting machine-generated forecast was provided to the participant. They found that forecasters who were provided with relevant time-series charts performed best. In general, machine forecasts did not perform as well as human forecasts; however, machines outperformed humans on a few questions that required data aggregation in a way that was not easily replicable by humans without technical skill.

12.3   Method

We restrict our analyses to data from IARPA's hybrid forecasting competition (HFC) collected by our team from March to September 2018. Forecasters had to solve Individual Forecasting Problems (IFPs) about real-world events in the following domains: conflict, economics, health, politics, science, and technology. The following are examples of IFPs in each domain:

- *Conflict*: How many battle deaths will ACLED (the Armed Conflict Location and Event Data project) record in Yemen in May 2018?
- *Economics*: What will be the FAO (the Food and Agriculture Organization of the United Nations) Sugar Price Index in June 2018?
- *Health*: How many positive influenza virus detections will FluNet record for Australia between July 30, 2018 and August 19, 2018 (epidemiological weeks 31-33, inclusive)?
- *Politics*: Which candidate will win Colombia's presidential election?
- *Science*: What will be the maximum sea ice extent on the Bering Sea between March 14, 2018 and April 10, 2018?
- *Technology*: How many "hacking or malware (HACK)" data breaches will Privacy Rights Clearinghouse record in July 2018?

The IARPA-provided IFPs were verifiable by the end of the time period specified in the description of the question. Participants were expected to provide an initial forecast and update it as many times as necessary based on information they searched for, updates of this information, or new information altogether. Each IFP had between two and five discrete, mutually exclusive outcome options. Outcome options had to be assigned a probabilistic forecast with probabilities over all options adding up to 1.

IFPs could be either binary or non-binary depending on the number of provided response options. This is an example of a binary IFP: Will [country/coalition] seize control of [contested city] by [deadline date]? Response options: Yes, No. Non-binary (multinomial) IFPs had more than two outcome options that were either discrete options, discretized quantities, or discretized ordered time periods. The following are examples of multinomial IFPs:

- Who will win the next [presidential/prime ministerial] election in [country]? Response options: Election Candidate A, B, or C
- How many battle deaths will the Armed Conflict Location and Event Data (ACLED) project record in [country] during [time period]? Response options: three or more numbers.
- What will the Food and Agriculture Organization of the United Nations (FAO) [selected food price index] be for [month]? Response options: three or more prices.
- When will [y] occur? Response options: Between Time 1 and Time 2; Between Time 2 and Time 3; etc.

12.3.1 Participants

The HFC tournament had a randomized controlled trial design, where subjects were recruited by IARPA and randomly assigned to the three research teams' systems. Thus, our team received approximately one-third of the participants recruited by IARPA. Two samples of participants were recruited for this study. The first sample consisted of volunteers with interest in geopolitical analysis. They were recruited through the Good Judgment open project (Ungar et al. 2012), social media, targeted advertisement articles in newspapers and word of mouth. Having experience in forecasting was not a prerequisite to participate. Volunteers were mostly US citizens (76%), males (82%), with an average age of 43, and with a relatively high level of education (53% had received a postgraduate degree). Due to attrition among this first sample of volunteers, a second sample of participants was recruited. They were members of the Web services Amazon Mechanical Turk and TurkPrime, typically referred to as workers. To simplify our language, we will refer to the participants from the first sample as *Regulars* and to the participants from the second sample as *Turkers*.

12.3.2 Performance Measures

Forecasting performance was measured with the Brier score, an accuracy score, and a performance score. The Brier score is well established in the forecasting literature, whereas the accuracy and performance scores were unique to Prescience and were more relevant to the competitive forecasting context of HFC. The Brier score (Brier 1950) provides a measure of the error of a probability forecast: The further a forecast probability is from the actual outcome, the larger the error:

$$\text{Brier score} = \sum (p_i - o_i)^2$$

where p_i is the probability assigned to answer i, and o_i is 1 if answer i is correct, or 0 if it is not. The Brier score is between 0 (perfect forecast) and 2 (worst possible forecast).

The accuracy score is a relative score based on one's Brier scores compared to the median Brier scores of all participants. The accuracy on a particular day is $c_d - y_d$, where y_d is the participant's Brier score on that day, and c_d is the crowd's *median* Brier score on that day. The accuracy score varies between -2 (worst) and 2 (best).

The performance score builds on accuracy to include an incentive to participate in more IFPs as well as less popular ones:

$$\text{Performance in IFP}_i = 1000 * \text{Acc}_i \div \sqrt{n_i}$$

where Acc_i is the accuracy on IFP_i and n_i is the number of participants who attempted IFP_i

12.3.3 Hybrid Features

The participants that IARPA randomly assigned to our team accessed a dedicated Web site (called "Prescience") designed to assist them in searching and navigating information related to the IFP at hand. The Prescience system is still being designed and developed. Some of its tools, such as the Query tool, are aimed at furnishing human analysts with the best possible information with which to formulate a judgment. Other tools operate at the level of the forecast itself, e.g., providing the human with an actual machine forecast which they can either accept/adjust/reject as they see fit. Lastly, Prescience includes "back-end" hybrid tools, in which the melding of human and machine forecasts occurs at the aggregation level. The use of the available features was optional to users. We assumed users would strategically (Kirlik 1993) choose the features they needed depending on what stage of the task they needed more support with (Huurdeman et al. 2019) or what costs and benefits they attributed to using automated tools (Pirolli and Card 2005).

Only a subset of these features was used in the first phase of the tournament and in the study that we report here. For example, Prescience included the ability to set customized alarms which notified a participant when information relevant to his or her forecast (e.g., the value of a particular indicator) had changed, as well as the ability to visualize and track the crowd average forecast for each IFP. This section describes the Prescience Web site and its hybrid features that were used in the study reported here.

The hybrid tools allow participants to seek information about an IFP and make a forecast. Figure 12.1 shows a page from a preliminary version of the Prescience Web site. The participants could access numerical indicators relevant to the selected IFP, other user forecasts, forum conversations, news, links, tabs, and so on.

The Question Details tab displays additional information about the IFP, including a more precise description of the prediction task and any clarifications about the problem ("the fine print").

The Crowd Forecast History provides information about how all forecasters have collectively answered the question (Fig. 12.2). This was intended to help the participants compare their own prediction to the average prediction. To minimize herding behavior, this tab was initially hidden and was made visible only after the participants entered their own first forecast for the IFP.

The Indicators tab displays a list of indicators, which are statistics relevant to the IFP. Indicators can be economic statistics, Internet search term frequency, information from conflict databases, and much more. A participant can monitor how their

Fig. 12.1 An example page of the Prescience Web site

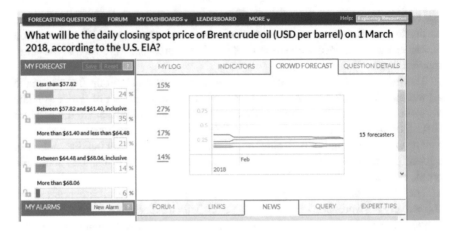

Fig. 12.2 Crowd forecast tab

indicators change over time to see when something changes about a question and decide to update their forecast (Fig. 12.3).

The Forum tab allows participants to discuss the question, comparing forecasting strategies, and share information.

The Links tab contains a list of useful links to sources relevant to the question. Participants were encouraged to examine these links and decide whether to update their forecast or not. The News tab is another way to find relevant links in Prescience. The news tab comes with a suggested set of search terms designed to provide relevant news articles. The participants can customize the search terms to refine the list of articles.

The Query tab allows the participants to extract data from several relevant sources. Query bots automatically access Web sites and databases providing the current and

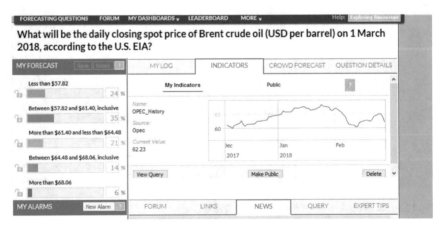

Fig. 12.3 Indicators tab

past trends of indicators underlying many of the questions. To guide participants to which queries would help them answer a given IFP, "Prescience" automatically recommends databases to participants. A set of databases was compiled by subject matter experts for each IFP category (e.g. conflict, economy, or health); when a question from a certain category is posted, Prescience automatically recommends the databases for that category. When a particular data source is mentioned in the description of the question, Prescience automatically recommends that source. Additionally, if the question matches a predefined template, the system recommends a query. For example, an IFP about number of deaths in battle in Afghanistan would suggest an ACLED query covering battle deaths over the past three years. Participants can edit a suggested query, for example, by modifying some of the suggested values. If an IFP does not match a template, but does mention a data source, the system will recommend that source to the participant. Participants can also manually add databases they deem relevant to a given IFP from the selection of databases collected and updated by Prescience. Then they can create queries on databases using a query editor that allows them to specify a date, location, type, actor, etc. In response to a query, Prescience displays recent events that match the query specifications.

Forecasters can save a query in order to automatically track its results in time. A saved query becomes an Indicator. Every six hours, the system automatically reruns the query. Forecasters can also manually rerun their queries. Indicators can be shared among forecasters by making them public. Indicators updated over the course of an IFP's lifecycle are viewable to participants as time-series graphs in the IFP Query tab (Fig. 12.4).

Another important feature of Prescience allows participants to create custom alarms (also called alerts) based on indicators. Alarms can alert a participant when key statistics have updated that may affect his or her forecast. Alarms in Prescience

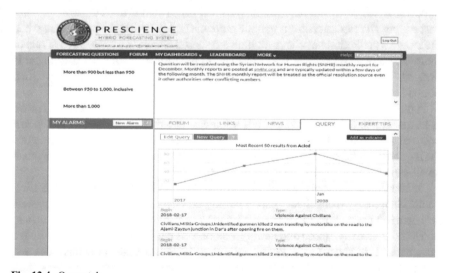

Fig. 12.4 Query tab

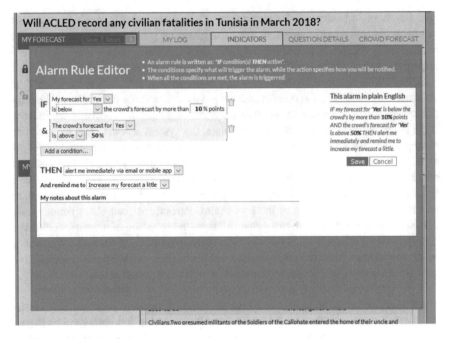

Fig. 12.5 Alarm rule editor

are created with the Alarm Rule Editor (Fig. 12.5). They are written in the form of IF condition, THEN action. That is, the participant specifies the conditions that trigger the alarm and what actions should be taken once the alarm is triggered (i.e., forecast recommendations). The participants can create three types of alarms: crowd-based, indicator-based, and time-based. Crowd-based alarms track the average forecast among all forecasters for a specific outcome and will alert the participant when the crowd's prediction has changed. Indicator-based alarms track the value of one or more indicators. Once an indicator reaches a pre-specified value, the participant is notified. Time-based alarms remind the user to review their forecast after a specified period has passed.

A more advanced version of the alarm tool is the rule-of-thumb (RoT) tool. A RoT is an alarm that not only recommends a forecast update but also makes the update automatically and notifies the user. The RoT tool was not implemented in Prescience during the first phase of the tournament (2018). We are currently running a separate small experiment to assess the value of the RoT tool.

In addition to the tools described above, email updates were sent to the participants when their alarms fired. Also, a weekly newsletter was sent to all forecasters with general news about the forecasting tournament and the Prescience system, and notes about recently closed and newly introduced IFPs. The newsletter ended with a personalized summary of the participant's contributions over the previous week and statistics of how they performed compared to the group. In addition to the newsletter, users could also sign up for immediate or daily emails with new forum posts for the

Table 12.1 Hybrid tools supporting information search and forecasting

Feature	Purpose/Function
Question details	Provide additional information about the question
Crowd forecast history	Provide aggregate information about how all forecasters have answered the question
Indicators	Display current value and time course of statistics relevant to the IFP
Forum	Allow participants to discuss the question and share information
Links	Display a list of useful links to sources relevant to the question
News	Suggest relevant news and allow news search
Query	Allow participants to extract data from relevant sources. Query bots automatically recommend relevant data sources and queries. Query editor supports creation and reruns
Customized alarm	Notify participant when relevant information (e.g., the value of a particular indicator) changes and recommend a forecast update
Customized rule of thumb	Detect change in relevant information, automatically update forecast, and notify the participant
Email updates	Provide participants with general information and customized recommendations and feedback about their forecasts

IFPs they forecasted on. Additionally, forecasters could provide notes on the alarms and rationales for their forecasts and see the history log of rationales associated with their forecasts for a particular IFP. Discussion forums were associated with each IFP (Table 12.1).

12.3.4   Variables Related to Personality and Behavior

Most of the participants completed the Cognitive Reflection Test (Frederick 2005), the Actively Open-minded Thinking scale (Stanovich and West 1997), and the Need for Cognition scale (Cacioppo et al. 1984). These variables were found in previous studies to correlate with forecasting performance (Mellers et al. 2015a). In addition, we collected extensive data on participant behavior, such as the number of IFPs forecasted, the number of forecast updates per IFP, and frequency of usage for each hybrid feature.

12.3.5   Hypotheses

We expected that the provided suite of hybrid features would improve forecasting productivity and quality, that is, the number of forecasts participants can generate the frequency at which these forecasts can be updated, and the accuracy of these forecasts. The hybrid features should allow participants to reduce the cognitive load associated with monitoring their forecasts and updates, which in turn should allow them to make more forecasts and focus on evaluating information quality and relevance. For example, when alarms trigger, they remind participants to update their forecasts, and a higher frequency of updating has in turn been linked to better forecasting performance (Tetlock and Gardner 2015). When users create alarms, they are implicitly encouraged to employ a top-down (model-driven) strategy. They need to develop intuitive causal models of what factors determine the occurrence of the event to be forecasted. Due to the nature of the forecasting task (discussed in Sects. 12.2.3 and 12.2.4), modeling and understanding the (hidden) causes of events are critical for performance. Furthermore, we expect that participants will access information from their fellow forecasters (from forums, rationales, and crowd forecasts), which might nudge them to consider alternative options and possibilities, further sharpening their own forecasts.

Hypothesis 1 In line with previous studies (e.g., Mellers et al. 2015a), behavior and personality variables (as defined in Sect. 12.3.4) will be associated with forecasting performance (as defined in Sect. 12.3.2). We use the term "behavioral variables" to refer to what participants do (e.g., update their forecast, use the query engine, click on links), whereas the term "performance" refers to the outcome of what participants do (i.e., whether they are successful or not).

Hypothesis 2 Hybrid features will increase forecasters' productivity by helping participants forecast more IFPs, update their forecasts more often, and attempt to forecast IFPs from domains that they may not be familiar with.

Hypothesis 3 More frequent use of hybrid features will be associated with better forecasting performance.

With regard to hypothesis 3, we tested two alternative explanatory accounts:

Hypothesis 3.1 Motivation predicts hybrid features usage, which in turn predicts forecasting performance.

Hypothesis 3.2 The availability of hybrid features predicts motivation to make forecasts and updates, which in turn predicts forecasting performance.

12.4   Results

In the analyses reported here we included all the participants who had complete data on the variables of interest (described above). No other procedures were used to eliminate or select data. We included 839 participants in total, of which 383 were Regulars and 456 Turkers. They worked on over 150 forecasting questions over the course of 7 months. On average, each participant produced forecasts for 20 questions.

12.4.1 Psychometric Variables

As in previous studies (Mellers 2015a), the Cognitive Reflection Test correlated significantly with the Brier score, $r(836) = -0.16$, $p < 0.001$. Similarly, the Actively Open-minded Thinking scale correlated significantly with the Brier score, performance, and accuracy, $r(835) = -0.08$, $p = 0.02$. However, the Need for Cognition scale did not correlate significantly with Brier score, performance, or accuracy.

12.4.2 Use of Hybrid Features and Forecasting Productivity and Accuracy

To evaluate if the use of hybrid features improved forecasting productivity and performance, we split the forecasters into two groups: one that used no hybrid features (queries, indicators, or alarms) composed of 519 participants and a group of participants who used one or more hybrid features, 319 participants.

The average number of forecasts per IFP was higher for participants using the hybrid tools, $t(371.67) = -6.44$, $p < 0.001$. Thus, participants who used hybrid tools made more forecast updates. The average number of IFP topics forecasted was also higher for participants who used hybrid tools, $t(737.78) = -8.81$, $p < 0.001$. Thus, the participants who used hybrid tools attempted to forecast a wider range of IFP topics. The total number of forecasts submitted was higher for participants who used hybrid tools, $t(328.61) = -4.89$, $p < 0.001$.

Forecasting performance as measured by the Brier score and the relative accuracy measure (describe above) was higher for the participants who used hybrid tools, $t(835.29) = 1.99$, $p = 0.05$ for Brier scores and $t(834.07) = -4.58$, $p < 0.001$ for relative accuracy.

Thus, as expected, forecasting productivity and accuracy were higher in those participants who used the provided hybrid features (Table 12.2). However, it remains unclear whether these findings are driven by the availability of hybrid features or by motivation. Mellers et al. (2015a) found that the frequency of forecast updating, which they considered to be a behavioral indicator of motivation, was a significant predictor of forecasting performance. Arguably, the direction of causality could go both ways: (1) The highly motivated participants made a larger number of forecast

Table 12.2 Differences between the participants who used one or more hybrid features ($n = 319$) and the participants who used no hybrid features ($n = 519$)

Variable	t value	p value
Number of forecasts per IFP	−6.44	<0.001
Number of IFP topics forecasted	−8.81	<0.001
Total number of forecasts	−4.89	<0.001
Brier score	1.99	0.05
Accuracy	−4.58	<0.001

updates and used the provided hybrid tools, which in turn increased performance, or (2) the hybrid tools increased the participants' motivation to make updates, which in turn increased performance. We address this issue in the following section.

12.4.3 Structural Equation Modeling (SEM)

To test hypotheses 3.1 and 3.2, we constructed and tested two SEM models attempting to explain the structural relations between hybrid tools usage (a sum of queries, indicators, and alarms used), psychometric measures (cognitive reflection and actively open-minded thinking), motivation (number of topics forecasted and average number of forecasts per IFP), and performance (Brier score and accuracy).

Model 1 hypothesizes a direct causal link between hybrid feature use and forecasting performance, whereas model 2 hypothesizes an indirect causal link (via motivation) between hybrid feature use and forecasting performance.

Model 1 assumes that motivation causes hybrid tool usage, which in turn causes increased performance. It also includes the known associations between psychometrics, motivation, and forecasting performance.

Model 2 assumes that hybrid tool usage causes motivation, which in turn causes increased performance. Similar to model 1, model 2 also includes the known associations between psychometrics, motivation, and forecasting performance.

We compared the two models using the Akaike information criterion (AIC) and Bayesian information criterion (BIC). Model 2 had AIC = 15913 and BIC = 15994, whereas Model 1 had AIC = 15941 and BIC = 16022; thus, Model 2 fits the data better than Model 1.

Model 2 supports the hypothesis that the use of hybrid tools has a direct effect on motivation. Email alerts about indicator changes and crowd changes motivated participants to update their own forecasts and perhaps do additional information searches. In agreement with previous studies, motivation had a direct effect on performance, as did the psychometric variables actively open-minded thinking and the tendency to engage in cognitive reflection.

12.5 Discussion and Conclusion

Previous studies (Mellers et al. 2015a; Tetlock and Gardner 2015) reported dispositional and behavioral predictors of forecasting performance. These findings were replicated in our study: Cognitively reflective and open-minded participants made better forecasts. Forecasters who are open-minded are more likely to consider information that contradicts their prior forecasts and to update their forecasts. Forecasters who are cognitively reflective are more analytical and perhaps less likely to fall victim to the cognitive biases described in Sect. 12.2.1.

In addition to cognitive ability, motivation is also an important predictor of forecasting performance. Mellers et al. (2015a) showed that participants who updated their forecasts more often achieved better forecasting performance. This finding was also replicated in our study. Frequent forecast updates reflect the participants' motivation to search for and process information relevant to the problem at hand. These results support our hypothesis 1.

Our study added a suite of hybrid feature to assist forecasters with the laborious tasks of information search, sense-making, and decision-making. The use of these tools was optional. We assumed users would act strategically (Kirlik 1993) and use these tools as needed. The expectation was that forecasters equipped with hybrid tools would become more productive and more accurate. The effect of the hybrid tools was expected to be independent of the effects that were already known (i.e., cognitive ability, cognitive style, and motivation). For example, hybrid tools were expected to be helpful above and beyond a participant's motivation or cognitive ability. What we found does not entirely support this expectation. We did find that the use of hybrid features improves forecasting performance, but this relationship is most likely mediated by motivation. The use of hybrid features increased the forecasters' productivity, as indicated by the number and the variety of IFPs they forecasted and the frequency of forecast updates. These findings support our second hypothesis.

Since the use of hybrid features was optional, the relationship between the use of hybrid features and forecasting performance must be interpreted with caution, as only a minority of participants used the provided hybrid tools (319 of 839) and the decision to use hybrid features might be confounded by other factors such as trust in automation and in other forecasters (Juvina, Collins et al., in press).

Regarding our third hypothesis, the interpretation that seems to be supported by the data is that the provided hybrid features encouraged the participants to do more work (i.e., information search, communication, reflection), which in turn resulted in improved forecasting performance. Thus, hypothesis 3.2 garnered more empirical support than hypothesis 3.1.

We focused here on a subset of hybrid tools that were implemented in Prescience in the first round of the hybrid forecasting competition (2018), namely queries, indicators, and alarms. They appear to be useful in driving improvements in forecasting performance. While it is not surprising that supporting users information foraging and sense-making improves forecasting performance, our unique contribution emphasizes the importance of engaging users in creating their own support tools. We provided the alarm editor to encourage participants to create customized alarms that would alert them when potentially relevant information changes and recommend a forecast update. The participants who chose to create an alarm had to specify the conditions that would trigger the alarm (i.e., specific changes in one or more indicators) and the action to be recommended (i.e., a specific change in the forecast). As a matter of fact, the alarm editor challenged participants to create their own intuitive models of information search and forecasting and turn these models into support tools. The results highlight the importance of providing tools that are not only useful and useable, but are able to engage users and enhance their cognitive activity, aiming to strike a balance between user effort and information search automation (Bates 1990), ultimately achieving the goals of human machine symbiosis and co-evolution (Licklider 1960; Ackerman 2000).

The environment participants used offered forums to facilitate discussions between participants, the possibility to share news stories, and the possibility to enter and share rationales for forecasts. These data will be reported elsewhere.

Currently, we are engaged in the second phase of the HFC. New hybrid tools have been added to the Prescience system such as rules of thumb (i.e., active alarms), base rate support (to counteract the base rate neglect bias), and personalized IFP recommendations. We are running a series of experiments to assess the potential of these features to improve forecasting performance.

The work reported here contributes to the area of human factors involved in information search and navigation tasks in information intensive environments (e.g., Pirolli and Card 1999; Pirolli and Fu 2003; Juvina and van Oostendorp 2008; Karanam et al. 2016). Our results so far demonstrate the importance of combining a thorough understanding of human cognition from decades of research in cognitive science and cognitive modeling with recent advances in information search technology to support human performance in complex socio-technical systems.

Acknowledgements The work reported here is part of a larger project involving the following companies and universities: Raytheon BBN Technologies, Lumenogic, Kairos Research, Wright State University, USC Information Sciences Institute, American Center for Democracy, Ipsos Public Affairs, Systems & Technologies Research, and Tufts University. This work is supported by the Office of the Director of National Intelligence (ODNI), Intelligence Advanced Research Projects Activity (IARPA), via 201717072100002. The views and conclusions contained herein are those of the authors and should not be interpreted as necessarily representing the official policies, either expressed or implied, of ODNI, IARPA, or the US Government. The US Government is authorized to reproduce and distribute reprints for governmental purposes notwithstanding any copyright annotation therein.

References

Ackerman MS (2000) The intellectual challenge of CSCW: the gap between social requirements and technical feasibility. Human-Computer Interaction 15(2):179–203

Amershi S, Morris MR (2008) CoSearch: a system for colocated collaborative Web search. Proc. CHI 2008:1647–1656

Baldonado MQW, Winograd T (1997). SenseMaker: an information-exploration interface supporting the contextual evolution of a user's interests. In Proceedings CHI 1997, pp 11–18

Bates MJ (1990) Where should the person stop and the information search interface start? Inf Process & Manag 26(5):575–591

Beger A, Ward MD (2018) Assessing Amazon Turker and automated machine forecasts in the Hybrid Forecasting Competition. In 7th Annual Asian Political Methodology Conference, 5–6 January 2019, Kyoto, Japan

Billman D, Bier EA (2007) Medical sensemaking with entity workspace. In Proceedings CHI 2007, pp 229–232

Brier GW (1950) Verification of forecasts expressed in terms of probability. Mon Weather Rev 78(1):1–3

Budescu DV, Chen E (2014) Identifying expertise to extract the wisdom of crowds. Manage Sci 61(2):267–280

Cacioppo JT, Petty RE, Feng Kao C (1984) The efficient assessment of need for cognition. J Pers Assess 48(3):306–307

Dekker SWA, Woods DD (2002) MABA-MABA or Abracadabra? progress on human-automation Co-ordination. Cogn, Technol & Work 4:240–244

Evans JSB, Stanovich KE (2013) Dual-process theories of higher cognition: advancing the debate. Perspect Psychol Sci 8(3):223–241

Fingar T, Fischhoff B, Chauvin C (2011) Analysis in the US intelligence community: missions, masters, and methods. In: Intelligence analysis: behavioral and social scientific foundations, pp 3–27

Fischhoff, B (2011) Judgment and decision making. Oxford: Routledge/Earthscan

Fitts PM (ed) (1951) Human engineering for an effective air navigation and traffic control system. National Research Council, Washington, DC

Frederick S (2005) Cognitive reflection and decision making. Journal of Economic perspectives 19(4):25–42

Gotz D (2007) The ScratchPad: sensemaking support for the web. Proc. of WWW 2007:1329–1330

Hirshleifer D, Levi Y, Lourie B, Teoh SH (2019) Decision fatigue and heuristic analyst forecasts. J Financ Econ

Huurdeman HC, Kamps J, Wilson ML (2019) The multi-stage experience: the simulated work task approach to studying information seeking task stages. In Proceedings BIIRRRR workshop at CHIIR 2019

Hyndman RJ, Khandakar Y (2007) Automatic time series for forecasting: the forecast package for R (No. 6/07). Clayton VIC, Australia: Monash University, Department of Econometrics and Business Statistics

Juvina I, Collins MG, Larue O, Kennedy W, de Visser E, de Melo C (in press). Toward a unified theory of learned trust in interpersonal and human-machine interactions. ACM Transactions in Interactive Intelligent Systems

Juvina I, van Oostendorp H (2008) Modeling semantic and structural knowledge in Web navigation. Discourse Process 45(4):346–364

Kahneman D, Egan P (2011) Thinking, fast and slow (vol. 1). Farrar, Straus and Giroux, New York

Kahneman D, Knetsch JL (1992) Valuing public goods: The purchase of moral satisfaction. J Environ Econ Manage 22(1):57–70

Karanam S, van Oostendorp H, Fu WT (2016) Performance of computational cognitive models of web-navigation on real websites. J Inf Sci 42(1):94–113

Keel P (2007) EWall: a visual analytics environment for collaborative sensemaking. Inf Vis 6:48–63

Kirlik A (1993) Modeling strategic behavior in human-automation interaction: why an" aid" can (and should) go unused. Hum Factors 35(2):221–242

Lee WY, Goodwin P, Fildes R, Nikolopoulos K, Lawrence M (2007) Providing support for the use of analogies in demand forecasting tasks. Int J Forecast 23(3):377–390

Licklider JCR (1960) Man-computer symbiosis. In: IRE Transactions on Human Factors in Electronics, volume HFE-1, pp 4–11

Mellers B, Stone E, Atanasov P, Rohrbaugh N, Metz SE., Ungar L, ... and Tetlock P (2015a) The psychology of intelligence analysis: drivers of prediction accuracy in world politics. J Exp Psychol: Appl 21(1):1

Mellers B, Stone E, Murray T, Minster A, Rohrbaugh N, Bishop M., ... Ungar L (2015b) Identifying and cultivating superforecasters as a method of improving probabilistic predictions. Perspect Psychol Sci 10(3):267–281

Morris MR, Horvitz E (2008) SearchTogether: an interface for collaborative Web search. In Proceedings UIST 2008, 3–12

Paul SA, Morris MR (2009) Cosense: enhancing sensemaking for collaborative web search. In Proceedings of the SIGCHI Conference on Human Factors in Computing Systems, ACM, 2009, pp 1771–1780

Pirolli P, Card S (2005) The sensemaking process and leverage points for analyst technology as identified through cognitive task analysis. In Intelligence Analysis, pp 2–4

Pirolli P, Card SK (1999) Information foraging. Psychol Rev 106:643–675

Pirolli P, Fu W-T (2003) SNIF-ACT: a model of information foraging on the World Wide Web. In: Proceedings of the Ninth International Conference on User Modeling. Johnstown, Pennsylvania. *LNAI 2702* (pp 45–54). Springer-Verlag, Berlin

Qu Y (2003) A Sensemaking supporting information gathering system. In Ext. Abstracts CHI 2003, pp 906–907

Rahwan I, Cebrian M, Obradovich N, Bongard J, Bonnefon JF, Breazeal C, Crandall JW, Christakis NA, Couzin ID, Jackson MO, Jennings NR, Kamar E, Kloumann IM, Larochelle H, Lazer D, Mcelreath R, Mislove A, Parkes DC, Pentland AS, Roberts ME, Shariff A, Tenenbaum JB, Wellman M (2019) Machine behavior. Nature 568:477–486

Sankar S (2012) The rise of human-computer cooperation. https://www.ted.com/talks/shyam_sankar_the_rise_of_human_computer_cooperation/transcript?language=en

Stanovich KE, West RF (1997) Reasoning independently of prior belief and individual differences in actively open-minded thinking. J Educ Psychol 89(2):342

Tetlock, Philip E (2005) Expert Political Judgment: How Good Is It? How Can We Know? Princeton University Press, Princeton

Tetlock Philip E, Gardner Dan (2015) Superforecasting: the art and science of prediction. Broadway Books, New York

Turner BM, Steyvers M, Merkle EC, Budescu DV, Wallsten TS (2014) Forecast aggregation via recalibration. Mach Learn 95(3):261–289

Tversky A, Kahneman D (1974) Judgment under uncertainty: heuristics and biases. Science 185(4157):1124–1131

Ungar L, Mellers B, Satopää V, Tetlock P, Baron J (2012, October). The good judgment project: a large scale test of different methods of combining expert predictions. In: 2012 AAAI Fall Symposium Series

Van Nimwegen C, Burgos D, Van Oostendorp H, Schrijf H (2006) The paradox of the assisted user: guidance can be counterproductive. In: Proceedings CHI 2006, 917–926

Chapter 13
Conversational Interfaces
for Information Search

Q. Vera Liao, Werner Geyer, Michael Muller and Yasaman Khazaen

Abstract Recent progress in machine learning has given rise to a plethora of tools and applications that rely on conversational interactions, from chatbots, speech-controlled devices to robots and virtual agents. Conversational interfaces are becoming widely accepted for utility tools, where a common function is to serve users' information needs. Albeit with much excitement, we are only starting to understand how users' information-seeking behaviors and design opportunities may transform moving from traditional graphical user interfaces to conversational user interfaces. In this chapter, we start by reviewing recent work in the emerging area of conversational interfaces and lay out their opportunities for supporting information search tasks. We then present insights from our experience deploying a chatbot supporting information search in a large enterprise, demonstrating how a conversational interface impacts user behaviors and offers new opportunities for improving search experience, in particular for user modeling.

13.1 Introduction

Conversational systems, with which users interact through spoken or typed natural language, are becoming ubiquitous thanks to the popularity of many commercial products such as Apple Siri, Google Assistant, and Amazon Alexa. We *talk* to these systems to find directions, choose products, troubleshoot technical problems, learn

Q. V. Liao (✉)
IBM Research AI, Yorktwon Heights, New York, NY, USA
e-mail: vera.Liao@ibm.com

W. Geyer · M. Muller · Y. Khazaen
IBM Research AI, Cambridge, MA, USA
e-mail: werner.geyer@us.ibm.com

M. Muller
e-mail: michael_endmathmuller@us.ibm.com

Y. Khazaen
e-mail: yasaman.khazaeni@us.ibm.com

© Springer Nature Switzerland AG 2020
W. T. Fu and H. van Oostendorp (eds.), *Understanding and Improving Information Search*, Human–Computer Interaction Series,
https://doi.org/10.1007/978-3-030-38825-6_13

about the latest news, and seek information for various decisions. This paradigm shift to conversational interactions on the one hand offers new opportunities to improve information-seeking tasks, on the other hand, requires developing new types of computational models and interaction techniques.

If a conversational system is seen as merely a text-based or voice-based search system, it makes sense to use search results to respond to user questions. For example, the following exchange is a common scenario in talking to a FAQ chatbot on a Web page of an insurance company:

> User: Is it mandatory to purchase collision coverage?
>
> Agent: Collision coverage pays for repair or replacement costs if your car crashes into an object or another car. This coverage is designed to fix up or replace your own car after a collision. Our customers will need to have comprehensive coverage before adding collision coverage. You can have comprehensive and not collision on your policy, just not the other way around. If you lease or finance your car, collision may be required by your leasing or financing company. Like comprehensive coverage, collision coverage will pay for damages to your car as long as they don't exceed the car's actual cash value...

However, such an interaction is not yet compatible with how humans engage in conversations. Much burden is still on the user to locate the answer from the lengthy texts of the search result. More problematically, the customer has to accurately formulate the question or the system would retrieve an irrelevant set of results. In that case, the customer would have to carefully read the large chunk of text, decide there is no useful information, and start over again by reformulating the question, leading to frustration or boredom. We envision that one day we could actually talk to intelligent systems as follows:

> User: Hi agent, I need some help
>
> Agent: Sure! How can I help you?
>
> User: Do I need to buy coverage for my own car?
>
> Agent: Are you considering collision coverage or comprehensive coverage?
>
> User: What is collision coverage?
>
> Agent: If your car crashes into an object or another car, collision coverage is designed to fix up or replace your own car.
>
> User: How is it different from comprehensive coverage?
>
> Agent: Well, collision coverage is to cover your own car after a collision, while comprehensive coverage pays for damage in events that are not collision-related, such as theft and vandalism.
>
> User: I see. Am I required to purchase collision coverage then?
>
> Agent: Collision coverage is optional. But if you lease or finance your car, it may be required by your leasing or financing company
>
> User: Okay thanks.
>
> Agent: You are welcome!

In such conversational interactions, information is given by the system in a succinct and precise manner. More importantly, an accurate understanding of the customer's problem is incrementally formed through various actions from the system such as clarification and explanation, which are made possible by having the customer well engaged in a natural and personable conversation. Conversational interface like this can reduce customers' cognitive workload to read, requires little learning to use, and might be the only viable solution in some contexts such as voice-based systems.

The agents in both examples have access to the same set of information sources. So how do we move from single-turn Q&A in Example 1 to multi-turn interactions in Example 2? By talking naturally, users should be able to express their information needs in a familiar way as in their everyday conversations, no longer required to learn the operation vocabulary of a search system or the output schema. This means that users would be offloaded from "direct manipulation" of computational models (Shneiderman and Maes 1997), instead relying on conversational interfaces to perform an *intermediary* role between the information seekers and information sources. Natural conversation offers the necessary devices to perform such an intermediary role, as we communicate through language to exchange information between our different minds, not through queries-and-answers, but nonlinear combinations of disclosure, elicitation, refinement, clarification, explanation, narratives, and so on. Conversational interfaces should take advantage of these devices

This is not to say that conversational systems should mimic entire human conversations, nor could we expect them to achieve human-level intelligence any time soon. Rather, our view is that we should start with the fundamental question—what aspects of conversations are pertinent and beneficial for performing information search tasks, and what are the necessary system capabilities to enable them?

We believe these questions should be addressed from two ends: From a systems point of view, i.e., how can conversational interactions extend current computational models for information search; from a cognitive point of view, i.e., what are the desirable and necessary properties of conversations to support information seeking. In the next section, we offer some perspectives by drawing on related work that answers the following questions: (1) How do conversational interactions fit and extend information search models? (2) Empirically, what have we learned about designing functionalities of conversational search systems, which are still very much in an exploratory stage? (3) Theoretically, what are the fundamental properties of human conversations, and how can they inform the design of conversational search to make it more cognitively compatible with how people converse?

With that, we lay out a space of functional goals for conversational search systems along two axes: stages of information search behaviors—query formulation, search result exploration, and repair (Bates 2002; Marchionini 1997; Wilson 2000); and fundamental principles of human conversations—efficiency, common ground, and recipient design (Bell 1984; Grice 1975; Clark and Brennan 1991; Sacks and Schegloff 1979). We also discuss empirical insights on how users converse with a conversational agent performing information search tasks from our own work deploying a chatbot that answers questions from employees of a large enterprise. The results demonstrate the rich conversational behaviors users engage with a conversational interface and the opportunities they offer for improving search performance and user experience.

13.2   Conversational Search

Conversational systems that support information-seeking tasks encompass systems with a one-shot question-and-answer (QA) model (as in most current commercial products), systems that can engage in free conversations to resolve a user's problem, and anything in between. To be excluded are systems that perform primarily chitchat, and systems that receive or give commands through voice or text. This chapter will not discuss 60-year history of dialogue systems and conversational agents. For interested readers, we recommend several books (Cassell et al. 2000; McTear 2004; McTear et al. 2016). We do not address with any particular computational solutions, whether rule-based, statistical, or more recent neural network models (Baeza-Yates and Ribeiro 2011; Li et al. 2018; Sun and Zhang 2018). Our focus is on designing *interactions* of conversational search.

While people have long been fascinated by "machines to talk to," migrating to a new interaction modality requires work to define new system functionalities and design guidelines. The information retrieval (IR) community responded with much enthusiasm–"*such a growth in natural language dialogue between users and search systems may even lead to the dominant interaction model of one-shot keyword queries being displaced with conversational systems*" (Radlinski and Craswell 2017). The IR community takes a system-driven approach and considers new opportunities offered by conversational interactions to extend existing IR frameworks (Azzopardi et al. 2018; Christakopoulou et al. 2016; Li et al. 2018; Radlinski and Craswell 2017; Zhang et al. 2018). The human–computer interaction (HCI) community, expressing equal enthusiasm, follows its user-centered design tradition by studying users' needs and behaviors to inform the design of this new type of interface (Liao et al. 2018; Luger and Sellen 2016; Myers et al. 2018; Porcheron et al. 2018). We draw on work from both communities as well as related social and cognitive science to reflect on how to best deliver the benefits of conversational interactions for information search tasks.

13.2.1   From Search to Conversational Search

Across academic communities, there is a long history of creating formal frameworks of users' information-seeking behaviors to guide IR system design (Bates 2002; Marchionini 1997; Wilson 2000). While details vary, these frameworks converge on three core stages of information seeking: query formulation from information needs, examination of search results, and query refinements or reformulation if necessary. Chapter 7 of this book provides a more detailed overview of these multi-stage search behavioral models. Earlier work sought inspiration from structures of information-seeking dialogues (e.g., with a librarian) to inform *interactive search*. Influential work includes Conversation Role Model by Sitter and Stein (1992) and conversational scripts by Belkin et al. (1995). Both aimed to provide idealized flows for an interactive search system to select next steps, but they were not considered specifically for conversational systems.

Recently, researchers started conceptualizing what actions can be made by users and systems if search becomes "conversational." In a perspective paper by Radlinkski and Craswell (2017), they identify properties of conversations pertinent to search settings to be: mixed-initiative, goal-oriented, maintaining memory, and adaptive. Accordingly, they offer a formal definition of conversational search system to be *"a system for retrieving information that permits a mixed-initiative back and forth between a user and agent, where the agent's actions are chosen in response to a model of current user needs within the current conversation, using both short- and long-term knowledge of the user"*.

Radlinkski and Craswell argue that a conversational search system should therefore have the following properties as advantages over traditional search systems: (1) User disclosure: Through conversations, it could help the user better express information needs; (2) System disclosure: It is convenient for the system to reveal its capabilities, building the user's mental model; (3) Mixed-initiative: The system and user can both naturally take initiative as appropriate; (4) Memory: The user can naturally reference past statements; (5) Set retrieval: The system can reason about the utility of a set of items in a conversation rather than having multiple search sessions as in traditional search system. Based on these requirements, Azzopardi et al. (2018) proposed possible actions that a user and a conversational agent could perform during query formulation and search results exploration stages, as well as mixed-initiative actions that can happen in the conversation (Fig. 13.1). This action spaces could be used to generate dialogue policies for performing conversational search.

To complement these theoretical perspectives, in the following, we discuss empirical work on developing functionalities of conversational search. We will organize the discussions by the three core stages of information-seeking behaviors. Currently, to handle free-form conversations remains an open challenge. Most work addresses only some aspects of conversational search. Another approach taken is to study how people naturally engage in information-seeking conversations (McDuff et al. 2017; Trippas et al. 2018), either with another human, or a wizard-of-oz agent (an unseen human simulating an agent). The premise is that these scenarios represent the ideal level of intelligence and that users prefer interactions consistent with their natural conversations. While such a view is debatable, it is a valuable approach to seek inspirations to define capabilities and actions of conversational search.

13.2.1.1   Query Formulation

Whether through a speech-controlled device or chatting with a chatbot, users' querying behaviors may naturally change when the interface becomes conversational. A number of studies examined user queries with spoken search systems and compared them to typed queries in a search box, showing that spoken queries are longer, more verbose, and have more varied language (Crestani and Du 2006; Guy 2018). For example, Guy conducted an analysis on half a million search logs and found

USER			AGENT		
	Query Formulation	**Reveal** Disclose Revise Refine Expand	**Inquire** Extract Elicit Clarify	*User Disclosure*	
Set Retrieval	Result Exploration	**Inquire** List Summarize Compare Subset Similar	**Reveal** List Summarize Compare Subset Similar		*Memory*
		Navigate Repeat Back More Note	**Traverse** Repeat Back More Record	*System disclosure*	
Mixed Initiative		**Interrupt** Interrupt	**Suggest** Recommend Hypothesize		
		Interrogate Understand Explain	**Explain** Report Reason		

Fig. 13.1 An action space of conversational search systems proposed by Azzopardi et al. (2018) based on properties of conversational search proposed by Radlinski and Craswell (2017)

that spoken queries have more formal grammatical structures (e.g., wh-words–what/why/who/where), types of parts of speech (while typed queries are mostly nouns), and tend to use full-sentence inquires (e.g., "I am looking for", "take me to") (Guy 2018). Trippas et al. conducted a study observing conversations between an information seeker and a human intermediary who had access to a search system (Trippas et al. 2018). They observed much variance—while some used query-like expressions, others used lengthy and complex sentences to describe their needs. These natural language expressions could include multiple actions (e.g., querying, navigation) in one turn, or complete one action with multiple turns, in contrast to a linear process with a traditional search interface.

Perhaps the most critical difference that a conversational system makes is that query formulation can be achieved through multi-turn interactions (Christakopoulou et al. 2018; Mahmood and Ricci 2009; Thompson et al. 2004; Zhang et al. 2018). It means that, for one, it is possible for the user to express complex information needs sequentially, yielding a more accurate representation of their real knowledge gap, which may be multi-faceted, multi-item, or inter-dependent (Radlinski and Craswell 2017). Second, the system could take an active role that resembles an intermediary, by asking questions back to the user depending on the previous information provided, thus offloading the user's effort to accurately formulate formal system input.

According to Azzopardi's model (Azzopardi et al. 2018), during the query formulation stage, a user may follow up by *revising, refining,* and *expanding* the original query, and a system can *"extract, elicit, and clarify."* Extracting key information and clarification are necessary actions to deal with the verbose, sometimes ambiguous queries in conversational forms. Eliciting user criteria, preferences, or constraints to refine search results has long been of interest to IR systems (Baeza-Yates and Ribeiro 2011; Chen and Pu 2004; Mcginty and Smyth 2006). Earlier work on goal-oriented dialogue systems also adopted a "slot-filling" approach that requests one criterion from the user at a time (Bobrow et al. 1977; Walker et al. 2001). The outcome, however, might be a long, tedious dialogue that does not feel natural (Zhang et al. 2018). This approach is also questionable outside narrow domains if the criteria have many candidates or cannot be pre-defined. An alternative approach is to acquire user criteria by eliciting feedback for sample items through critiquing (Mcginty and Smyth 2006), comparing (Christakopoulou et al. 2016), or grouping similar items (Chen and Pu 2004). By suggesting items and eliciting feedback, it could also help build users' mental models of the search space. These approaches could face challenges with traditional search system as users may be unwilling to provide feedback by repeatedly filling out forms. Conversational interfaces could be a natural fit, as example-based discussions are common in conversations, and with natural language the user input can be incremental and flexible.

There are a number of computational challenges to enable query formulation through conversations. First, extraction and pre-processing techniques are necessary to bridge natural language queries and input for the underlying computational models. Currently, to handle variations in conversational input, rule-based or machine-learning-based intent models are often used to first map a user utterance to a query category for system input. Arguello et al. showed that conversational queries yield worse retrieval performance if issued unmodified to search APIs (Arguello et al. 2017). While Crestani and Du suggested that simple processing by extracting nouns, adjectives, and verbs can improve the retrieval performance (Crestani and Du 2006), the challenges are likely beyond keywords extractions. For example, one may need to breakdown multiple moves in one utterance, understand user needs from multiple turns, and accommodate greater individual variances in querying behaviors. Second, optimizing the dialogue flow for elicitation questions remains a computational challenge. To efficiently reduce the search space (sometimes relaxing if over-specified) involves multiple complex optimization problems, such as selecting elicitation methods to use, criteria to elicit for, and considering the trade-off between further elicitation and revealing results.

13.2.1.2   Search Results Presentation

How to present search results in conversational forms is an under-studied area. Most existing systems simply either read out the top result or a condensed version of a ranked list. Such designs are not conversational and can be problematic for speech generation and users' attention span (for listening and reading). Also many key elements of traditional search systems, such as search snippets and graphic information, cannot be easily presented in conversational forms. It is important to recognize that, compared to graphical user interfaces, conversations represent a "narrower" and thus ideally more precise information channel—a turn of a dialogue is expected to be succinct, informative, and relevant (Grice 1975). Therefore, additional processing mechanisms are required on top of document retrieval.

One such mechanism is summarization. Trippas et al.'s study shows that the human intermediary naturally chose to provide document summarization to the information seekers, sometimes summarizing across multiple documents (Trippas et al. 2018). The counterparts of summarization—drilling-down for details—would also be necessary, which are embodied in various actions in natural conversations, mainly paraphrasing, defining, explanation, and elaboration (Schegloff 2007). Azzopardi et al.'s model emphasizes the presentation of multiple documents, suggesting that users should be able to request presentation of multi-documents in overview–*summarization, listing*, etc., or in details–*subsets, comparison between documents*, etc., and to navigate between documents–*forward, backward*, and *repeat* (Azzopardi et al. 2018).

The technical challenge here is to create representations of varied granularity for a document or a set of documents, from high-level summarization to different types of details. In their book on design patterns for conversational systems, Moore and Arar suggested patterns to decompose document content, such as a FAQ page, for conversational interactions (Moore and Arar 2019). While a search engine may simply retrieve a document (e.g., health insurance coverage), a conversational system should not only recognize subtopics within the document (e.g., copay, deductible), but also respond to different types of follow-up requests—paraphrasing, examples, and definitions, by either generating or extracting such contents from the document.

Conversational interfaces are especially suitable for driving the user down a focused navigational path. The drawback is that the user may lose awareness of alternate information and risk forming a narrow understanding or inaccurate mental model of the search space. This is another place where the system should take initiative. Azzopardi et al. suggest that the system should always keep a representation of users' current information needs, past information needs, as well as alternate information needs, and provide recommendations that the user may not have explicitly requested (Azzopardi et al. 2018). However, technical challenges remain to be solved, not only on how to infer alternate information needs, but also when to suggest them. For example, one needs to consider the trade-off between access to more information and the increasing complexity of the conversation.

13.2.1.3 Query Reformulation and Repair

In search behavior models, query reformulation is the step following dissatisfying search results exploration. This definition is worth revisiting in a conversational search setting. On the one hand, in conversational search the querying process can be incremental, i.e., query formulation and search result presentation can happen multiple times in series (e.g., to elicit further feedback), thus blurring the boundaries between query formulation and reformulation. On the other hand, conversational systems introduce new types of errors in addition to suboptimal retrieval performance, such as errors in the steps of speech recognition, speech to text, or language understanding. Hence, it may be more appropriate to use the term "repair" to consider user and system actions when there is breakdown in conversational search.

Recent work investigated how users naturally reformulate queries with conversational search systems (Hassan et al. 2015; Jiang et al. 2013; Myers et al. 2018; Shokouhi et al. 2014). For example, with a spoken search system, Jiang et al. showed that users engaged in various ways of lexical reformulation (e.g., addition, substitution, removing, reordering) and phonetic reformulation (e.g., emphasizing parts of the query) (Jiang et al. 2013). However, it creates problem when users make blind attempts of reformulation, which sometimes contradicts with practices in natural conversations. For instance, while it is natural for people to elaborate with more information when talking to another person, reformulating queries with more details may adversely harm the retrieval performance (Myers et al. 2018). This is due to a mismatch between how humans perform natural language understanding and how computational systems work. Users often do not understand this mismatch because conversational interfaces are misleadingly "natural" and thus opaque in disclosing the underlying computational models.

A system may fail both the search task and creating a truly conversational experience if solely relying on users to repair, as conversation should be a two-way process to resolve uncertainty (Clark and Brennan 1991). Recent work started addressing system-initiated repairing processes (Balchandran et al. 2009; Paek and Horvitz 2000). In Ashktorab et al. (2019), the authors propose a framework for repair design of conversational QA with three levels of increasing contributions from the system: explicitly acknowledging the breakdown (e.g., asking for confirmation or rephrasing), making the system model transparent to assist user repair (e.g., explaining current understanding), and proactively suggesting query reformulation. The research shows that user satisfaction increases with a higher level of contribution from the system.

The technical challenge for the three levels of system-initiated contributions, however, remains largely unsolved. First, there is often no precise way for a system to recognize a misunderstanding or retrieval error. Currently, machine-learning-based systems rely on a confidence level to infer a potential breakdown. Such methods cannot identify "unknown unknown" errors where the training data have blind spots. Paek and Horvitz explored using Bayesian networks to infer uncertainty (Paek and Horvitz 2000), but it has not been adopted as a scalable solution. Second, explaining language understanding or search results is a pressing problem that has raised much interest lately (Gunning 2017; Miller 2018). The challenge is on how to make the explanation actionable to support the end goal of successful query reformulation. For example, a system can explain its current understanding by keywords it identified for search results, and the user should be able to respond by incrementally correcting misunderstanding without starting all over. Lastly, as with traditional search systems, query suggestions may fail, and such failures are likely more detrimental if presented as a single turn in a conversation.

13.2.2 Toward Conversational User Experience

Now that we have reviewed work on the functionalities of conversational search systems, we consider some fundamental properties of natural conversations. These properties could inform the design of conversational search systems to make them more cognitively compatible, and help assess what search functionalities are necessary to deliver the benefits offered by conversational interactions. Social and cognitive science provides rich insights into the general patterns of how people engage in conversations. Three basic principles are commonly recognized for governing these patterns (Moore and Arar 2019): *efficiency* (Grice 1975; Sacks and Schegloff 1979), *common ground* (Clark and Brennan 1991), and *recipient design* (Bell 1984; Clark and Murphy 1982; Sacks and Schegloff 1979). We advocate incorporating these principles into the design space of conversational search at each stage. Many of the functionalities discussed in the previous section can be seen as to serve these principles. In Table 13.1, we map them in this design space and suggest additional functional goals that may be necessary to create a truly conversational experience. While each of these principles is backed by a large volume of research, in the following we discuss high-level ideas and implications for designing conversational search.

Efficiency: Also referred to as minimization, the efficiency principle guides speakers to achieve necessary informativeness with minimum effort, e.g., using as few turns and number of words as possible. To minimize user's effort, this principle suggests the system to *maximize its initiative as allowed by the intelligence*, and *simplify the content as allowed by understandability*. System-initiated actions to support query formulation and repair, including extracting system input from user utterances, optimizing elicitation dialogues for user preferences, criteria or constraints, and contributing to repair, can be considered to serve the goal of minimizing user's effort. Additionally, the system should in general aim to *support natural language expressions that may be minimal, implicit and incremental*, for example, by memorizing contexts and long-term user models to make inference about user's information needs. For presenting information in a conversational form, this principle supports the idea of *starting from the lowest granularity of details that most targeted users can understand*, meanwhile providing rich navigational paths for details.

Common ground: This principle views conversation as a form of collective action to achieve mutual knowledge. Speakers constantly assess if there is good enough mutual understanding through evidence (e.g., explicit acknowledgment or relevant next turn), and if not, a grounding process (i.e., repair) will be initiated. When the dialogue partner is a machine, its model of understanding is significantly mismatched from the human speaker. Therefore, in applying the common ground principle for human–computer interactions, the general goal is to *make the system model more*

Table 13.1 A design space of functional goals for conversational search

	Efficiency	Common ground	Recipient design
Query formulation	• Extract system input from natural language • Optimize elicitation dialogue flow • Maintain context and user model for inference	• Clarification to bridge user input and system model • Incrementally suggest examples and elicit feedback	• Support different querying behaviors • Tailor elicitation dialogue flow
Results exploration	• Minimize complexity • Start from summarization or low granularity, with navigational paths for details	• Make capabilities and navigational paths discoverable • Support follow-up inquiries (paraphrasing, definition, examples, elaboration) • Suggest alternate information	• Tailor search algorithms • Tailor presentation and interaction styles
Query reformulation and repair	• Maximize system initiative for repair • Support incremental repair	• Signal breakdown • Make system model and status transparent • Suggest reformulation	• Tailor repair assistance strategies

transparent, and actively *bridge between the user model and system model*. This principle is most relevant to functionalities for clarification and repair, and provides theoretical support for the three levels of system contributions we discussed for query repair: showing evidence (signaling potential misunderstanding or breakdown), making the system model (especially current understanding) transparent, and bridging mismatched user and system models (e.g., suggesting query reformulation). Equally important is to equip the system with capabilities to handle common types of user-initiated repair, including paraphrasing, providing definition, examples, and elaboration (Moore and Arar 2019). The principle also highlights the importance of *system disclosure to help build users' expectation and mental models* of the search space at all stages, such as suggesting examples for feedback, recommending alternate information, and making the system capabilities and the navigational paths discoverable.

Recipient design: Speakers constantly tailor the ways they talk according to the particular recipient(s), based on their knowledge, social relations, personalities, and so on. The principle of recipient design governs all aspects of human conversations, from choices of topics, to levels of details, to the organization of the conversation and linguistic styles. It is not surprising that incorporating awareness and knowledge of the user has long been a focus for research in dialogue systems and conversational agents (Cassell et al. 2000), and many argue that demonstrating adaptiveness is necessary to achieve human-like conversational interactions. Work on conversational search, however, has not yet given much attention to this area. Of course, personalization and adaptation have their place in IR work (Ghorab et al. 2013; Kelly and Teevan 2003; Teevan et al. 2005), but mostly with a narrow focus on tailoring search algorithms based on users' interaction history or user profiles.

We argue that *recipient design should take a more central role for conversational interfaces*. First, besides *retrieval algorithms*, there are more properties of interactions to tailor for individual users to deliver a truly conversational experience. When presenting the search results, adapting *interaction styles* such as the level of details, language use, linguistic styles, and other social and communication designs for individual users could improve user engagement with agent systems (Cassell et al. 2000; Szafir and Mutlu 2012; Thomas et al. 2018; Xiao et al. 2007; Zhao et al. 2016). During the process of query formulation and reformulation, many decision points in a dialogue flow, such as choices of elicitation methods, desired precision level, and repair strategies (Ashktorab et al. 2019), could also account for individual differences.

Second, compared to traditional search systems where user interactions are limited to typing queries and selecting results, conversational interfaces allow users to give free-form natural-language input and thus enable much richer forms of user disclosure. Importantly, signals or user profiles obtained from the disclosure are the prerequisite for user modeling and system adaptation. In conversational interactions, the disclosure can not only be achieved through explicit inquiry, but also inference from users' conversational behaviors, just as how people engage in recipient design in everyday conversations based on subtle cues from the other speaker(s). These subtle cues may not only reveal who they are and what they prefer, but also how they feel about the interactions. In other words, conversational interfaces may enable new user modeling techniques for improving search experience based on feedback signals in users' conversational interactions that are beyond click-through patterns used by traditional IR systems. In our work developing conversational agents and studying how users interact with these agents, we take great interest in identifying such user signals in conversational interactions to work toward the goal of system capabilities for recipient design. In the following section, we give an overview of our recent work to demonstrate some exciting opportunities in this area.

13.3 Recipient Design with a Conversational Search System

Starting in 2015, with a group of colleagues, we developed a conversational agent in IBM to answer employees' questions related to the work environment, such as "tell me about health benefits" or "how can I find IT help". The agent answers these questions using a hybrid model combining pattern-based retrieval of curated answers and output from a search engine for IBM internal Web pages (Chandar et al. 2017; Liao et al. 2018). The agent is called Cognitive Human Interface Personality (Chip). In summer 2016, Chip was deployed to 337 new hires who used Chip for 5–6 weeks. The deployment resulted in a chat log dataset with more than 6,000 messages. The dataset provides a valuable resource to study how users converse with a conversational agent *in the wild.*

We analyzed the dataset with two goals in mind. First, we intended to provide an empirical account of the types of conversational interactions users have with an information search agent. This complements prior work on conversational search in two ways. First, instead of conversing with a human intermediary or a wizard-of-oz system, we examined interactions with a real chatbot in a real-world setting. Second, besides information queries, we also paid attention to conversational interactions that perform communication or social functions, most of which are not covered by the existing models of information behaviors for conversational search (Azzopardi et al. 2018; Radlinski and Craswell 2017).

Our second goal was to explore recipient design, i.e., adapting the system, based on users' conversational behaviors, where we consider both tailoring its *search functionalities* and *interaction styles.* In this section, we discuss insights from our work as an example to demonstrate the new opportunities that conversational interfaces offer for encouraging user disclosure and hence enabling recipient design. The technical details of the system and the methodological details of the analysis are presented in our recent papers (Chandar et al. 2017; Liao et al. 2016, 2018). Before discussing the two areas of recipient design, we briefly describe the types of conversational interactions users had with Chip.

13.3.1   Conversational Behaviors with a QA Agent

Despite Chip being a QA agent for IBM internal information, we found that more than 35% of the chat logs were dedicated to non-queries. 85% of users sent at least one of these non-query messages. By performing content analysis, we categorized these non-query interactions into four general areas:

- **Opening and closing**: Instead of simply querying the agent, users showed anthropomorphizing behaviors by opening and closing the conversations as if chatting with another human. More than 57% of users had at least once formally opened the interaction (e.g., "hi", "hello"). 46% of users also had at least once closed the querying by acknowledging the agent's answers (e.g., "ok", "got it"), and 11.6% of users had at least once closed the conversations with farewell.
- **Agent ability checking**: There was a category of user questions concerned with capabilities of the system, by asking "what can you do" or "can you do [function]?". These inquiries carried distinct meaning from other anthropomorphizing inquiries, as in serving the goal of reducing uncertainty about the system.
- **Feedback giving**: We found that users actively commented on the agent's performance. This is interesting considering that it is a known challenge to obtain feedback in traditional search systems. During the deployment, we suggested participants to use "#fail" to give negative feedback if unsatisfied with Chip's answers. 42.4% of users did it at least once. In addition, 11.9% users had at least once

complimented Chip (e.g., "you are helpful"), and 21.1% made some forms of complaints (e.g., "you are stupid").

- **Chitchat**: Some users engaged in chitchat with Chip, representing playful inter-actions by intentionally anthropomorphizing the agent (Luger and Sellen 2016). Types of chitchat included asking about the agent's status ("what are you up to") or traits (e.g., "what do you like?"), making off-topic requests, and talking about oneself.

Based on common patterns identified in Conversation Analysis, Moore et al. proposed a design framework for interaction patterns of conversational agents (Moore and Arar 2019). The framework differentiates between interactions that perform goal-oriented activities (inquire, respond, etc.), sequence management (e.g., repair), and conversation management. The main categories of conversation management interactions include opening, closing, capability checking, and disengaging (e.g., request to transfer to a human agent). The non-query conversational interactions we identified are generally consistent with these patterns of conversation management, with two additional areas–providing feedback and having playful chitchat. Both can be considered unique to the setting of interactions with a personified conversational agent.

13.3.2 Recipient Design by Tailoring Search Functionalities

A longstanding theme in IR work is to adapt search functionalities to individual pref-erences based on feedback in the interaction history. For example, based on what a user liked or disliked, one can learn the user's topical interest to adapt the ranking algorithm (Ghorab et al. 2013; Teevan et al. 2005). Prior work also explored adapt-ing information presentation or providing query assistance for those less satisfied users (Song and He 2010; Zhai and Lafferty 2006). Because it is costly and some-times not feasible to obtain explicit user feedback, implicit feedback is often inferred from user behavior, such as click-through patterns or dwell time (Feild et al. 2010; Fox et al. 2005; Kelly and Teevan 2003; Kim et al. 2014). However, the challenge is that these behavioral signals may be sparse and unreliable. In viewing conversational interactions users had with Chip, it was encouraging that users actively commented on its search performance (e.g., "#fail"). It motivated us to further explore what feedback signals existed in their conversational interactions that can be leveraged for adapting search functionalities.

We adopted a data-driven approach by statistically modeling what features in conversational interactions predict a user's self-reported satisfaction with Chip's search performance, gathered by a survey. Details of the model are discussed in (Liao et al. 2018). The results show that, after controlling for the system performance, users with lower *subjective* satisfaction tended to engage in conversational interactions in the categories of *feedback using #fail*, *agent ability checking*, *closing by farewell* and *off-topic requests*. These are the users that might have distinctive information needs and thus recipient design should target. A number of words or terms were also found to be associated with more positive user opinions, such as "tell me about", "should I", "what does", "where is", "who is", and "how to".

Based on these results, we summarize three areas in users' conversational interaction to obtain feedback signals for adapting search functionalities: *conversational feedback*, *implicit complaints*, and *question structure keywords*:

- **Conversational feedback**: Conversational interfaces may encourage users to provide more feedback for the search performance. We found that using "#fail" was a strong indicator of dissatisfaction. In contrast, compliments such as "you are smart" or blunt complaints did not show significant association with user satisfaction, but instead might have been playful interactions. It highlights the complication in obtaining reliable feedback signals in conversational interactions and the necessity to identify them by empirical analysis.

- **Implicit complaints**: A conversational interface enables users to freely "talk," expressing feedback in ways that were not possible with traditional search systems. Statistical modeling allowed us to explore these less obvious signals. The result showed that the occurrences of *agent ability check* and *closing with farewell* predict user dissatisfaction. A closer look into the data revealed a pattern of users asking "what can you do" after encountering errors. Many have recognized that a critical drawback of conversational interface is its unclear affordance of capabilities (Luger and Sellen 2016; Shneiderman and Maes 1997). Agent ability check can be considered signals of user struggling with such unclear affordance. Similarly, we observed users closing the conversation after errors, signaling frustration and refusal.

- **Question structure keywords**: It is reasonable to expect that users who are satisfied with the system performance are more likely to keep using it for information needs and less so for *off-topic requests*. Among the lexical features predicting user satisfaction, we saw a group of wh-words (what/where/who), which indicate typical questioning structures. With conversational interfaces, users tend to ask question in full sentences instead of using keyword-based queries (Crestani and Du 2006; Guy 2018). Therefore, one can possibly infer user satisfaction by tracking these structure keywords for questions.

This part of our work explored new opportunities offered by a conversational interface for user modeling to enable recipient design, i.e., adapting search results for individuals. We focused on informing ways to know *for whom* to adapt search functionalities. For addressing *how* the system should adapt, one can refer to the large volume of IR work that tapped into user feedback signals to adapt search algorithms (Baeza-Yates and Ribeiro 2011; Ghorab et al. 2013; Teevan et al. 2005). The general idea is that one could track user feedback signals for search results of different features (e.g., topics) to learn about user preferences. Future work could explore applying similar approaches to adapting features that are important for a conversational search setting, such as level of details in search results presentation. Another approach is to provide additional query assistance for less satisfied users, such as tailoring the dialogue flows for query elicitation and repair assistance strategies as suggested in Table 13.1.

13.3.3 Recipient Design by Tailoring Interaction Styles

In conversations, recipient design is reflected in more aspects than tailoring information content—in addition to *what* to talk about, one also constantly tailors *how* to talk. Therefore, besides search functionalities, we also attempted at adapting interaction styles for individual users. Interaction style is unarguably an enormous design space with many dimensions (Szafir and Mutlu 2012; Thomas et al. 2018; Xiao et al. 2007; Zhao et al. 2016). We explored one dimension of core interest in studies of human–agent interaction—individuals' orientation to view an agent as a sociable versus utilitarian tool. Prior work suggests that people tend to have different mental models interacting with a conversational agent (Lee et al. 2010, 2011). Those who see an agent as a sociable tool are inclined to engage in human-like interactions and exhibit relational behaviors such as chitchat and politeness. Recent work also uses the term "playfulness" to refer to intentional engagement of anthropomorphizing behaviors with an agent system (Luger and Sellen 2016). In contrast, those with a utilitarian orientation may see in an agent nothing more than an information search tool. Our hypothesis is that this orientation could govern a user's preference for interaction styles that are more social versus ones that resemble traditional search systems.

To validate such a hypothesis and explore how to provide recipient design for social versus utilitarian interaction styles, we started with a qualitative study interviewing the users of our pilot deployment of Chip (Liao et al. 2016). We developed a self-reported scale to measure one's *social agent orientation* by asking if one enjoys conversational interactions and chitchat with an agent. Then we contrasted user preferences for those on different sides of the scale. In general, we found that those with high social orientation *desire properties of natural conversations*, such as abilities to handle multi-turn conversation and tailoring the level of details for individual needs. They also prefer agents with *rich personality designs*. In contrast, those with utilitarian orientation repeatedly *favor common features in traditional search systems*, such as handling query-like input and providing a ranked list of answers. They also desire more *transparency of the information source* and consider *human-like features to be unnecessary* in the conversation content and visual design.

The above results suggested *how* to tailor interaction styles for users with social versus utilitarian orientation. We also leveraged a statistical modeling approach to explore signals in conversational interactions to infer the orientation of an individual user, i.e., *for whom* to adapt the interaction style. We found the following categories of conversational interactions to predict more social orientation: *chitchat about the agent's status* and *agent's traits*, *chitchat talking about oneself*, and *giving compliments*. We also found a number of words or terms associated with more social orientation: "how do you", "are you", "do you know", "search", "information", etc.

We examine these results and summarize three areas to obtain signals for recipient design of social versus utilitarian interaction styles: *playful chitchat, agent-oriented conversations* and *casual testing*.

- **Playful chitchat**: Three categories of conversational interactions were strong signals of users with high social orientation—chitchat asking about the agent's traits, status, and talking about oneself. They confirm that chitchat carries explicit anthropomorphizing intentions. It is notable that conversation management actions such as opening and acknowledging did not show significant association. It suggests that, in the context of a text-based QA agent, they may be more of habitual behaviors with the chat interface instead of consciously anthropomorphizing the agent.
- **Agent-orientated conversations**: An evident pattern in lexical features signaling social orientation is the frequent occurrence of second-person pronouns. This agent-oriented interest is consistent with the tendency to anthropomorphize the agent. This suggests that a simple way to identify socially oriented users could be monitoring the usage of second-person pronouns.
- **Casual testing**: The lexical features predicting social orientation suggest less formality but more casual asking, such as "do you know" or "tell me". We also found the words "information" and "search" to be strong signals. A close examination of the conversations revealed a pattern of repeatedly asking Chip to retrieve different kinds of information (e.g., *"search information about my manager"*). These behaviors suggest the less utilitarian-oriented users, who may see Chip differently from a traditional search system, exhibited curious behaviors by casually testing its intelligence.

With these studies, we aim to inform recipient design of conversational search with more social versus utilitarian interaction styles. For example, based on the above signals, one can distinguish users with social or utilitarian orientation, interacting with natural conversations and rich social designs for the former group, while presenting information like traditional search system for the latter. Besides recipient design for search results presentation, one may also improve the search task by anticipating differences in users' querying behaviors. For example, it is likely that a socially oriented user would express information needs in natural language, while a utilitarian-oriented user would use keyword-based queries, and thus different processing techniques should be applied. Our work demonstrates that recipient design should take a more central role for conversational interfaces because the rich design issues involved, for not only improving search algorithms, but also interaction styles, which could be concerned with information presentation, conversation organization, or linguistic styles.

13.4 Summary

Conversational interfaces are an emerging area of research for search systems. It is important to recognize that human conversation is a metaphor for this type of user interface. The benefit of an interface metaphor is to give users instantaneous knowledge on how to interact with the system in a familiar way, while leaving the interface to bridge these familiar actions and the underlying computational models. To take full advantage of such a metaphor, this chapter aims to provide perspectives on properties of natural conversations that fit and benefit information search tasks, in order to identify functional goals of conversational search systems. By reviewing relevant work, we start from two ends: system actions to extend models of traditional search systems to conversational search, with regard to query formulation, search results exploration, and query repair; and the fundamental properties of natural conversations including efficiency, common ground, and recipient design. The two threads converge at a design space for the functional goals for conversational search systems. We identify a gap and an area of opportunity to put user modeling and adaptation in a more central place for conversational interfaces, and discuss insights from our own work on making search systems conversational and adaptive.

References

Arguello J, Choi B, Capra R. (2017). Factors Affecting Users' Information Requests. In SIGIR 1st International Workshop on Conversational Approaches to Information Retrieval (CAIR'17) (Vol. 4)

Ashktorab Z, Jain M, Liao QV, Weisz, J (2019). Resilient Chatbots: Repair Strategy Preferences for Conversational Breakdown. In Proceedings of the (2019) CHI Conference on Human Factors in Computing Systems (CHI'19). ACM, New York, NY, USA

Azzopardi L, Dubiel M, Halvey M, Dalton J. (2018). Conceptualizing agent-human interactions during the conversational search process. In The Second International Workshop on Conversational Approaches to Information Retrieval

Balchandran R, Rachevsky L, Sansone L, Sicconi R. (2009, September). Dialog system for mixed initiative one-turn address entry and error recovery. In Proceedings of the SIGDIAL 2009 Conference: The 10th Annual Meeting of the Special Interest Group on Discourse and Dialogue (pp. 152-155). Association for Computational Linguistics

Baeza-Yates R, Ribeiro BDAN. (2011). Modern information retrieval. New York: ACM Press; Harlow, England: Addison-Wesley,

Bates MJ (2002) Toward an integrated model of information seeking and searching. The New Review of Information Behaviour Research 3:1–15

Baeza-Yates R, Ribeiro BAN. (2011). Modern information retrieval. New York: ACM Press; Harlow, England: Addison-Wesley,

Belkin NJ, Cool C, Stein A, Thiel U (1995) Cases, scripts, and information-seeking strategies: On the design of interactive information retrieval systems. Expert systems with applications 9(3):379–395

Bell A (1984) Language style as audience design. Language in society 13(2):145–204

Bobrow DG, Kaplan RM, Kay M, Norman DA, Thompson H, Winograd T (1977) GUS, a frame-driven dialog system. Artificial intelligence 8(2):155–173

Cassell J, Sullivan J, Churchill E, Prevost S (Eds.). (2000). Embodied conversational agents. MIT press

Chandar P, Khazaeni Y, Davis M, Muller M, Crasso M, Liao QV, ... Geyer W. (2017). Leveraging conversational systems to assists new hires during onboarding. In IFIP Conference on Human-Computer Interaction (pp. 381-391). Springer, Cham

Chen L, Pu P (2004) Survey of preference elicitation methods (No. EPFL-REPORT-52659)

Christakopoulou K, Radlinski F, Hofmann K. (2016). Towards conversational recommender systems. In Proceedings of the 22nd ACM SIGKDD International Conference on Knowledge Discovery and Data Mining (pp. 815-824). ACM

Christakopoulou K, Beute, A, Li R, Jain S, Chi EH. (2018). Q&R: A two-stage approach toward interactive recommendation. In Proceedings of the 24th ACM SIGKDD International Conference on Knowledge Discovery & Data Mining (pp. 139-148). ACM

Crestani F, Du H (2006) Written versus spoken queries: A qualitative and quantitative comparative analysis. Journal of the American Society for Information Science and Technology 57(7):881–890

Feild HA., Allan J, Jones R. (2010). Predicting searcher frustration. In Proceedings of the 33rd international ACM SIGIR conference on Research and development in information retrieval (pp. 34-41). ACM

Fox S, Karnawat K, Mydland M, Dumais S, White T (2005) Evaluating implicit measures to improve web search. ACM Transactions on Information Systems (TOIS) 23(2):147–168

Ghorab MR, Zhou D, O'connor A, Wade V, (2013) Personalised information retrieval: survey and classification. User Modeling and User-Adapted Interaction 23(4):381–443

Goodwin C, Heritage J (1990) Conversation analysis. Annual review of anthropology 19(1):283–307

Grice HP. (1975). Logic and conversation. In Cole, P.; Morgan, J. Syntax and semantics. 3: Speech acts. New York: Academic Press. 41–58

Gunning D. (2017). Explainable artificial intelligence (xai). Defense Advanced Research Projects Agency (DARPA), nd Web

Guy I (2018) The Characteristics of Voice Search: Comparing Spoken with Typed-in Mobile Web Search Queries. ACM Transactions on Information Systems (TOIS) 36(3):30

Hassan AA, Gurunath KR, Ozertem U, Jones R. (2015). Characterizing and predicting voice query reformulation. In Proceedings of the 24th ACM International on Conference on Information and Knowledge Management (pp. 543-552). ACM

Heritage J, Atkinson, JM. (1984). Structures of social action. Studies in Conversation Analysis

Jiang J, Jeng W, He D. (2013). How do users respond to voice input errors?: lexical and phonetic query reformulation in voice search. In Proceedings of the 36th international ACM SIGIR conference on Research and development in information retrieval (pp. 143-152). ACM

Jiang J, Hassan AA, Jones R, Ozertem U, Zitouni I, Gurunath KR, Khan OZ. (2015). Automatic online evaluation of intelligent assistants. In Proceedings of the 24th International Conference on World Wide Web (pp. 506-516). International World Wide Web Conferences Steering Committee

Kelly D, Teevan J. (2003). Implicit feedback for inferring user preference: a bibliography. In Acm Sigir Forum (Vol. 37, No. 2, pp. 18-28). ACM

Kim Y, Hassan A, White RW, Zitouni I. (2014). Modeling dwell time to predict click-level satisfaction. In Proceedings of the 7th ACM international conference on Web search and data mining (pp. 193-202). ACM

Mahmood T, Ricci F. (2009). Improving recommender systems with adaptive conversational strategies. In Proceedings of the 20th ACM conference on Hypertext and hypermedia (pp. 73-82). ACM

Mcginty L, Smyth B (2006) Adaptive selection: An analysis of critiquing and preference-based feedback in conversational recommender systems. International Journal of Electronic Commerce 11(2):35–57

McTear MF. (2004). Spoken dialogue technology: toward the conversational user interface. Springer Science and Business Media

McTear M, Callejas Z, Griol D. (2016). The conversational interface: Talking to smart devices. Springer

Clark HH, Murphy GL. (1982). Audience design in meaning and reference. In Advances in psychology (Vol. 9, pp. 287-299). North-Holland

Clark HH, Brennan SE (1991) Grounding in communication. Perspectives on socially shared cognition 13(1991):127–149

Lee MK, Kiesler S, Forlizzi J. (2010). Receptionist or information kiosk: how do people talk with a robot?. In Proceedings of the 2010 ACM conference on Computer supported cooperative work (pp. 31-40). ACM

Lee N, Shin H, Sundar, SS. (2011). Utilitarian vs. hedonic robots: role of parasocial tendency and anthropomorphism in shaping user attitudes. In Proceedings of the 6th international conference on Human-robot interaction (pp. 183-184). ACM

Li R, Kahou SE, Schulz H, Michalski V, Charlin L, Pal C. (2018). Towards Deep Conversational Recommendations. In Advances in Neural Information Processing Systems (pp. 9748-9758)

Liao QV, Davis M, Geyer W, Muller M, Shami NS. (2016). What can you do?: Studying social-agent orientation and agent proactive interactions with an agent for employees. In Proceedings of the 2016 ACM Conference on Designing Interactive Systems (pp. 264-275). ACM

Liao QV, Hussain MM, Chandar P, Davis M, Crasso M, Wang D, ... Geyer W. (2018). All Work and no Play? Conversations with a Question-and-Answer Chatbot in the Wild. In Proceedings of the 2018 CHI Conference on Human Factors in Computing Systems (CHI'18). ACM, New York, NY, USA (Vol. 13)

Luger E, Sellen A. (2016). Like having a really bad PA: the gulf between user expectation and experience of conversational agents. In Proceedings of the 2016 CHI Conference on Human Factors in Computing Systems (pp. 5286-5297). ACM

Marchionini, G. (1997). Information seeking in electronic environments (No. 9). Cambridge university press

McDuff D, Thomas P, Czerwinski M, Craswell N. (2017). Multimodal analysis of vocal collaborative search: a public corpus and results. In Proceedings of the 19th ACM International Conference on Multimodal Interaction (pp. 456-463). ACM

Miller T. (2018). Explanation in artificial intelligence: Insights from the social sciences. Artificial Intelligence

Moore RJ, Arar R. (2019). Conversational UX Design: A Practitioner's Guide to the Natural Conversation Framework. Morgan & Claypool

Myers C, Furqan A, Nebolsky J, Caro K, Zhu J. (2018). Patterns for How Users Overcome Obstacles in Voice User Interfaces. In Proceedings of the 2018 CHI Conference on Human Factors in Computing Systems (p. 6). ACM

Paek T, Horvitz E. (2000). Conversation as action under uncertainty. In Proceedings of the Sixteenth conference on Uncertainty in artificial intelligence (pp. 455-464). Morgan Kaufmann Publishers Inc.

Porcheron M, Fischer JE, Reeves S, Sharples S. (2018). Voice Interfaces in Everyday Life. In Proceedings of the 2018 CHI Conference on Human Factors in Computing Systems (p. 640). ACM

Radlinski F, Craswell N. (2017). A theoretical framework for conversational search. In Proceedings of the 2017 Conference on Conference Human Information Interaction and Retrieval (pp. 117-126). ACM

Sacks H, Schegloff EA (1979) Two preferences in the organization of reference to persons in conversation and their interaction. In: Psathas G (ed) Everyday language: Studies in ethnomethodology. New York

Schegloff EA. (2007). Sequence organization in interaction: Volume 1: A primer in conversation analysis (Vol. 1). Cambridge University Press

Shneiderman B, Maes P (1997) Direct manipulation vs. interface agents. interactions 4(6):42–61

Shokouhi M, Jones R, Ozertem U, Raghunathan K, Diaz F. (2014). Mobile query reformulations. In Proceedings of the 37th international ACM SIGIR conference on Research & development in information retrieval (pp. 1011-1014). ACM

Sitter S, Stein A (1992) Modeling the illocutionary aspects of information-seeking dialogues. Information Processing & Management 28(2):165–180

Sun Y, Zhang Y. (2018) Conversational Recommender System.In The 41st International ACM SIGIR Conference on Research & Development in Information Retrieval. ACM

Szafir D, Mutlu B. (2012). Pay attention!: designing adaptive agents that monitor and improve user engagement. In Proceedings of the SIGCHI conference on human factors in computing systems (pp. 11-20). ACM

Teevan J, Dumais ST, Horvitz E. (2005). Personalizing search via automated analysis of interests and activities. In Proceedings of the 28th annual international ACM SIGIR conference on Research and development in information retrieval (pp. 449-456). ACM

Thomas P, Czerwinski M, McDuff D, Craswell N, Mark G. (2018). Style and Alignment in Information-Seeking Conversation. In Proceedings of the 2018 Conference on Human Information Interaction&Retrieval (pp. 42-51). ACM

Thompson CA, Goker MH, Langley P (2004) A personalized system for conversational recommendations. Journal of Artificial Intelligence Research 21:393–428

Trippas JR., Spina D, Cavedon L, Joho H, Sanderson M. (2018). Informing the Design of Spoken Conversational Search: Perspective Paper. In Proceedings of the 2018 Conference on Human Information Interaction&Retrieval (pp. 32-41). ACM

Walker M, Aberdeen J, Boland J, Bratt E, Garofolo J, Hirschman L, ... Pellom B. (2001). DARPA Communicator dialog travel planning systems: The June 2000 data collection. In Seventh European Conference on Speech Communication and Technology

Wang WY, Finkelstein S, Ogan A, Black AW, Cassell J. (2012 July). Love ya, jerkface: using sparse log-linear models to build positive (and impolite) relationships with teens. In Proceedings of the 13th annual meeting of the special interest group on discourse and dialogue (pp. 20-29). Association for Computational Linguistics

Wilson TD (2000) Human information behavior. Informing science 3(2):49–56

Song Y, He, L W. (2010). Optimal rare query suggestion with implicit user feedback. In Proceedings of the 19th international conference on World wide web (pp. 901-910). ACM

Xiao J, Stasko J, Catrambone R. (2007). The role of choice and customization on users' interaction with embodied conversational agents: effects on perception and performance. In Proceedings of the SIGCHI conference on Human factors in computing systems (pp. 1293-1302). ACM

Zhai C, Lafferty J (2006) A risk minimization framework for information retrieval. Information Processing & Management 42(1):31–55

Zhang Y, Chen X, Ai Q, Yang L, Croft WB. (2018). Towards conversational search and recommendation: System ask, user respond. In Proceedings of the 27th ACM International Conference on Information and Knowledge Management (pp. 177-186). ACM

Zhang Y, Liao QV, Srivastava, B. (2018, March). Towards an Optimal Dialog Strategy for Information Retrieval Using Both Open-and Close-ended Questions. In 23rd International Conference on Intelligent User Interfaces (pp. 365-369). ACM

Zhao R, Sinha T, Black A, Cassell J. (2016). Automatic recognition of conversational strategies in the service of a socially-aware dialog system. In Proceedings of the 17th Annual Meeting of the Special Interest Group on Discourse and Dialogue (pp. 381–392)

Printed in the United States
by Baker & Taylor Publisher Services